FIRST VICTORY

BRITAIN'S FORGOTTEN STRUGGLE IN THE MIDDLE EAST, 1941

ROBERT LYMAN

CONSTABLE • LONDON

Constable & Robinson Ltd
3 The Lanchesters
162 Fulham Palace Road
London W6 9ER
www.constablerobinson.com

First published in the UK by Constable,
an imprint of Constable & Robinson Ltd 2006

A copy of the British Library Cataloguing in
Publication Data is available from the British Library

ISBN-13: 978-1-84529-108-2
ISBN-10: 1-84529-108-5

Printed and bound in the EU

This book is for Montague and Phineas

Contents

Acknowledgements

I am grateful to a wide range of people, libraries and museums for their various kindnesses in assisting me to complete this book. In no particular order I would like to thank the Revd Philip and Mrs Isla Brownless, Major Gordon Graham MC and Bar, Mr Gaby Kiwarkis, Mr Michael Skeet, Captain Dick Hennessy-Walsh, Colonel W.H. Gerard Leigh CVO MBE, His Grace The Duke of Wellington KG LVO OBE MC DL, Dr Christopher Morris (of the RAF Habbaniya Association), Mrs Naida Davies (née Smart), Mr Peter Bindloss, Mr Bob Maslen-Jones, Mr Andrew 'Latin' Brown of Lambrook Haileybury School and Mr Jim Glass.

For their mastery of the hyphen, dash and comma, the eager destruction of long sentences and the elucidation of the mysteries of the subjunctive, I am especially grateful to the careful labours of both Dr David Preston and Isla Brownless. Both took their formidable editorial red pens to the manuscript, to its great profit. Their enthusiasm for the story was a tremendous encouragement to me during the long months of its gestation. I am very grateful also to David for providing me with his view of General Charles de Gaulle from a Francophile English perspective, a useful balance to General Spears' post-1941 bitter anti-Gaullist prejudice. Needless to say, all remaining errors, either of fact, judgement or grammar, are entirely my own.

The public record depositories in the United Kingdom are a superb national treasure. I wish to record my special thanks to all who helped me with ideas, advice and access to material, especially the long-suffering staff at Prince Consort's Library (Aldershot); Alistair Massie at the National Army Museum, the Departments of Documents and Photographs at the Imperial War Museum, Hugh Alexander at the Image Library of the National Archives, the British Library, the Liddell Hart Centre at King's College (all in London); the John Rylands Library (Manchester); Major Gerald Davies of the Gurkha Museum (Winchester); the Household Cavalry Museum (Windsor); and the Middle East Centre Archives at St Anthony's College, University of Oxford. I am very grateful to the librarians, archivists and trustees of all institutions for their kindness, and for permission to quote from material in their care. I have sought but have been unable to identify all the copyright holders for the material from which I have quoted. If I have infringed any copyright I have done so accidentally. If this is the case, I crave the indulgence of the owner, and respectfully seek permission now.

I am indebted to the superb team at Constable & Robinson, who guided me through the publishing process with quiet professionalism. My special thanks go to Dan Hind (now Editorial Director at Duckworth) for sponsoring the project from the outset, to Hannah Boursnell for taking over the job from Dan at such short notice and without blinking an eyelid, and to my editor Nicola Chalton for her enthusiasm, support and careful attention to detail. Max Burnell has once again provided a superb cover. Last, but by no means least, I wish to thank my wife and family for putting up with the long absences – both of mind and body – that accompanied the writing of this book.

A Note on Proper Names

Throughout, I have followed the example of one of the most famous Arabists of them all, T.E. Lawrence, who, in the *Seven Pillars of Wisdom*, wrote:

> Arab names will not go into English, exactly, for their consonants are not the same as ours, and their vowels, like ours, vary from district to district. There are scientific systems of transliteration, helpful to people who know enough Arabic not to need my helping, but a wash out for the world. I spell my names anyhow, to show what rot the systems are.

Maps

Introduction

Winston Churchill famously remarked that 'Before El Alamein Britain never had a victory: after El Alamein she never suffered a defeat.' This, of course, was not true, but Churchill's characteristic literary hyperbole met his need at the time to describe the welcome upward movement of Britain's fortunes in a war, which until then had seen little obvious signs for rejoicing. General Montgomery's victory at the second battle of El Alamein in October 1942 was undoubtedly a significant turning point in the war as a whole: it signalled the beginning of the end in the long struggle in North Africa, an end to the defensive fighting that had pushed Great Britain back on to its heels since 1940, and represented the start of a slow return by British forces to the offensive, although both Arakan (in Burma in 1943) and Arnhem (in Holland in 1944) were significant defeats for British arms after El Alamein.

Other such 'turning points' in the war – key battles or campaigns in which the future course of the war was determined – included the Battle of Britain, which prevented a German invasion of Britain; the Battle of the Atlantic, which secured Britain's sea-lanes of communication with North America; and the Battle of Normandy, which secured the Allies' foothold on continental Europe. Another, the subject of this book, took place in the Middle East during the five months between April and August 1941. By virtue of three military successes that year – first against Iraq, then against Vichy-held Syria and then finally by the invasion and occupation of Iran – Great Britain secured her sources of oil and established unequivocally the security of her eastern Mediterranean flank, hitherto dangerously vulnerable to Axis pretensions in the Middle East.

In the popular historiography of the Second World War these short but decisive wars have been forgotten in favour of subsequent and more dramatic events elsewhere. Even at the time the loud and savage battles for Greece, Crete and Libya made a sound that drowned out almost everything else. However, it is the contention of this book that these three forgotten victories in the summer and autumn of 1941 were a crucial turning point in Great Britain's fortunes during the war. The campaigns themselves were not large, they were conducted without much fanfare and each with laughably limited resources, and they were all quickly overtaken in the publicity stakes by the broader course of the war. But they were crucial for Britain's survival and ability to continue fighting in a year when Britain, together with her empire and commonwealth, stood alone against Nazi tyranny.

The context of these victories needs to be recalled. It is easy to forget just how desperate was Great Britain's plight at the time. The year 1941 was probably the worst in Britain's modern history. The country stood on the very edge of defeat in the European war. France had fallen in June and the rump French state based in Vichy sided openly with Germany. Until June 1941 the Soviet Union was an uneasy ally of Hitler, and the United States was not to join the war on Britain's side until mid-December. Although the Royal Air Force had averted a German cross-channel invasion in the summer of 1940, things still looked very bleak. The pre-war professional British Army, along with all its equipment, had been destroyed in France and it was taking an inordinately long time to recover from two decades of military impoverishment. Even worse, the substantial gains by Wavell, Britain's Middle Eastern Commander-in-Chief (C-in-C), in the Libyan Desert against the Italians in 1940 had been reversed by March 1941 at the hands of the *Deutsches Afrika Korps*, and the British were unable to stop the German seizure of Greece in April and Crete in May. At the end of the year Japan joined the war and within six months had imposed, by means of the military humiliation of both European and United States empires, her 'Greater Asia Co-Prosperity Sphere' across the whole of the Asian rim.

The contention of this book is that, through the loss of Iraq, and the German capture or domination of Syria and Iran, Great Britain could well have lost the war in 1941. The continuance of Britain's strategic position in the Middle East was therefore crucial to her survival in 1941. There are a number of reasons for this, of which two are pre-eminent. First, the Middle East was at the time the linchpin of British imperial interests, the Suez Canal representing both a physical and psychological conduit between Europe and Asia, the lifeline between the scattered outposts of the British diaspora. If Egypt with its precious Canal were lost, the glue that joined together Britain's strained sinews of empire, connecting the Mediterranean with India, and thence Asia and Australasia, would have been broken. Second, the Middle East provided Great Britain with the only sources of oil, that essential lubricant of modern, mechanical warfare, under her direct control. Indeed, without oil, she could not fight. Nor, for that matter, could Germany.

Iraqi and Iranian oil was therefore an important element in Britain's continued ability to fight in 1941, and had been since the Royal Navy had begun to convert her warships to oil at the end of the nineteenth century. At the onset of the First World War 75 per cent of all British oil had come from the region. By 1941, the United States dominated world production. Some 83 per cent of the world's oil was produced in the United States, nearly 5 per cent was produced in the Middle East with the remainder coming from Romania and Russia.*

In 1941, the loss of Iraq would have inevitably led also to the loss of Iranian oil. The principal Iranian oil fields lay just to the east of the Iraqi frontier at Abadan, some thirty-two miles south-east of Basra. Iraqi and Iranian oil together, through the auspices of the Iraq Petroleum Company (IPC) and the Anglo-Persian Oil Company (APOC) respectively, provided Great Britain with virtually all of her non-American supplies of this most precious of commodities.

Without Middle Eastern oil Britain would have been forced to rely entirely on the continuing supply from the United States and, to a lesser extent, South America. This posed a number of difficulties. The first was that this oil had to be paid for from the fast-dwindling supplies of cash in Britain's treasury at far from advantageous prices (unlike that sourced from Iraq and Iran), money that was desperately needed at the time to buy war materiel for her armed forces, and food for her

---

* Southern Iran produced 8.6 million tons of oil in 1940 and Iraq some 4.3 million.

population. Second, it had to run the gauntlet of the Atlantic sea-lanes, and brave the perils of the U-boat menace.

But more critically, in early 1941 Great Britain could not guarantee the continued support of the United States. At the time, Britain's strategic relationship with the United States was weak. America was neutral, and strong domestic political pressures were arrayed against the possibility of her becoming embroiled in yet another bloody European war. To Churchill's frustration, Roosevelt consistently rejected every attempt to commit the United States to a more active role in the war against Germany.* The only real guarantor at the time of Great Britain's supplies was control of her own means of production and supply. This meant the retention, at all costs, of the Middle East. A year later, in 1942, the United States had become the guarantor of Britain's oil supplies. By 1943 there was no prospect of Germany managing to win its war in Russia and thus renewing its interest in the Middle East. As a result the strategic importance of this theatre diminished commensurately. However, in the difficult spring of 1941 the situation was for Great Britain starkly different. There was no guarantee that the United States would come to her aid if the Middle East were lost. If all sources of oil were denied to her, Britain would no longer be able to fight and would be forced to sue for an ignominious and unimaginable peace. The efforts of the previous eighteen months to hold the Nazi monster at bay would have come to nought and Britain, the last European bastion to stand up to Hitler, would have failed. By 1940 and 1941, therefore, when Britain stood alone in Europe against a rampant Nazi tyranny, her survival as an independent nation would have been severely compromised without Middle Eastern oil.

Equally, what Great Britain had in abundance as a consequence of her position in the Middle East, Hitler desperately craved. Even the relatively small amount produced in the Middle East in 1940 proportionate to the dominance of US production would have met all of Germany's petroleum needs. In 1941 Germany's only sources of oil were Romania and Russia, but it was anticipated that she would need to draw on sources further afield. Indeed, the need to secure the Caucasian oil fields was a significant factor in Hitler's drive into Russia

---

* Churchill's long struggle in 1941 to persuade Roosevelt to declare war on Germany is cleverly told by Michael Dobbs in *Churchill's Hour* (London: HarperCollins, 2004).

that summer and the denial of oil to Germany a critical factor in Great Britain's contingency planning during 1940.[1]

If Britain were able to retain her oil and simultaneously deny it to Germany, the omens for eventual British success in the war were good. General Archibald Wavell, as C–in–C Middle East, articulated this logic in May 1940. His judgement was that Great Britain's access to oil, and its ability to ship it (and protect it while so doing) would inevitably lead to Britain's ultimate success in the war and Germany's failure. Wavell's thinking ran along the following lines:

1. Oil, shipping, air power, sea power are the keys to this war, and they are interdependent.
   Air power and naval power cannot function without oil.
   Oil, except in very limited quantities, cannot be brought to its destination without shipping.
   Shipping requires the protection of naval power and air power.

2. We have access to practically all the world's supplies of oil.
   We have most of the shipping.
   We have naval power.
   We have potentially the greatest air power, when fully developed.

   Therefore we are bound to win the war.

3. Germany is very short of oil and has access only to very limited quantities.
   Germany's shipping is practically confined to the Baltic.
   Germany's naval power is small.
   Germany's air power is great but is a diminishing asset.

   Therefore Germany is bound to lose the war.[2]

Ensuring that it could secure its sources of oil whilst at the same time damaging or removing German influence in these areas was thus a critical strategic requirement for Great Britain at this juncture of the war.

This book is an account of how Great Britain, by frighteningly narrow margins, succeeded in preventing this calamity in the months between April and August 1941. Surprising as it may seem in retrospect,

1941 was in fact a year of victories for Great Britain as strategic in their outcome as Midway, El Alamein, Stalingrad and Kohima. It was the year in which Britain guaranteed, using Wavell's logic if not his methods, that it would eventually win the war.

1

Cairo

As the steamship *Devonshire* slipped through the still waters of the Persian Gulf, escorted by HMS *Cockchafer* and *Falmouth* of the Royal Navy's Gulf Flotilla, together with the Australian sloop HMAS *Yarra*, Captain Jack Masters, adjutant of the 2nd Battalion 4th Prince of Wales's Own Gurkha Rifles, stood in what patchy shade the deck of the troopship offered him, watching the sweaty exertions of his troops as they practised loading and unloading from the ship's boats. It was 5 May 1941. Masters' expectation was of an opposed landing at Basra. Had he known it, he would have chuckled on Harry Hopkins' observation that 'the Persian Gulf is the arsehole of the world, and Basra is eighty miles up it.'[1] It would not take him many days before he was to agree wholeheartedly with this sentiment. Iraq played a prominent role in the history of Masters' regiment. His battalion had fought in General Maude's successful campaign in 1918 and had helped to capture Baghdad, celebrating thereafter 'Baghdad Day' as its annual anniversary holiday. This year, Masters would experience the reality of war in the desert for himself, instead of merely as long distant history.

The day was unbearably hot: Masters recorded the temperature at 110 degrees Fahrenheit. The prospect of an opposed landing was grim for troops originally loaded at Karachi for Malaya:

No assault landing craft, only the ship's lifeboats. No covering fire, except from the Armed Merchant Cruiser. No rehearsal. No communication channels. Where in the hell was the reserve ammunition packed? The mortar bombs? Who was responsible for this bloody mess anyway . . . ?

We steamed on. The brigade staff issued orders for the landing, detailing the various waves of assault, and the lifeboats allotted to each. I sub-allotted them to our companies . . . The riflemen clambered cheerfully in and out of the lifeboats, armed, if not to the teeth, at least to the waist. We thought that we would not meet very heavy opposition, since the bulk of the Iraqi Army was upcountry near Baghdad. The enemy at Basra would be mostly armed police, who had already attacked the near-by RAF base [RAF Shaibah].[2]

Masters' fears were relieved with the welcome signal received on the day of the convoy's arrival off Basra: *'Deflate balloon. Dock area in our hands.'*[3] The three thousand Indian and Gurkha troops of the three ship convoy, part of Major General William Fraser's 10 Indian Division, disembarked quickly and safely into the town, occupied in part by 20 Indian Brigade following its arrival on 18 April.

The opening shots of this war had in fact been fired under a week before, at the Royal Air Force base at Habbaniya, west of Baghdad. Even as Masters and his battalion were disembarking 300 miles to the south-east at Basra, the tiny British garrison at Habbaniya was fighting for its life against ground and air attack by the Iraqi Armed Forces. The landing of elements of 10 Indian Division at Basra in mid-April and early May, together with the battle for Habbaniya, were the opening salvoes in a short war for the control of Iraq in the spring of 1941, a war quickly forgotten amidst the noise and scale of a global conflict, but with profound implications at the time for Britain's survival.

In the ocean of books about the Second World War that fill the shelves of our bookshops and libraries it is rare to find any comment about the war that convulsed Iraq in May 1941, the prospect of which confronted the young Jack Masters on that sweltering day of his arrival. Captain Basil Liddell Hart ignored it completely, not mentioning Iraq at all in the 825 pages of his *History of the Second World War*, first published, soon after his death, in 1970. Likewise it did not come close to registering in Major General J.F.C. Fuller's three volumes of the *Decisive Battles of the Western World*, which first emerged between 1954 and 1956. Most other historians follow this lead, Sir John Keegan being a notable exception, dedicating a paragraph to the subject in his *The Second World War*, published in 1989. General Sir David Fraser's seminal analysis of the British Army in the Second World War, *And We Shall Shock Them*, gives Iraq a passing sentence, and then only in reference to General Archibald Wavell. Those who do mention it, such as Martin Gilbert in his colossal *Second World War*, often get the details wrong.[4] In many respects the speed with which historians pass over events around Baghdad in the early summer of 1941 is understandable. It was, after all, a short war, dwarfed at the time by climactic events elsewhere, such as the dramatic German victories in Yugoslavia, the humiliating British eviction from Greece and the reversal of earlier British success against the Italians in Libya by Lieutenant General Erwin Rommel's *Deutsches Afrika Korps*, which drove Wavell's weakened forces out of Libya altogether (except for one small bastion at Tobruk) and penetrated the Egyptian frontier. Of course, *Operation Barbarossa*, which thrust Hitler's forces into Russia at the height of the dusty eastern summer in June 1941, rapidly eclipsed all else in the war until the arrival of Japan on the Axis side in mid-December. In the grand scheme of things, therefore, the small war that shook Iraq a month before the opening curtain of *Barbarossa* seems to deserve not much more than a footnote in the accounts of the titanic global struggle between the free world and fascist totalitarianism that was the Second World War.

But as the British traveller, writer and roving Ministry of Information propagandist Freya Stark emphasized, it was 'a turning point in the Middle Eastern war'.[5] Her claim was not exaggerated. The war was a victory of Churchillian determination against overwhelming odds, bitter wrangling at the highest levels of political and military command mixed with courage, improvisation and sheer bluff by the soldiers and airmen forced to fight against enormous odds across Iraq's shifting sands. The story of the war in Iraq would have been instantly recognizable to the 1930s film makers of the imperial bastion genre: a weak cantonment filled with women and children; a vigorous defence by a lightly armed and heavily outnumbered garrison; a flying column of aristocratic and sublimely confident cavalrymen advancing through dust and heat to the rescue (ably assisted by British-officered and loyal

Arab and Assyrian troops); the collapse and flight of the aggressor and the raising of the Union flag once more where it had been so grievously imperilled. The extraordinary thing about this story in Iraq in 1941, however, is that it was not a work of creative fiction: it was all absolutely true.

The result of this brief conflict was as fortunate to Britain as any other in her history. Had Iraq been lost, Great Britain may have been forced to sue for peace. As we have seen, the region's oil was a critical determinant in Great Britain's ability to continue to wage war independent of a yet uncommitted United States. Iraq was important to the survival of Great Britain for other reasons, too. The first was the psychological boost an Iraqi victory would have provided for Arab nationalism elsewhere in the Middle East at the time. Iraq had been, since the late 1930s, the home of a new brand of militant Arab nationalism which, building on a hatred of Great Britain, France and Jews in equal measure, sought both to thwart plans to create a Jewish homeland in Palestine and to create a new, unified Arab state from the patchwork of tribes and states left by the collapse of the Ottoman Empire in 1918. Had Great Britain been defeated in Iraq, its hold on both Palestine and Egypt, and thus the ability to defend these strategically sensitive countries from simultaneous external and internal threats, would have been much more difficult. The Arabs in Palestine had already revolted in 1936, and there were plenty of nationalists in Egypt willing and prepared to rise up against the British.[6] This nationalistic volatility made the region easy prey for Axis propaganda and influence; combined with Rommel's success in the Western Desert, it might have proved enough to eject the British from Egypt altogether, with all the implications this would have meant for the loss to Britain of the Suez Canal.

Iraq was also important because of the danger its loss would have represented to the security of Egypt's north-eastern flank through Turkey, Syria and Palestine. Following the collapse of France, Syria remained under the control of a Vichy regime that was increasingly pro-German, and Turkey's neutrality would not have stood for much against a determined attack by Hitler intent on securing the Suez Canal. In late 1940 Great Britain was fearful of the possibility of a German attack on Palestine and Suez directed through Turkey. Additionally, of course, the loss of Iraq would have broken the vital line of communication between the Mediterranean and India, and a crucial supply route to Palestine from the east if Egypt were to fall to Rommel. On 5 November 1940 Churchill and his cabinet considered the question of what would happen if Germany seized control of Greece, Turkey, and then Syria. It was agreed that if Turkey and Syria fell, plans would need to be constructed to demolish the Iraqi oil fields and the pipelines that transported the oil for some 1,200 miles from Kirkuk through Transjordan and Palestine to the Mediterranean.[7] The British had already cut off the French pipeline through Syria to Tripoli (in Lebanon) following the fall of France.

Negating these malign pressures could reap significant strategic benefits for Great Britain, including the dampening of pan-Arab (and pro-German) nationalism in Palestine, Egypt and Iraq, the quietening of Turkish fears and strengthening of Ankara's will to resist Berlin, and the securing of Britain's vital line of communication to India and the Far East.

Iraq has long held a significant place in British interests, for both good and ill. During the First World War, as Mesopotamia, it was scene to the fumbling British attempt to eject the Ottoman Turks from their long-held desert hegemony. This was a task that, despite the adventures of Captain T.E. Lawrence and his rebel-rousers, took three years to achieve as an ill-prepared and poorly led British Army struggled to advance north along the Tigris from Basra to Baghdad.* A number of the senior British and Indian officers who found themselves with responsibility for British operations in Iraq in 1941, such as Generals Archibald Wavell, Claude Auchinleck and Bill Slim, had served in Mesopotamia during the Great War. During the 1920s Iraq, a territory mandated to Great Britain by the League of Nations in 1920, attracted archaeologists, antiquarians, diplomats, travellers and assorted romantics of every description to explore the archaeological and cultural vastness first popularized by the likes of Gertrude Bell and Lawrence during the opening decade of the century. A distinct Arabist School developed

---

* Basra was captured in November 1914, but Baghdad was not taken until March 1917 after the ignominious siege and defeat of the British expeditionary force at Kut al-Amara in 1916.

within the British foreign policy elite, building on a wider and older Orientalist base. A significant role for Britain in the region had been secured by reason of its support for the Arab rebellion against the Ottomans and the various promises it had made regarding Arab independence. The key commitment was the promise in 1915 to the Arab leader, Sharif Husayn of the Hijaz, that Great Britain would support the creation of an independent Arab state, under British protection, encompassing Iraq, Syria, Jordan and parts of the Arabian Peninsula. However, these promises – together with widespread goodwill towards Britain – were fatally undermined by publicity in 1920 that revealed the hitherto secret Sykes–Picot Agreement of May 1916, in which Britain ceded control of Syria and northern Iraq to France, thus preventing the achievement of this unity. Solidifying their grip on power the French drove Faisal, Sharif Husayn's son, from Damascus, where the British had installed him as king at the end of the war. In recompense Britain attempted to make good this loss by making Faisal King of Iraq and by carving out a piece of Palestine in 1921, called Transjordan, and giving it to his elder brother, Abdullah.

Granted independence in 1932, a compliant Iraqi Government (described by one British diplomat as an 'Arab façade') bound itself through a mutual assistance agreement to Great Britain for twenty-five years, signing the Anglo-Iraq Treaty in 1930. The primary British interest in the country was, of course, her precious oil, pumping steadily from the oil fields around Kirkuk in troublesome self-proclaimed Kurdistan. A single pipeline took the oil from Kirkuk to Haditha, on the Euphrates, before bifurcating, one pipeline going via Syria to Tripoli on the Syrian coast, and another via Transjordan to Haifa in Palestine.* The sale of oil became a significant element of Iraq's export income and thus provided investment for the modernization of her physical infrastructure. In exchange for Iraq's friendship and protection of the oil flowing towards the Mediterranean, Great Britain committed

---

* The San Remo Agreement of April 1920 gave France a 25 per cent stake in the output of the Iraq Petroleum Company. The French then built a pipeline from Kirkuk through Syria to Tripoli to export the crude oil to the Mediterranean, after which it was shipped to France for refining. The pumping stations along each pipeline were named after each respective terminus, hence H1, H2 for example were *en route* to Haifa and T1, T2 to Tripoli.

herself to the defence of Iraq from foes both external and domestic. To achieve these aims Great Britain was granted the right, amongst other things, to maintain two air bases in the country and to recruit local 'Levies' to assist in their security. In due course, a large RAF base was constructed at Lake Habbaniya on the Euphrates, some fifty-five miles due west of Baghdad, to replace the RAF cantonment at Hinaidi, on the outskirts of Baghdad. The long-established base at Shaibah, sixteen miles south-west of Basra, was retained, together with base and port facilities at Basra. Habbaniya also became an important staging post on the aerial route to India and the Far East for the military transport aircraft and civilian airliners of their day (flying boats of Imperial Airways) and a potential route by which Egypt could be reinforced in time of emergency.

Britain also provided support and training to the nascent Iraqi Army and Royal Iraqi Air Force (RIAF) through a small military mission based in Baghdad. The Iraqi Army consisted of four divisions with some 60,000 troops. The *1st* and *3rd Divisions* were based in Baghdad, the *2nd Division* at Kirkuk and Mosul, and the *4th Division* at Diwaniya with detachments in the Basra area. An independent Mechanized Brigade, with a company of Fiat light tanks, a company of fourteen British-built Crossley six-wheeled armoured cars and two battalions of motorized infantry was also garrisoned in Baghdad. The RIAF boasted a total of 116 aircraft although only about 60 were reported to be in a serviceable condition in early 1941, most of which were based at Rashid airfield in Baghdad.* In addition, facing the slowly approaching convoy containing Jack Masters and the 3,000 Sikhs and Gurkhas of 20 Indian Brigade, were the six gunboats of the Iraqi Navy based in the Shatt al-Arab waterway.

Despite the Anglo-Iraq Treaty and the ending of the British mandate, the relationship between Iraq and Great Britain remained, on reflection, tenuous. Superficially, Iraq remained at least nominally a British ally and relations between Britain and King Faisal were warm. The country was made up of a variety of competing tribes and religious groupings – Shi'ite Muslims, Sunni Muslims, Kurds, Assyrians, Bedouin Arabs, Christians and Jews amongst others – none owing loyalty for long to anything other than their own distinct identity. The

* Previously known as Hinaidi airfield.

Royal family was itself an external imposition: Faisal was a Sunni Muslim whereas most of his subjects were Shi'ites. He had substantial minorities with which to contend, few of whom felt any natural affinity to him as their ruler.

The latter years of the 1930s had changed the attitude of many Iraqis to Great Britain in a way that British policy makers, on the whole, failed to see – London relying on the old certainties of joint endeavour against the Turk, British support for Iraqi independence and the fact that the Iraqi Royal Family owed its position to British patronage. Beneath these diplomatic givens, however, turbulent undercurrents ran in directions opposite to those assumed or desired by Great Britain and the Iraqi Royal Family. During this period German intrigue grew strongly. Those who had eyes to see recognized that British policies on wider issues in the Middle East had gravely influenced views amongst the political elite in Iraq about the desirability of continuing to support Great Britain at all. The rebellion in April 1920, supported by Shi'ite and Sunni alike against the imposition of direct colonial rule by Great Britain, burst into violence almost as soon as the ink was written on the San Remo Agreement. Great Britain had assumed for itself, as conquering power, the mandates for both Palestine and Iraq. The rebellion proved to be a signal to those who had presumed that Iraq would bow meekly to an outsider's will, particularly now that the country was free of the Turk. After a time the rebellion was savagely crushed, but the dissent remained.

Following independence in 1932 this emerging antagonism towards Great Britain was exacerbated by three other ingredients in the pan-Arab political pot. The first was Britain's promise in 1917, through the 'Balfour Declaration', to provide a Jewish homeland in Palestine. The second was Great Britain's failed promises with respect to pan-Arab nationalism, complicated by Britain's friendship with France, given the latter's occupation of the Levant (Syria and Lebanon). The third was the ever-growing influence of Germany and Nazi propaganda during the 1930s, activity that was well organized, well resourced and well received across the region. These three issues more than anything else galvanized political opposition against Britain inside Iraq as the Second World War began.

The crisis that came to a head, therefore, in April 1941, had been a long time in development. It came to many in Britain, however, as a surprise. Successive British administrations had never thought of the country as anything other than a friend, at times strongly supportive of British interests and at others exercising merely a benign neutrality. Even more damagingly, the tell-tale signs of increasing Iraqi hostility – and even hatred – towards Great Britain were not detected early enough for appropriate counteraction, either military, political or both, to be taken. Much of this hostility was generated from within a younger generation of military officers who resented the continuing influence of British neo-colonialism and the retention of power by a closed circle of elderly politicians. It was this new generation who committed themselves to pan-Arab nationalism and anti-colonialism, albeit within a domestic political arena that still largely excluded them.

In Baghdad on 17 April 1941 Freya Stark, visiting the British Embassy, confided to the privacy of her diary:

> I believe there is a large body of opinion here opposed to us only *accidentally* – young Nationalist opinion, which has become anti-British chiefly because the older generation was pro-British and kept all the power in its own hands. This young opinion has been caught by the Nazis, but a divorce should not be beyond our skill. Its strongholds are: Pan Arab-ism and the Mufti.[8]

Two days later she made the same point in a long letter to her friend Rushbrook Williams at the Ministry of Information in London:

> There is no doubt that, under Hitler, the Mufti is the main immediate cause of trouble: his removal or pacification entails action far beyond the scope of the wretched propagandist and I feel I must add the usual wail to my report – namely that the Palestine question lies at the root of all our troubles.

The radicalism of Iraqi politics in the late 1930s was bound up, as Stark observed, with the fortunes of Palestine, but was based on much deeper foundations that related to the desire for a pan-Arab federal state, something which Arab nationalists argued was denied by the continuation of French colonialism in the Levant, and British neo-colonialism elsewhere. As Stark observed to Williams:

For years I have been unable to see why our Government should not take every public opportunity to give a blessing to the Pan-Arab cry. What are they frightened of? The sentiment would please every Arab, even if the realization remained as Utopian as ever.[9]

Haj Amin el-Huseini, the 'Grand Mufti' of Jerusalem, a title bestowed in 1920 by the British on the leader of Muslims in Palestine, led the Arab rebellion between 1936 and 1939, a revolt prompted mainly by Jewish immigration. After its collapse he fled with his Syrian, Iraqi and Egyptian supporters first to Beirut, and then in 1939 to eventual sanctuary in Baghdad. There, el-Huseini's fiery, anti-Jewish pronouncements merged well with the pan-Arabism of leading figures in the Iraqi Government. To British chagrin he delighted in the retention of his exalted title. Stark met him in the lobby of a Baghdad hotel on 5 April 1941, 'a young-looking though white-haired, handsome man, wearing his turban like a halo, his eyes light blue and shining and a sort of radiance as of a crest-fallen Lucifer about him.'[10] Through the Grand Mufti's sponsorship pro-Axis intrigue grew dramatically, under the noses of a British Foreign Office concerned only with issues that would help Great Britain win the war, and for the most part blissfully unaware not just of the depth of anti-British feeling in Iraq but of the implications that this might have for Britain's long-term situation in the region more generally.[11]

British soldiers have rarely had anything good to say about the experience of fighting wars in Iraq. Across much of the country the topography and climate are extreme, and campaigning is less than pleasant at any time of the year. To those who had fought there under General Maude in the First World War it was 'Mespot!' an almost pejorative description that evoked heat like the opening of an oven door, flies, pack-mules, heatstroke and dysentery in 'a kind of delirium, a brown and yellow nightmare.'[12] The country south of Baghdad extending all the way to the Persian Gulf is a vast plain of alluvial clay, rarely reaching one hundred feet above sea level at any place, serving as the seabed of the Persian Gulf which at one time stretched nearly as far as the Mediterranean. This huge river delta drains two of the world's mightiest rivers, the Euphrates and the Tigris, which join forces fifty miles north of Basra. When mixed with rainwater, the consistency of the terrain turns quickly to mud of a glutinous consistency, leading seventh-century Arab conquerors to call the place appropriately enough 'Iraq ul Arab', or 'The Arab's mud bank'. In 1941 flooding and rainfall made movement other than by boat almost impossible, particularly where breaching destroyed the few roads. Indeed, both the roads between Basra and Baghdad, one running alongside the Euphrates and the other the Tigris, became unserviceable for several days after only moderate rainfall. It was in this region that the campaign of 1941 was fought. North of Baghdad the plain gradually reaches a height of between 500 and 1,000 feet above sea level, with intermittent hill ranges leading to the first mountain folds of Asia Minor, comprising the self-proclaimed Kurdistan at the point where Turkey, Iraq and Iran meet. The mountains which form the Iranian border in the north-west, from whence the Tigris rises, are remarkable for the violence of their scenery, the mountains reaching 10,000 feet and the steep gorges cutting a path for torrents of water on the start of the river's 1,150 mile journey to the sea. Halfway between Mosul and the Persian Gulf, as the Tigris flows inexorably southwards, it passes through the City of the Caliphs – Baghdad.

By virtue of its commanding location Baghdad was (and remains) the natural communications node for the whole of Iraq. All routes led to and departed from the city. Westwards, a road of sorts took travellers some 560 miles to Haifa in Palestine, should they have wished to traverse that far. The quality of the road changed dramatically across the course of its route. The distance to Habbaniya, some 55 miles, enjoyed a thin layer of tarmacadam, and crossed an iron bridge over the Euphrates at Falluja. The road then ran to Ramadi and from thence across the desert floor to Rutba Fort, equidistant between the pumping stations H2 and H3 on the Kirkuk to Haifa pipeline owned by the Iraq Petroleum Company. At Rutba the road forked, one route leading north-west to Damascus and another south-west to Amman, capital of Transjordan, and thence on to Haifa.

With the exception of mountain ranges separating Iraq from Syria in the north-west of the country, the borders in the remainder of the country are, on the whole, vast expanses of sand and rock that until more modern times caused topographers to write on their maps exasperated phrases such as 'barren wilderness', 'uninhabited wastelands' or 'featureless desert'. The Euphrates travels for some 1,600 miles from Turkey in a south-easterly direction through Iraq, reaching the alluvial plain at Hit, some thirty miles north of Habbaniya, flowing from there to its junction with the Tigris north of Basra. Both rivers are subject to annual spates, rising from December to their highest peaks in April for the Tigris and May for the Euphrates, before falling again to their lowest levels in September. The rivers are contained for the most part by artificial embankments known as 'bunds' that keep the water-level from spilling, when it rises above the height of the surrounding plain, but in the days before damming it was necessary occasionally to relieve the pressure and height of the Euphrates at Ramadi by cutting the bunds, allowing surplus water to drain into Lake Habbaniya. If the bund had to be cut, the surrounding area would remain flooded and thus inaccessible by foot or wheel-based transport for anything between fifteen and thirty days.

The intensity of the heat in the southern region of Iraq takes unsuspecting visitors by surprise. Daytime temperatures in the shade can easily reach 130 degrees Fahrenheit and the mean temperature in August in the country south of Iraq is 119 degrees. By some freak of nature 1941 was the hottest year for a quarter of a century. Sandstorms (*Khamsin*) ripped through the desert in five days out of every seventeen, with winds of up to fifty miles per hour carrying sand and flint in a destructive fury and halting operations during the hours of daylight. But for the British, Gurkha and Indian soldiers who fought there between 1914 and 1917, and again in 1941, the climate was the least of their problems. Campaign reports from the First World War and a 1938 reconnaissance of Iraq by officers of the Indian Army examining the state of the line of communication to Palestine described the extent of the difficulties faced in the country:

> From the point of view of health and sanitation, Iraq has little to recommend it. Plague, smallpox, malaria, sandfly fever, dysentery and Baghdad boils are not uncommon, while cholera, typhus, scurvy and heatstroke also occur. Sickness is spread by insects, mosquitoes, sandflies and an incredible number of flies. There is an element of truth in the Arab saying, 'when Allah made hell, he found that it was not bad enough, so he made Iraq and added flies.' Basra is the most malarious town in Iraq, due to the numerous

creeks, seepages and floodwaters. The high prevalence of fevers of the enteric group renders the provision of a pure water supply of great importance. No man or animal is ever really free from diarrhoea.[13]

The three principal towns in 1941 were Baghdad, Basra and Mosul. Towns of lesser significance were Kirkuk and Khanakin in the north, Karbala, Kut al-Amara and Hilla in the central region, and Nasiriya, Diwaniya, Amara and Samawa in the south. Baghdad was the seat of government, the old town lying on the western bank of the Tigris, with the more modern city, together with the principal public and commercial buildings, lying on the eastern bank. In 1941 Basra was a modern port, able to accept ocean-going ships, despite the fact that it was situated 56 miles above the mouth of the Shatt al-Arab waterway, as Hopkins had so expressively observed. The principal form of communication between Basra and Baghdad was by river: plying the Tigris in 1941 were some 86 steam and motor craft, together with upward of 433 barges, ranging in size between 10 and 300 tons. A metre-line gauge railway that linked the 354 miles between the two cities acted as a secondary communication vehicle. Beyond Baghdad the railway went both to Mosul and thence to Syria through Turkey in the west, and to Khanakin in the east. In the north, Mosul occupied a site of key strategic significance on the right bank of the Tigris, looking over the remains of ancient Nineveh on its west bank.

In the years since independence from Great Britain in 1932, Iraqi politics had been far from stable. Coups and political assassinations became a regular feature of the internal political landscape. A military *coup d'état* in 1936 by General Baqir Sidqi, which resulted in bombs being dropped on Baghdad and the murder of the Prime Minister, provided evidence of the increasingly stratified nature of political allegiance. These divisions were exacerbated by the long-running Palestinian problem, the development of Baghdad as the hub of the radical Arab diaspora, the baneful growth of the army as a political instrument in its own right and the coming of war. The constitutional monarchy was carefully modelled on that which had developed in Britain in the 717 years since the Magna Carta and was ill suited to the mutually antagonistic tribes in a country created by artificial international construct rather than by internal assent.[14] John Connell,* biographer of two senior British figures in 1941 – Generals Archibald Wavell and Claude Auchinleck – described Iraq's infant parliamentary institutions as an 'indecorous farce'. He was certain that the importation by Great Britain of an alien constitutional monarchy in the form of the Hashemite dynasty of King Faisal was 'doomed to tragedy'.[15] Certainly the Royal family itself suffered from a series of unfortunate events that contributed to its declining influence in 1939 and 1940. Following Faisal's death in 1931, his nineteen-year-old son, Ghazi, took the Hashemite throne, but was himself killed in a car accident in 1939. Ghazi was not a natural supporter of Britain, and his death spawned conspiracy theories in Iraq speculating that he had been murdered by the British so that his pro-British uncle – Prince Abdullah – could be installed in his place as Regent. At the onset of the war the throne was in the control of Ghazi's brother, who as Regent ran Iraq on behalf of Ghazi's five-year-old son, Faisal II. Because of his friendship with Great Britain the Regent was the subject of political intrigue by extreme nationalists determined to undermine his position.

A central element in the endless wrangling between family, political interest and tribe lay in the domestic power play of a group of influential army officers who detested Iraq's closeness with Great Britain, in part because of their desire to be free of the neo-colonialism that, they believed, denied them a united pan-Arab state and in part as a product of the grandiloquent claims of Nazi propaganda. This cabal, nicknamed 'The Golden Square' by Iraqis, comprised four colonels in the Iraqi Armed Forces who by 1940 exercised real power in Iraqi politics, successive governments depending on the support of the military for their survival.† This virulently anti-British clique had long looked to Germany for support for their cause, enthusiastically encouraged since the mid-1930s by Dr Fritz Grobba, the German Ambassador, whose sophisticated and well-organized propaganda

---

* John Connell was the *nom-de-plume* of the Canadian, John Henry Robertson.

† Led by Colonel Salah ed-Din es-Sabbagh, commander of the 3rd Iraqi Motorized Division, Kamal Shahib (1st Division), Fahmi Said (Mechanized Force) and the Air Force chief, Colonel Mahmud Salman.

activities in Baghdad made Freya Stark frustrated and angry at the lack of any effective British counteraction. This early relationship between Arab nationalism and Nazism, in Iraq at least, gave the pan–Arab movement from the outset a distinctly militarist and racist flavour.

When Britain declared war on Germany on 3 September 1939, Iraq reluctantly followed suit, with politicians such as Rashid Ali el-Gailani, an ex-lawyer, judge and Anglophobe, demanding concessions from the British on Palestine and Syria as a condition for declaring war. The Prime Minister, General Nuri es-Said, announced Iraq's commitment to the Anglo-Iraq Treaty,[16] Dr Grobba left the country for Tehran, and German citizens were interned and deported to India. However, the recurrent political instability carried on into 1940 as the pro-Axis faction vied for political supremacy. Nuri es-Said played the difficult game of being both pro-British as well as nationalist and pan-Arabist. His cabinet was evenly balanced between pro- and anti-British members. When Rustum Haidar, the Finance Minister, was assassinated in early 1940, a new government was formed on 31 March and Rashid Ali replaced Nuri es-Said as Prime Minister. Nuri es-Said remained in the cabinet with the Foreign Affairs portfolio and amongst the other seven members were General Taha el-Hashimi (Defence) and Naji Shawkat (Justice). Only Taha el-Hashimi and Nuri es-Said were generally well disposed towards Great Britain and the Anglo-Iraq Treaty, with the remainder generally hostile.

During the year that followed, relations between London and Baghdad declined markedly. At the outset of war in September 1939 London had requested Iraq's military support in the war against Germany, but this had been declined, Iraq agreeing merely to cut off diplomatic relations with Berlin. However, the cracks in the relationship appeared starkly when Iraq refused to break off diplomatic relations with Rome on Italy's entrance into the war on 10 June 1940, despite the strenuous efforts of the British Ambassador, Sir Basil Newton, to persuade her to do so. The truth was that the majority of pan-Arabist politicians in Iraq were quickly convinced that Britain's days as a regional superpower were numbered and that the defeat of both Britain and France would help to achieve the wider political goals of Arab unity and freedom for Palestine. Thus by the spring of 1940 the majority view amongst the Iraqi political establishment was that Britain's demise was only a matter of time, that the treaty obligations with Great Britain should only be respected in the minimum way and that a neutral stance ought to be adopted towards the war.

There were strong grounds for this view. Britain stood on the very precipice of defeat in the year following the fall of France in June 1940. The bulk of Britain's deployable pre-war professional army had been destroyed in France and its equipment left at Dunkirk – 12,200 artillery pieces, 1,350 anti-aircraft and anti-tank guns, 6,400 anti-tank rifles, 11,000 machine guns, 75,000 vehicles and virtually all its tanks.[17] German military strength was awesome and unmatched, and had sliced through northern France, adding it to the startling series of German victories between 1939 and mid-1941 that included Poland, Norway, Denmark, Belgium, Holland, Yugoslavia and Greece. Only the heroism of a few had stood in the way of German hegemonic ambitions during the Battle for Britain, but even that was insufficient, it seemed, to halt the seemingly inexorable march of the victorious German legions elsewhere in Europe, especially in Crete and North Africa.

Dunkirk underlined the enormity of the disaster that had befallen Europe since Hitler had launched his assault on the West. In Great Britain the RAF was outnumbered three to one, and the bulk of the *Luftwaffe* was flying day and night sorties over British cities. Britain was threatened by invasion from France and the Low Countries, and faced starvation through the destruction of the Atlantic sea routes to North America and desertion by her allies. True, the Commonwealth had responded quickly to the threat faced by Britain, but with its ignominious collapse France, the old ally, now represented by Vichy, not only turned its back on Britain but also actively sought to support the victor. Nowhere was this more apparent than in the old French colonies and protectorates in Syria, Tunisia and Morocco. Likewise Italy challenged British domination in the Nile Valley, where some 415,000 Italians with 500 aircraft in Libya to the west and Abyssinia and Eritrea to the south faced at most 55,000 British troops and 200 obsolete aircraft.

Sir Arthur Bryant comments:

> It was hardly surprising that most of the American Service chiefs regarded Britain at this time as a bad risk. The French High Command, conscious of how quickly its own army had collapsed, predicted that within three weeks her neck would be 'wrung like a chicken's'.[18]

Unsurprisingly the prevalent Arab view at the time reflected these sentiments. In a wonderfully elegant piece of rhetoric Churchill used this phrase to his advantage in a speech to the joint session of the Canadian Parliament on 31 December 1941, remarking to a roar of approval, 'Some chicken, some neck!'

As the pro-British element in the Iraqi Government began to be isolated politically, the formal relationship with Great Britain moved from one of spirit to one of word only. For instance, on 21 June 1940 the British Ambassador, Sir Basil Newton, requested permission for the transit of British troops from Basra through Iraq to Haifa in Palestine. The Rashid Ali government was unwilling to comply, agreeing finally only on the basis that these forces be moved through the country as quickly as possible, and in small groups. An attempt to reduce the widening gap between London and Baghdad was made in mid-1940. Pro-British Arab politicians and pro-Arab Britons sought to gain concessions for Palestine (including the implementation of Chamberlain's White Paper of May 1939, which had proposed constitutional reforms in Palestine), the re-arming of Iraq and independence for Syria, in exchange for Iraqi support for Britain in the war. The British delegate at these meetings was Colonel S.F. Newcombe, a colleague of T.E. Lawrence during the Arab Revolt against the Ottoman Turks. Churchill's government, however, cognisant of Jewish threats to rebel in Palestine, ruled out any concessions on Palestine and rejected the so-called 'Baghdad propositions' at the end of August. The failure of the Newcombe Mission undoubtedly reinforced nationalist prejudices about the possibility of ever extracting concessions from Great Britain, and served to bolster the arguments of those who were even then initiating tentative discussions with the Axis powers.

Indeed, the Iraqi Government was already in secret communication with both Italy and Germany, through both the Italian Consul and the Grand Mufti, Haj Amin el-Huseini. Iraq had long been a centre of anti-British intrigue in the pre-war period — lavish German gifts, flattery and propaganda making substantial inroads into popular Iraqi consciousness — although in 1939 and 1940 Hitler had no direct military interest in the region. He had bigger fish in sight. Exploratory feelers towards Italy by Rashid Ali on 26 June regarding the status of French Syria after the fall of France received a favourable though half-hearted response from Mussolini's Foreign Minister, Count Ciano, who indicated that Italy favoured 'the complete independence [and] territorial integrity of Syria and the Lebanon, and, moreover, of Iraq itself, together with other countries under British mandate.'[19] Whilst Iraq's nationalists knew of and feared Italy's own colonial pretensions, they began a dialogue with Rome in the hope that the Axis Powers as a whole might reward Iraq for the ejection of the British. At the same time Haj Amin el-Huseini also tried to open up communications with Hitler through the German Ambassador to Turkey, Franz von Papen. Von Papen met the Iraqi delegation, led by Naji Shawkat, in Constantinople on 5 July 1940. On this occasion Shawkat profusely apologised for Iraq's declaration of war on Germany, congratulated Germany on its string of victories and announced that he looked forward to the time when the British yoke could be thrown off and Iraqi troops would fight alongside the Germans. Haj Amin el-Huseini's personal secretary, Usman Kemal Haddad, likewise travelled to Turkey in August 1940 and thereafter to Berlin for discussions. In both places Haddad pressed the Germans and their Italian partners for a formal declaration supporting Arab rights, for which he promised in exchange Iraq's wholehearted support for the Axis cause, including access to its oil.

Despite Germany's general courting of its potential new mistress, her approach to the explorations by Arab nationalists was initially cautious. Germany had no intrinsic interest in supporting the pan-Arab movement at the time except for what it could exploit for its own purposes. Hitler even admired the British Empire and believed, until 1941 at least, that it was a force for good in Middle Eastern and indeed world stability, and did not want to dismantle it in favour of self-sponsored and radical forms of nationalism. Von Papen could therefore offer Shawkat nothing more than encouragement and an exhortation to Iraqi nationalists to keep their powder dry until an opportunity arose to rise up against the British, although carefully avoiding any firm commitment in the form of arms or troops. In any case, Germany was content at this point to allow the Middle East to remain within Italy's sphere of influence. Nevertheless, while her war plans in 1940 prevented her at the time from active involvement in the region, there was broad acceptance in Germany of the idea that support for Iraq was a good thing. It would ensure Iraq's strict neutrality, prevent her from meeting her treaty obligations with Great Britain and allow the Axis Powers access to her oil. Indeed, some elements of the German political and military machine had long supported the idea of undermining British influence in the Middle East by supplying arms and advisers to friendly Arab states, and of supporting anti-British nationalist movements. The German Foreign Office* had been active in the Middle East since August 1940 following the fall of France, and an envoy – Otto Werner von Hentig – had been despatched to Vichy-occupied Syria to evaluate the threat posed to the Levant by Great Britain. Von Hentig reported enthusiastically to Berlin that German representation in Syria would reap significant benefits for the Third Reich. It could protect German interests, defend their political friends, control and eventually prevent British trade, collect and transmit useful political and military information, and support anti-British activity amongst the Arabs. This message was reinforced as a result of a second visit by Usman Haddad to Berlin in February 1941, in which he carried a letter to Hitler offering the rich pickings of the Middle East as a lure for supporting the nationalist Arab cause.[†]

In October 1940 – with *Operation Sea Lion*[‡] postponed indefinitely and Great Britain apparently determined not to face the inevitable and capitulate – at Iraq's prompting, Germany approached Italy about drafting a joint declaration in support of Arabism. Italy was, however, cool to the idea, not wanting to empower the Arab states and concerned at Germany's developing interest in what Italy regarded as her 'patch'. Nevertheless a declaration of sorts was agreed and broadcast in Arabic on Radio Rome and Radio Berlin on 23 October 1940. It was published in the German and Italian press in December. It is clear, however, that Germany and Italy said only as much as they thought they could get away with. They wanted to secure Arab support but not necessarily to meet demands for an Arab state. Consequently the more militant Arab nationalists were disappointed that the declaration went no further than warm words.

The failure of the Newcombe Mission and Iraq's evident ambivalence towards Great Britain began to cause concern in both

---

* The *Auswärtiges Amt*.

[†] This letter is contained as an annex to Dharm Pal, *Official History of Indian Armed Forces in the Second World War. The Campaign in Western Asia.* (Delhi: Combined Inter-Services Historical Section, 1957).

[‡] Hitler's planned invasion of Britain in 1940.

London and Cairo in the autumn of 1940, although it was not considered that Iraq might actually transfer allegiance to the Axis Powers. It was assumed nonetheless that a primary German objective (this was long before any hint that Hitler might be casting longing eyes at the Russian oil fields and the great prize of capturing Moscow) would be the seizure of Turkey, followed by Syria, Iraq and then Iran, in part to secure Middle Eastern oil for her own use. As soon as the *Abwehr* codes revealed that Greece was to be the next victim of German aggrandizement, this assumption was reinforced. It was this objective that made sense of a projected German move into Bulgaria and the Balkans. In an attempt to pressurize Iraq away from a liaison with the Axis Powers, the War Cabinet decided on 7 November 1940 to impose economic sanctions on the country, and the ambassador was instructed to be more forthright to the Regent about British concerns. A follow-up to the Newcombe Mission was proposed, whereby a senior politician with experience of the country would visit Baghdad in an attempt to persuade the Iraqi Government to play a more pro-British tune. Unfortunately this mission never transpired and the opportunity was lost. Newton, however, warned the Iraqi Government to sever the surreptitious talks that the British knew the Iraqis were maintaining with Italy and Germany (because London had broken the Italian diplomatic codes), to break off diplomatic relations with Italy and not to resume relations with Germany (as popular rumour was then speculating), a charge which the Iraqi Government strenuously though falsely denied.[20] Newton then informed the Regent that Britain had no confidence in Rashid Ali's government. He insisted that Iraq choose between British friendship and the extreme nationalism of the incumbent government. On 29 November Newton met with the Foreign Minister, Nuri es-Said, and the Regent to seek Rashid Ali's removal. At the same time the United States envoy, Paul Knabenshue, informed Iraq that the United States was in complete support of Great Britain. This pressure on the Regent to act against the Rashid Ali government came, however, at a time when the Regent's own authority and influence were in decline and these heavy-handed British tactics ultimately failed to bear any fruit.

Some indication of the limited impact of these diplomatic manoeuvrings was given by the discovery that in December 1940 Rashid Ali asked, through the Italian envoy in Baghdad, for captured

British weapons. His shopping basket included 400 light machine guns with ammunition, 50 light armoured cars, 10 anti-aircraft batteries with ammunition and equipment, explosives, anti-armour missiles, mines and 100,000 gas masks. Germany agreed to release impounded French weaponry held in Syria. The route chosen for the delivery of equipment was by train via neutral Turkey, labelled for delivery to Iran and Afghanistan. At the same time Germany took the decision to reverse its earlier policy and take the lead in dealing with the Arabs rather than leaving this to the Italians, as the latter were reluctant to engage the Arabs on issues relating to self-determination and pan–Arab unity. However, there were concerns at the time that Germany's agreement with the Grand Mufti's wild demands might have unsettling consequences for Vichy-held Syria, which, it was felt, might turn itself over to the Gaullists.

All the while the power play between pro–British and pro–Axis politicians in Baghdad continued. For his part, Rashid Ali protested hotly though hollowly that his intentions were not hostile, merely that he wanted Iraq to remain neutral. The Regent, pressed hard by the British and Americans, now attempted to force Rashid Ali to resign. But the Regent's calculations misfired; the whole cabinet resigned in late January 1941 and the government was thrown into turmoil. The Regent appointed two new ministers on 28 January, a power struggle ensued and the Regent fled in fear of his life that evening, seeking safe haven with friendly tribes 100 miles south of Baghdad. Accepting the possibility of civil war in Iraq, Rashid Ali resigned and on 31 January 1941 General Taha was placed in power by the now dominant Golden Square.

Despite Rashid Ali's voluntary relinquishment of power, relations between Iraq and Great Britain failed to recover, in part because of Rashid's continued manipulation of affairs behind the scenes. The scale of Rashid Ali's dialogue with both Italy and Germany was by now abundantly clear to London. Some attempts were made to counter Rashid's obvious machinations and to appear to support the interests of the Regent, who now returned to Baghdad. Anthony Eden, Britain's Foreign Minister, visited the Middle East in February and March 1941, and met the Iraqi Foreign Minister, Tawfik es-Suweidi, in Cairo on 6 March. Eden forcefully pressed him to break off relations with Italy and to take a more supportive line towards Great Britain and her interests generally. Tawfik es–Suweidi, whilst not wanting to antagonize Britain, was nevertheless hamstrung by the power of the Golden Square. Returning to Baghdad on 17 March he persuaded Taha to attempt to clip the Golden Square's wings. In the backlash that followed, nationalist hostility to all things British accelerated pace and exploded in a military *coup d'état* by the Golden Square that placed Rashid Ali back in power at the end of the month.

The anti-British and pro-German agitation of Rashid Ali, the Grand Mufti and members of the Golden Square saw increasing success through March 1941. By early 1941 German political and military opinion had moved in favour of providing practical support to the Arab world and where appropriate of doing this over the objections of Italy. The hope was that this would provide enough prompting for Arab nationalists to rise up against the British in Iraq, Palestine and Egypt. Both Hermann Goering, the quixotic head of the *Luftwaffe*, and Admiral Raeder, the German Naval C–in–C, pressed Hitler in late 1940 and early 1941 to consider the opportunities provided by capturing Britain's weakly defended and widely dispersed imperial possessions in the Mediterranean and the Middle East. These included the capture of the Suez Canal, which would have forced Britain's shipping back around the Cape route, as well as securing Britain's sources of oil in Iraq and Iran. A modest commitment of troops, aircraft and logistical support might reap substantial dividends by stiffening the backbone of the Iraqis and encouraging them to strike out at British interests. Through the simple expedient of words, promises and limited commitment, the prospect existed for the whole of the British imperial edifice in the region to tumble down without the expenditure of much undue effort. That, at least, was the hope.

In their new, more proactive and aggressive approach to Iraq, Germany decided to make the radical cleric Haj Amin el–Huseini their principal contact. They determined that diplomatic and practical relations with the Iraqi Government and Syrian nationalists would be stepped up, as would German propaganda to the region. Ninety minutes of Arabic broadcasts were to be made every day from both Berlin and Paris; newspapers, pamphlets and other publications were to be supported financially and pre-prepared articles were to be distributed to newspapers across the Arab world. Espionage activity was also to be increased, including active support for anti-British sabotage and uprisings. On 9 April a joint German and Italian statement of support was sent to Rashid Ali promising military and financial assistance but without being specific about when this would be forthcoming. It declared:

1. That Italy and Germany followed his actions with the greatest sympathy.
2. That Italy and Germany advise armed resistance against England as soon as the relationship of the forces involved offers promise of success.
3. That Italy and Germany even at this time are actively preparing assistance in the form of arms and ammunition . . . The Italian and German governments are also prepared to give the Iraq government financial support and would like to be informed of its present wishes in this respect.[21]

Although hardly a definitive statement regarding Germany's commitment to any future Iraqi military struggle with Great Britain, the ever-optimistic members of the Golden Square believed that, in this event, the Axis Powers would come swiftly to Iraq's aid. The same message – one of potential, future assistance in which Germany would *support* rather than *lead* an uprising against Britain – was repeated in a declaration that reached Iraq on 16 April 1941:

Germany, who has never possessed Arab territories, has no territorial aims in the Arab area. She is of the opinion that the Arabs, a people with an old civilization, who have demonstrated their competence for administrative activity and their military virtues, are entirely capable of governing themselves. Germany therefore recognises the complete independence of the Arab states, or where this has not yet been achieved, the claim to win it. Germans and Arabs have common enemies in the English and the Jews and are united in the struggle against them . . . [Germany] is glad to cooperate in a friendly manner with the Arabs and, if they are forced to fight England in order to achieve their national aims, to grant them military and financial assistance in so far as is possible. *In order to assist the Arabs in their preparations for a possible struggle against England, Germany is also prepared to supply them with war material at once, in so far as a route for transporting it can be found.*[22] [my italics]

Both statements led Iraqi nationalists to believe that German assistance would be instantly forthcoming in the event of war. All the signs that they would do so – German victories in the Balkans and North Africa – appeared propitious. The Italian legate in Baghdad reported to Rome on 10 April:

> The victorious advance of the Axis armies on the Balkan and Libyan front is seen here as evidence that the decisive phase of the war in the Mediterranean has begun. Nationalist military circles in Iraq see in this the confirmation that the *coup d'état* carried out by the army has occurred at the right moment, not only from the point of view of the country's interest, but also in relation to the overall situation . . . There is a widespread conviction that Axis forces will soon put in an appearance in this area, either from the north or from the south, and that the inevitable decisive battle of the Mediterranean theatre will be fought in Mesopotamia.[23]

The developing relationship between nationalist Arabism and fascist militarism in Germany and Italy is only incongruous if it is assumed that anything other than deep, self-serving pragmatism lay at the root of pan-Arab politics at the time. Extreme Arab nationalism was willing to seek the support of any power prepared to meet its demands, even from a German regime constructed uncompromisingly on the principle of Aryan racial dominance and an Italian dictatorship intent on revisiting the bloody military expansionism of the old Roman Empire. But in treading the path of pragmatism rather than principle, Arab nationalists entirely failed to see that the Axis had no interest *per se* in either a pan-Arab state or an independent Palestine and that such ideas would be supported by the Axis Powers only for as long as they suited their own strategic purposes. In retrospect it was a suicidal policy, but Arab nationalism was blind to the illogicality of many of its pretensions. There is no reason to believe that swapping French colonialism or British neo-colonialism for that of Germany would not have brought with it the enslavement and murder of millions in an ethnic levelling of the type and scale which swept the occupied countries of Europe between 1938 and 1945. Because of their hatred of the Jew, however, pro-Axis Arabs were content to accept a superficial knowledge of Nazi totalitarianism, one that in fact displayed profound ignorance of Nazism's true nature and failed to recognize Nazi contempt for their own race. Promising Arabs their independence in a context which ignored Italian militarism and German racial intolerance would have required, as Hitler himself acknowledged, 'a grandiose fraud'.[24] Because the Arabs appeared so gullible when it came to swallowing Nazi propaganda and promises this was precisely the policy Germany pursued. It very nearly came off.

As a result of the willingness of much of the pan-Arab movement to side with the Axis Powers, Great Britain's strategic position in Iraq – and as a consequence the whole of the Middle East – was extremely dangerous in the late spring and early summer of 1941. Her unwillingness to deal with issues of Palestine and pan-Arab unity whilst the war was underway, and her inability to counter the effect of unchecked Nazi propaganda, provided exactly the reason the most disaffected elements across the region sought as justification to engage with Britain's enemies. It was an opportunity they grasped with an enthusiasm that brought Great Britain within a whisker of losing control of the Middle East altogether, and which had wider and more profound implications for Britain's survival as a whole in the Second World War.

In the early spring of 1941, whatever else was happening in the British Isles and North Africa at the time in the war against Hitler and his Axis bed-fellows, large tracts of the British Empire continued somnolently in their easy slumber in much the same way that they had done in times of peace. At RAF Habbaniya life continued undisturbed in its well-ordered patterns. The airbase and cantonment, laid out between 1932 and 1937 by the Knightsbridge contractor, Messrs Humphries & Co, was by early May a blaze of botanical colour. The intense scents of the eucalyptus, pepper and casuarina trees, hibiscus and oleander shrubs, rose beds, sweet peas and bougainvillaea wafted through the shaded offices, hangars and mess accommodation, whilst from the skies above, during the cooler parts of the day, came the drone of the far-off engines of the ancient training aircraft of Number 4 Service Flying Training School.

The war was far away and had little real impact in these peripheral localities. Few, if any, felt a need to change this situation. Mobilizing for war in Europe and the Middle East was an enormous undertaking in itself, especially at a time when Great Britain could count on few real friends, and no specific requirement existed to defend every part of Britain's overseas possessions or interests. Winston Churchill's quite sensible dictum was that *actual* war should take precedence over *potential* war.[25] This approach, however, did provide real problems in locations as yet uncommitted to war, as sensible defensive precautions were neglected in the forlorn expectation that the conflict would never reach them. Of course, the Empire was slowly galvanizing itself in defence of the Motherland, as troops, equipment and supplies travelled along the vast sea, land and aerial lines of communication that linked every part of the global network making up the assorted patchwork of Great Britain's friends and Commonwealth. The urgent imperatives of action that dominated the British Isles, Egypt and the Horn of Africa at the time, however, were not felt everywhere. These war-like motivations were certainly not felt in Iraq, which in early 1941, to the British at least, was as far off from the war as could be imagined.

The RAF had played an important role in imperial policing in Iraq since October 1922, when it was decided, for reasons of economy, to ensure order in the newly mandated territory, not by a large and expensive standing army, but by aircraft, supported on the ground by armoured cars and backed up by locally recruited Levies.* Where the only opposition was recalcitrant tribesmen equipped with horses, camels and bolt-action rifles (or even flintlock *jezails*), the approach worked well, and throughout the 1920s and 1930s, supported by the nascent Iraqi Army, security of a sort was maintained. The British-commanded 'Iraq Levies', whose original purpose was to relieve regular British troops in Iraq and Kurdistan, were established in 1921 and provided lightly armed land forces able to meet immediate emergencies. In 1941 the Levies formed by far the largest land force element at RAF Habbaniya, some one thousand two hundred in six companies, Arab, Kurdish and Assyrian. The Assyrians were members of the ancient Nestorian Christian community from central Iraq who had

---

* Running Britain's Empire, let alone defending it, was expensive. British policy was always to do it on the cheap. As it was, however, the cost of running Iraq, in 1921, amounted to £23 million, more than the total British health budget at the time. Niall Ferguson, *Empire: How Britain made the Modern World* (London: Allen Lane, 2004), p. 317.

no love for the Arabs with whom they shared the country, regarding Arabs to be interlopers and Muslims to be heretics. They were the direct descendants, recalled Captain John Frost (later of Arnhem fame, who served with them in 1939 and 1940), 'of those who "swept down like a wolf on the fold" in Biblical times, and bore the old names like Nimrod, Sennacherib and Tilgath-Pileser.'[26] The British found them to be natural soldiers and disciplined fighters. Their loyalty was never in doubt. The Arab Levies were another matter entirely, however, and proved to be a source of worry before the war, a concern that happily dissipated with the onset of fighting, as all were to prove their loyalty beyond doubt.[27] The Levies and their families, together with Indian and Arab labourers, brought the population of the cantonment in the spring of 1941 to some 9,000 souls.

When internal policing came to an end with the onset of Iraqi independence, the two original RAF bases at Mosul and Hinaidi (Rashid) were handed over to the Iraqi forces and the two new bases at Habbaniya and Shaibah were constructed and occupied. Shaibah became home to 244 Bomber Squadron RAF operating ancient Vincent bombers. The purpose of the bases was to act in part as the military guarantor of Britain's commitment to the Anglo-Iraq Treaty, the most important element of which for Great Britain was the uninterrupted provision of Iraq's oil. For its part, the Iraqi Government committed itself to protecting the installations from tribal or any other form of harassment or attack.

In the otherwise turbulent milieu of Iraqi politics during April 1941, Squadron Leader Tony Dudgeon, who arrived for a rest posting from the Western Desert on 3 April, recalled that everything on the surface appeared calm at Habbaniya at the start of the month. No thought appeared to be given by the authorities at the airbase that their staid and somewhat comfortable existence was under threat, despite the *coup d'état* and the hostility of Rashid Ali to the British presence in his country. Dudgeon recalled:

There were some rumours of a potential rebellion sixty miles away in Baghdad but it was apparently not serious, just a local uprising. No one paid much attention. Everybody from the Air Vice-Marshal downwards carried out their normal duties, blissfully careless of any dangerous situation in brew.[28]

A variety of obstacles stood in the way of a successful defence of Habbaniya at the time. It was never expected, for instance, that these airbases would find themselves in the front line of battle. RAF Habbaniya was hopelessly sited for defensive purposes. Between the base and Lake Habbaniya lay a steep escarpment leading to a wide plateau some 150 feet high, which entirely dominated the base. Immediately below the escarpment lay the airfield and the Habbaniya cantonment itself, a vast camp of around 500 acres, secure behind a 7-mile-long steel fence guarded by the Levies and regularly sited brick block houses. The rear of the base was formed by the mighty Euphrates River, in spate at this time of year. Habbaniya was a cantonment built on the self-contained Indian model, and included everything that those stationed there, both military or civilian, might require without having to venture outside the wire. Adjacent to the airfield were the aircraft hangars for Number 4 Service Flying Training School and the Iraq Communications Flight, behind which the base was carefully and methodically laid out to reflect a little British oasis in the desert: broad avenues named after places back home – Piccadilly, The Strand and Regent Street amongst a pantheon of RAF heroes – were bordered by trees, shrubs, lawns and ornamental gardens, all watered by the Euphrates. Tony Dudgeon recalled that Habbaniya possessed quite impressive off-duty amenities:

> There were playing fields for rugger, soccer, and hockey. There was a golf course. Riding stables held the ponies for hacking, or playing polo on the polo pitch. Both polo-pitch and golf course were beside each other, right in the middle of the camp. The lake, just up and over the escarpment on the other side of the airfield, could be used by the local RAF Yacht Club and for open-water bathing. Within the camp, there was also the finest swimming pool in the Service. The gymnasium was superb and there were fifty-six tennis courts.[29]

Dudgeon failed to recall the hounds and horses of the Royal Exodus Hunt, which tended to be the preserve of the seconded British Army officers. Captain John Frost was the master and Captain Alistair Graham the whip, the pack hunting wild jackal out across the expanse of plateau between the Euphrates and Lake Habbaniya.[30] Those who designed the cantonment never conceived that it would ever be subject to attack, and certainly not by a government bound to Great Britain by a formal treaty of mutual non-aggression. The most that could be expected was perhaps a civilian riot, or a foray against it by disaffected tribesmen; the presence of the Iraq Levies and the ancient but still serviceable Rolls Royce Silver Spirit armoured cars of World War One vintage were considered sufficient to fend off threats of this nature.

A second obstacle to the successful defence of Habbaniya was that as a relatively comfortable training station it was commanded by men who, whilst brave in their time, were far from their prime in 1941. The two senior RAF officers at Habbaniya, Air Vice-Marshal H.G. 'Reggie' Smart and Group Captain W.A.B. Savile, despite being well decorated pilots from the First World War, were entirely unsuited to the desperate challenge they were about to face. Slow, conservative and conventional, they were unprepared mentally for the pace and fury of modern war. By 1941 Smart had relaxed into the comfortable routines of peacetime flying training and revelled in the petty bureaucracy typical of the unstretched, complacent military mind. Dudgeon recalled that Savile marched in cadence with Smart, following rules and regulations slavishly and frowning on the exuberance and imagination of the more youthful officers. The army officers seconded to command the Iraq Levies had a similarly jaundiced view of their RAF superiors, Captain John Frost recalling that these men 'were very fixed in their ideas, the main one of which was to live as quiet a life as possible'.[31] Time was to show that it was to the younger and more dynamic officers – both RAF and army – that the eventual survival of the base was due.

A third obstacle to the defence of Habbaniya lay in the complete absence of any aircraft suitable for fighting a modern war. Of the variety of aircraft found at Habbaniya, not all could be used for offensive operations and none could be described as modern. Likewise, many of the eighty-four airframes on the base could not be flown or used offensively, and at the start of the battle the station boasted only thirty-nine pilots. The inventory comprised a mixed assortment of obsolete and obsolescent bombers, fighters and trainers. Habbaniya boasted three superannuated Gladiator biplane fighters, used as officers' runabouts, and thirty Hawker Audaxes, which could also carry eight 20-pound bombs. There was no belted ammunition for the Gladiator and Audax guns, so when the need arose many thousands of belts had to be constructed by hand, a long and laborious process carried out by ground crew.

The bombing fleet included seven early 1920s vintage Fairey Gordon biplane bombers and twenty-seven twin-engined Oxfords. Long made redundant from acts of war, the Gordons were used to tow targets for aerial gunnery practice at speeds of some eighty miles per hour. Although slow, their chief virtue was that they could carry a couple of 250-pound bombs. The Oxford was a cheaply constructed training aircraft, built out of plywood, never designed for action, containing space to drop eight 9-pound smoke practice bombs. There were also twenty-five Hawker Harts – the bombing version of the Hawker Audax – which could carry two 250-pound bombs. Finally, there were some twenty-four or so Hart-trainers, but despite desperate attempts nothing could be done to fit any form of weaponry to these aircraft, Dudgeon recording that their sole useful purpose in the coming emergency was that 'which entailed swoops and noises'.[32]

With the imminent possibility of action Dudgeon and a group of officers, together with Wing Commander Hawtrey who until recently had been head of the Royal Iraqi Air Force Training School, sought Smart's permission to prepare the aircraft for war, including making adjustments where possible to allow aircraft to carry bombs. Each 20-pound bomb carried by an Audax, for example, contained the same amount of explosive as a 6-inch artillery shell, and Dudgeon wanted to try to see whether he could increase the bomb load on the Audax to that of the Hart, from 160 pounds (eight 20-pound bombs) to 500 pounds (two 250-pound bombs). Such a modification would dramatically increase the offensive capability of the aircraft. Both Smart and Savile were reluctant to divert their aircraft from their primary duty of training, however, and forbade absolutely any experimentation on aircraft payloads. Fortunately Dudgeon and others, in secret, ignored these instructions, made the requisite adjustments and tested the aircraft with their new payloads under cover of darkness. When it was proven that these adjustments could be easily, simply and safely made, permission was grudgingly granted to convert as many Audaxes as possible. Dudgeon was eventually able to convert twelve Audaxes providing, together with the seven Gordons, a total of nineteen aircraft each with the capability to carry a 500-pound bomb load.

Dudgeon was faced with the same obstruction by Savile when attempting to fit 250-pound bombs to the Oxfords, so he had to make do with designing a rack to enable them to carry eight 20-pound anti-personnel bombs instead of the smoke bombs. Both Savile and Smart refused even this proposal, until Dudgeon secretly tested the new arrangement himself and proved that it was safe. By late April the twenty-seven Oxfords had been converted to carry 160 pounds of bombs each, which meant that the whole Oxford fleet could take to the air carrying a total complement of 216 bombs. This effort to increase the bomb payload on otherwise weakly armed aircraft was to prove decisive in the battle for Habbaniya: in a mere matter of weeks the number of aircraft at Habbaniya provided with an offensive capability was doubled, as was the total bomb carrying capacity of Smart's motley air force. Smart accepted other proposals to make the base ready for war, and the hallowed polo pitch and golf course were levelled by bulldozers to make a relatively safe runway inside the wire, as the main airfield did not even enjoy that protection. These preparations, both sanctioned and furtive, were all critical factors in enabling the puny garrison not merely to stand against the coming storm but, in spite of all its deficiencies and inadequacies, to conquer.

2

New Delhi

From the outset of his arrival in New Delhi as Commander-in-Chief India on 27 January 1941 (after the retiring General Sir Robert Cassels) Lieutenant General Claude Auchinleck was deeply worried about wider threats to India's security. India had long been concerned about its perimeter, formed in the north-west by the rich, oil-bearing regions of Iraq and Iran and in the south-east by Britain's weakly defended possessions in the Far East. Auchinleck, a long-standing and distinguished son of the Indian Army, accepted completely the view that Indian security was inextricably part of a strategic continuum that extended uninterrupted from the Mediterranean and Middle East (Gibraltar, Malta, Libya, Egypt and Palestine) through India (Iraq, Iran and Afghanistan) to the Far East (Burma, Malaya and Singapore). Each element was as important as the other, and a concentration upon one part at the expense of another would necessarily weaken the whole front. There was by no means universality of agreement on this view, but it had its strengths, and a succession of Indian Viceroys and Commanders-in-Chief trusted it as the overarching context of India's strategic position in the great curve of empire that stretched from Great Britain through Gibraltar to Singapore and thence on to Australasia. Any threat to this strategic conception was resisted fiercely, and Auchinleck, with his deep knowledge of India behind him, was no different from those he followed.

Contingency plans had existed in India since August 1939 to send forces to the Persian Gulf in the event of a threat to the Iranian oil fields, the primary predator at the time being Russia, the old protagonist in what Rudyard Kipling described as the 'Great Game' of British and Russian imperial rivalry in the Middle East.* The War Cabinet's 'Middle East Policy Directive' of 15 January 1940 recognized the threat to both Iran and Iraq from the old enemy by ordering the preparation of contingency plans based on deploying troops from India Command to Basra. Three plans were rapidly drawn up. *Operation Trout* was to involve the despatch to Basra of an Indian division;† *Operation Salmon* went a step further and envisaged the creation of a base organization at Basra necessary to sustain a whole corps of three divisions; *Operation Herring* considered the requirements for one British and two Indian divisions that could operate across the whole of both Iran and Iraq if needed. In the course of 1941 as the nature of the threat changed, particularly with the prospect of an Axis attack on Iraq through Vichy-held Syria, these three plans were changed and their appellations with them: *Herring* became *Sabine, Trout* became *Sybil*. The formations allocated to *Sabine* were to be 6, 8 and 10 Indian Divisions.‡

In March and April 1941, as the German war machine bore down on Yugoslavia, Egypt and Greece, the prospect of a German breach of Turkey and thrust into Syria, Iraq and Palestine became ever more a possibility. Auchinleck became increasingly fearful that the lack of robust action by Britain – both political and military – could lead to the loss of Iraq altogether, with disastrous consequences for India. The results would have been profound. Not only would Axis occupation of Iraq close the reinforcement route from India to Palestine, immobilize the Royal Navy through the loss of Iraqi and Iranian oil, and disrupt British use of the Persian Gulf, but it would also, in the words of the Indian Official Historian, turn India from being an asset to London into a liability.[1] New Delhi was fearful of the negative impact inaction might have on nationalist opinion in India. Looking

---

* An excellent account of this rivalry is Anthony Hopkirk, *The Great Game: On Secret Service in High Asia* (London; John Murray, 1990).

† An infantry division typically comprised some 15,000 troops in two or three brigades, and was commanded by a Major General.

‡ 6 Indian Division comprised 26, 27 and 28 Indian Infantry Brigades; 8 Indian Division comprised 17, 18 and 19 Indian Infantry Brigades; 10 Indian Division comprised 21, 24 and 25 Indian Infantry Brigades.

back over the activity of recent months Auchinleck came to the conclusion that both London and Cairo were failing to display the leadership necessary to manage the impending crisis. He determined, with the Viceroy, Lord Linlithgow, to take on this responsibility himself. His immediate concern was to ensure both that a friendly government remained in power in Baghdad and that in the event of an Axis attack Britain would already have deployed substantial forces to the region and would therefore be in a strong position to protect its interests not just in Iraq, but also in Iran. On 8 February he wrote to General Sir Archibald Wavell, the Commander-in-Chief Middle East, in Cairo, to register his concern that the arrangements made so far about *Sabine* were both operationally and administratively deficient because they failed to make clear who – Cairo or New Delhi – would control operations if either plan was activated. This was a responsibility that he believed should fall to India Command. 'Time' he wrote, 'is getting short and the situation in Iraq looks none too pleasant. I am therefore most anxious to clear the air on major problems as soon as possible so that we can get down to detailed planning here in India.'[2]

Letter writing was a slow way of communicating at the time, it not being unusual for mail to take three weeks to get from London to New Delhi, and given the pressures on Wavell during this period, with the deteriorating situation in both Libya and Greece, he did not reply immediately.* In any case Wavell failed to see why the matter was so urgent. His view was that Iraq was a sideshow to the main arena of war in North Africa and the Mediterranean, where he was confronted by strong enemy forces in the field, and that if the situation demanded it firm political action alone would be required. In the absence of any immediate response from Wavell, Auchinleck wrote on 21 February directly to the Chief of the Imperial General Staff, General Sir John Dill, who was then undertaking a brief tour of the Middle East. He copied the letter to Wavell.

Auchinleck pressed Dill for a decision to allow the following:

---

* In peacetime flights from London to Baghdad took four days and a further two days to get to New Delhi. Regular flights were operated by Imperial Airways, KLM, Air France and Ala Littoria air services. In wartime, however, most mail went by sea, much of it via the Cape.

1. The initial occupation of Basra and its vicinity on the assumption that the landings might be opposed both by Iraq and Iran with the aid of enemy forces whether German or Russian.
2. A plan for the early reinforcement of the leading echelon and for the establishment of a base at Basra.
3. After the occupation of Basra and its vicinity and the establishment of a base at Basra alternative plans were required for
   (a) Further operations in Iraq.
   (b) Operations in the oil fields of south-west Iran, should they be necessary.

His preferred solution, he explained to Dill, would be to make New Delhi solely responsible for the planning and mounting of operations in Iraq:

I feel that it would be far sounder to delegate the task, at any rate of occupying Basra, entirely to this HQ. If it were necessary at a later date to place the Force under the operational control of Mideast I should offer no objection provided I were given an opportunity of expressing my views as to the plans adopted. As A.H.Q [Army Headquarters] India will be responsible for maintenance and reinforcement, and will naturally be blamed for any breakdown, I regard this as essential . . .

Whatever the decision on the question of operational control it is in my opinion necessary, if the operation is considered a serious possibility, to assemble at an early date a nucleus Corps H.Q to carry out the planning in detail. It is also essential that the officer who is to command the Force should be nominated in order that he may take charge of the preparation of the Plan of Operations. If, as I anticipate, this officer is to be found from India, I should be glad of very early authority to submit my proposals.[3]

Auchinleck already had a commander in mind: Major General Edward Quinan, then the General Officer Commanding (GOC) Western District, based in Quetta. Dill and Wavell discussed Auchinleck's ideas, and in separate letters to Auchinleck both men expressed general agreement. On 8 March Wavell sent his long-awaited response to Auchinleck. In this he cautiously supported India's proposals, particularly those that related to the insertion of a force into Basra in an emergency, agreeing that initial planning for operations in Iraq should reside with India. Dill also publicly supported Auchinleck's plans, adding that he was convinced that the activation of *Sabine* was only a matter of time. Writing from Cairo on 13 March, he mused:

> Conditions in Iraq are, as you know, bad and show little sign of improving. We have had that nasty little red fox, Tewfiq Suwaidi [sic], the Foreign Minister, over here. He has been all honeyed words but is obviously quite unreliable. The Regent, they tell me, is good, but can he control or deal with the soldiers who have gone political?[4]

It is clear, nevertheless, that Wavell did not give vent to the full range of his views on Iraq at this time, leaving Auchinleck in the dark about the depth of his antipathy to the idea of pre-emptive military intervention. For his part the Secretary of State for India (in London), Sir Leopold Amery, was under no illusion about the threat. In a letter written to Auchinleck on 19 February he wrote: 'It is difficult to foresee what is going to happen in that part of the world, but it may well be that sooner or later you may have to face the necessity of sending troops to Basra.'[5] Auchinleck agreed. His reading of the situation made him pessimistic about the prospects of keeping the lid on the Iraqi political cauldron, believing that the British would be drawn into some kind of action in Iraq sooner or later, particularly if the Germans or Italians became involved. The long struggle against the Turks in Mesopotamia twenty-five years earlier continued to cast a shadow over Indian security. Auchinleck wrote in reply to Amery on 17 March:

> I feel more and more certain that it will not be long before we shall have to send troops to Iraq and that this alternative L of C [Line of Communication] via Basra, Baghdad, Mosul and Aleppo may become really important strategically before the war is much older. However, as you know, we are preparing for that contingency and planning has now started in earnest.[6]

The week before, on 13 March, Auchinleck had written again to Wavell, reinforcing his concerns about Iraq. 'I shall feel', he wrote, 'much easier in my mind when we have got something concrete on which we can work at short notice, because I feel, myself, that with events moving at the pace they are the notice we shall get may be very short.'[7] Whilst agreeing to the sensibleness of planning for *Sabine*, however, Wavell still could not see the need for military action in Iraq in the current circumstances. He was not convinced that Auchinleck's arguments about the threat posed to Iraq were sound and consequently was opposed to any kind of military intervention in Iraq other than the pre-emptive plans underway for *Sabine*. Two factors drove Wavell's attitude towards Iraq at this time. The first was the argument, common in Arab Bureau and Foreign Office circles, that precipitate military action in Iraq might serve to inflame anti-British passions across the region, and by causing revolts and rebellions could serve to weaken yet further Britain's hold on its interests in the Middle East. The second was that Wavell had too few resources available to him to risk diverting any to an unnecessary (in his view) expedition to secure Basra. He was simply too preoccupied with pressing concerns in both Greece, Libya and the defence of Egypt to pay any detailed attention to the potential for a flare up in Iraq.

Wavell nevertheless agreed to the need for a meeting to update the plans for *Sabine*. Auchinleck proposed to send his Chief of Staff, Lieutenant General Sir Thomas Hutton, to Cairo for the purpose. Hutton was briefed by Auchinleck in New Delhi on 15 March and thereafter travelled to Egypt with explicit instructions from his chief to prepare the plans for the despatch of *Force Sabine* and to reinforce the strong view of the Indian Government that decisive pre-emptive action was needed in Iraq to preserve, amongst other things, the all-important line of communication from India to Palestine and the Suez Canal. 'I am most anxious', he told Hutton, 'to gain a foothold in Iraq. The sooner we begin to get control, militarily, in Iraq, the better. It is very necessary to gain the Euphrates tribes on our side.'[8]

The Cairo planning conference, however, proved to be something of a disaster for India. As soon as Hutton arrived in Cairo, Wavell did his utmost to wean him away from what he clearly believed to be India Command's foolhardy ideas about military intervention. He was successful. Hutton, when exposed to the full force of Wavell's arguments, decided to side with Cairo against the firm instructions of his own chief. Accordingly, the view of the conference was that the Indian forces prepared for *Operation Sabine* should be deployed not to

Basra but to Transjordan or Palestine where they could be used against Baghdad should the need arise. After all, the argument went, he who held Baghdad held Iraq, and Basra was too far from Baghdad to be able to influence events in the capital. Wavell made it clear that he was convinced that Auchinleck's prescription was wrong, that a commitment to Palestine rather than to Basra was the correct way forward and that potential problems in Iraq could be speedily resolved through the use of strong diplomatic and political action rather than the use of force. Hutton agreed.

When he was formally in receipt of these proposals on 29 March, Auchinleck was furious. This was very far from the plan that India had proposed. He was angry that Hutton had so clearly and quickly come under the spell of the Cairo camp and had so rapidly moved away from 'the object which was decided after careful consideration and agreed to',[9] namely GHQ (General Head Quarters) India's strong conviction that an unsecured Iraq posed a serious threat not just to India but to Great Britain's long-term interests, and that military action to secure the oil fields of the upper reaches of the Persian Gulf was a serious strategic objective to which India was completely committed. He was equally annoyed that Wavell had apparently agreed to Auchinleck's plan whilst Dill was on his visit to Cairo in March, only thereafter to undermine the decision weeks later once Dill had returned to London. In his firm view Wavell's proposal failed entirely to recognize the threat to India of non-intervention in Iraq. The issue was not what could be done *after* war had broken out in Iraq, but what needed to be done to prevent it, *before* conflict arose. Throughout this period the virtues of pre-emption were repeatedly rejected by Wavell. Auchinleck ordered Hutton to return to New Delhi immediately.

The difference of opinion that now divided Cairo from New Delhi was stark. Wavell did not accept the threat to the security of British oil by a hostile government in Baghdad, nor that British strategic interests in Iraq could only be secured by the interposition of military force, which was the clear and unequivocal object of *Sabine* and the driving imperative of the Indian Government.

The political chaos in Iraq failed to improve through February and March 1941. General Taha el-Hashimi, the man whom the Golden

Square managed to place in power, was weak and failed to take a hard enough line with the British as the radicals demanded. Accordingly, as the Regent tried in vain to persuade Taha to reduce the power of the Golden Square, Taha was himself deposed in a *coup d'état* on 1 April, Rashid Ali being appointed Prime Minister by the dominant military clique in his stead. The Regent, recognizing just in time what was about to happen, fled for protection to the American envoy, who took him to safety at RAF Habbaniya under a carpet in the back of his car, after which he was flown to Basra and the protective hull of the elderly British river gunboat HMS *Cockchafer*. He was to spend much of the interregnum in Jerusalem. Stark relates how the officers of the Golden Square:

> had taken over the post offices and radio station; every word spoken over the telephone was listened to; and on April 1st they had searched the palace for the Regent with – it was said quietly – four doctors and a certificate of death by heart failure already written out.[10]

Rashid immediately declared himself leader of a 'National Defence Government' and proceeded to arrest many leading pro-British citizens and politicians, although a good many also escaped by various means and routes, most to Amman in Transjordan.

Announcing that Rashid Ali had assumed the premiership 'in accordance with the requests of the people and the army', the coup leaders' immediate plans were to refuse any further concessions to Great Britain, retain diplomatic links with Italy and expel the most prominent pro-British politicians from the country. Their aim at this stage appears not to have been to mount a military confrontation against Britain. Instead, insofar as the Golden Square's plans can be ascertained, the intention was to exert maximum political and diplomatic pressure on Great Britain to persuade the ex-mandatory power that counteraction against Iraq would be futile, and if possible to eject the British without necessarily resorting to force. The coup was evidence of the Golden Square's conviction both that Britain was a spent force and that Germany would make good its promises of aid to Iraq in the event that a military clash became inevitable. This belief was strengthened by the encouraging noises emanating from Berlin following Haddad's trip to the German capital in February. Despite Britain's widespread interests in the country, all plotters believed that as a result of her increasing military weakness Great Britain would not resort to military force but would instead attempt to negotiate with the new government, regardless of its legality.

A vituperative propaganda campaign was launched almost immediately against both the Regent and Great Britain, which did much to exacerbate popular anti-British prejudice on the streets of Baghdad. Stark travelled through the capital city on 3 April in the midst of an atmosphere, as she described to her diary, which was 'frothing like milk about to boil'.

> Crisis as usual only a bit more so. The army has got post office and radio station: Government resigned, and Rashid Ali Gailani [sic] has seized it; Regent disappeared, some say to the British at Habbaniya.[11]

The tone of the new regime was immediately apparent. Writing four days later, Stark recorded:

> Everyone is watching the crisis get worse in a fascinated way. The Big Four seem very competent in the management of news: the Regent's broadcast is jammed; Reuter's fatuous message about 'perfect tranquillity' in Baghdad is already scattered by them in leaflet form; anxiety to continue British friendship stressed, though the German tone of Press and Baghdad wireless are already more pronounced . . .
>
> HMS *Falmouth* reached Basra full steam. Rashid Ali protests that no permission was asked: H.E. [British Ambassador, Sir Kinahan Cornwallis] says he doesn't recognize the right of the present government to be asked. They are being marooned in the Embassy. No Iraqis have been to see them there.[12]

As the storm clouds gathered over Iraq, an increasingly nervous Smart asked Cairo on 6 April for reinforcements at Habbaniya. Wavell and his Air Officer Commanding (AOC) Middle East, Air Marshal Sir Arthur Longmore, however, believing Iraq to be a low priority compared with Greece and Libya, rejected the request. Habbaniya remained vulnerable and alone.

Stark complains that not enough was done by London or Cairo to counter the propaganda effort made by the Germans and Italians during the spring of 1941, and to stand firmly in defence of the Regent.[13] She had a point. Worse, no military or political planning had taken place to prepare for a *coup d'état*, should it come. It was not as though there had been no warnings. During February and March 1941 the British Secret Intelligence Service reported that Rashid Ali and his clique were working hard to bring pressure on the government through political and pro-Axis agitation, and that Britain's failure to support the Regent was making the rebels bolder by the day. Italian diplomatic traffic likewise indicated that a crisis was brewing. Warnings had been made as early as December 1940 about the danger of Rashid Ali seizing power, and the Foreign Office had asked that additional forces be sent to Iraq as an insurance against any untoward development in the country. Whitehall did not always speak with a single voice, however. When Smart repeated his request to Cairo for a bomber squadron and a 'modern aircraft flight' to be based in Basra to support and protect the landings of *Force Sabine,* Longmore agreed to send a squadron of Wellingtons to Basra (two-thirds of the bomber force available to him at the time) together with six Gladiators. However, the Air Ministry in London, out of touch with both the weakness of Smart's position and with the rapidly increasing prospect of war, refused to authorize the deployment. Ignoring London, Longmore nevertheless despatched six time-expired Gladiator biplanes to Iraq accompanied by a single Wellington bomber (loaded with Gladiator spares) to cover the landings at Basra.

The struggle during March between Wavell and Auchinleck saw no let up after Rashid Ali's *coup d'état*, and if anything increased slightly in intensity. The dispute was exacerbated by London's insistence that Cairo, rather than New Delhi as had recently been agreed by Dill, responded to the unfolding events in Iraq. It remains unclear why London took this line. It may have been because this new domestically inspired threat was different from that which formed the original rationale for *Herring* (invasion by Russia) or *Sabine* (invasion by Germany through Syria). Yet, whilst it is true that a threat emanating from within Iraq had not been anticipated, it offered no less severe a danger to British interests in the country and should not have been treated any differently from one emanating externally. Nevertheless, the War Office asked Wavell on

3 April what military forces he could provide in the event that intervention in Iraq might be required. From the outset Churchill urged an aggressive response to the illegal government in Baghdad, advocating a policy of non-recognition of Rashid Ali's new National Defence Government. On 5 April it became clear from intercepted signal traffic from the Italian legation in Tehran that Germany was planning the despatch of arms shipments to Iraq through Syria, information that reinforced Churchill's viewpoint. Wavell had, of course, already come to firm conclusions about the possible use of force in Iraq and saw no reason at this stage to change his mind. Accordingly, he urged London to restrict itself to diplomatic pressure and at the same time asked the Joint Intelligence Committee for an appreciation of Soviet and Iranian reactions to any military intervention in Iraq by Britain. On 8 April he received the verdict: Iran and Russia were unlikely to respond unfavourably to British military action.

In the meantime Britain's newly arrived ambassador, Sir Kinahan Cornwallis, who had the misfortune to arrive at Habbaniya on 2 April, the day on which the Regent managed to escape the clutches of his would-be assassins in Baghdad, gave London his own appreciation of the situation. Cornwallis was an old Iraq hand who had spent twenty years in the country as adviser to the late King Faisal. He knew Rashid Ali well, as he had been removed by Rashid from his post in 1935 when the latter had been Minister of Internal Affairs.[14] He identified three options for action by Great Britain. First, it could attempt to restore the Regent by armed action. Second, it could publicly reject the Rashid Ali regime in the hope that this would weaken its internal position. Finally and unthinkably, it could recognize the new regime and learn to live with it. The only option with any hope of succeeding was the first, but it would need to take place quickly to prevent Rashid Ali from consolidating his power base. Cornwallis was firmly of the view that a failure by Britain publicly to stand up for the deposed Regent would dangerously damage Britain's prestige amongst ordinary Iraqis as well as in the wider Arab world. This was precisely the view already taken by both Churchill in London and Linlithgow and Auchinleck in India. It was not, however, the view taken by Wavell.

On 7 April Wavell replied to London's request to the effect that all he had to spare in an emergency was a single British battalion in Palestine, and that 'any other action is impossible with existing resources.'[15] He concluded that the only alternative was for Iraq to be contained by strong diplomatic action and an aerial 'demonstration' by the RAF in Iraq. Otherwise, he could do nothing else to help. It is not clear what Wavell meant by a 'demonstration', but short of a massive aerial bombardment of strategic targets in Baghdad it was unlikely to prove decisive. So it transpired. It may have been that Wavell believed that all he faced in Iraq was a bunch of unruly tribesmen on scraggy horses armed with ancient flintlocks, the sort of audience that aerial 'demonstrations' had been designed to counter on the frontiers of the Empire in an earlier age. Surprisingly, in the absence of anything else that seemed likely to work, at Habbaniya Smart grasped the straw Wavell offered. He ordered his Training School to desist from daily duties on 8 April in order to mount an aerial demonstration over the Euphrates. It stretches credulity to believe that Smart thought it would frighten Iraq into compliance with Britain's wishes, particularly when he had no intention of even flying over Baghdad itself. The result was a farce. A motley collection of some forty-eight obsolete planes flew repeatedly along the Euphrates between the villages of Ramadi and Falluja in an operation that served merely to burn fuel, bemuse camel herdsmen and scatter wild gazelles far below. There is no evidence that any Iraqis in positions of responsibility even saw or heard, let alone registered any concern, about the entire strength of RAF Habbaniya flying seemingly aimless patterns in the clear blue of the desert sky.

It is possible to discern a variety of motives for Wavell's opposition to London's demands for strong action in Iraq during April and May 1941 in addition to the factors that led him earlier to reject Auchinleck's analysis of the threat facing Britain from an unguarded Iraq. First, Wavell was determined to resist any move that would require the sending of troops to Iraq and the diminution of other priorities in North Africa and the Mediterranean. This was understandable given the wide range of his other commitments. In late March 1941 his forces stretched between the Horn of Africa, through Egypt, Libya, Palestine and Greece. Malta needed reinforcing and Wavell was fearful for his northern flank of the German domination of Syria. He feared perhaps that a military commitment to Iraq might also become open-ended and impossible to sustain for the long term. This new commitment being pressed upon him by Churchill and Auchinleck could not have come at a worse time. Indeed, April 1941 was the lowest point so far in British fortunes in the Middle East. Rommel captured Mersa Brega on 1 April, Benghazi on 3 April and Derna on 7 April, pushing back Wavell's forces into Egypt (except for those besieged at Tobruk) by 13 April. Salonika was taken on 8 April and Belgrade fell on 17 April, the British being forced to evacuate from Greece entirely by the end of the month. Britain stood alone against the German tidal wave, and every new threat impinged in some way on Wavell and his fast-depleting resources. In the face of such pressures Wavell prioritized the resources available to him, deciding on 6 April that his first task was to hold Egypt, the Suez Canal and Palestine: Iraq was a very low priority indeed. The period was described by Wavell's biographer, John Connell, as one 'of supreme challenge, of a complex mingling of triumph and disaster, of bold decisions and nightmare risks, above all of overwhelming responsibility.'[16] The situation was so grave at the end of April that Roosevelt anticipated a British withdrawal from the Middle East.[17] These fearsome pressures all coloured Wavell's perspective and his judgement.

Second, it is more than probable that Wavell regarded the call to intervene in Iraq as yet another example of the Prime Minister's aggressive impetuosity, a characteristic he had already seen in Churchill's calls to send troops from Libya to Greece.* In an appreciation sent by hand to London on 24 April Wavell articulated what he described as his 'Worst Possible Case', a scenario that included the prospect of strong German attacks from the west from Libya, from the north through Turkey and Syria, and from the east by the Iraqi Army supported by German airborne troops, as well as severe air and sea attacks on both Crete and Cyprus. A threat very clearly existed, in Wavell's eyes, from Iraq, but his task at the time was to apportion the limited resources he had to their best effect, and the threat from Iraq did not appear urgent, existing in the possibility not of an attack by Germany but merely of an 'anti-British rising'. A potential *political* threat to British interests in Iraq, Wavell considered, did not constitute an urgent *military* priority on his slender resources. He did not accept

---

* Wavell had sent 50,000 troops and 8,000 vehicles to Greece in early March 1941, thus dangerously denuding North Africa of the resources necessary to prevent Libya and Egypt being over-run by Rommel's newly arrived *Afrika Korps*.

Auchinleck's arguments about the virtue of pre-emptive military intervention.

Wavell was not therefore concerned whether active military intervention in Iraq was or was not necessary, but whether he had the wherewithal at the time to meet the demands of yet another of the increasing number of tasks thrown at him. His primary concern was how to defend what he already had, marshalling and prioritizing his already dispersed and depleted forces between Libya, Egypt, Greece and Palestine, rather than attempting to counter any further threat to British interests in the region. It is clear, therefore, that Wavell was concerned not with political imperatives *per se*, but with military realities. Criticism of Wavell throughout April and May 1941 needs to take this vital point into account, despite the nature of his role, which demanded the highest degree of political astuteness. His position as military Commander-in-Chief conferred on him a requirement to act both as a politician and as a soldier: the two functions were necessarily intertwined. In addition to being the Commander-in-Chief Middle East, a position he assumed in August 1939, he had been instructed to maintain:

'close touch and sympathy' with the rulers of Egypt and Iraq; with the High Commissioner for Palestine and Transjordan and the Governor-General of the Sudan; with the Governors of Cyprus, Aden and British Somaliland, the Political Resident in the Persian Gulf, the British Ambassadors in Cairo, Baghdad, Istanbul and Athens, together with the chief representatives of Britain's allies adjoining his area of command. [18]

It was this point that made Major General R.J. Collins entitle his biography *Lord Wavell, A Military Biography* in recognition of the fact that Wavell saw his primary responsibility as military rather than political decision-making.* It was an uncomfortable reality that until 1943 British commanders-in-chief were forced to be both politicians and soldiers, without the sort of clear distinction between these two functions that was to prevail later in the war, and that military decision-

* R.J. Collins, *Lord Wavell (1883–1941) A Military Biography* (London: Hodder & Stoughton, 1948)

making suffered as a result. Wavell was thus required to think politically and direct forces operationally. Balancing the competing imperatives of each of these two quite different functions, combined more often than not with imprecise or even conflicting instructions from London, grew more and more difficult as the months passed and as responsibilities increased. The quite proper distinction between the two functions became a daily dilemma and one that Wavell, alone, could never hope or be expected to solve.

Arguably, responsibility for political as against military action needed to have been separated, but in Britain's conduct of the war there was no clear divorcement of these two functions until late 1942 in the Mediterranean, and late 1943 in the Far East. At the time, to expect Wavell to have made political judgements and then to apply military resources to resolve them was asking too much of any man, no matter how gifted. That said, there is an equally powerful argument which states that, as Wavell was invested with both political and military responsibility, he could not abrogate one in favour of the other, a point that Major General Sir John Kennedy, Director of Military Operations in the War Office for much of the war, makes in his account, *The Business of War.**

There was also another distinct nuance to Wavell's appreciation of the threat from Iraq at the time. It might be construed from his actions that he regarded the only motive for using military force to retain British control over Iraq to be a physical threat from Germany: German troops, German tanks and German aircraft. He deprecated, on the other hand, any use of military force against home-grown rebel activity partly because he underestimated the damage well-organized Iraqis could do to the weak British position in Iraq. One of Wavell's marked characteristics as a commander was an unfortunate underestimation of his non-German enemies, a failing that was to identify itself starkly during his tenure a year later as Commander-in-Chief India when faced with the onslaught in the Far East from Japan. It was a failing that evidenced itself with regard to Iraq. This was unfortunate because Britain's interests in Iraq were threatened in the first case by the incumbent (illegal) Iraqi regime, which was determined to strip her of her special rights and to hand these to Germany. Iraq was well able, if

* Sir John Kennedy, *The Business of War* (London: Hutchinson, 1957)

it wished, to defeat the weak British forces in Iraq and to open the door for Germany. The Germans would need only to have *exploited* rather than *initiated* an attack on British interests in Iraq. If Wavell had waited until Germany had occupied Iraq, Britain's position could only have been recovered by the overwhelming use of military resources of the sort that simply did not exist in Wavell's armoury in early 1941. One must accept what Churchill saw as inalienable logic: Britain could not do without Iraqi and Iranian oil and was forced to mount a pre-emptive military response to prevent the loss of these strategically vital assets regardless of the type or origin of the threat. The imperative of pre-emption, therefore, so clear to Auchinleck and Churchill, moved Wavell not one bit. It may be that in the midst of the immediate military pressures facing him elsewhere in the Mediterranean and North Africa, Wavell did not recognize how tenuous was Great Britain's hold on its oil at the time, a perspective that was only too clear to Churchill and the War Cabinet in London, viewing the war on a broader canvas. In the absence of a proper *political* appreciation by Wavell, it was relatively easy for the Arabist camp in his HQ in Cairo in April and May 1941 to convince him that diplomacy would win the day against Rashid Ali, and that the use of force in Iraq would in any case be provocative, counter-productive and something to be avoided at all costs.

In emphasizing these immediate military pressures faced by Wavell, Harold Raugh, in his exhaustive study of Wavell's generalship in the Middle East, judges him exclusively on the basis of the military resources available to him. This, however, is to judge Wavell's performance only in part. Expressing surprise at Churchill's apparent failure to grasp the enormity of these difficulties, Raugh concludes that Churchill was myopically blind to the 'complexity of Wavell's commitments . . . or the paucity of his resources', and ignorant of 'the precariousness of the British position in the Middle East'. Furthermore, he alleges that Churchill was frustrated by Wavell's 'indecisiveness, lethargy, and an unwillingness to take risks.'[19] These charges are an exaggeration and an over-simplification. Churchill was impetuous, forceful and emotional, certainly, but he was not unaware of the difficulties Wavell faced and quite definitely not blind to the precariousness of the British presence in the Middle East. Indeed, it was his realization of what was at stake with the defence of British interests in Iraq that led him so forcefully to lean on Wavell in the first place. Nor was he frustrated by Wavell's 'lethargy', but with his failure to see beyond – understandably perhaps – the daily desperation of battle, compounded by his rigid adherence to the 'Arabist' argument that British military operations in Iraq would fuel a wider anti-British uprising and his determination to resist any notion that the threat from Rashid Ali was real and dangerous. All that can justifiably be laid to Churchill's charge was the complaint levelled by Ronald Lewin, one of Wavell's biographers, that the Prime Minister 'was blind to the fact that he had overloaded the Commander-in-Chief Middle East like some Arab's donkey.'[20]

Churchill had, nevertheless, identified a deficiency in Wavell's exercise of command that was an uncomfortable characteristic of much of British generalship in the first half of the war. Wavell was a deeply intellectual soldier, well versed in the art of war, whose approach to tactics was eminently sound and whose analysis of the *military* problems he faced was always thorough and perspicacious. He was first and foremost a soldier, bound by the conceptual constraints of his own personality, training, upbringing and military experience. But whether it was the combination of age, or tiredness, the competing and seemingly irreconcilable demands of policy and of military resources or simply the fact that he was worn down by the pressures of command, it was clear to many observers that by 1941 Wavell's exercise of command lacked the sparkle of imagination with which he had previously been blessed, together with a visible slowing of his reflexes. Air Marshal Arthur Tedder, with whom Wavell did not enjoy the easiest of relationships, captured the nature of the problem in his diary entry for 28 May 1941:

I like Wavell – he is intellectually – and in every other way – honest, but he does move so slowly. Even now I don't think he realises the need for speed . . . [He] is a nice, solid, sound, honest old thing.[21]

Brigadier Francis ('Freddie') De Guingand, who was to become Montgomery's long-serving Chief of Staff, and was at the time the General Staff Officer Grade 1 (GSO1) Intelligence in GHQ Cairo, believed that a change was needed at the top: 'There is no question that many of us working at GHQ Cairo about then felt that the Commander-in–Chief was losing his grip and wanted a rest.'[22] Wavell had been the right man for 1940, but Churchill was right in realizing that he was the wrong man for 1941. He had run out of reserves of the imaginative energy necessary to turn the tables on the extreme risk-takers with whom he was faced on the German side, that of the operational gambler Rommel in the Western Desert and that of the strategic gambler – Adolf Hitler – in the Balkans and Dodecanese.[23] Britain's military effort in the Middle East required a commander able to concentrate forces to meet *political* necessities, move rapidly to take *military* risks and think outside the logical methodologies and logistical certainties which had been sufficient to overcome the Italians in the previous year.[24] Wavell was not that man. That said, it is also clear that no such commander then existed in British service who could have fulfilled such a demanding role.

Churchill, Dill, Amery, Linlithgow and Auchinleck were undoubtedly correct in their judgement about the urgent need to despatch military forces to Iraq in April 1941. The political imperatives associated with action or inaction in Iraq in their view clearly outweighed the struggle to find the appropriate resources to meet this new and unwanted requirement, thrust rudely on to an unwilling HQ Middle East. Churchill's policy in these circumstances was to take the most decisive strategic action the circumstances required, without regard for any unintended consequences. Iraq constituted a very definite threat to wider British interests, requiring stern and decisive pre-emptive action. Wavell's apparent inability to recognize the political implication of not taking strong action surprised Churchill. We have already acknowledged, however, the impossible situation in which Wavell found himself, having to judge between political and military imperatives which would seldom co-align. It was extremely fortunate that at this time Auchinleck was not faced by the increasingly intolerable burden suffered by Middle East Command, that decisive action in Iraq to forestall an Axis counter-action and to protect strategic British interests in the country had been at the forefront of Auchinleck's mind for some months, and that he had the troops available for immediate despatch to Basra.

On 8 April 1941, the day British troops came into contact with Germans in Crete for the first time and the day on which Wavell suggested that Britain respond to Rashid Ali's *coup d'état* by an ill-defined aerial 'demonstration', Churchill wrote a note to Amery, the Secretary of State for India, asking whether India could divert troops to the defence of Basra. His call for support from Cairo had been rebuffed, and he turned to New Delhi instead:

> Some time ago you suggested that you might be able to spare another division from the frontier troops for the Middle East. The situation in Iraq has turned sour . . . I am telling the Chiefs of Staff that you will look into these possibilities. General Auchinleck also has had ideas that an additional force could be spared.[25]

Amery telegraphed Linlithgow on the same day, stressing the critical nature of the situation in Iraq and the importance of retaining Great Britain's influence in the country, and asking what support India might provide in order to make a show of force. Some hours later, another telegram from London changed Amery's request for information to one asking for action to be taken to send a force immediately by sea to Basra and for the rapid insertion of an infantry battalion by air to RAF Shaibah. On the same day the German Foreign Office issued what Rashid came to regard as a letter guaranteeing German support for any anti-British action he undertook 'as far as possible in case of any war undertaken by the Arabs against the British for their freedom.'[26]

The fruit of India's planning and of Auchinleck's dogged insistence paid off. On receipt of the telegram from the War Office in London, Auchinleck sent a message to Wavell on 10 April explaining what he intended to do:

> First. Propose to divert to Basra one infantry brigade and one field regiment with ancillary troops now in ships at Karachi and destined for Malaya. This force not tactically loaded so naval and air support will be necessary if landing likely to be opposed.
> Second. Between 13/4 and 22/4 we will send one . . . Hospital and base stores.
> Third. We are convinced that force in and around Basra should be brought up as soon as possible to equivalent of at least one division. We would follow first brigade group by two further

brigade groups and base units for 'Sybil'. Second echelon could probably be embarked after twenty one days.

Fourth. We can send approximately four hundred British infantry with twelve L.M.G.s [Light Machine Guns] and six Vickers guns by air to Shaibah starting move 13/4 and completing in seven to eleven days.

Fifth. We are examining possibility of sending infantry brigade group to Palestine but unless it is to have priority over troops for Basra or special shipping can be provided it will have to sail after division is established at Basra. Ends.[27]

This was to be the long-planned *Sybil,* the vanguard of *Sabine.* In command was the 55-year-old Major General William Fraser, General Officer Commanding 10 Indian Infantry Division.[28] Churchill was grateful for such a swift and positive response from New Delhi. 'His Majesty's Government appreciates your immediate and most effective response to their urgent request for help in Iraq,' cabled Amery after talking to the Prime Minister, 'and they gratefully accept your offer. Proceed at once with the despatch of force to Basra and Shaibah as you propose.'[29] Observing this exchange of signals Wavell injected a note of scepticism and repeated the line he had already made to Churchill: 'It is just possible that this force might suffice to swing the scales in Iraq. I am fully committed in Cyrenaica and can spare nothing for Iraq.'[30]

London was not prepared, however, to let Wavell off the hook. Despite India's willingness to commit substantial forces to the Iraq cause and to play the major and most willing part in the venture, Churchill and Dill insisted that operational control of northern Iraq (which included Baghdad) remain with Wavell, and that the southern area (based upon Basra) stay with Fraser under the direct command of Auchinleck in New Delhi. Ignoring Wavell's protests, the Chiefs of Staff on 11 April took the unusual step of over-ruling the Commander-in-Chief and ordered Wavell to despatch a 'sizeable force' from Palestine to Habbaniya. At the time this order was given, Wavell was in the Western Desert visiting his troops arrayed against the fast encroaching threat posed by Rommel, and his Chief of Staff, Major General Arthur Smith, deputized for him in Cairo. On receipt of this signal Smith replied to London, repeating his chief's earlier reply that there were insufficient troops available in Palestine to do what London had asked, forces there comprising but a weak infantry battalion and 'the partially equipped Cavalry Division'.[31]

Fraser's convoy duly set off from Karachi on 12 April, with the following orders:

1. To occupy the Basra–Shaibah area in order to ensure the safe disembarkation of further reinforcements and to enable a base to be established in that area.

2. In view of the uncertain attitude of the Iraqi Army and local authorities, to face the possibility that attempts might be made to oppose the disembarkation of his force . . .

3. Should the embarkation be opposed, to overcome the enemy by force and occupy suitable defensive positions ashore as quickly as possible.

4. To take the greatest care not to infringe the neutrality of Iran.[32]

Cornwallis' judgement of a week earlier that Rashid Ali would seek to consolidate his power at Britain's expense as quickly as possible was soon seen to be accurate. Britain's military strength in the region was weak. The garrison at Habbaniya as we have observed was not designed to have an offensive capability and the Royal Navy had only a limited presence in the Persian Gulf, boasting four small warships at the start of April, increasing to seven as the month progressed, including the cruiser HMS *Emerald* and the carrier HMS *Hermes*. The new Iraqi regime acted swiftly to limit the effectiveness of these forces, weak as they were. On 6 April British military personnel were prevented from travelling between Habbaniya and Baghdad and the British Military Mission was stripped of its radio transmitters.

Ironically, the newly agreed arrangements between London and New Delhi for Iraq were very nearly unseated by Cornwallis himself. Cornwallis was, from the start, a staunch proponent of strong action in Iraq. Indeed, so thoroughly did she trust his judgement and his experience of Iraqi politics that Freya Stark was convinced that had Cornwallis 'come earlier, the April *coup d'état* might perhaps have been avoided'.[33] Cornwallis was appointed to the post on 13 February 1941 but owing in part to a failure by the Foreign Office in London to appreciate the urgency of the situation in Baghdad it took seven weeks for him to arrive. On 11 April, however, following a passionate declaration to the Iraqi Senate by Rashid Ali of his commitment to abide by the spirit and letter of the Anglo-Iraq Treaty, Cornwallis suggested to London that Rashid Ali might be given the opportunity to prove his good intentions and that the arrival of Fraser's troops be delayed. He feared that a British landing at Basra might play into the rebels' hands, as they could claim that they were the victims of unprovoked aggression, which itself could be used as the trigger or excuse for German intervention. An empire-builder of the consensual, diplomatic school, Cornwallis was eager to give positive, proactive diplomacy a chance. In any case Wavell had warned him, as he had passed through Cairo, that he should not count on receiving any military assistance from the Middle East if force was required in Iraq.[34] Amery asked India for its view. Auchinleck and Linlithgow were both unanimous in opposing the idea. Auchinleck's views were recorded in a memorandum he penned for Linlithgow on 12 April, with Fraser's convoy already at sea:

My own opinion is that the acceptance of the Ambassador's advice to defer action for the securing of Basra may very well result in our never getting Basra at all.

I have already informed His Excellency of my considered opinion that it is essential for us to establish ourselves in Basra so as to secure its use for us as a base as soon as we possibly can. I am convinced myself that the possession of a base at Basra may make the difference between success and failure to us in the Near and Middle East during the next six months . . .

In my opinion, the time for diplomatic parleying has passed. I think there is a very definite danger that Rashid will use the breathing space Cornwallis proposes to consolidate his position and, probably, to invoke German aid, which might even take the form of airborne troops and aircraft.

I am convinced that, if we are to prevent a general deterioration of the situation in Asia generally, and especially in Turkey, Iran, Iraq and Arabia, we must show now that we are prepared to maintain our position by force.[35]

Later events during 1941 were to vindicate Auchinleck's position. Britain was eavesdropping on the communications between the Italian Legation in Baghdad and Rome and, although little of this intelligence made it into the hands of commanders and diplomats on the ground, the advantage that this information gave London was considerable. This source indicated that on 17 April Rashid Ali had asked for Axis assistance, particularly in the area of air support. A week later on 23 April he went further and asked not merely for weapons but for active intervention by German forces in the event of a war with Great Britain, a situation that he felt certain would come about in a matter of days. It is difficult not to conclude from this decryption that Rashid Ali was planning military action against the British at least a week before it occurred, and that the landings in Basra served to unnerve him into acting precipitately. It was common knowledge in the oil community within the country that the Iraqi Government had also asked the Iraq Petroleum Company to stockpile nearly a million gallons of motor fuel in two dumps near Baghdad, presumably and in the absence of any other explanation, ready for arrival of the hoped-for Teutonic legions.[36] Within the new administration in Baghdad it was not difficult to see who was master: in the last week of April the Secret Intelligence Service reported that Rashid Ali 'had been given an ultimatum by the Iraqi Army: it would take over from him unless he turned out the British forces and established relations with Germany within a week.'[37]

Happily, Cornwallis' well-intentioned suggestion was not followed up. London accepted India's strongly pronounced views and Fraser's force was instructed to proceed, following a long and forthright telegram from Linlithgow to Amery on 13 April stressing that Arab opinion came second to the need to prevent Axis threats to the Persian Gulf being translated into an uncomfortable reality. Linlithgow was later to record that he regarded the decisive intervention on 13 April by Auchinleck and himself in persuading London to act with strength and courage in Iraq as 'one of the turning points of the war', recalling that the problem in Iraq was caused in part by 'the stubborn failure of the Foreign Office to comprehend the nature of the emergency and to provide adequate support in coping with it.'[38]

Unhappily, the Air Ministry's influence remained such that on 13 April the Defence Council, whilst authorizing the despatch of troops by air and sea from India to Iraq, pressed Wavell to consider again the need for an 'Air Demonstration', this time over Baghdad.[39] Unsurprisingly, following Smart's experience of a week earlier, the suggestion was quickly and quietly forgotten. It appeared that the 'Air

Demonstration' theory of tribal pacification, *de rigueur* in the 1920s and 1930s, continued to hold unwarranted sway in some parts of the Air Ministry as late as 1941.

As it was, the government of Rashid Ali was taken entirely by surprise by the cool matter-of-factness of Cornwallis' announcement, on 16 April, that under the terms of the Anglo-Iraq Treaty Great Britain would shortly be landing troops at Basra. On the following day the first of 364 officers and men of the 1st Battalion The King's Own Royal Regiment landed in Shaibah. Their journey from Karachi had taken four days by air, via Sharjah Fort in Trucial Oman and Bahrain in what was in all likelihood the first-ever strategic airlift by British forces in war. The troops travelled courtesy of 31 Squadron RAF, whose pilots were long used to patrolling the skies of the North-West Frontier from Peshawar. The airlift was conducted using twelve obsolescent Vickers Valentia biplane transports, together with five high-wing Armstrong Whitworth Atlantas lent to the RAF for the operation, along with their pilots, by Imperial Airways. Later on in April, 31 Squadron was re-equipped with the new American Douglas DC2, and the 1,300-mile flight from Karachi was conducted in the much shorter period of thirteen hours.[40] Colonel Ouvry Roberts, Quinan's chief staff officer in 10 Indian Division, managed to find himself a place on one of the planes as part of the divisional reconnaissance party. Once deposited safely in Shaibah, the troops of the King's Own were then flown north-west on 29 April to reinforce the vulnerable air station at Habbaniya. Roberts joined them on 1 May. They expected to conduct merely static defensive duties and to remain in Iraq for about six weeks.

Escorted by the Australian sloop HMAS *Yarra*, on the morning of 18 April the first ships of convoy BP.1, which had left Karachi on 12 April, nosed carefully into the port at Basra, bringing Brigadier Powell's 20 Indian Brigade,* 3 Field Regiment Royal Artillery and Fraser's divisional headquarters into the Shatt al-Arab waterway. Two hundred men of 2/7 Gurkha Rifles secured the dock area that day, allowing the remainder of the force to disembark on 19 April. It was fortunate for Powell's troops that the landing was unopposed, as the brigade was only partly trained and poorly equipped. This feat was

---

* 2/8 Gurkha Rifles, 2/7 Gurkha Rifles and 3/11 Sikh Regiment. The convoy also included 1 Anti-Tank Battery RA, 10 Field Company RE and 41 Field Park Company Royal Army Service Corps (RASC).

brought about by the urgent personal diplomacy of Major General G.G. Waterhouse, head of the British Military Mission to Iraq, who travelled to Basra with Colonel Roberts to persuade the local military authorities not to oppose the convoy's arrival.

The BBC announced the peaceful landing on the radio, describing 'that the new Iraqi Government was affording full facilities' to the troops, who had arrived in accordance with the long-standing Anglo-Iraq Treaty, and 'that a warm welcome had been given to the Imperial troops by the local population'.[41] When the news broke in Baghdad Stark recorded in her diary:

> Electrical effect of our landing. The new Government tried to keep it dark and even denied it, so that our broadcast describing the cordial reception by local officials, etc, came as a surprise. Most people seem pleased.[42]

At the time of these landings the prevailing opinion in London was that they would serve forcefully to keep the lid on any potential Iraqi uprising and were principally a deterrent. When pressed by Air Vice-Marshal Longmore for the prioritization of effort on 17 April, Churchill had replied: 'Libya counts first, evacuation of troops from Greece second, Tobruk shipping unless indispensable to victory must be fitted in as convenient, Iraq can be ignored and Crete worked up later.'[43] The following day the Chiefs of Staff repeated this message to Wavell: 'Don't worry about Iraq for the present' was the advice he was proffered. 'It looks like going smoothly.'[44] These views, as time was shortly to tell, were dangerously ill conceived. It is not hard to sympathize with Wavell when he received this advice: if scarce military resources were to be redeployed to Iraq (against his will), where no actual fighting was expected, would not those forces be better employed where there was at least some expectation of action? The truth was, of course, that whilst the deployment of *Sybil* was preventative, its aim was to make a serious political point to Iraq: namely, that Britain would defend its interests in the country with force if necessary.

In fact the rapid insertion of Indian and British troops into Shaibah and Basra between 17 and 18 April 1941 had a profound effect on the war in the Middle East. Pre-emptive military action to solve an impending crisis worked decisively in Great Britain's favour, vindicating the efforts of those such as Auchinleck and Linlithgow who had long advocated a show of force against an illegal regime that was growing bolder by the day. Rashid Ali reacted immediately by notifying Cornwallis that whilst the treaty permitted the arrival of the troops the Iraqi Government insisted that the troops transit quickly through Iraq to Palestine, and that they do so in small contingents. He was obviously rattled, having on 16 April received the letter from Berlin assuring him of German support in the event of war with Britain. Not for a moment did he believe that Britain had the will or the wherewithal to fight a war in Iraq. In a note to London on 18 April, Cornwallis recorded his view that the Iraqi 'Army leaders having been caught by surprise will now do everything they can to nullify our initial advantage.'[45] This fact was only too obvious to Churchill who, scenting that Iraq might retaliate forcibly, urged the Chiefs of Staff on 20 April to ensure that the full terms of *Operation Sabine* be executed, namely that a whole Indian Division of three brigades be despatched at once to support the initial toe-hold at Basra. On the same day, in receipt of his telegram of 18 April, Churchill urged the Foreign Office to impress firmly on Cornwallis that the landings were a significant part of the wider Middle East war effort, and that more was at stake than just the manoeuvrings of the Iraqi regime, or even of the importance of Iraqi oil, the treaty injunctions having been used as a cover for more pressing motives. One of these was the suggestion that the Persian Gulf might be useful as an area for the receipt and despatch of air reinforcements to the Middle East from the United States, should the Suez Canal Zone fall to Rommel.[46] Cornwallis was instructed to reject Iraq's demands and not to 'entangle himself by explanations'.[47] Furthermore, Britain would be prepared to use force against Iraq if the government insisted upon the removal of the Basra base.

London was, through all of this, continuing to eavesdrop profitably on discussions between Baghdad and Rome, and by extension, Berlin. On 18 April Luigi Gabrielli, the Italian Ambassador, told Rome that Rashid Ali wanted:

to learn as soon as possible from the Axis governments: first, whether the Iraq army could count on support from the air force of the Axis powers; the airfields of Iraq would of course be placed at the disposal of the Axis powers. Second, whether the Iraq army could count on receiving rifles and ammunition by air transports.[48]

Churchill's desire to launch *Sabine* immediately came as a profound relief to both Linlithgow and Auchinleck, and another convoy containing more of Fraser's 10 Indian Division arrived at Basra on 29 April.* India's enthusiastic response took Churchill by surprise, used as he was by this stage to his generals explaining why things could not get done. Amery cabled Linlithgow on 26 April:

> Please convey to Commander-in-Chief and his staff my heartiest congratulations on splendid way in which they have risen to emergency over despatch of troops to Iraq. I am sure that promptitude and secrecy with which they were sent off were in no small measure responsible for Iraq incompetence in their landing.[49]

In a separate note to Auchinleck, Churchill minuted much more succinctly: 'We are greatly obliged to you for the alacrity with which you have improved on your previous arrangements.'[50]

The arrival of the second convoy in Basra on 29 April came as a severe shock to Rashid Ali. Cornwallis deliberately refrained from passing him the diplomatic note informing Iraq of the imminent arrival of the remainder of Fraser's troops until the day before the landings. Rashid Ali was by now a very nervous man. By 24 April he had not yet received a reply from Germany to his urgent request of 18 April, and he berated Gabrielli for the lack of a response. Gabrielli reported:

> The situation, which is already extremely delicate, could in three or four days become downright critical. The annoyance is all the greater since [Haddad] brought back with him from Berlin the most optimistic impression about the possibility of obtaining such aid.[51]

On 26 April Rashid Ali warned Gabrielli that Iraq intended to act against Great Britain within days and followed this on 28 April with

---

* The remaining troops of 10 Indian Division arrived at Basra on 10 May 1941.

a request for financial support amounting to 3 million Iraqi dinars to compensate it for the loss of oil income from Britain in the event of war.* In addition to requesting that in the forthcoming war Germany take responsibility for attacking British shipping in the Persian Gulf, allowing it to operate from the airbases at Habbaniya and Shaibah and promising the Axis' use of the airbases at Mosul, Baghdad and Mikdadia, he also asked for further substantial aid. The list he gave Gabrielli included 10 squadrons of planes and 50 light armoured cars. The Iraqis asked for captured British infantry weapons with which the Iraqi Army were familiar, including 400 half-inch Boys armour-piercing rifles (with 50,000 rounds of ammunition), 60 armour-piercing cannons (with 60,000 rounds of ammunition), 10,000 hand-grenades, 600 Bren Guns and 84 Vickers machine guns.[52]

Rashid Ali's instinctive reaction to Cornwallis' note was to refuse the British request outright. After all, had not the Germans promised their support and would they not underwrite Iraq's bellicosity? Cornwallis, however, refused to budge, insisting that the troops would unload as planned under the terms of the treaty between the two countries, and that any intervention by Iraq to prevent this would be regarded by Great Britain as a hostile act. Rashid's response came as no surprise to Cornwallis. By now the atmosphere in Baghdad was tense and threatening and on 29 April he ordered the evacuation of 250 British women and children from Baghdad, rejecting simultaneously the suggestion that an attempt be made to assassinate Rashid Ali.[53] The evacuees made their precarious way out of the city in RAF trucks and with a solitary unarmed Oxford Trainer flying top-cover in the skies above. As they travelled they were confronted by an ominous sign: crowds of Iraqi soldiers also making their way out of the city along the road to Falluja.

Squadron Leader Dudgeon was struck by the dramatic increase in anti-British rhetoric and hostility amongst the populace, which at the start of the month was largely confined to Baghdad. Gossip in the bazaars during April was of the Iraqi Army destroying Habbaniya and evicting the effendis once and for all. Late on the afternoon of 29 April a signal sent from RAF Habbaniya reached New Delhi:

---

* Equivalent to £1 million sterling.

Unmistakeable signs treaty may be repudiated. Ambassador asking Rashid Ali this morning for safe conduct women and children from Baghdad to Habbaniya with further evacuation by air to Basra and thence by air to India. Three D.C.2 aircraft now transporting troops Habbaniya are being retained for this purpose.[54]

The 'unmistakeable signs' [sic] referred to the movement of large numbers of Iraqi soldiers out of Baghdad westward along the road towards the Euphrates at Falluja and beyond, and the simultaneous cutting of the Euphrates embankments which, because the river was in spate at this time of the year, flooded the low lying areas around Habbaniya and effectively cut it off from the east. The British Embassy reported these troop movements at 3 a.m. on the morning of 30 April. That day an estimated two brigades of Iraqi troops made their way towards Habbaniya and a further brigade occupied the town of Ramadi, fourteen miles west of Habbaniya on the Euphrates. The troops involved had been instructed to deploy on a training exercise to the high ground between Lake Habbaniya and the RAF Air Station. The only thing to arouse the suspicions of the inquisitive was the fact that they were instructed to take live ammunition. In Baghdad tension mounted and some 350 British subjects fled for safety to the British Embassy, whilst the American Legation provided shelter for another 150. Freya Stark, returning from a trip to Tehran, was also arrested and interned in the embassy. The Iraqis then placed the British Embassy under a virtual state of siege and the road from Baghdad to Falluja was closed. The operation was clearly pre-planned, as the mobilization of this number of Iraqi troops would necessarily have taken some time. Iraqi troops simultaneously seized the oil fields at Kirkuk, promptly shutting down the flow of oil to Haifa and opening up that to Tripoli, a flow that Britain had originally closed down with the collapse of France nearly a year before. Such moves, Rashid Ali believed, would cow Britain into negotiated emasculation. By luck rather than by judgement on Britain's part, Rashid Ali was to be proved badly wrong.

3

Habbaniya

During the last two weeks of April Air Vice-Marshal Smart comforted himself with the certainty that any anti-British activity by the new Iraqi Government was certain to show itself against the build-up of Indian troops in Basra and that Habbaniya would be allowed to remain in its perpetual state of semi-somnolence. Smart had failed to appreciate that Habbaniya was ideally placed to allow Rashid Ali to blackmail Britain into negotiating a complete withdrawal from Iraq, and that he needed to act before the forces at Basra could be built up. Surrounding Habbaniya by strong military forces would enable the Iraqis to threaten the cantonment and its occupants and by this means secure compliance with their demands. Iraqi assumptions were well founded. They knew the base had significant defensive weaknesses, was heavily populated with civilians, possessed a virtually non-existent offensive capability and that the nearest British forces were cut off by flood waters and a disabled railway three hundred miles away in Basra. With so many mouths to feed they needed no detailed analysis to appreciate that food stocks would be limited (in fact, to twelve days for the garrison and a mere four days for the cantonment). Palestine was five hundred miles away to the west across a desert that no conquering army in history had ever traversed. Equally, Britain was known to be on its knees against the Axis Powers and would undoubtedly accept terms quickly. What would have confirmed this approach to the Golden Square, had they but known it, was the knowledge that the British Commander-in-Chief

Middle East was arguing strenuously for a diplomatic solution to the developing difficulties between Britain and Iraq, and was firmly opposed to any form of military action.

It needs little imagination to see that if Wavell had had his way, the Golden Square would have won a spectacular victory. RAF Habbaniya would have been held to ransom and Great Britain ejected without a fight. Rashid Ali's ill-gotten power would have been consolidated not just with his own people, but also with the wider radical Arab nationalist community, and with the clique's German and Italian allies as well. To the Golden Square it was most definitely a policy worth pursuing. If 'negotiations' with Britain failed to bring about the result they desired, the occupation of Habbaniya by Iraqi troops would be relatively easy, with an exhausted cantonment eager for relief. Habbaniya, with its superb location, its extensive hangars, workshops and fuel, would be of inestimable benefit to the Germans as a base in the Middle East.

The news in the early hours of 30 April of the troop deployments from Baghdad came as something of an unexpected surprise to Smart. At 4.20 a.m. the general alarm was sounded and as the early dawn broke just over half an hour later it was with considerable consternation that the Habbaniya garrison discovered that it was being overlooked from the escarpment by a large number of troops, clearly visible to the naked eye, preparing defensive positions. An Audax sent up to report came back with the information that at least 1,000 troops with field guns, howitzers and armoured vehicles were dispersed across the plateau and long lines of vehicles could be seen on the road that stretched back towards Falluja and, beyond that, Baghdad. At the height of their strength the Iraqi force was put at 9,000 troops with 28 guns and armoured cars.

Smart had no time to consider his options before an Iraqi officer arrived at the main gate at 6 a.m. with the following message:

For the purposes of training we have occupied the Habbaniya hills. Please make no flying or the going out of any force or persons from the cantonment. If any aircraft or armoured car attempts to go out it will be shelled by our batteries, and we will not be responsible for it.

Undoubtedly struck by the incongruity of a training exercise being conducted with live ammunition, Smart had the presence to reply:

Any interference with training flights will be considered an 'act of war' and will be met by immediate counter-offensive action. We demand the withdrawal of the Iraqi forces from positions which are clearly hostile and must place my camp at their mercy.[1]

When he saw a copy of the reply the next day Sir Miles Lampson, Britain's ambassador to Egypt,* rejoiced to his diary at this 'splendid' response: 'It is refreshing to hear something of that kind coming from our people these days . . . If only we can bring off something quick and dramatic, it will have an enormous effect everywhere, especially in Egypt.'[2] The Iraqi action placed Smart in a quandary. Despite the rapid decline in formal relations between Great Britain and Iraq over the previous month, Smart was not expecting any form of military threat to develop against Habbaniya. He was certainly not prepared for a physical threat against the base and was understandably not prepared to declare war without higher authority. The soldiers of the King's Own had arrived by air from Shaibah on 29 April, but even with the six companies of the Iraq Levies the total ground forces available to Smart amounted to a mere one thousand four hundred, strengthened by some eighteen thin-skinned Rolls Royce armoured cars. He had rations for twelve days for the garrison, but only four days supply for the civilian cantonment. Nevertheless it was plain to Smart that an aggressive defence of Habbaniya was required.

During that day, one of intense but dry heat with the mercury well over 110 degrees Fahrenheit, frantic preparations for battle took place across the cantonment. Trenches were dug to ensure that if shelling did begin some shelter could be had in the otherwise entirely defenceless station. Whilst troops and aircrew were pressed into this task, the pilots manoeuvred the aircraft out of sight of the Iraqi guns and a battle roster was organized. The aircraft were split into three squadrons. The twenty-one Audax 'bombers' were placed under command of Wing Commander Larry Ling and were to operate from the polo field out of sight of the Iraqis on the plateau whilst the remaining forty-three aircraft under Squadron Leader Tony Dudgeon were to operate from the main runway in full view of the enemy. Dudgeon's group comprised a flight of twenty-seven Oxfords, a second flight of nine

* Later Lord Killearn.

Gladiators and a third flight of seven Gordons. The lack of suitably trained pilots, however, was acute. Eventually, only thirty-nine were found, eighteen to fly the Audaxes and nineteen for the remainder. Some had not flown for a considerable period of time and many had never flown in battle before. Within fourteen hours of the start of battle a quarter of these pilots had been lost.

The likely opposition in the air was formidable. Dudgeon records:

We knew full well that the Iraqis had a substantial and more modern Air Force with many British-trained pilots. Their nominal strength was seven squadrons. They had over seventy operational aircraft – with crews. They had Italian Savoia bombers and Breda fighters. They had American Northrop fighters. All those were fast, modern monoplanes. They had Audaxes with more powerful engines than ours.[3]

Apart from preparing defences and organizing his aircraft into operational 'wings', what else could Smart do? Smart was pre-eminently a bureaucrat, content to run an efficient training organization pushing out new pilots for a far-distant war. Now, suddenly and unexpectedly, war was on his doorstep, and he was required to act, and to do so decisively. At 8.55 a.m. on the morning of 30 April a rattled Smart signalled to Cornwallis in Baghdad:

Intention appears to immobilize Habbaniya and use as a political lever. I considered alternative of issuing ultimatum for withdrawal but in view of policy to date and improbability of early reinforcements this area decided to defer taking offensive action until Iraqis open fire. Request immediate directive and possibility of immediate reinforcements.[4]

Smart was understandably concerned lest he inadvertently and illegally started his own little war. He asked Cornwallis to put all possible pressure on the Iraqis to withdraw, and to warn them that their provocative action might force him to take action to protect the base. During the morning Iraqi activity continued across the escarpment in full view of the cantonment. Smart reported to Cornwallis that Iraqi artillery pieces were being aimed directly at the base and that enemy troop numbers were increasing, repeating his earlier plea for immediate reinforcements. By mid-morning Cornwallis replied. Before Smart launched any action he must first have the approval of the Foreign Office in London.

Then, at 11.30 a.m., the Iraqi military envoy returned to the front gate. He now stated that training flights had to cease, citing Britain's blatant disregard for the Anglo-Iraq Treaty for this new demand. The specific area of default in terms of the treaty was not made clear, but in all likelihood referred to the second Basra landing on 29 April. This situation put Smart in a very difficult position. Iraqi pressure was increasing but he lacked specific instructions as to what to do, and those that he would receive in the coming hours, from a variety of sources, were wildly contradictory. He knew that he was extremely vulnerable to ground attack, and that if he were to retain the initiative he would have to launch his own pre-emptive attack before the Iraqis felt that they were in a position of complete dominance. And yet all the imperatives from Cairo in recent weeks had been to secure stability in Iraq through diplomatic methods, Wavell and Longmore being unwilling to use the threat of force to secure the continuance of British interests in the country. On the other side of the coin, a pre-emptive air strike could not guarantee that the Iraqi forces would not retaliate in force against the vulnerable cantonment. At least 250 women and children, shipped hastily out of Baghdad in RAF trucks the day before, were still on the base, as well as the large civilian population, many of whom were Iraqis, whose reactions to firm military action by Smart were difficult to gauge. The only certainty was that Habbaniya was vulnerable and likely to become more so if he did nothing about it.

Without clear orders Smart decided to do nothing. At midday he gave the Iraqi envoy his answer, which was a polite request to remove his forces from the plateau and to leave their respective political masters on either side to sort out the impasse. By this time twenty-seven guns could be counted on the escarpment, only one shell from which could disable the water tower or destroy the power station, which would bring the defence of Habbaniya to a sudden and ignominious end. Immediately following this meeting, Smart sent his third signal of the day to Cornwallis, repeating his request for reinforcements, asking for a firm directive, and explaining his reasons for not taking military action at that stage.

An afternoon of confusion then reigned. The Iraqi commander on the plateau told Smart that he would not act against Habbaniya so long as Smart took no unilateral action himself. In Baghdad Cornwallis' attitude now hardened, telling Smart by radio that although he was waiting instructions from London, he believed that a pre-emptive attack against the Iraqi positions on the plateau was warranted should Smart feel it necessary.

Early on the morning of Thursday 1 May a quick succession of signals arrived for Smart, none of which, however, alleviated his difficulties by making the decision for him. At 5.25 a.m. the long-awaited Foreign Office instructions arrived for Cornwallis: Smart was instructed to take what steps he thought were necessary to seize the initiative.

Position must be restored. Iraqi troops must be withdrawn without delay. You have full authority to take any steps you think necessary to ensure this, including air attack on these troops. Air Officer Commanding must act on his own authority if you have no direct communication with him.

Here, at last, were firm, unambiguous instructions. Now that he had received them he had to decide not *if*, but *when*, to act. Cornwallis told Smart that he would support anything he decided to do: Auchinleck signalled to the effect that he believed that Smart should attack at once; however, Major General Fraser in Basra told him that he would be unable to assist as the Iraqis had breached the flood defences and had made northward movement by his troops on land impossible. Immediate aid for Habbaniya would not be forthcoming from the lone Indian Brigade now in Basra.

Smart still assumed that an ultimatum to the Iraqis to withdraw their troops, made directly by the ambassador to the Iraqi Government, would work. He wanted to ensure also that, if he did launch military action, he had the whole day available to prepare. He therefore asked Cornwallis to demand an ultimatum to the Iraqis, giving them three hours to withdraw, and delivering the message at 5 a.m. local time. Cornwallis replied at midday to the effect that the time for ultimatums was past, and that he had advised London that he was expecting air action against the Iraqis on the escarpment at Habbaniya that very day.

Finally realizing the danger of the situation in Iraq, Longmore in

Cairo on 1 May ordered eighteen Wellingtons from Egypt to Shaibah (eight from 70 Squadron and ten from 37 Squadron) to supplement the single Wellington and six Gladiators that had arrived from the Middle East on 19 April. Longmore's belief was that if action was called for the strategic priority would be to attack Baghdad, in the hope that this would be sufficient to persuade Rashid Ali to back down. It is clear from his memoirs that Air Vice-Marshal Tedder, Longmore's deputy and successor, also took this line.[5] Longmore accordingly told Smart either to continue flying training or to attack at once, hitting not the forces that lay at Habbaniya, but rather the government buildings and barracks in Baghdad itself. Fortunately Smart ignored this advice, which if acted upon would have brought an immediate and devastating attack on the cantonment by the overwhelming ground forces on the escarpment. If Habbaniya's air assets were to be deployed, their most sensible use was to destroy those forces that posed the most direct and immediate threat. Apart from the advice received from Longmore, Cairo was silent, reflecting the harsh reality that the need for immediate and forceful action in Iraq was recognized only by London and New Delhi.

During the afternoon of 1 May it became increasingly apparent to Smart that he had but one option: to do what Cornwallis advised and to strike hard against the Iraqi forces on the plateau at first light the following morning. A telegram from Churchill with advice that was characteristic and uncompromising, strengthened his resolve: 'If you have to strike, strike hard. Use all necessary force.'[6]

At a conference held at 8 p.m. that night, Smart briefed his officers. They would launch an attack at 5 a.m. the next morning, with the newly arrived Wellington bombers from Basra joining in. The attack would secure complete surprise, and would be decisive. Smart's attitude now swung from desperate pessimism to hopeless optimism. The orders were:

> Concentrated bombing, without warning, will be very demoralising for them. It won't last long. They should be in full flight within about three hours. Do the best you can. Have every aircraft in the air before light, and start bombing as soon as you can distinguish targets on the ground – 5.a.m.

'None of us got away to our rooms before midnight,' Dudgeon recalled, 'and the last man was back at his aircraft by 0315.'[7] At 2.45 a.m.

Smart sent the local Iraqi commander an ultimatum to the effect that if his forces were not withdrawn forthwith he would be forced to take immediate action. No response to this ultimatum was received.[8]

In the relative coolness of the pre-dawn darkness the aircraft were prepared for action, parked on the main runway and the polo field facing their direction of take-off. Lifting into the still inky darkness just before 5 a.m., the entire armed aircraft complement at Habbaniya launched itself one by one into the air. Once airborne the aircraft grouped above the plateau, joining the Wellingtons that had travelled 300 miles north-west from Basra, and then threw themselves determinedly against the Iraqi positions. The objectives of the attack were artillery, machine-gun positions and armoured vehicles, although as the day progressed any suitable target was attacked. The principal aim was to hit the Iraqis hard enough to prevent a ground assault on the otherwise defenceless base. Tony Dudgeon recalled the confusion of the skies above the escarpment during those first few hours:

> As the daylight got stronger we could see that the air above the plateau was like the front of a wasp's nest on a sunny morning. The ten Wellingtons were there from Basrah [sic] making a total of forty-nine aircraft of five different types and speeds, clustering and jockeying over an area not much bigger than a minor golf course. It was a hairy experience. In my Oxford I would peer down into the dusk, trying to distinguish a juicy target like a gun-emplacement – and an Audax would swoop past at some crazy angle. Or a Wellington would sail majestically across my bows, giving me heart failure and leaving my machine bucketing about in its slipstream. Luckily, no one hit anybody else, but there were some very close shaves indeed.[9]

The attack came entirely as a surprise to the Iraqi forces on the escarpment, as it was intended. Despite the live ammunition they carried, many soldiers still thought that they were on a training exercise. For their part, the fact that the British were prepared to fight rather than negotiate a peaceful surrender came to Rashid Ali and the Golden Square as something of a shock. It was simply not what they had expected. To compound it all, the first attacks took place on Friday, and the largely Muslim army was preparing for morning prayers. On news of the attacks reaching Baghdad, an enraged Grand Mufti immediately declared a *jihad* against Great Britain, the *Fatwa* being pronounced on German and Italian radio:

I invite you, O Brothers, to join in the War for God to preserve Islam, your independence and your lands from English aggression. I invite you to bring all your weight to bear in helping Iraq that she may throw off the shame that torments her. O heroic Iraq, God is with Thee, the Arab Nation and the Moslem World are solidly with Thee in Thy Holy Struggle![10]

More practically, the flow of oil through the remaining pipeline to Haifa was severed through the sequestration of the Iraq Petroleum Company oil plants.

Nevertheless, Iraqi artillery was quick to retaliate, shells firing indiscriminately into the cantonment only minutes after the first bombs began to fall. In the early half-light of the morning these guns revealed their positions by their muzzle flashes and proved easy targets for the bombers overhead. Captain Alistair Graham of the Green Howards, on Loan Service with the Levies, recorded in his diary:

The planes seemed to skim over the Plateau – tracer bullets and shells reached out but never quite touched them, while clouds of black dust and smoke rolled up from the bombed enemy positions.

A routine now began. As aircraft divested themselves of their bombs they would scoot back to Habbaniya, either to the airfield or to the polo ground, and whilst one of the crew would bomb up the other would rush to Group Captain Savile's operations room to report on the last sortie and receive target instructions for the next. Any halt to the operation would invite attack from the ground, and everyone fighting that day at Habbaniya knew that they had to keep the bombardment going without end until the Iraqis broke.

Pupils and ground crew volunteered to act as crew for the departing aircraft and the novice bomb-aimers and machine-gunners proved remarkably accurate. Dudgeon recalled:

Ground fire was both intense and accurate. Over the plateau, the Oxfords were cruising at about 1,000 ft. One would fly steadily on a bombing run . . . sitting and watching bullet holes being punched up through the wings from underneath. Most aircraft received several bullets strikes through the cockpit itself.[11]

During that first day of battle several aircraft were lost, including a Wellington, which managed to land on the airfield but was hit by Iraqi artillery and destroyed. Many others were peppered with holes from bullet strikes. Additionally, Iraqi Northrops, Bredas, Savoias, Audaxes and Gladiators made a number of attacks on Habbaniya, bombing and strafing, albeit inaccurately. On the ground, strong offensive action had also taken place by the Levies and troops of the King's Own to identify enemy gun emplacements and to cover the perimeter with machine guns from the blockhouses. These efforts involved fighting patrols sent out to locate and destroy an enemy gun emplacement behind the Burma Bund across the Euphrates, and acted successfully to repel a foray towards the camp from the south early in the day by eight Iraqi armoured cars and three light tanks, using anti-tank rifles. Aggressive action during this first day did much to temper Iraqi ardour and no further penetrations by armour were attempted against the perimeter during the siege. The blockhouses kept up a constant fire on all observed Iraqi movement and although Iraqi artillery targeted these positions the attacks were surprisingly ineffective. None were put out of action.

As dusk fell late on that first day of fighting and the darkness stopped operational sorties until the morning, Smart evaluated the results. They were worrying. The Iraqis were still on the plateau, apparently unmoved. The only consolation to the scattered and vastly outnumbered infantrymen guarding Habbaniya was that there was no sign yet of a ground assault developing. Smart's hope that it would all be over in three hours had proven to be widely misplaced. Of the sixty-four aircraft that had begun the day, twenty-two had been shot down and ten of the thirty-nine pilots had been killed or wounded. Two Vincent bombers had also been shot down during a sortie near Shaibah. During fourteen hours of flying, one hundred and ninety-three official sorties were counted – about six for each aircraft – but according to Dudgeon many more went unrecorded. Disconcertingly, whilst Smart's actions had been correct (though belated), the universal view in Cairo remained that Smart should have launched an all-out attack on government buildings in Baghdad. This view, as we have observed, would have been a political *faux pas* of the greatest magnitude, providing an easy justification for Iraqi retaliation against the cantonment and even perhaps a Cawnpore-like slaughter.* But it coloured Longmore and Tedder's view of Smart's ability to manage the crisis effectively.[12]

During the first night, the aircraft helpless on the ground, the Iraqi gunners lobbed some 200 shells into the cantonment between midnight and 3 a.m., fortunately without hitting the precious water tower or electricity generator and causing only a small number of casualties. The airbase facilities had no back-up, and if the water tower or electric plant had been hit, life would have very quickly become extremely uncomfortable for the besieged. Despite this bombardment, aircraft were repaired and bombed up in preparation for another assault at dawn on the morning of Saturday 3 May. During the night Habbaniya's hard-pressed infantrymen sent out fighting patrols to dominate no-man's-land around the perimeter and successfully frightened off Iraqi patrols. Thereafter the Iraqis kept their distance at night, withdrawing their standing patrols at dusk and making few attempts to raid the cantonment in the days or nights that followed.

On the second day of the battle the re-organized squadrons at Habbaniya were made ready at 4 a.m. for a 5 a.m. lift-off. On this day the DC2s of 31 Squadron, temporarily based in Basra, arrived to fly the remaining women and children to Basra and then India. As the slow and defenceless transport aircraft flew out of Habbaniya, Audaxes flew violent sorties against the Iraqi positions to prevent them targeting the lumbering planes and their precious cargoes.

On 1 May, Colonel Ouvry Roberts flew into Habbaniya from Basra in a Vincent with instructions to establish contact between the two bases and to report the situation back to Fraser. It was not his intention to remain in Habbaniya. Pressed nevertheless by Wing Commander Hawtrey and others to stay, he did so, ignoring requests from Fraser to

---

* Cawnpore was the site of the notorious massacre of women and children during the Indian Mutiny of 1857. As the cantonment in Iraq was built on the Indian model, the threat to the women and children would have been viewed by those Europeans present in the context of the collective memory of the Cawnpore tragedy.

return to Basra. It was fortunate that he did so, as he was able to take effective command of the base on Smart's enforced departure some days later.

During Saturday 3 May aerial attacks from Habbaniya were extended to include not just the immediate presence of Iraqi forces on the escarpment, but Iraqi airfields around Baghdad and the Baghdad–Falluja–Ramadi road by which the forces on the escarpment were receiving supplies and reinforcements. Three Wellingtons of 37 Squadron off-loaded some 7,100 pounds of explosives on to Rashid airfield in Baghdad. On Sunday 4 May eight Wellingtons continued the attack dropping 15,700 pounds, destroying hangars, dispersed aircraft, magazines and ground defences. Entirely unexpectedly, four Blenheim twin-engined fighters from 203 Squadron arrived from Egypt, making a powerful and welcome addition to the offensive capability of the base. These aircraft conducted an immediate low-level machine-gun attack on Rashid airfield and Baghdad civil airport. These strikes proved extremely effective in limiting the offensive capability of the Iraqi Air Force and in severely undermining the fragile morale of Iraqi troops on the ground. In the days that followed, attacks continued against Iraqi airfields in Baghdad and at Ba'quba (north of the city) with considerable success, and against Iraqi vehicles attempting to supply the troops on the plateau. All the while the Iraqi guns on the plateau fired indiscriminately but relatively ineffectively into the Habbaniya compound.

So far, the Habbaniya forces had done well to prevent the Iraqis on the escarpment from mounting any form of serious retaliation. In Cairo, however, Wavell remained deeply pessimistic about the outcome. During the morning of 3 May Lampson was horrified to hear Wavell casually comment that he saw no alternative but to begin negotiations with the Iraqis: he had no troops to deal with the problem and the only answer was to parley.[13]

That night attempts were made to prevent Iraqi artillery firing on the cantonment during the hours of darkness. A blackout was imposed across the cantonment and delayed-action bombs, dropped by aircraft during the day, were designed to explode at various times during the night. Additionally, although possessing neither night-navigational instruments nor lights, a number of aircrew flew sorties against the plateau at night, a hazardous undertaking that cost the lives of at least one Oxford crew. Aircraft had to take off blind, the pilot trusting to experience to judge when to lift off, and landing solely with the support of the landing light switched on briefly shortly before landing.

At dawn the following morning – Sunday 4 May – attacks continued unabated from both Habbaniya and Shaibah. Freya Stark, a prisoner with 350 others in the besieged British Embassy in Baghdad, described with elation her first sight of a bombing raid against the city by bombers of 37 Squadron, which had flown up from Shaibah in the early morning dawn:

> About 4 a.m. in faintest beginning of light, five of our bombers came over to plaster Rashid camp and machine-gun the airfield – wild and ineffectual popping of Iraq firearms. A very beautiful sight – a great Wellington, slowly sailing along at about 1,000 feet, up the river from south to north, very dark against the green sky and the sleeping houses. The dull sound of bombs dull but clear: the A.A. very sharp and crackling . . . The raid lasted about three hours.[14]

The attack on Rashid airfield that morning cost the Iraqi Air Force some twenty-nine destroyed aircraft and that on Ba'quba another thirteen. Leaflets were also dropped over Baghdad assuring the population that Great Britain's fight was with the usurper government rather than the people of Iraq, and the Regent broadcast from Jerusalem appealing to the population not to be led astray by 'falsehood and lies which had brought the country from the blessings of peace to the horrors of a venomous war.'[15]

Two elderly World War One-vintage 18-pounder field guns graced the entrance to Air Headquarters (AHQ) at RAF Habbaniya. They had not been used in anger since fighting the Turks and it was assumed that they had been disabled. This was not so. Although they had been decommissioned for over two decades and had been painted liberally over the years, Roberts believed that it could be possible to press them back into service. They were stripped and cleaned, by a Royal Artillery artificer flown in from Basra, and 4.5-inch ammunition arrived courtesy of the 31 Squadron DC2s. Not only did the weapons work but they proved to be surprisingly effective. The BBC ran a special report for propaganda purposes explaining that specially equipped aircraft had flown in heavy artillery. Tony Dudgeon recalled:

> We later learned that they had had a tremendous effect on our enemies which far outweighed their material achievements. The soldiers, up on the plateau, were convinced that guns in quantity were now being flown in from Basrah [sic].[16]

Four full days of fighting provided a heavy toll on Habbaniya's dwindling air force. By the evening of Monday 5 May, only four of the Oxfords were 'flyable', Dudgeon recording that:

> one of those sported well over seventy fabric patches pasted over bullet holes. The Audax, Gladiator and Gordon squadrons were no better off. In addition to the dead pilots and those in hospital or evacuated to Basrah [sic], four others from my original nineteen had had to be taken off flying because their nerves had cracked.[17]

One of the casualties evacuated to Basra on Monday 5 May was Smart, who suffered the indignity of chest and facial injuries in a motor accident caused by the blackout.[18] The pressure and worries of those early days had also made him over-wrought, and a number of eye-witnesses claim that he suffered some kind of breakdown at this time, although this remains hotly disputed by his family. Lady Holman, whose husband Adrian served at the embassy, and who stayed with Smart for several days at Air House in Habbaniya, was little surprised that this peacetime bureaucrat had collapsed under the weight of the responsibilities placed upon him:

> when the attack started he became quite hysterical. He went absolutely berserk. It was so serious that the senior doctor from the hospital gave Reggie a knockout injection so that he was totally unaware of what was going on and could be evacuated quietly.[19]

Tedder used the same language to describe Smart's breakdown, commenting somewhat unfairly that 'Smart's handling of the attack [on 2 May], which failed, and his despatch of somewhat hysterical messages, led me to think his judgment might be affected.'[20] Dudgeon writes caustically about his superiors, commenting that 'many of the elderly officers had no *will* to fight'[21] although Colonel Ouvry Roberts could find no evidence when he arrived that Smart had broken down.[22] On 29 May the unfortunate Smart and his family were evacuated from Basra to India by boat.

Until this time there had been no indication that the British attacks had made any significant impact on the Iraqi troops manning the positions on the escarpment, although the Iraqis continued to make little use of their tremendous topographical advantage. The infantrymen defending the base were stretched, concentrating on manning the blockhouses with their antiquated Lewis guns and dominating the ground around Habbaniya at night. On 5 May a patrol of the King's Own failed to drive off the Iraqi troops defending Sin-el-Dhibban village,* four miles south of the cantonment and the ferry point over the Euphrates – which the Iraqis were using to reinforce their positions on the escarpment – although substantial Iraqi casualties were claimed.

On the morning of Tuesday 6 May, it became clear from aerial reconnaissance that a massive reinforcement of the plateau was underway. This news was accompanied by the heaviest raid by the Iraqi Air Force to date, and it appeared that an all-out effort was about to be made to finish off the Habbaniya defenders. Then, unaccountably, the forces on the plateau decided that they had had enough, and began to stream away from their positions. Signals intelligence indicated that Rashid Ali was appealing for Axis support. On 6 May the Italian diplomatic cipher revealed that 'Rashid Ali had failed at Habbaniya, that his stocks of bombs and ammunition were exhausted and that he was desperately entreating the Germans and Italians to send him bomber and fighter aircraft.' As a result London was able to assure Wavell that there was 'an excellent chance of restoring the situation by bold action, if it is not delayed' because the British landings at Basra had forced Rashid Ali 'to go off at half-cock before the Axis were ready.'[23] The unremitting British air attacks, coupled with the fact that the Iraqi troops had deployed without rations or fresh water, had led to a dramatic loss of morale on the escarpment amongst the Iraqi conscripts. It may also have been the

* Arabic for 'Teeth of the Wolf'.

case that some of the soldiers had never been entirely comfortable with waging war on their erstwhile allies.

This withdrawal, however, was not followed by the troops at Sin-el-Dhibban, who proved more difficult to budge. During the day three successive attacks by troops of the King's Own and the Levies, supported by the Rolls Royce armoured cars, finally forced the remaining defenders from the village. Then, at about 4 p.m., troop reinforcements with armoured vehicles were spotted heading for the ferry point from the area of Falluja. Every available aircraft was thrown into the sky to meet this new threat. Dudgeon recalled:

> We made 139 aircraft sorties and when the last aircraft left, its pilot reported that the road was a strip of flames, several hundred yards long. There were ammunition limbers exploding, with cars and lorries burning by the dozen. We lost one Audax shot down.

The Iraqis retaliated with an air attack at 5 p.m., destroying two Oxfords, a Gladiator and an Audax, and killing seven and wounding eight.

The end of the siege was close. During 6 May troops of the garrison took 408 prisoners. On Wednesday 7 May RAF armoured cars reconnoitred the top of the plateau and reported it deserted. The siege was over. The estimate of Iraqi losses was put at anything between 500 and 1,000, although precise figures are impossible now to estimate. The plunder seized from the escarpment was substantial and provided a welcome relief for Roberts. The garrison captured six Czech-built 3.7-inch howitzers with 2,400 shells, an 18-pounder gun, a tank, ten modern armoured cars, three anti-aircraft guns with 2,500 shells, forty-five Bren light machine guns, eleven Vickers heavy machine guns, 340 rifles and 500,000 rounds of ammunition. The light arms were all British and far superior to those with which either the Indian Army or British troops in Palestine were equipped, who had to rely on ancient Lewis and Hotchkiss guns their fathers and grandfathers had used in an earlier era. The ancient Hotchkiss was described as 'an inferior gun even in the first flush of its youth some thirty years before.'[24] British pre-war arms sales had ensured that the modernization of the Indian Army and imperial garrisons came a distant second to export earnings, even when these earnings came from Britain's prospective enemies.

It had been an extraordinary week. Dudgeon calculated:

During those hectic 5 days our hastily armed, outdated training machines had dropped well over 3,000 bombs, totalling over 50 tons, and we had fired 116,000 rounds of ammunition. The ops-room had recorded 647 sorties, but we had completed, unrecorded, many more than that . . . Our losses [from 4 Training School] were 13 killed and 21 too badly wounded to carry on – and 4 more grounded from nerves gone.[25]

Losses from pilots and crews from other units who joined the battle on an *ad hoc* basis were never recorded. Habbaniya's gallant defenders had achieved an extraordinary victory, one that policy makers in London and Cairo had never imagined possible. Through their bold and determined attacks they had achieved a remarkable moral ascendancy over both the Rashid Ali regime and the Iraqi Armed Forces. Churchill cabled the defenders of Habbaniya on 7 May 1941:

Your vigorous and splendid action has largely restored the situation. We are watching the grand fight you are making. All possible aid will be sent. Keep it up![26]

Churchill's message was the first occasion that the defenders at Habbaniya had heard that a relief expedition was planned. If they believed that assistance was imminent, they were nevertheless to be disappointed. Dudgeon recalled:

Delighted with Churchill's signal, we of course imagined that a fine and cohesive fighting army unit from Egypt had been launched forth with all speed as soon as it became known that we were under duress – and long before we began to be shelled. Succour, with tanks and guns, had to be almost on our doorstep.

But Dudgeon had little inkling of the battles that had been and were being fought between London, Cairo and New Delhi regarding the nature, source and purpose of reinforcements for Iraq. Many years later he recalled:

Ignorance is bliss. It would have been a grave blow to our morale had we known that, far from being on our doorstep, nothing would leave the shores of the Mediterranean before 11 May – five days after we had defeated the hostile army by ourselves.[27]

In the two days following the debacle on the plateau a number of vigorous attacks from the air had virtually destroyed the remaining elements of the Iraqi Air Force, thirteen aircraft being destroyed on the ground, and a further twenty damaged. Further reinforcements dribbled into Habbaniya over the ensuing days. On about 11 May five more superannuated Gladiator fighters from 94 Squadron arrived from Ismailia on the Suez Canal.

During the siege the besieged had heard nothing from the embassy in Baghdad, and an attempt was made on the evening of 8 May to regain communication: an Audax dropped a message-bag into the embassy garden. However, machine-gun fire prevented the same Audax from collecting a response using the tried-and-tested hook and cable method the following night, and so the base and the embassy remained incommunicado. Ensconced precariously inside her ambassadorial prison the prescient Freya Stark wrote in her diary on 7 May:

must admit that in the map of the whole Middle East we are not so very important, but console ourselves by reflecting that our neighbourhood to Oil will prevent us from being forgotten.[28]

The prisoners in the embassy had a grandstand view of the aerial warfare that occurred as a daily routine over Baghdad and particularly the Rashid airfield, Baghdad's primary air base. On 17 May she exclaimed:

Yesterday I saw my first Messerschmitt of the war – a locust creature buzzing out north-west against the white clouds on the tail of two of ours that had come over. This morning two Germans were seen to fall in flames over Rashid camp.[29]

The results of the Habbaniya battle were threefold. First, the cantonment was not overrun, and the defenders not defeated. As a consequence, Rashid Ali's aim to use the threat to the cantonment as a bargaining chip in negotiations with Great Britain was decisively thwarted. This political stratagem was the most likely reason for the

Iraqi failure to attack Habbaniya on 30 April and 1 May. It seems that Rashid Ali wanted to create a political crisis and to drag out the resulting impasse through negotiation. He did not believe for one moment that in its straitened circumstances Great Britain would defend its interests in Iraq by force, and considered that the resulting period of negotiation would give Germany time to bring arms and aircraft into the country. Another reason perhaps, was the expectation that the arrival of strong German forces would do the job for the Iraqis. In either event Rashid Ali's policy failed dismally. Third, the Iraqi Armed Forces received a severe and demoralizing beating. In five days of incessant aerial bombardment the Iraqi Army was dealt a devastating blow from which their morale never recovered. In the process Iraq's air force was largely destroyed. The public standing of Rashid Ali's government was also dealt a severe blow, caused in part by his failure to overcome the Habbaniya problem and by his inability to ensure the timely arrival of the much-vaunted German legions, about which he had boasted to his supporters for so long.

As Smart had begun to prepare for his own lonely and unexpected battle around Habbaniya on 1 May, the onset of hostilities with Iraq intensified the battle between Wavell and Auchinleck over the issue of intervention in Iraq, and that of the command arrangements of forces sent to the country.

On 1 May, worried by Cairo's continuing lack of action in what he correctly saw as a rapid descent into war in Iraq, Auchinleck decided to take the situation into his own hands and assume command himself, something which he felt entitled to do as a result of the decision in February to allow India to assume operational responsibility for Iraq in time of war. Accordingly, Auchinleck sent the following signal to Wavell at 6.20 p.m. on 1 May:

General Fraser now reports that he has assumed command in Iraq from A.O.C [Air Officer Commanding] and in accordance with the decision of H.M.G. [His Majesty's Government] responsibility for defence of British interests in that country now rests primarily with C-in-C India. General Quinan will take over from General Fraser on approximately May 6. General Fraser is therefore the responsible adviser of H.M.G., of the Ambassador and of India on all matters of defence policy but will maintain the closest possible consultation with A.O.C India.[30]

There is no record of a response to this from Cairo. One assumes that Wavell was grateful perhaps that Auchinleck had assumed responsibility entirely for the Iraqi situation and by doing so had relieved him of yet another unwanted burden. In any case, Wavell regarded the whole problem of Iraq to have been one of India's doing, as without the provocative landings at Basra the situation might never have deteriorated as quickly or to the extent that it had done.

Auchinleck followed up his note to Wavell with a directive to Quinan on 2 May, which instructed him in no uncertain terms: 'You will command all British Empire land forces in Iraq from the time of your arrival. You will be under my orders.'[31]

London, however, had different ideas. Auchinleck's attempt to take control spurred London to action, concerned at the potential imperilment of an area of decisive economic importance to Great Britain. At 10.15 p.m. on 2 May the Chiefs of Staff sent a signal to Wavell, copied to Auchinleck, as follows:

In view of current situation in Iraq which is not that which we visualised when India took responsibility it seems operational command should now pass temporarily to Middle East whence alone immediate assistance can be given. This will take place forthwith unless you see strong objections.

Wavell took the decision badly. He was undoubtedly frustrated that Churchill appeared to have completely ignored his arguments of early April and that a repetition of this debate was about to be revived. Wavell simply did not accept the need for this extra commitment. He did not have the resources to do what Churchill demanded, he believed that the use of military force in Iraq was a dangerous over-reaction to an internal Iraqi political problem, and he could not understand why anyone could regard Iraq as of equal if not greater importance than either Palestine or Egypt at the current time. What is more, he had made these points repeatedly in the past. In response to Churchill's signal Wavell replied on 3 May, forcefully repeating arguments he had now been making for several weeks:

I have consistently warned you that no assistance could be given to Iraq from Palestine in present circumstances and have always advised that commitment in Iraq should be avoided.

Nothing short of immediate action by at least a brigade group with strong support of artillery and AFVs [Armoured Fighting Vehicles] could restore situation. There are no guns or AFVs in Palestine and to send forward weak and unsupported forces of cavalry or infantry seems merely asking for further trouble.

My forces are stretched to limit everywhere and I simply cannot afford to risk part of forces on what cannot produce any effect.

I do not see how I can possibly accept military responsibility for force at Basra of whose disposition and strength I am unaware, and consider this must be controlled from India.

I can only advise negotiation with Iraqis on basis of liquidation of regrettable incident by mutual agreement with alternative of war with British Empire, complete blockade and ruthless air action.

Longmore has seen this cable and agrees there is no alternative to above.[32]

It is not difficult to sympathize with Wavell's predicament. His command could not have been more stretched, and to ask it to do any more was, to Wavell, to ignore some inalienable military principles regarding the adequacy of resources to carry out the tasks demanded of him.

London saw the problem as one that centred on Baghdad rather than Basra, the alleviation of which would be best served by troops with transport based in Palestine (500 miles away) rather than those without transport in Basra (300 miles away). Was this a mistake? In light of the increasingly bitter disagreements between London, Cairo and New Delhi during the previous month it would seem to have made much more practical sense to leave responsibility for Iraq with Auchinleck. Wavell appeared to have neither the troops nor the will to intervene, whilst Auchinleck had both. This is the argument propounded by John Connell. Was this extra pressure on Wavell therefore unnecessary, given the willingness of India Command to take on the mantle of responsibility for Iraq at this time? In other words, was Churchill *right* to insist on rigorous action in Iraq, but *wrong* to expect it from Wavell? The answer must assuredly be 'no'. India Command, whilst keen to contribute decisively in Iraq, was still too weakly positioned to be able to act in adequate strength in the time available. It had but one brigade in Basra (comprising only two lightly armed infantry battalions) and one brigade still *en route* in the Persian Gulf and not expected to arrive until 6 May at the earliest. The brigade in Basra had an enormous task in itself to subdue hostile elements in the region and to protect the base area. It had no transport, armoured cars or aircraft, and the routes north to Baghdad, along road, railway and river, with the Iraqi destruction of the railway and river transport and widespread flooding, would prove extremely difficult to negotiate. Only Wavell had the wherewithal to do anything to help, even though these resources were limited. This reality was reluctantly recognized by both London and New Delhi.

After briefly discussing London's telegram with Linlithgow, Auchinleck accepted the decision to place responsibility in Wavell's hands, but insisted that this arrangement should only be temporary and asked at the same time that he retain responsibility for the control of forces in southern Iraq.

Auchinleck drafted a personal signal to Dill in which he set out his appreciation of how the strategic situation in the Middle East could soon develop, and its impact on India, reinforcing arguments he had rehearsed with both London and Cairo in the previous weeks:

If Alexandria and the Canal should be closed to us by enemy action, loss of Egypt would not be a major disaster, though importance of continuing to hold it cannot be minimized.

Even if we lose Egypt we should be able to hold Sudan and deny use of Red Sea to enemy.

To support Turkey and to stop enemy penetrating Asia, it is essential to deny to him Syria, Palestine and Iraq, and this may soon become our primary strategic object in this theatre.

Basra and Iraq are assuming major strategic importance as a base and line of communications area for operations in Middle East. Development of Basra and communications leading thence north and north-west is urgent necessity.

Consolidation, by force if necessary, of our position in Iraq is urgent need.

At present India alone can produce troops for occupation of Iraq but these troops cannot perform task unless provided with modern weapons and aircraft which India cannot give them. Provision of these is exceedingly urgent.[33]

Despite Wavell's anger, he nevertheless did as he was told. A few hours later he despatched another telegram to London explaining that he would put in place the appropriate preparations for a relief column to make its way from Palestine to Habbaniya, using what few resources he could rustle up. He warned, however, that this process would take time, the column would be weak in anti-tank and anti-aircraft weapons and would leave Palestine ill-defended. During 3 May Wavell had heard also from London that Turkey had offered to mediate in the resolution of the dispute between Britain and Iraq. Should not, he asked, Turkish or Egyptian offers of mediation be accepted?

It was clear to London, given his heated response on 3 May, that Wavell's usually broad strategic comprehension had failed him at this time of unparalleled stress. So discordant did Wavell appear that Ronald Lewin suggests that Wavell must have appeared, 'even to a wise old friend like Major General Hastings Ismay, the Secretary of the Chiefs of Staff Committee, as naively out of touch with reality.'[34] Wavell did not appear to comprehend the nature of the threat posed by Rashid Ali's rebellion, for here was not an isolated revolt by an insignificant dictator in a fly-bitten corner of the Empire, but an attempted assault on the very sinews of British power: the oil that fuelled her ability to continue to wage war. The Defence Committee ordered that these realities be impressed on Wavell. Accordingly, the Chiefs of Staff responded in a carefully argued telegram (Number 88) sent at 7.35 p.m. on 4 May 1941. None of these points were new, merely re-stated clearly and simply:

1. We much deplore extra burden thrown upon you at this crucial time by events in Iraq. A commitment in Iraq was however inevitable. It was essential for us to establish a base at Basra and to put ourselves in control of port of Basra and to be ready to safeguard Iranian oil in case of need . . . Had we sent no forces to Basra the present situation at Habbaniya might still have arisen under Axis direction . . .

2. With reference to your reluctance to assume responsibility for operations in Basra, the Iraq problem is admittedly divided by

geography into (a) Basra and (b) Habbaniya and oil. Control of operations in northern area must be in your hands as help can only come from Mideast . . . This responsibility cannot be divided and orders will therefore be given by C-in-C direct to General Basra, C-in-C India being kept informed.

3. There can be no question of accepting Turkish offer of mediation. For reasons in para. 1 above we can make no concessions . . . Essential that we should do all in our power (a) to restore situation at Habbaniya and (b) to place ourselves in a position to control pipeline to Mediterranean. Nothing in way of a demonstration is likely to be effective, and positive action as soon as forces can be made available will be necessary.

4. Your actions will therefore now be directed to implement the following policy: .

(a) The active defence of Habbaniya must be maintained by all possible means.

(b) Preparations for sending a force to restore situation as given in para.3 above must be pressed on . . .

(c) Our Ambassador in Iraq is being instructed to continue to exercise all possible pressure on Iraqi Government. For this purpose he can threaten the following action should situation develop into active war:

(1) Air bombardment of Baghdad.

(2) Destruction of Akrutiyah dam (we are advised this is possible by air action).

(3) Destruction of oil pumping stations.

(4) Complete blockade of Basra . . .[35]

At the same time, Churchill made clear to Turkey the response to the offer of mediation. The Turkish Government was asked to warn Iraq that if it persisted in its current path, Iraq would become a battleground as severe as anywhere else in Europe, with desperate consequences for its infrastructure and its people. There was to be no negotiation, only compliance or the threat of destruction.

Churchill's telegram arrived in Cairo in the early hours of Monday 5 May, Wavell's fifty-eighth birthday. Wavell exploded in uncharacteristic fury when he received it, exclaiming to Colonel Eric Dorman-Smith, who had brought him the message, that Churchill 'must face facts'. He repeated this phrase in his response to Churchill later that morning, but was perspicacious enough to recognize this message for what it was: a direct instruction from the Prime Minister that brooked no dissent. Wavell's facts related to the extreme paucity of his available resources, relative to the unrelenting pressure placed on him at a multitude of different and diverse battlefields across the length and breadth of his command. Churchill's facts, however, were, on this occasion at least, unassailable: lose the oil fields and risk losing the war. The only choice for Churchill was to re-prioritize strategic necessities and, for Wavell, to obey. It is fair to say that Wavell's concerns were also practical. How could a puny relief force from Palestine be able to save Habbaniya from the Iraqi crush around it? No one in their right mind expected Habbaniya to be able to save itself without relief.

During the day Wavell discussed the subject of Churchill's telegram with Sir Miles Lampson. Wavell was certain that tragedy would result for Great Britain from involvement in Iraq, to which Lampson countered that tragedy would also result from negotiation. The choices were stark, but Wavell could not be moved from his pessimism, one that Lampson could not personally understand.[36] Lampson had begun to notice a distinct character trait in many military men that he suspected was also true of Wavell, which was to 'announce dogmatically that such and such can't be done' at the outset of a debate only thereafter to find that something might be possible after all. Wavell's categorical assurances that no troops could be found for Iraq soon proved to be less than uncompromising when in fact, as Lampson observed, some were quickly forthcoming. They were not the massive force that Wavell may well have liked, but they were still troops. Lampson was also worried that Wavell could not see the political necessity for action, apparently calmly letting 'the situation slide on the argument that it [Iraq] was only an additional commitment. That may be all right militarily (though I doubt if it is), but it certainly isn't all right from the political side.'[37]

Wavell refused to accept Churchill's arguments, although he continued nevertheless to make arrangements for the relief force demanded by London for RAF Habbaniya. Accordingly, he explained what he was doing to meet London's demands. Following Churchill's instructions on 3 May, Wavell had immediately tasked Major General George Clark, temporarily in command of Palestine, to assemble a column – to be called 'Habforce' – from whatever troops he had remaining, following the earlier departure of 6 Infantry Division to both Greece and the Western Desert. Later that day he reported the results of Clark's plans to London:

I am arranging to assemble at H.4, near Transjordan – Iraq frontier, force consisting of the following: mechanized cavalry brigade (incomplete), one field regiment (less one troop), fifteen RAF armoured cars, three squadrons Transjordan Frontier Force, 1st Essex Regiment. It cannot be assembled before 10th May at earliest and could not reach Habbaniya till two days later even if no resistance met at Rutbah [sic] or elsewhere.

Very doubtful whether above force strong enough to relieve Habbaniya or whether Habbaniya can prolong resistance till its arrival. I am afraid I can only regard it as outside chance.

I feel it my duty to warn you in gravest possible terms that I consider prolongation of fighting in Iraq will seriously endanger defence of Palestine and Egypt. Apart from the weakening of strength by detachments such as above, political repercussions will be incalculable and may result in what I have spent nearly two years trying to avoid, serious internal trouble in our bases.

I therefore urge again most strongly that settlement should be negotiated as early as possible . . .

As regards para. 4(c), I feel that particular threats are most unwise unless they can be carried out in decisive fashion. Surely threat of war with British Empire is most effective.

Will do my best to control Basra situation, where fighting appears to have broken out, and am sending liaison officer to ascertain situation as soon as possible. I still feel that India, where reinforcement possibilities are known and whence force is maintained, is better placed to exercise effective control.[38]

This long response, the carefully compiled arguments and his continuing refusal to accept Churchill's arguments, riled the Prime Minister. At 5.15 p.m. that day Wavell signalled to his old friend General Sir John Dill:

Nice baby you have handed me on my fifty-eighth birthday. Have always hated babies and Iraqis but will do my best for the little blighter. Am hatching minor offensive in Western Desert but not sure yet can bring it off.[39]

Wavell's case was inadvertently weakened by a telegram to Churchill from Auchinleck on 5 May offering 'reinforcements of up to a total of five infantry brigades and ancillary troops by 10th June if shipping could be provided.'[40] Churchill's perception of Wavell, whose reticence was now unfavourably compared with Auchinleck's enthusiasm, had reached its nadir. His public criticism of Wavell now lacked even the pretence of objectivity. Churchill expressed surprise that given the fact that he had been advised initially of a potential operation in Iraq in early April Wavell had not even organized the Cavalry Division in Palestine into something resembling a mobile column, suggesting that, having been surprised on both western and eastern flanks, Wavell was obviously tired out. 'Why should the force mentioned, which seems considerable, be deemed insufficient to deal with the Iraq Army?' he asked Ismay in a memo drafted in the early hours of 6 May.[41]

On the last day of the siege of Habbaniya, 6 May 1941, the Chiefs of Staff in London devoted the whole morning to the question of Iraq and Wavell's refusal to accept Churchill's arguments for immediate intervention. London's conclusion was to reiterate its arguments to Wavell and to take responsibility for the consequences. Major General Ismay morosely recorded that this telegram was 'the first occasion in the war on which the Chiefs of Staff overruled the commander on the spot, and took full responsibility for the consequences.'[42] Later that day Churchill penned yet another chapter in what was becoming something of a saga:

Your telegram of yesterday has been considered by Defence Committee. Settlement by negotiation cannot be entertained on the basis of a climb down by Iraqis, with safeguard against future Axis designs on Iraq.

Realities of the situation are that Rashid Ali has all along been hand in glove with Axis Powers, and . . . was merely waiting until they could support him before exposing his hand. Our arrival at Basra forced him to go off at half-cock before the Axis were ready. Thus there is an excellent chance of restoring by bold action if it is not delayed.

Chiefs of Staff have therefore advised Defence Committee that they are prepared to accept responsibility for despatch of the force specified in your telegram at the earliest possible moment. They would like to see some light tanks and Bofors added if possible but there should be no delay on this account. Telegraph command arrangements.

Defence Committee direct that AOC Iraq be informed that he will be given assistance and in the meanwhile it is his duty to defend Habbaniya to the last.

Subject to security of Egypt being maintained, maximum air support possible should be given to operations in Iraq.

Reflecting Auchinleck's newfound status in Churchill's eyes the Commander-in-Chief India was sent a decidedly more positive response by the Prime Minister:

Your bold and generous offer greatly appreciated. Please prepare forces as a matter of urgency. Notify dates by which they will be ready to sail and we will confirm before despatch.[43]

Wavell's responses later that day dealt with operational concerns only. To Dill he reported:

Concentration of Habforce for relief of Habbaniya proceeding as rapidly as possible. Have ordered immediate occupation of Rutbah [sic] to be attempted, it seems to be only lightly held. Situation in Habbaniya apparently stable and signs that enemy may be short of gun ammunition and waiting Axis aid.[44]

Then, to the Chiefs of Staff on the same day he tabled the following:

Now that Iraqi force appears to have withdrawn from Habbaniya require urgently guide to policy. Is RAF to continue attacking military objectives throughout Iraq? Have no knowledge situation Baghdad, is Rashid's Government still in power and is there any sign of change of attitude? AOCinC [Air Officer Commander-in-Chief] is issuing instructions to confine air action to Iraqi aerodromes and troops in immediate neighbourhood Habbaniya, Shaibah or Basra.

But the war of words between Cairo and London was not yet over. On Wednesday 7 May no fewer than four 'Most Immediate' telegrams were sent from London to Wavell, three from the Chiefs of Staff and one from the Prime Minister. Churchill himself recalled that he 'continued to press Wavell hard'. Rather than diminish, the fault line between London and Cairo grew and in the process Wavell's own position grew progressively weaker. Emboldened by news of the success at Habbaniya, but fearful of the imminent arrival of potentially large numbers of *Luftwaffe* aircraft, Churchill signalled Wavell on 7 May:

> We must forestall the moral effect of their arrival by a stunning blow. I presume that if Rutba and Habbaniya are clear [our] column will take possession of Baghdad or otherwise exploit success to the full.[45]

Such a thought turned Wavell cold. On 8 May he responded acerbically to the Prime Minister, repeating the arguments he had wielded repeatedly over the previous weeks:

> I think you should appreciate the limits of military action in Iraq during next few months without a favourable political situation. Forces from India can secure Basra, but cannot, in my opinion, advance northwards unless the co-operation of the local population and tribes is fully secured. Force from Palestine can relieve Habbaniya and hold approaches from Baghdad to prevent further advance on Habbaniya, but it is not capable of entering Baghdad against further opposition or maintaining itself there . . . In order therefore to avoid a heavy military commitment in a non-vital area, I still recommend that a political solution be sought by all available means.[46]

Tired of this long-running battle with his Middle East C-in-C, Churchill rebuffed Wavell strongly, his mind already made up to replace him in Cairo with Auchinleck. On 9 May he told Wavell tersely:

> Our information is that Rashid Ali and his partisans are in desperate straits. However this may be, you are to fight hard against them. The mobile column being prepared in Palestine should

advance as you propose . . . having joined the Habbaniya forces. You should exploit the situation to the utmost, not hesitating to try to break into Baghdad even with quite small forces, and running the same kind of risks as the Germans are accustomed to run and profit by. There can be no question of negotiation with Rashid Ali unless he immediately accepts . . . terms . . . Such negotiation would only lead to delay, during which the German Air Force would arrive.[47]

On 8 May Wavell assumed operational control in southern Iraq and instructed Quinan to secure the Basra–Shaibah area, effectively cancelling Auchinleck's earlier instructions to Quinan to develop a forward policy in Iraq and make every effort to reach Baghdad. This approach was, in Wavell's view, dangerously presumptuous and not to be undertaken until the Basra base was secure and the Tigris tribes pacified, neither of which could be expected to take place quickly.

Command of 10 Indian Division now changed hands. When, on 10 March 1941, Auchinleck had instructed Quinan to prepare to take command of *Sabine* he told Quinan that he had hand-picked an Indian Army brigadier by the name of William Slim to be his chief staff officer: 'I think his recent war experience ought to be of great value to you', he wrote.[48] Auchinleck confirmed the appointment a few days later in a note to Wavell: 'I have nominated Quinan as Commander of the Force and have sent his name home to the War Office. I propose to give him Slim as his BGS [Brigadier, General Staff] and I think the combination should be a good one.'[49] Quinan and Slim left India for Iraq together on 4 May 1941.[50]

The opportunity for Slim to command his own division came far sooner than anybody expected.* On 11 May 1941, Auchinleck wrote to the Viceroy, Lord Linlithgow, advising that he was removing Fraser from command of 10 Indian Division at his own request, and was replacing him with Slim: 'I have every reason to expect that Slim's

---

* See Robert Lyman, *Slim: Master of War* (London: Constable, 2004). Many officers who were to play significant roles in the forthcoming Burma Campaign such as Wilfred Lloyd, Bill Slim, Ouvry Roberts, Alf Snelling, 'Sunny' Lomax and Douglas Gracey cut their teeth in the Middle East in 1941.

energy, determination and force of character generally will prove equal to the task', he wrote.[51] Slim accordingly took up the appointment on 15 May 1941 in the temporary rank of Major General.

Slim was a Gurkha officer of immense ability who was to play a conspicuous and important role in forthcoming operations in Iraq, Syria and Iran. Of that, more anon. On leaving Iraq in March 1942 he was destined to spend the remainder of the war forging the weapon to defeat the Japanese in India and Burma. Soon after rejoining 10 Indian Division, Ouvry Roberts listened to Slim talking *en masse* to the assembled officers of the division, and was immediately impressed by him. Roberts was to find himself under Slim's command, in various guises, for the remainder of the war. Jack Masters also listened:

> Slim was squarely built, with a heavy slightly undershot jaw and short greying hair. He began to speak, slowly and simply, with no affectation. He told us first that we had done a good job in the Iraq campaign. But no one could call that a very serious business. He had already seen enough of our fighting spirit and our technical competence to know that we needed little teaching there. What he wanted to do was to prepare us, practically and above all mentally, for the heavier fighting that we must soon meet.

Slim's strictures on individual discipline, the centrality of morale to a soldier's willingness and determination to continue fighting in conditions of extreme danger and hardship and the certainty of hard fighting ahead left Masters musing: 'Slim's sort of battle wouldn't be much of a lark, after all.'[52]

Although he by now had no operational control over the situation in Iraq, Auchinleck was fearful lest Wavell drop the baton he had been given, now that the gallant garrison of Habbaniya had secured its perimeter, at least for the time being. On 9 May he reinforced his concerns about the situation in Iraq in a long message to Dill:

> Although control of forces in Iraq now rests with Mideast it is impossible for India to disassociate herself from the formulation of policy in that area. Not only is success or failure in Iraq vital to the

safety of India but most of the forces and material employed in that theatre must come from India. I gather also that it is intended that control of operations will eventually revert to India.

We are prepared to make great efforts and to take great risks to support a sound policy which in our opinion has some prospect of success and also will continue as in the past to give all help possible to Mideast. The opportunity for controlling the situation in Iraq by means of a force stationed in northern Palestine is however past and the main advantage of that proposal is now nullified by the fact that we are firmly established in Basra. In our opinion there is now only one policy which will call a definite halt to German penetration into Iraq, Iran and possibly Turkey and Syria. As you are aware German influence is already firmly established in Iran and failing some positive action on our part will no doubt greatly influence the situation both in Iraq and elsewhere.

This policy is to establish ourselves with the minimum delay in sufficient force at Baghdad and other key points such as Mosul and Kirkuk so as to be able to resist any attack internal or external by the Axis. These forces must have a secure L.of.C. [Line of Communication] and this must in our opinion lead from Basra. Except as very temporary alternative the Baghdad–Haifa L.of.C is too difficult and too vulnerable to Axis forces based in Syria.

The present time when Iraq forces have suffered a serious setback, are short of ammunition and indecisive of purpose is ideal for obtaining our objective with the minimum effort and if we act boldly and employ suitable personnel and suitable methods we may do it with the support rather than the opposition of the tribes.[53]

Auchinleck's view therefore was that Iraqi disarray as a result of their defeat at Habbaniya had to be exploited quickly and comprehensively across the whole of Iraq. Wavell had trouble hiding his irritation at this restating by Auchinleck of what he had long regarded as foolishness. Convinced of Churchill's dangerous folly in further dividing the scarce forces available to him, in not appreciating the virtues of political negotiation or the dangers of the type of open-ended commitment to Iraq seemingly advocated by Auchinleck, Wavell continued obstinately to press his case, seemingly unaware of just how angry Churchill had become with his endless prevarication in the face of clear orders. In due course Wavell was to recognize that his arguments in favour of political negotiation failed to acknowledge the military objectives of the Rashid Ali regime, but in early to mid-May 1941 he could not see why Iraq should take military precedence over either Egypt or Palestine. In an extensive telegram on 10 May he argued that operations in Iraq be limited to the minimum possible:

> There is obviously some divergence of view between C.-in-C. in India and myself on Iraqi policy . . . At this critical period essential that our limited resources be concentrated on our really vital military interests. In Iraq these are . . . (a) Avoidance of major conflict with Arabs (b) Security of oil supplies from Abadan (c) Security of oil supplies from Iraq and (d) Maintenance of air route to India.
>
> All these are of minor importance compared with the security of Egypt and Palestine.

Wavell was concerned that the beating of the war-drum from Simla (whither Auchinleck's GHQ had moved to escape the heat of the New Delhi summer), represented in part by Auchinleck's signal to Dill on 9 May, ignored the widespread negative repercussions that military intervention would precipitate across the Muslim world.

> India naturally does not appreciate fully effect on military position in Middle East which large-scale Arab uprising against us in Iraq would have. It would have repercussions in Palestine, Aden, Yemen, Egypt and Syria which might absorb very large proportion of my Force in maintaining internal order. Firmness in dealing with enemy attack on Habbaniya will have on whole good effect but unless we can get back to normal relations with well-disposed Iraqi Government at very early date suggestions that we propose to occupy country and suppress Iraqi independence will be exploited by enemy with serious results . . . Hence my anxiety for political solution as early as possible.
>
> Supply of oil from Iraq to Haifa can only be obtained by Iraqi goodwill. Iraqis are at present in position to destroy refineries

and cut off supply and to imagine that we could by military occupation secure this long and vulnerable supply is to my mind illusory.

Security of Abadan oil depends largely on having force available at Basra to protect refinery and to keep open Shatt-el-Arab [sic]. Anti-aircraft defence will be required and will be difficult to provide.[54]

It is clear that Wavell's view failed to appreciate that Iraq was determined to seek an Axis-supported confrontation with Britain and was not in the least bit interested in a long-term political settlement. Not understanding the nature of this threat, therefore, Wavell argued that operations should be limited to the following:

(a) To do everything possible to secure political settlement … as soon as possible and to resume normal relations with Iraqi government.
(b) Force at Basra to secure and organize base and endeavour to establish good relations with tribes but not to move forward till strong enough to be effective which I do not feel will be for some little time.
(c) HABFORCE will move from Palestine to Habbaniya and thence if situation permits to Baghdad with view to influencing political situation.[55]

Auchinleck did not respond directly to Wavell. He had found the endless debate by telegram wearying and did not believe that the arguments of either party would be advanced by further communication of this sort. In a note to Linlithgow on 11 May he stated that he believed that Wavell's viewpoint was insufficiently broad and remained parochial and that until all parties worked 'to a common end, we shall waste much of our effort in voicing our divergent views one against the other'. He concluded:

I had considered cabling General Dill on these lines, but I feel I have done a lot of cabling lately and I wondered whether Your Excellency thinks it worth while trying to press this point of view any further at the moment.[56]

In part Wavell was right: the pre-eminent task for Great Britain was to install a friendly government in Baghdad. Indeed, all sides of the increasingly bitter dispute agreed with this imperative. The disagreement revolved around the *means* of achieving this end and the *scale* and *source* of the means utilized. It was the basis of Wavell's logic with which both Churchill and Auchinleck disagreed. Wavell's starting point, as we have seen, was to calculate the military resources available to him and then to decide whether this sum would be sufficient to achieve the ultimate political objective required. From the equation that he calculated his firm conclusion was that the military force available would not be sufficient to achieve the desired outcome and that a negotiated settlement was the only reasonable option in the circumstances. It is not difficult to understand why he should take this line, as he had been in this situation before and was determined not to accept any more impossible tasks from Churchill on slender or insufficient resources again.

Wavell was later to accept that in this judgement he was wrong, proving clearly that had not Churchill bullied him mercilessly and had not the Chiefs of Staff overruled him on 9 May, the results for Britain could have been calamitous. After 4 May, wrote Wavell:

> I was inclined to accept the Turkish offer of mediation. But Winston quite rightly refused to have anything to do with it and said we must deal with the matter by our own military force . . . I told Winston that I was doubtful whether the force ordered across to Habbaniya was strong enough to effect its purpose, and it would leave me without any reserve whatsoever for any eventuality in Syria. *He ordered me to send it, a bold and correct decision, which I always felt I really ought to have taken myself.*[57] [my italics]

In the case of the Rashid Ali government in Iraq every risk had to be taken as early as possible to prevent an escalation (leading to armed German intervention in the country), something that Britain would then be unable to control. Rashid Ali's gauntlet had to be accepted, and although the tiny number of troops available to take up the challenge was regrettable, both Churchill and Auchinleck believed that immediate military action was essential, if only to signal Britain's political determination to use military force to resolve the issue in her favour. A firm hand in Iraq was a necessary precursor to any subsequent political action precisely because Rashid Ali, as

Auchinleck and Churchill correctly surmised, had no intention of doing anything but overturning the established order, handing over Iraqi oil and resources to Germany, allowing the establishment of strong German military bases across the country for the pursuance of her war aims elsewhere in the region and removing Great Britain and her influence entirely. If Britain had caved in to Rashid Ali's threats by seeking a negotiated settlement, as Wavell so strenuously advocated, it would have seriously weakened Britain's standing in the region as a whole, and made it more rather than less difficult for her to deal with Arab nationalist claims in other parts of the Middle East: her reputation for not bowing to violent blackmail would have been fatally compromised.

What motivated Wavell to take the line that he did? One supposes that not a little was the result of a natural stubbornness exacerbated by what he regarded as Churchill's unreasonable demands and Auchinleck's ill-judged warmongering. Wavell, like both Churchill and Auchinleck, possessed a formidable though taciturn personality combined with powers of logic that were rooted in a deep intellect. When he knew he was right, he was hard to move; when he knew someone else to be wrong, the stubbornness became persistent and even rebellious. These were the traits that were to express themselves to a degree so dangerously to Wavell's position as Commander-in-Chief in that exceptionally hot summer in 1941, and which were to contribute to his removal in early July.

In an attempt to douse Wavell's flames Churchill wrote reassuringly in the early hours of 13 May:

About Iraq – you do not need to bother too much about long future. Your immediate task is to get a friendly Government set up in Baghdad and to beat down Rashid Ali's forces with utmost vigour. We do not wish to be involved at present in any large-scale advance up the river from Basra, nor have we prescribed the occupation of Kirkuk or Mosul. We do not seek any change in the independent status of Iraq, and full instructions have been given in accordance with your own ideas on this point.

Like a lurcher after his hare, however, Churchill pressed Wavell hard on the importance of the current action:

What matters is action, namely the swift advance mobile column to establish effective contact between Baghdad and Palestine. Every day counts, for Germans may not be long. We hoped ... that column would be ready to move 10th and would reach Habbaniya 12th, assuming Habbaniya could hold out, which they have done and a good deal more. We trust that you will do your utmost to accelerate this movement.

On receipt of this message Wavell replied on 13 May, by coincidence the day in which Moscow announced belated recognition of Rashid Ali's government:

We will do our best to liquidate this tiresome Iraq business quickly. Shortage of transport is causing difficulty. Flying column should reach Ramadie [sic] and Falluja which may make it difficult to approach Baghdad. German Air Force now about to take hand, hope RAF can arrange to deal with them. Am sending my CIGS [Chief of the Imperial General Staff] to Basra tomorrow to see GOC [General Officer Commanding]. Will try to meet Auchinleck later but do not like leaving here at present.[58]

Auchinleck's argument that British strategy should consider the occupation of Iraq and secure its oil fields, a notion that had been rejected outright by Wavell on 10 May, was also dampened down by the Prime Minister in a friendly note he sent to the Commander-in-Chief India on 14 May:

We are most grateful to you for the energetic efforts you have made about Basra. The stronger the forces India can assemble there the better. But we have not yet felt able to commit ourselves to any advance (except with small parties when the going is good) northward towards Baghdad and still less to occupation in force of Kirkuk and /or Mosul . . . We are therefore confined at the moment to trying to get a friendly Government installed in Baghdad and building up the largest possible bridgehead at Basra. Even less can we attempt to dominate Syria at the present time though the Free French may be allowed to do their best there. The defeat of the Germans in Libya is the commanding event and larger and longer views cannot be taken till that is achieved, and everything will be much easier then.[59]

4

Baghdad

Sitting in the back of his Chevrolet staff car, moving at a strict fifteen miles per hour across the desert floor in the empty vastness of eastern Iraq, Captain Somerset de Chair of the Household Cavalry Regiment stared through the rear window at the black speck in the sky far to the rear of the seemingly endless column of assorted lorries that stretched to the horizon, lumps of grey and black through the sandy haze dotted across the rock-strewn plain. It was 15 May 1941.

> I saw, with surprised eyes, two black tulips of smoke blossom far down the line, and while the bomb bursts still hovered in the air, I saw the bright white-hot flash of anti-aircraft fire stream upwards across them. We had been discovered at last.[1]

Although de Chair was told that the culprit was a British-built Blenheim of the Royal Iraqi Air Force, the attack was actually carried out by a German Heinkel 111 of the newly arrived *Fliegerführer Irak* flying out of Mosul. What confused the troops on the ground was that the aircraft carried Iraqi markings, and to those without access to the intelligence provided by secret transcripts of the German Enigma transcoding machines (who indeed, were very few), the idea that the *Luftwaffe* was this far east was frankly preposterous.[2] Rumours, however, were rife and spoke of a yet unseen reality. As Intelligence Officer and chief navigator to the advance column of the relief force despatched overland to Iraq from Palestine, de Chair knew full well of the fears that Germany was preparing to use Greece or Crete as the base for an airborne assault on Cyprus and Syria, with the object of attacking British forces in Iraq:

> Was this the advance guard of the 22nd Airborne Division which I knew to be ready for action? Was it going to be sent through Syria to assist the Iraqis, to whom lavish promises of German assistance were hourly made by Axis propaganda? . . . It looked rather as if we were for it.[3]

Until 15 May, however, this was mere speculation. A few days earlier de Chair described the first ominous news that German aircraft would soon be prowling the Iraqi skies, information derived (although de Chair did not know this) from decrypts of Enigma messages on 9, 12, 13 and 14 May as well as from the British Consul in Aley, near Beirut, who heard the distinctive sounds of German aircraft flying over in the early hours of 8 May:

> While we were at Rutbah [sic], disturbing intelligence reached me . . . Seven unidentified aircraft had passed over Aley, near Beirut, heading for Iraq. Another seventeen were reported to be refuelling at Mezze. We knew they were Germans . . . Then Squadron Leader Dudgeon arrived in a Blenheim from Habbaniya where our Air Force cantonment was surrounded by Iraqi forces and told me that one of our pilots on reconnaissance over Mosul had been fired at by a Messerschmitt 110.[4]

On 14 May, just as the air threat to the garrison at Habbaniya appeared to be diminishing, a Blenheim pilot, on patrol in the area of Mosul, was surprised to find himself being attacked by a German Bf.110 fighter, and on the following day de Chair's column was struck.

General Sir Henry Wilson,* known to all as 'Jumbo' for his ample girth, found himself in Cairo on 2 May prior to proceeding to take command

---

* Later Field Marshal Lord Wilson of Libya.

of British forces in Palestine. Days earlier he had been evacuated with British forces from Greece, following yet another decisive German advance and dispiriting British withdrawal. Whilst waiting on the seashore on 30 April next to Malemi airfield on Crete, Wilson recalled Wavell saying to him, shortly after arriving for a conference to discuss the defence of the island: 'I want you to go to Jerusalem and relieve Baghdad.'[5] It seems likely that Wilson's memory failed him on this occasion. Although this was the day on which the two Iraqi brigades positioned themselves on the escarpment overlooking Habbaniya, Wavell was insistent at this time in his refusal to consider launching any form of intervention in Iraq and indeed had to be ordered to do so by Churchill. These orders, as we have seen, did not arrive until the morning of 3 May.

In answer to Wavell's instructions Major General George Clark, General Officer Commanding (GOC) of the still largely horsed 1 Cavalry Division – popularly though sardonically known in the British Army at the time as 'Hitler's Secret Weapon' – had cobbled together a force on paper some 6,000 strong for the expedition into Iraq.[6] Based around Brigadier Joe Kingstone's 4 Cavalry Brigade, 'Habforce' as it became known was to comprise the Household Cavalry Regiment (Life Guards and Blues), the Royal Wiltshire Yeomanry, the Warwickshire Yeomanry and 1 Battalion The Essex Regiment, together with 237 Battery of 60 Field Artillery Regiment. The problem was that many of these troops were not in Palestine at all: the Royal Wiltshire Yeomanry was still in the Western Desert* and 237 Battery had recently arrived in Suez. Although equipped with the fabulous 25-pounder, they had had no time to calibrate their guns before going into action.[7] Those troops still in Palestine after the despatch of forces to Greece were ill-trained and poorly equipped. The Household Cavalry had only recently converted from horses and had seen no action to date. This transformation from horse to inferior trucked infantry with paltry training, and given the label 'mechanized', was itself a demoralizing experience for which the cavalrymen were 'untrained, unenthusiastic and unfit'.[8]

---

* After recall from the Western Desert the Yeomanry covered 1,200 miles from Sidi Barrani to Habbaniya in 9 days. Their role was to guard the line of communication between Palestine through Transjordan to Iraq against the depredations of guerrillas and saboteurs.

In addition Habforce included a mechanized squadron of the Transjordan Frontier Force (TJFF*), No. 2 Armoured Car Company RAF with eight Fordson armoured cars† commanded by Squadron Leader Cassano (also in the Western Desert), an anti-tank troop of the Royal Artillery with 2-pounder guns, a troop of 2 Field Squadron Royal Engineers and a detachment of 166 Field Ambulance. It had no tanks. On 5 May Cassano's armoured cars were 1,000 miles to the west guarding airfields in the Western Desert. Nor did Habforce possess modern machine guns. What it lacked in training and equipment, however, Habforce made up for in an infectious though naive enthusiasm for the adventure ahead.

Major John Bagot Glubb, otherwise known as 'Glubb Pasha' or, to the Arabs amongst whom he had spent the previous twenty years, 'Abu Hunaik' ('The Father of the Jaw' after an indentation in his jaw caused by a wound sustained in the First World War), was attached to Clark's force as political officer. Glubb had long before resigned his commission in the British Army in order to live amongst the Arabs 'in a ruined castle of the wilderness where the Jinns bring him the desert news.'[9] At great political risk, when it seemed that the whole of the Arab world supported Hitler, Transjordan's King Abdullah (who was angry about the treatment of his brother, the Regent, by Rashid Ali) gave permission for Abdullah's private army, the Arab Legion, led by ex-British officers like Glubb, to join Habforce. Because of lack of transport, however, Glubb could only contribute 350 men of the Desert Mechanized Regiment as personal escort. Equipped with 1915-vintage Lewis Guns they travelled in a mixture of civilian Ford trucks and home-made armoured cars. 'Will the Arab Legion fight?' Wilson enquired of Glubb at the King David Hotel in Jerusalem. 'The Arab Legion will fight anybody,' Glubb replied. 'Were not these my brothers in arms, with whom I had lived for ten years past?'[10] Glubb had by this time made for himself a reputation amongst Arabs that far surpassed even that of Lawrence. Somerset de Chair came under his spell at once:

* Unlike the Arab Legion, the TJFF was a British imperial unit, paid for by Great Britain and led by officers on loan from the British Army.

† The Fordson was a more modern remake of the original Rolls Royce Silver Spirit armoured cars, with which RAF Habbaniya was equipped and which had been in the Middle East since 1915.

his whole background was glamorous, and I felt that the Glubb legend was more surely rooted in the hearts of the Bedouin than was Lawrence's. Glubb had led them for twenty years . . . and the Desert Patrol was his own creation. His men came from tribes all over the Levant (including Iraq) and were proud to serve under him. His command was more official than Lawrence's, for it had the authority of the established Emirate of Transjordan behind it. I had mentioned Lawrence's name in gatherings of Arabs, perhaps in a village perched high on some crag, accessible only to men on horses, and seen the flicker of recognition which passed around the circle of dark faces at the mention of Lawrence's name. But much of this fame had come after the event from the publicity which it received in books, newspapers and cinemas. Lawrence was a name to conjure with in the Near East, but Abu Hunaik's was accepted as of the Near East itself.[11]

On 6 May Wilson arrived in Jerusalem prior to assuming command in Palestine on 7 May and was briefed by Clark on the plans made over the previous three days. Air Commodore John D'Albiac, who had also been in Greece with Wilson, as Air Officer Commanding (AOC), had already arrived in Palestine. Wavell, Wilson, Clark and D'Albiac met in Jerusalem on 11 May to finalize plans for the operation, and it was here that Clark was told that his secondary objective was the relief of the embassy in Baghdad. His protest that this would not be possible with the supply resources at his disposal led to Wavell ordering the despatch of a further transport company from Egypt to support Habforce. Bidding farewell to Clark at the King David Hotel in Jerusalem, Wavell remarked: 'It's a long odds bet, but I think you will make it.'[12]

Clark's relief expedition, although that was now a misnomer given Habbaniya's plucky self-defence, had to travel some four hundred and sixty miles further east from the railhead at Mafraq in Transjordan. One hundred and twenty miles along this journey lay H4, the Iraq Petroleum Company's pumping station thirty miles from the Iraqi border. The tarmac ended forty-five miles after H4. Sixty miles further on from the frontier was Rutba Fort. H3 lay ten miles over the Iraqi border, between H4 and Rutba. Rutba, described as comprising 'the normal squalid collection of Arab hutments with its quota of bedraggled children and dogs', nevertheless had significant value as a source of water and an airfield.[13] From Rutba the traveller faced another two hundred and twenty miles on an ill-defined track across the desert to Ramadi and thence to Habbaniya. Only a march on a compass bearing could guarantee that a traveller, unused to the vagaries of direction finding in the desert, would be able to make sense of the mass of tracks, ancient and modern, animal and man-made, that criss-crossed the desert floor to tempt the unwary.

Members of the Iraqi Desert Police, a force with whom Glubb had himself worked in the past, had recently seized Rutba Fort and reportedly had been joined by the Arab guerrilla leader Fawzi Qawujki, long a thorn in the side of governments of Palestine, Iraq and Transjordan.* These elements had in fact fired the opening shots in the war when they attacked a British road survey party on 1 May. Instructed by Clark to seize the fort, the mechanized squadron of the TJFF, based at H4, refused, and were promptly marched back to H3 and disarmed. At this inauspicious start Clark decided to divide Habforce into two parts, despatching a flying column ('Kingcol') under Brigadier Kingstone and ordering it to make best haste to H3 to make contact with Glubb's Arab Legion, and then to capture Rutba. Kingcol comprised the Headquarters 4 Cavalry Brigade, the Household Cavalry Regiment and Cassano's eight vintage Rolls Royce armoured cars. To these forces were added the battery of 25-pounder field guns, two companies and two Bren gun carriers of the Essex Regiment under the command of Major K.F. May, an independent anti-tank troop with 2-pounder guns and the section of 166 Field Ambulance.

Glubb and the men of the Arab Legion were ordered to join Kingcol at H4. Glubb explained his role to Somerset de Chair:

> I was originally detailed to go to Iraq on a purely political job, to rally the Iraqis hostile to the Rashid Ali Government. I was originally to go alone, but I asked permission to take some men of the Arab

---

* Fawzi Qawujki served in the French–Syrian Army in the 1920s but deserted to join the Druze rebellion in 1925–7. He remained an outlaw thereafter but was pardoned by Vichy France in 1941 if he agreed to fight against Great Britain. He did so until being wounded on 24 June 1941, when he was evacuated by German aircraft to Athens. After the war he led the Palestinian Liberation Army in the war of 1947, in which Glubb Pasha fought on his side.

Legion as a personal escort. This task had originally no connection with the military operations, and I very nearly left for Iraq alone. When however it was proposed to send a military column across the desert, it was decided that we might as well go together.[14]

With some two thousand men and five hundred vehicles Kingcol took with it four days' worth of water and five of fuel. The immediate objective was to secure Rutba Fort. Whilst there were enough vehicles to transport the troops, those required to carry supplies had to be requisitioned in Palestine, most of which also retained their civilian drivers. Every kind of vehicle could be found in the column, from flatbed lorries to buses taken from the streets of Haifa and Jerusalem. Sir Alec Kirkbride, the British Resident Transjordan and a veteran of Lawrence's adventures, saw the column depart from Mafraq on 12 April:

The British units had sufficient transport to move themselves, but nothing over for supply purposes, so resort was had to the requisitioning of civilian lorries in Palestine regardless of their condition. The result was a transport train made up of dozens of different types of cars, with practically no spare parts or tyres, and manned by civilian drivers who were openly rebellious. As a car broke down, and many did, it was pushed into the ditch and abandoned. I saw this amazing piece of improvisation, which was called KINGCOL, leave Mafraq with four hundred miles of desert to cross before it could engage an enemy several times more powerful than itself, and my heart sank.[15]

On 9 May Blenheims from 203 Squadron attacked Rutba Fort. The Arab Legion, waiting expectantly in the desert for the fort's surrender, were disappointed at the outcome, the defenders spiritedly attempting to drive off the aircraft with their rifles, and succeeding in shooting down a Blenheim and killing the crew. Glubb was forced to withdraw to H3 on 9 May whilst Baghdad triumphantly announced that Abu Hunaik had been killed. Rather prematurely, his obituary was published in London. On the night of 10 May, however, following the arrival of Cassano's armoured cars, the fort was found abandoned and the way to Habbaniya open.

Kingcol left Mafraq in Transjordan on 12 May, arriving at the captured Rutba Fort on the following day. De Chair described first meeting members of the Arab Legion in the fading light at Rutba Fort after its capture:

> Here were trucks, armed with Lewis guns, and cars outside the gates. As we drove up to these and dismounted, the lofty oak doors swung open and in the glare of our headlights we could see the tall white-robed figures of the Bedouin framed in the darkness of the archway. Their black faces glinted under pink head-dresses. They were swathed in cross belts of ammunition, of which the pointed bullets gleamed like necklaces of shark's teeth. Long silver-handled knives sparkled in their girdles. Many had rifles slung over both shoulders.[16]

The British soldiers immediately dubbed the members of the Desert Patrol as 'Glubb's Girls' after their long hair and the effect created by their swirling desert robes.

Now that Rutba had been taken, Kingcol's task was to race across the desert to reach Habbaniya as soon as possible. Leaving the fort on 15 May, Kingcol's objective was now Kilo 25, a point on the Baghdad road some fourteen miles west of Ramadi, on the Euphrates, to which a brigade of Iraqi troops had been deployed. The two hundred and twenty miles to Habbaniya were expected to be crossed in two days of driving. On the advice of Colonel Roberts in Habbaniya the column was to turn south-east at Kilo 25, thus avoiding a confrontation with the Iraqi brigade at Ramadi, to skirt underneath Lake Habbaniya and advance on the cantonment across the bridge at Mujara village. It was on this day that Kingcol, spread like locusts on the plain, was attacked by the lone Heinkel, providing de Chair with worrying visions of a German airborne armada. Having safely navigated the column to Kilo 25, Somerset de Chair, on 16 May, turned the column off the main route. Disaster then struck, as the inexperienced drivers took their vehicles into the gullies between the sand dunes and hit soft sand. Having sent the knowledgeable Arab Legion off on a reconnaissance to the north, Kingstone faced the embarrassment of failure so close to his objective.

The whole column halted, many of the trucks wallowing in sand up to their axles, like beached whales unable to return to the sea. Much of that day was spent in recovering vehicles from the sand in temperatures of some 120 degrees Fahrenheit, the tempers of the vehicle crews frayed by the effort required in the intense heat. 'The vehicles dragged wearily back over the morning's route,' recalled de Chair, 'the men anxious only to murder each other, and fall asleep where they chose to stop.'[17] Fortunately the Messerschmitts did not find them and exploit their embarrassment. That night, with their objective tantalisingly close, and with Glubb having returned from his reconnaissance, Brigadier Kingstone addressed his commander's conference with, as de Chair described it, a sorrowful countenance: 'We have enough supplies of water to stay here one more day,' he said. 'After that we go on or go back.' The nearest water was at Rutba Fort, now some 200 miles behind. Kingstone turned to Glubb: 'I shall want your dusky maidens to help us find an alternative route.'[18]

Fortunately Glubb's men successfully reconnoitred another route and the column eventually and laboriously made it at the end of the following day through Mujara (during which it was visited by three angry Bf.110s), across a single bridge beneath which flowed a great rush of water emptying from Lake Habbaniya, astonishing the soldiers who had not seen flowing water since leaving Nathanya on the Mediterranean coast. Soon after Mujara the vanguard of the column reached an outpost eight miles south of the cantonment manned by soldiers of the King's Own Royal Regiment. To de Chair's disgust these men showed no reverence at all for Kingcol's achievement, which was hardly surprising given the fact that nearly two weeks had passed since the Habbaniya garrison had single-handedly ejected the besiegers from their perch on the escarpment, using their own resources. Nevertheless it was a feat of historic significance, as de Chair was all too willing to explain to a war correspondent waiting at Habbaniya. He declared emphatically:

> You can say with confidence that it is one of the greatest marches in history, and that it is the first time since the days of Alexander the Great that an army has succeeded in crossing the desert from the shores of the Mediterranean to the banks of the Euphrates.[19]

Somerset de Chair had romantically cast Kingcol, in his own mind at least, as an 'all-conquering British Column' despatched to secure the relief of Habbaniya and of Baghdad by means of an advance from the

Holy Land through 500 miles of sand and rock to the City of the Caliphs. De Chair was, after all, a Member of Parliament for South-West Norfolk with a temporary commission, a romantic outlook, poetic vision and a reputation for vanity. In some respects he was right, but the defenders of Habbaniya had very different views of the claim that Habforce was 'all-conquering', regarding this to be at best hyperbole and at worst dishonest.[20] Nevertheless Glubb agreed with de Chair's sentiment at least, describing Kingcol's transit of the desert by compass 'one of the most remarkable examples of military daring in history.'

The arrival of German aircraft in Iraqi skies on 14 May was the direct result of fevered consultations between Baghdad and Berlin in the days following Smart's pre-emptive strikes on the forces occupying the high ground above Habbaniya. On the outbreak of hostilities in the dawn of 2 May Rashid Ali's brother, the Iraqi minister in Ankara, despatched a note to Franz von Papen, pleading for immediate support from Germany:

> The Iraqi government requests that Minister Grobba be sent to Baghdad at once so that diplomatic relations may be resumed. It also requests immediate military aid. In particular a considerable number of airplanes in order to prevent further English landings and to drive the English from the airfields [sic].[21]

The speed with which German support for the Iraqi regime developed was astonishing and contrasted favourably with the slowness of British decision-making at the time. With the impending invasion of Russia, however, the resources allocated to operations in Iraq were severely limited. Von Papen immediately passed the request to Berlin and on the following day, 3 May, the German Foreign Minister, Joachim von Ribbentrop, persuaded Hitler that Dr Fritz Grobba* be secretly returned to Iraq to head up a new mission charged with channelling support to the Rashid Ali regime. Then, on 6 May, *Luftwaffe* Colonel Werner Junck received instructions in Berlin that he was to take a small

---

* Under the pseudonym of Franz Gehrcke.

force of aircraft to Iraq, operating under Iraqi markings out of Mosul, some 240 miles north of Baghdad. *Fliegerführer Irak* was to comprise a squadron (twelve aircraft) of Messerschmitt Bf.110s and one squadron (also of twelve aircraft) of Heinkel 111s. To help him get his force to northern Iraq he was lent some thirteen Junkers 52 and ninety transport aircraft, all but three of which were to return to Greece immediately to prepare for the invasion of Crete. Junck was ordered to conduct an operation designed to have an effect far wider than the limited resources allocated to it, 'leading eventually perhaps to an Arab uprising, in order to start a Jihad, or Holy War, against the British', carrying on a theme initiated during the First World War by Kaiser Wilhem II, who sought to overthrow Great Britain's imperial dominions by means of inciting religious rebellion from within.[22] Colonel Junck was accompanied by Major Axel von Blomberg, whose task was to integrate the *Fliegerführer* with Iraqi forces in operations against the British. The British quickly discovered these arrangements through both the Italian diplomatic cipher and Enigma decrypts.[23]

On the same day Berlin arrived at an agreement with the Vichy regime in France that allowed the French colonial administration in Damascus to recover 25 per cent of the weaponry impounded under the terms of surrender in July 1940 in exchange for turning over the remainder to Iraqi use. These so-called 'Paris Protocols' allowed Germany and Italy, amongst other things, full landing and provisioning rights in Syria, the right to establish a *Luftwaffe* base at Aleppo, permission to use ports, roads and railways for transport of equipment to Iraq and to train Iraqi soldiers in Syria with French weapons. Simultaneously Germany despatched a second envoy to Syria – Rudolf Rahn, a Foreign Office envoy from the embassy in Paris – who arrived on 9 May with specific responsibility for despatching French war stores by train to Iraq. In this he was very successful, the first trainload arriving in Mosul via Turkey on 13 May. The train was met at the Iraqi frontier by the *aide-de-camp* of General Dentz (the Vichy French High Commissioner in the Levant) and a German officer.[24] Enigma decrypts told London that the train had left Damascus on 11 May, transiting through Aleppo by 10 a.m. the following day. The first train to Iraq included 15,500 rifles with 6 million rounds of ammunition, 200 machine guns with 900 belts of ammunition and four 75-millimetre field guns together with 10,000 shells. Two further consignments reached Iraq on 26 and 28 May. In addition to the weaponry transported on 13 May, the French shipped eight 155-millimetre field guns together with 6,000 shells, 354 machine-pistols, 30,000 hand-grenades and 32 trucks.[25] Ironically these shipments served no useful purpose for those who sent them, as the Iraqis stockpiled these gifts carefully, not using them at all. Their absence from Syria in the following month was to be greatly felt by the Vichy regime. They denuded the Vichy-French in Syria of critical equipment they could usefully have employed against the British themselves.

Flying via the Greek island of Rhodes, Dr Grobba and his mission reached Aleppo on 9 May and Baghdad on 11 May, accompanied by two Bf.110 fighter aircraft. The bulk of Junck's force arrived in Mosul on 13 May after a flight that had taken them some 1,200 miles in 36 hours. In her diary for 13 May, Stark recorded an ominous new sighting in the skies above Baghdad:

Yesterday an aeroplane with strange new markings came down upon the airport. No one knows her: may be Iranian though not the usual weekly mail. One of our Gladiators flew over, low, and examined and we then heard machine-gunning and the foreign aircraft has not re-emerged into the sky.[26]

Over the following days these aircraft became increasingly frequent visitors to Baghdad.

Dr Grobba brought with him part of the dowry to seal the new marriage of convenience between Nazism and Arab nationalism: £10,000 in gold for Rashid Ali and US$15,000 in bank notes for the Grand Mufti. A further £10,000 in gold and $10,000 was delivered on 21 May to each man respectively. A planned consignment of £80,000 in gold never arrived, only reaching Athens by the time the war in Iraq was over. It was duly returned to Berlin.

On 14 May Junck's transport aircraft began staging through Aleppo to Mosul, and a further three He.111 bombers and three Bf.110 fighters arrived in Mosul, two over-laden He.111 aircraft having been left with damaged rear wheels at Palmyra in central Syria. These aircraft were then attacked by roving British fighters and disabled on the rough runway of the airfield. Junck himself arrived in Mosul on 15 May with a further nine aircraft. At the time he knew that Habforce was on its way to Habbaniya, and that Kingcol had taken Rutba Fort on 11 May. So as to be seen by his Iraqi hosts to make an immediate impact he despatched a lone Heinkel to find Kingcol at Rutba, successfully bombing the column as described above and alerting the British to a worrying new dimension in the whole Iraq equation.

On the same day Junck sent von Blomberg to Baghdad to make arrangements for a council of war with the Iraqi Government planned for 17 May. However, an Iraqi soldier guarding a bridge in Baghdad, not recognizing the shape and silhouette of the He.111, and believing it to be British, placed a few well-aimed rounds into the fuselage as it cruised low overhead, making its way to the airport. One of those stray rounds killed von Blomberg, the *Luftwaffe* liaison officer, instantly, although the aircraft made a safe landing at the civil airfield on the eastern edge of the suburbs.

By the end of that day Junck had assembled a force in northern Iraq comprising five He.111 bombers, twelve Bf.110 fighters, a communications flight with light aircraft, a section of anti-aircraft cannon and three JU52 transports. Junck himself visited Baghdad on 16 May in place of von Blomberg and held a meeting with Dr Grobba, Rashid Ali, General Amin Zaki, Colonel Nur ed-Din Mahmud and Mahmud Salman. They agreed a number of immediate priorities for *Fliegerführer Irak*. The first was to prevent Kingcol arriving to succour Habbaniya. The second was to capture Habbaniya itself, it being tacitly assumed by Junck that the Iraqi Army would make the actual assault whilst the Germans provided air cover. The overall aim was to provide what the Germans tellingly described as 'spine straightening' for the Iraqi Army, which had become terrified of bombing by British aircraft.

Possibly in an attempt to impress his new hosts with teutonic industriousness, Junck decided to launch a surprise attack that very day on Habbaniya, deploying six Bf.110 fighters and three He.111 bombers. The attack took the base by surprise, killing a number on the ground and shooting down two RAF aircraft, an Audax and a Gladiator, the raiders losing a Heinkel in exchange. Relaxing in the garden of the Officer's Mess, Dudgeon recalled the event:

> Suddenly, there was the noise of aircraft engines that I had never heard before. Then the noise of cannon-shells being fired, and exploding in the camp . . . unluckily they seemed to be well placed

among our parked aircraft on the airfield and the polo pitch. I picked the aircraft out at once. There were six Me110 fighters [sic], strafing us with their multiple-cannon . . . [Then there] was a sound of strange engines, again. I looked up, in case I needed somehow to find some cover. To my total incredulity I saw the impossible. Three German aircraft at about 6,000 ft, with the unmistakeable curved planform of wings which proclaimed them as Heinkel 111 *bombers!* Still, today, I remember clearly the thoughts flashing through my mind; 'It can't be true! They haven't the range. They couldn't get here. What the hell goes on?[27]

Shocked but undaunted the little Habbaniya air force took the air war to the newly arrived *Luftwaffe*. On 17 May RAF aircraft reinforcements arrived unannounced from Egypt in the form of four more Gladiators from 94 Squadron and six Blenheim bombers from 84 Squadron. Although the nine remaining Wellingtons in Basra had been withdrawn to Egypt on 12 May to assist in the war against Rommel, two new long-range cannon-firing Hurricanes had also arrived from Aboukir in Egypt. Together with the Blenheims they made a daring, long-range sortie to hit back at the *Luftwaffe* at Mosul on 17 May, destroying two and damaging four aircraft for the loss of a Hurricane. On the same day two Gladiators from Habbaniya, loitering around Rashid airfield at Baghdad, encountered two Bf.110s attempting to take off, and destroyed them both, much to the joy of the two British sergeant pilots responsible. Thus within two days of arrival, and despite the surprise attack on Habbaniya on 16 May, Junck's force had been whittled down to four He.111 bombers, eight Bf.110 fighters and two JU52 transport aircraft, a loss of 30 per cent. This rate of attrition did not augur well for the continuance of a strong *Luftwaffe* presence in Iraq. Indeed, by the end of May Junck had lost fourteen Bf.110s and five He.111s, an overall loss of 95 per cent of his original fighter and bomber strength. With few replacements available, no spares, poor quality fuel and aggressive attacks by the RAF out of Habbaniya, the mathematics of attrition went in only one direction, and the eventual withdrawal of the *Luftwaffe* in these circumstances was inevitable.

In the week following the end of the Iraqi investment of Habbaniya Colonel Ouvry Roberts, the *de facto* commander of the Habbaniya garrison, took control of ground operations, putting plans together to attack the town of Falluja as the first stage in striking out in the direction of Baghdad. Roberts' attack was planned for 19 May. His plan was to use the troops available to him in the garrison, and the arrival of Kingcol at Habbaniya on 18 May gave him welcome reinforcements, especially the artillery which usefully supplemented that which he had captured from the Iraqis as they fled the plateau and the field guns he had recovered from their ornamental resting-place at the front of Air Headquarters.

Both Air Vice-Marshal John D'Albiac and Major General George Clark arrived by air in Habbaniya on 18 May to find that Roberts had well advanced plans to capture Falluja. Clark agreed to leave Roberts to carry out his operation without interference, although he failed to live up to his promise, pestering Roberts in the following days to seize Falluja without delay. Despite his Military Cross, won during the First World War, Clark did not have a reputation as a field soldier, unlike the stubbly-chinned Joe Kingstone, late of the Queen's Bays, who commanded Kingcol. Somerset de Chair gently lampooned Clark after meeting him briefly in Habbaniya following his arrival on 18 May:

> A cool brain this, under a rather bald head. It was wise for a General to remain cool in the heat, but his habits did not endear him to the junior officers; and the troops did not know him by sight. So, as soon as Kingcol had crossed the desert, General Clark arrived by air, keeping very cool and went into the most comfortable billets obtainable. These were in Air House, a luxurious white villa, where electric fans stirred the air lazily and the footfalls of booted warriors were deadened upon soft Persian carpets.[28]

Falluja sits astride the Euphrates River. Its 177-foot long iron bridge was a key strategic feature, linking Habbaniya with Baghdad only thirty miles further on. However, most of the western approaches to Falluja and its precious bridge were all under water, a consequence of the deliberate flooding by the Iraqis of the low-lying areas under the Euphrates' 'bunds'. The incomplete Mujara–Falluja road (Hammond's Bund) had been cut in half by Iraqi demolitions and a roaring torrent flowed through the gap, resisting all but the most serious attempts to cross it. This limited the options available to Roberts as he contemplated how best to secure the bridge without its first being destroyed. A traditional ground assault was out of the question as the direct approaches were all under water, and surprise was essential to prevent the Iraqis blowing up the bridge before it could be secured. Roberts was also keen to ensure that street fighting in the town should be avoided at all costs. A different approach was therefore required.

The plan he came up with was one of brilliant improvisation. He envisaged two phases to the attack. In the first he intended to shower the Iraqi defenders with leaflets encouraging them to surrender before they were swallowed up by the vast (albeit imaginary) British Army advancing from the west and the south, that same army that had so decisively bettered the forces on the plateau at Habbaniya two weeks before. He would follow up this leaflet raid with a heavy aerial strike on the town, in an effort to reason with the defenders both physically and psychologically. The leaflets were to be dropped first on 18 May, advising the Iraqis to surrender and warning of bombing attacks if they refused. At the same time he cut off the town from telegraphic contact with Baghdad. This was achieved by the simple but dangerous expedient of flying Audaxes through the telephone lines. Where there was more than one line the pilot would land and cut the wires by hand whilst his passenger chopped down the pole.

Air attacks were fully co-ordinated with land operations in the advance out of Habbaniya. Wing Commander Casey had taken responsibility for air operations alongside Roberts, and the two dimensions had for some time now been fully integrated.[29] The relationship between land and air was a thoroughly modern and enlightened one, but one that sadly was still rare at this stage of the war and, in this instance, probably accidental. On his arrival as the in-coming Air Officer Commanding on 18 May, D'Albiac expressed his unhappiness at this apparent 'mis-employment' of air power, as it set 'an undesirable precedent'. He didn't seem happy that army officers were in a position to command air assets and sought to regain control of a situation that had been allowed to lapse so grievously since the departure of Smart fifteen days earlier.

In particular he was unhappy that Roberts had placed such an emphasis on the air component of the attack, and in his report to Cairo said as much, although he had the grace to accept Roberts' plan as it stood, as preparations for the attack on Falluja were so well advanced. He regarded the job of his aircraft to be to seek out and destroy the *Luftwaffe* threat, 'not the assault of land objectives whose capture could be effected by land forces'.[30] Even with his experience in Greece behind him, D'Albiac still remained a member of a dangerously reactionary group within the RAF who could not see that all operations were joint affairs, and required an appropriate blend of air and land power (and if appropriate, sea power as well), something that later in the war would become thoroughly routine. But it was still 1941 and the doctrine of the tactical use of air power was in its infancy. Auchinleck had already raised the subject of air–land co-operation with Dill. The lack of integrated air support to the Indian brigades was a worry to him. He had to contend both with a dire lack of aircraft and what he regarded to be an inadequate RAF air power doctrine for the sort of campaign he envisaged in Iraq. In his long letter to Dill on 29 May Auchinleck wrote:

> The prime need of all is some form of support in the air and here it seems that A.O.C.-in-C Middle East cannot help us. I feel that, in the circumstances, Quinan must have an air component at his disposal, however repugnant this may be to Air Force ideas of fluidity and mobility. We feel here in India that we cannot afford for our own sakes to leave this force, predominantly Indian as it is, without at least some support in the air. It is for this reason that I have pressed . . . so hard for the return of our two Blenheim squadrons from Malaya.[31]

Dill recognized the problem. Writing to Auchinleck on 26 June 1941 he remarked of air–land co-operation:

> Nowhere is it good. Nowhere have we had sufficient training. You will find the 'Air' out to help, but they have no complete understanding of what is required of them from the purely Army point of view and how necessary training is. Also, to ensure that our military and air strategy works in complete harmony is uncommonly difficult.[32]

D'Albiac's view was disappointing but reflected the uncomfortable norm. Irritatingly for Roberts it indicated a thorough mis-appreciation of the reason for the outstanding success of the Habbaniya battle, namely the powerful psychological effect of massed aerial bombardment on conscripts, combined with effective pressure on the ground. In truth, air and land forces were entirely complementary, and needed to be planned and operated together as two distinct dimensions of the same operation. Roberts had seen this at first hand (whilst D'Albiac had not) and believed, correctly as it transpired, that a repeat of these tactics would also reap dividends at Falluja.[33]

The second phase of Roberts' plan was a three-pronged assault on Falluja, the primary objective of which was to secure the bridge. If the Iraqis failed to heed the written warnings dropped by leaflet, or were insufficiently cowed by his aerial and artillery bombardment, troops would advance along Hammond's Bund and cross the gap by improvised ferry, rushing the bridge at dawn on 19 May. At the same time a force would cross the Euphrates at Sin-el-Dhibban (where the Iraqis had previously used a ferry) and then threaten Falluja from the north-west. The river at Sin-el-Dhibban was 750 feet wide with a strong current, and the Madras Sappers and Miners brought up from Basra to build a ferry did so with 1,500 feet of wire hawser. Further south, a wide assortment of pleasure boats from Lake Habbaniya had been brought up to cross the flooded breach at Hammond's Bund. Such was the importance of this hawser in enabling troops to cross the river that General Clark was later to observe that the campaign was 'won on two ropes'.[34] In the third phase, troops were to be transported by air in a daring airborne manoeuvre to cut the road between Falluja and Baghdad, thus preventing Iraqi reinforcements from assisting the town's defenders.

Air attacks began as planned in the early hours of 18 May on targets around Falluja and the road to Baghdad. During the night of 18 May a force of Levies, 2/4 Gurkha Rifles, Rolls Royce armoured cars and captured Iraqi howitzers crossed by the raft at Sin-el-Dhibban and approached Falluja from the north-west, but were held up by floodwaters before the town. Troops also began laboriously crossing the flood gap at Hammond's Bund in the darkness. It took all night to get the troops into position. Air attacks involving fifty-seven aircraft began again at dawn on 19 May. Roberts' aim was to give the Iraqi defenders time to surrender or escape. In the early dawn light a company of the King's Own Royal Regiment were flown to a position on the

Fallujah–Baghdad road to cut off the town and prevent the arrival of reinforcements, landing on the desert floor by four Valentia aircraft flown up from Basra for the purpose. The aircraft landed blind on the desert and took only a matter of minutes to disgorge their occupants before taking off again for the safety of Habbaniya.

Clark's nervousness now began to get the better of him and, despite his promise to keep out of the battle, he pestered Roberts all morning to push troops into Falluja. Roberts ignored these calls. He wanted to avoid a pitched battle in the town at all costs and he hoped that artillery and air pressure, together with the knowledge that they were surrounded, would persuade the defenders to melt away. After a break during the morning a short but furious dive-bombing air attack took place on Falluja at 2.45 p.m., followed by a rush on the Falluja bridge by the Levies who had crossed Hammond's Bund, supported by a troop of 25-pounders. The bridge and the town were successfully secured with some 300 enemy prisoners captured. The RAF had thrown nearly 10 tons of bombs at the town in 134 sorties, and when the Levies attacked they suffered not a single casualty: the enemy had melted away as Roberts had hoped, discarding their uniforms and merging with the civilian population if they could not get out of the town itself.

When the news reached the embassy in Baghdad the next day, Freya Stark was overjoyed:

> Now, four in the afternoon, just heard that Fallujah [sic] is taken, bridge, town and all. Thank God. No details except surrender of town; leaflets were dropped, air and ground attack, and the whole given over. Really brings relief in sight. Hope Ramadi and tribes may follow.[35]

Earlier that day Stark had observed one of the almost daily air attacks over Baghdad:

> Events today began with the scrunch of heavy bombs over Rashid [airfield] and twenty-six of our fliers in the sky. The little Gladiators sail over us in threes, their black made grey by the sunlight shining from above them so that in size and colour they look very like the grey and white doves that circle agitated from the garden trees. Over Rashid the bombers sail and dip and the dull noise follows; they circle in far wide curves in the early sky.[36]

Despite the interventions of Clark and the unhappiness of D'Albiac, Roberts had succeeded completely in a very difficult task. His job over, Roberts returned south to Shaibah to rejoin 10 Indian Division on 21 May.

Unexpectedly fierce Iraqi counter-attacks were made against Falluja by an Iraqi brigade with light tanks on 22 May in an attempt to destroy the bridge over the Euphrates. There were reports afterwards from Iraqi prisoners that German 'technicians' had played a 'spine-stiffening' role in these attacks.[37] British forces in the town had thinned out already and only a light defensive screen was in position facing the road to Baghdad. It appears that this counter-attack was in fact patterned on one of the exercises set for the Iraqi Army senior officers' school in 1939 and that the attack had been carried out according to the Directing Staff solution.[38] Joe Kingstone rushed forward to take personal command of the defence of Falluja, bringing with him reinforcements in the shape of the two Essex Regiment companies and 'C' Squadron of the Household Cavalry. These troops quickly crossed the gap in Hammond's Bund and marched the seven miles into Falluja with anti-tank rifles, Hotchkiss guns and ammunition on their backs, wading neck-deep in some places through the floodwaters. Makeshift rafts were built to cross areas under water. Major May of 1 Essex recalled:

> The operation involved complete stripping, and swimming and wading about 600 yards. With improvised rafts of old oil drums and planks made up by Indian Sappers, first 'A' Company crossed. We piled arms and ammunition and all clothing on top and got over in parties of ten to fifteen; it took about two hours to get the company over.[39]

Despite the attempt on 16 May to co-ordinate the efforts of *Fliegerführer Irak* with Iraqi forces, none was apparent during this critical battle. A co-ordinated assault on the town by ground and air forces may well have tipped the balance in Iraq's favour even at this stage and recovered the bridge. However, the counter-attacks on Falluja were beaten back, six light tanks were captured and over one hundred prisoners taken. The route to Baghdad was opened up on 23 May and Joe Kingstone was awarded an immediate bar to his Distinguished Service Order. Roberts, however, received no recognition for his work in winning this critical battle, nor indeed that of Habbaniya, receiving merely a brief mention in D'Albiac's report, filed in 1948.

During this period Glubb's Arab Legionnaires were dominating the tribal country to the north between the Euphrates and the Tigris, an area known as the 'Jezireh'. Glubb had been instructed to persuade the local tribes to desist in supporting the Baghdad government, and with a combination of propaganda and raids against government posts he proved remarkably successful. The influence amongst the tribes of the Arab Legion was such that German propaganda broadcasts continued to broadcast that 'Colonel Glubb' of the Arab Legion had been killed, a stratagem designed to spread despondency amongst the many tribes people loyal to the Regent and to persuade them not to support the British forces.[40]

Whilst the battles on the ground were continuing to splutter, the war of words between London, Cairo and Simla regarding wider strategies for Iraq continued unabated. The argument had now moved on from the original intervene or not-to-intervene debates to consider for what purpose troops should be used within Iraq. It was now: should the object of intervention in Iraq be the domination of the whole of Iraq for wider military purposes (as advocated by India), or should it be merely the installation of a friendly government in Baghdad? Lord Linlithgow pressed India's case very strongly with the India Office. On 13 May he penned a personal letter to Amery in which he balanced the arguments between the two perspectives:

> The last thing . . . that we in India want is military occupation of the whole of Iraq. What is however essential is that we should have our lines of communication, and that of course involves . . . arrangements to ensure that those lines of communication are properly held and not cut . . .
>
> I am quite sure that if we are to avoid [German] infiltration on a scale that may be very dangerous indeed to us, given the vital importance of this area and of the head of the Persian Gulf, we must be pretty strongly represented on the spot. Even if we can get rid of Rashid Ali and get the Regent back with a Cabinet sufficiently responsive to our control, we shall have to buttress

them against German intrigue, and to do that effectively we must be on the spot in sufficient strength . . .

I am not at all happy at the thought of the dangers which may confront us if we miss the present opportunity, and I do feel on that side, with every admiration for Wavell, that he is (perhaps not unnaturally) disposed to under-estimate the critical significance of the Iraqi area.[41]

On 14 May Major General Arthur Smith, Wavell's CIGS, flew to Basra to meet Quinan. He reported back to Wavell two days later that Quinan believed his task to be the security of Basra and that extensive flooding made a move northwards impracticable, perhaps for as long as three months. This was by no means Auchinleck's view, however, who expected Quinan to make every endeavour to press northwards towards Baghdad, whatever the impediments posed by floods, broken railway lines or pockets of Iraqi resistance. In an attempt to resolve the differences between Cairo on the one hand and London, Delhi and Simla on the other, it was agreed that Wavell and Auchinleck should meet to discuss the ongoing crisis in Iraq and the most appropriate way to respond to it. A week later, on the morning of 24 May, Wavell met with Auchinleck in Basra.

Despite London's wishful thinking, the Basra Conference failed to resolve Wavell and Auchinleck's differing viewpoints, although it did lead to agreement as to the way forward. Wavell's attitude had not changed over the previous month. If anything it had grown stronger. He believed that the British should now concentrate on holding Habbaniya and Basra, not to make any attempt to seize Baghdad and to give up all hope of recovering the Kirkuk oil fields for the duration of the war. He considered that a German occupation of Iraq would be far less worrisome than their occupation of Syria, and it was to the latter problem that he wanted to address himself. Auchinleck was perplexed by this view. If the Germans managed to occupy land bases in Iraq as well as the air bases they had already garrisoned in the north, they could easily secure Baghdad and, by moving through Iran, outflank the weak Indian forces at Basra and thus threaten the crucial oil fields at Abadan. He was therefore keen to move his forces on Baghdad at the earliest opportunity in order to pre-empt any German moves in that area.

Despite these differences both men agreed that Habforce would be allowed to push on towards Baghdad and that 10 Indian Division in Basra be instructed to open up immediate land communications with Habbaniya. Wavell agreed that once Auchinleck's troops had reached Baghdad, India Command could resume control of operations in Iraq. Both men agreed to the following text, sent to London by Wavell on 25 May:

From discussion with Auchinleck it is obvious that we regard Iraq from somewhat different angles. My main task, defence of Egypt and Palestine, would be made more difficult but would not be greatly jeopardised by hostile control of Iraq, whereas hostile control of Syria would affect me much more closely and dangerously. So long as my resources are inadequate I am bound to be influenced by the closer and more threatening danger. India on the other hand regard Iraq as absolutely vital outpost of their defence since they consider that hostile Iraq would mean hostile Iran and Afghanistan and compromise whole defence of Indian Empire. From point of view of greater interest it seems therefore desirable that India should control operations in Iraq.

Middle East is already fully occupied with Western Desert campaign, defence of Crete, danger to Syria and Cyprus, besides East Africa campaign. Troops in Iraq are mainly Indian, maintenance must be from India and administration can more easily be done from India . . .

From political point of view it is better that all Arab affairs should be under one control, which can only be Mideast, also if Iraq becomes line of communication to Turkey there are advantages in Mideast, which must be closely concerned with Turkish operations, exercising control. By good liaison, however, both above difficulties could probably be overcome if India took over Iraq.

To sum up, it seems that in view of her greater interest and greater stake in Iraq operations, India should resume control as soon as possible. This seems to be when force at Basra is in position to control and maintain operations from Habbaniya against Baghdad, and this can presumably only be when communications can be established between Basra and Habbaniya.[42]

Auchinleck regarded the meeting to be a complete vindication of the approach to the problem of Iraq that he had taken since his arrival in February 1941. On 25 May, flying back to Karachi in India, he wrote to Dill:

I am very glad we were able to meet as I know now what I always thought was the case, namely, that Mideast have never really had time to think of Iraq in its relation to India and the maintenance of our position in Southern Asia generally, but have so far looked at it as a nuisance area on their eastern flank . . .

I think, as a result of our talk, Wavell sees our point of view and agrees that we must take bold action in Iraq if we are ever to regain our position there, and he has given orders to Quinan accordingly. We must take and keep Baghdad if we are to have any hope of stopping German infiltration, and, having got it, we must, in my opinion, then secure the key points in the north such as Mosul, Kirkuk, Erbil. That this can be done by bluff and boldness I have little doubt, if we act now. We must run big risks to gain our objects . . .

Wavell and I discussed the question of control . . . I did not think it was any use trying to take over until touch has been established between Quinan and 'Habforce', as, until this happens, Quinan cannot really influence the situation round Baghdad, except by sending reinforcements to Habbaniya by air, which he is now doing. It is a slow process, owing to the scarcity of troop-carrying aircraft. We have sent over all we have from India. I admit that I was greatly tempted to take over then and there and, between ourselves, I feel that Wavell would be glad to be rid of this additional commitment.

I feel, however, that as soon as we get to Baghdad, the reopening of road and rail communications between that place and Basra is likely to follow quickly and that then I can take over with some hope of being able to do something . . .

I think that Quinan now understands the situation and that he will get on with the job, which is one which calls for unorthodox and opportunist methods.[43]

Wavell returned by plane to Lydda near Jerusalem. The strain of recent weeks was beginning to show, exacerbated by the German attack on

Crete, which began on 20 May. The battle was not going well and news everywhere was bad. His *aide-de-camp* recorded:

> We just made Lydda, and, as we thankfully clambered out of the plane, the Chief had a bad giddy spell; staggered and fell against me. He recovered in a minute, but he is exhausted, I fear, mentally as well as physically.[44]

Somerset de Chair was gleefully scathing about the impact of *Force Sabine* as the advance of which he was part made its way towards Baghdad. He was entirely unaware that Wavell had forbidden anything of the division other than defensive operations in the Basra area, and that 10 Indian Division started, therefore, with a significant disadvantage. He opined:

> Far to the south from the slowly stirring headquarters of the Indian Division forming at Basra, there were the first signs of animate existence. This redoubtable army, which arrived with its tents and its baths, its polo sticks and fishing rods, and was preparing for a two-year campaign on the model of General Maude's, had actually penetrated as far up the lower Euphrates as Nasariya [sic] . . . The Basra Elephant, with its toppling howdah of Staff Officers, penetrated as far as Ur of the Chaldees, but this interesting peep into ancient history does not seem to have affected the course of the present campaign.[45]

Once again de Chair was engaging his pen in literary hyperbole. The effort to land and establish a division in the Basra area and there to form a base from which future operations in Iraq could be launched and the Iranian oil refinery at Abadan protected, was no mean feat, and in the circumstances of 1941 proved to be a considerable achievement. Although the successive British convoys bringing Brigadier Powell's 20 Indian Infantry Brigade from Karachi landed without opposition and occupied the port and power station in Basra, the local atmosphere was sullen and unco-operative. The dock labourers went on strike, forcing soldiers to unload their own ships before labourers could be brought in from India. When, on 2 May, hostilities commenced at Habbaniya, operations had also to be undertaken in the Basra area to safeguard the growing base area, disarm local military units and constabulary, and to prevent any outbreaks of violence and lawlessness amongst the population.

The situation around Basra, however, was difficult as no transport had yet arrived from India and the Iraqis had worked hard to deny the road, rail and river routes north–west towards Baghdad, locomotives and river-craft being removed northwards and rail and telegraph lines uprooted and destroyed. It was clear that the relief of Habbaniya could not come from this source. Indeed, it was not until 6 May that the second brigade of *Force Sabine* containing 2/4 Gurkha Rifles, of which Jack Masters was adjutant, landed at Basra. Commanded by Brigadier C.J. Weld, 21 Indian Brigade* doubled the size of the Basra base and allowed the occupation of key buildings in the town. A firm base in the Basra area was gradually established by 20 and 21 Indian Brigades and the HQ of 10 Indian Division, and through offensive action across the region they removed any threat of Iraqi interference to operations in the north. This was by no means what Auchinleck had wished, but a useful role was played nevertheless by the two brigades, subduing localised dissent and sponsoring the creation of regional government favourable to the rule of the Regent. Responsibility for the defence of Shaibah was given to 20 Indian Brigade, whilst 21 Indian Brigade protected Basra itself and the port area. The division was complete when on 30 May the final of its three brigades – 25 Infantry Brigade – disembarked from its convoy in Basra port.[†]

The pitifully small Habforce was by now advancing on Baghdad in what was a dangerous game of bluff. The most direct route to Baghdad was from the west along the Falluja–Baghdad road, but it was also the most obvious. Iraqi defences there were likely to be strong. Another option was to attack from the south and for troops to be diverted

---

* 4/13 Frontier Force Rifles, 2/4 Gurkha Rifles and 2/10 Gurkha Rifles. The convoy included two troops of 13 Lancers with armoured cars and a detachment of Indian Army engineers.

† 25 Indian Infantry Brigade comprised 3 Jat Regiment, 2 Royal Sikh Regiment and 1 Mahratta Light Infantry.

through the holy city of Karbala, perhaps linking up with 10 Indian Division advancing north from Ur. A third alternative was to advance on Baghdad from the north, along the direction of the Mosul road. The plan eventually adopted was chosen in order to maintain the momentum gained by the capture of Falluja on 23 May and in the expectation that the Iraqis had no idea about how small and vulnerable Clark's forces actually were. To wait for Slim's division to advance from the south would substantially have delayed the operation: indeed, 10 Indian Division was only given orders to advance on 25 May. Clark decided that in addition to a thrust from the east a strong detachment would cross the desert north-east to cut the Baghdad–Mosul road and railway, Slim would continue to threaten from the south, and that maximum pressure would be exerted from the air.

It was, nevertheless, a high-risk plan: indeed, Glubb regarded the campaign to be 'mad' and 'most rash'.[46] Clark had but some 1,450 men including about 250 of the Arab Legion; the Iraqi Army had at least 20,000 troops in the Baghdad area, including a brigade to the west at Ramadi, German aircraft were active in the skies above, and substantial water obstacles lay between Falluja and the gates of Baghdad. However, Clark judged that if the impetus of operations could be sustained across the country, both on land and in the air, this plan might just pay off. After all, bluff and high stakes had already paid off handsomely at Habbaniya, in Kingcol's advance across the desert and in the capture of Falluja, and there was every reason to expect that they would be successful again.

One reason why a bold attack at this time had a strong possibility of success was that Iraqi support for the rebel government in many areas was waning. Boldness at the right time and the maintenance of the momentum gained by the little Habbaniya air force could bring substantial dividends, as Freya Stark observed in her prison within the Baghdad Embassy. By the time that Falluja had fallen on 22 May, Stark recorded that the previous rebel-inspired antipathy to the British and support for the Axis Powers, gushing relentlessly from Baghdad Radio, had changed significantly. She had a conversation with her Iraqi Police guards on the evening of 23 May:

'The Germans are of the family of Satan' [they said].
'I have heard,' said I, 'that we have brought six of them down between Habbaniya and Syria.'

'Praise be to God,' said the enemy, under cover of darkness. 'But we have burnt forty of yours,' they added as an afterthought.

'I take refuge with God from your untruthfulness,' said I; to which they agreed with laughter.[47]

Brigadier Kingstone took a column directly along the Falluja–Baghdad road, whilst a column commanded by Lieutenant Colonel Andrew Ferguson of the Household Cavalry traversed the desert to join the main road to Baghdad from Mosul in the north at Meshahida. The forces in both columns were tiny, Kingstone's comprising a squadron of the Household Cavalry, two companies of the Essex Regiment, three Rolls Royce armoured cars and a troop of 25-pounders, a total of only some seven hundred and fifty men. Ferguson's column boasted the remainder of the Household Cavalry Regiment, a troop of 25-pounders, three further armoured cars and two hundred and fifty men of Glubb's Arab Legion, a total of only seven hundred.

Kingstone made steady progress during 28 May, slowed only by pockets of resistance along the road and by the flooding. The fort at Khan Nuqta was seized after a show of force and his column finished the day some twelve miles from Baghdad at the demolished bridge over the Abu Ghuraib Canal. At noon on 29 May elements of Kingstone's column managed to cross the bridge and Iraqi positions in front of Baghdad were pounded by artillery and aerial bombardment. The advance to Baghdad was resumed on 30 May. Crossing the Euphrates on 27 May, Glubb's legion guided the men of Ferguson's column through the desert until they met the Mosul–Baghdad road. Ferguson missed a chance to drive straight into Baghdad on the evening of 27 May, instead bivouacking six miles north of the city that night. Had his small force pressed on, it would have undoubtedly managed to seize the city, as they were entirely unexpected, the government being taken by surprise by the advance from the north. A strong Iraqi infantry force prevented their movement the next morning, and the element of surprise was lost. Thereafter, apart from cutting portions of the railway line leading north to Mosul, the column made slow progress against stiff opposition in the brickworks of Al Khadimain, near the al-Askari shrine, one of the holiest sites in Shi'a Islam.

Following the agreement in Basra on 25 May between Wavell and Auchinleck, Slim's division began to move out of Basra on 27 May. The first move, prior to arranging an advance on Baghdad along the course of both the Euphrates and the Tigris rivers, was the securing of the ancient city of Ur, birthplace of Abraham. This was achieved successfully by Weld's 21 Indian Brigade, which moved north on the afternoon of 28 May with ten days' rations and 14,500 gallons of water. The few opportunistic attacks made on the brigade were dispersed with artillery fire and de Chair's 'Basra Elephant' made its first tentative but confident steps up the Euphrates.

Habforce's apparently slow progress caused some nervousness in London. Dill telegraphed Wavell on 28 May to say that the Defence Council meeting that day had been 'disturbed by delays which are attending advance of Hab Force on Bagdad [sic].'[48] By this stage, however, Clark had created a feeling of superiority over the enemy that would soon translate itself into a decisive victory. The impression the advance had created, together with intensive British air activity, was such that Baghdad would soon be surrounded. British troops had managed to cut off the road to Mosul (although the Iraqis had no appreciation of the extreme weakness of Ferguson's position), the main body of the British force was advancing from Falluja after having successfully crossed 500 miles of desert from Palestine, and 10 Indian Division in the south had broken out to capture Ur and was making steady progress northwards, despite the hindrances posed by flooding and sporadic attacks. Certainly the sounds of war were creeping closer to Baghdad. On the morning of 29 May Freya Stark recorded:

> Gunfire has been thudding steadily since four this morning, coming gradually nearer. They think it is by Aqqa Kuf and may be cutting across country towards Kadhimain [sic]. Now (8 a.m.) it begins to shake the window-panes slightly. Small arms they say have been heard from the direction of the iron bridge.[49]

In Baghdad wild rumours were spreading about the strength of the British advance. On 28 May Grobba sent a panicked message to Berlin reporting that the British were close to the city with more than a hundred tanks, Junck had been reduced to two He.111s with only four bombs and none of his Bf.110s were serviceable.[50] At 2 p.m. on 29 May, in confirmation of the reports of steady British progress on virtually every point of the compass, the rumours in the city of British tanks were fortuitously reinforced by Somerset de Chair's Arabic interpreter who managed to use a captured telephone at Khan Nuqta to contact the *3rd Infantry Division* and convince the Iraqi signaller on the other end of the approach of large numbers of British tanks ('at least one hundred') along the Falluja road.[51] These reports, amongst others, panicked the city and contributed to the final collapse of government, being sufficient to persuade Rashid Ali and a group of forty others, including the Grand Mufti, to flee under cover of darkness on the night of 29 May to Iran, where Sir Reader Bullard, the British Ambassador, reported their arrival the following day to Cairo.[52] One commentator records with satisfaction the fact that: 'The total number of this émigré party, it may be noted by those familiar with the tale of Ali Baba, amounted to precisely forty.'[53]

In fact the Iraqi Government had lost its nerve well before this, senior officials and their families fleeing to Iran and Turkey as early as 21 May. The German military mission to Syria was evacuated and on 30 May Fritz Grobba himself left for Mosul.

After repairing the Abu Ghuraib bridge, Kingstone's column continued its advance on Baghdad on 30 May, the only obstacle between him and Baghdad now being the Washash Canal, which boasted elaborate defences and a well-defended bridge. That afternoon the column's armoured cars came under heavy artillery and machine-gun fire, attacks which were in turn successfully subdued by the fire of Kingstone's 25-pounders. By now, to all intents and purposes, the British had created a stranglehold on the city: what the Iraqi defenders had no means of knowing was just how small Clark's forces were. In Cairo, with desperate news from Crete, Wavell still remained deeply pessimistic about the chances of success in Iraq.[54] However, the advance was about to be proved decisive. With Ferguson's column five miles to the north, Kingstone's three miles to the east, incessant air attack and rumours sweeping Baghdad, the Mayor of the city, together with the Chief of Iraqi Military Operations, Lieutenant Colonel Nur-ud-Din, who had assumed command of the army, approached Cornwallis in the British Embassy to seek terms for surrender at about 8 p.m. that evening. Communications were immediately opened up between Cornwallis and Clark and a parley was arranged for the following morning. Early the next morning, 31 May 1941, the Mayor led a delegation to meet at the Washash bridge, arriving at the stated hour:

4 a.m. At 3 a.m. Clark had sent a signal to 'Jumbo' Wilson in Jerusalem with surprise and delight: 'Iraqis have asked for a flag of truce. Allah be praised!'[55]

Glubb recorded the scene. The British party, including Clark and D'Albiac, nervously went forward through the British front line in the early morning darkness and met 'two Iraqi officers, bearing a bath towel on a pole'. The Iraqis were sent back into the city to collect Sir Kinahan Cornwallis. 'The Iraqis had cut all the canal banks in the vicinity and water was lapping the road . . . With water birds flapping overhead the scene was more suggestive of the Norfolk Broads than the City of the Caliphs.' Once the Iraqis had returned with the British ambassador, 'armistice terms were drafted on the back of a telegram form, sitting in the General's car, and were carried back to Baghdad by the British ambassador. The A.O.C. and G.O.C. returned to Cavalry Brigade Headquarters for breakfast, and the campaign was at an end.'[56] Sir Miles Lampson commented to his diary the following day without any hint of smugness: 'It makes one smile when one remembers that it was not so long ago – about 10 days – that Archie Wavell was quite prepared to throw in his hand and make any terms with the Iraqis.'[57]

The terms of the surrender were straightforward and were discussed by Anthony Eden, the Foreign Secretary, and the Chiefs of Staff in London during the day.[58] For the soldiers on the ground the aim was to keep the terms simple so that the responsible Iraqi authorities would agree quickly and thus allow the rapid re-establishment of the Regent in power in Baghdad. A long drawn-out process of agreement could easily have been disastrous, given the numerical weakness of Clarke's tiny army.[59] On the magnanimous basis that the war had been a political contest against Rashid Ali, rather than a war against the Iraqi people, the Iraqi Army was allowed to return to its peacetime locations with all its weapons and equipment, the terms of the Anglo-Iraq Treaty were to be restored, Germans and Italians were to be interned at RAF Habbaniya, Prisoners of War on both sides repatriated and the Iraqi garrison in Ramadi evacuated.[60] To the fury of the British and Indian troops who had managed to capture gold-dust-like Bren guns, Bren gun carriers and other equipment from the Iraqi Army, they were ordered to return them to their erstwhile owners. Unsurprisingly, many did not. One, a Bren carrier captured at Falluja, rechristened 'Southend-on-Sea' and painted in desert-coloured paint to disguise its giveaway Iraqi Army olive-green, somehow found its way on to the equipment inventory of 1 Essex and completed its war service in the British Army.[61]

In the embassy Stark's rescuers were a troop of 'Gay, swaggering, dusty and nonchalant' Arab Legionnaires. 'With a fine untidy arrogance of the wilderness they strolled about the decorous but weary purlieus of Chancery, glancing at us – pallid and rather deplorable effendis – with friendly and tolerant amusement.'[62] Grabbing the chance, Stark managed to jump into one of the cars leaving the embassy early that morning for the iron bridge. 'We have done all this with only two battalions', she mused, '– colossal bluff.'[63] For his part, too, Joe Kingstone was concerned that the Iraqis might find out that the 'army' encamped on the outskirts of Baghdad comprised no more than 750 men, and had no tanks, and efforts were made to hide the weakness of the British force. The truth perhaps dawned on the Iraqis in the ensuing days that they had been the victims of a gigantic hoax, but by then it was too late, the armistice was being enforced and the terms of the Anglo-Iraqi Treaty restored.

The Regent returned to Baghdad on 1 June, having waited at Habbaniya for several days in anticipation of the collapse of Rashid Ali's regime. Partly in order to disguise the weakness of Kingstone's force, the decision was made not to occupy Baghdad immediately. Instead, the Regent was to be restored without having to admit by public demonstration that this had been brought about by British force of arms. It was an unfortunate though understandable decision. In the hiatus that followed Baghdad was torn apart by rioting and looting, the violence being channelled against the wealthy and despised Jewish mercantile elite. Some 120 Jews lost their lives and 850 were injured in the violence that followed as the Jewish Quarter was sacked, until the otherwise complacent Iraqi Police were ordered to restore order with live ammunition.[64]

Mosul was occupied on 3 June and Kirkuk a few days later following an airlift of troops from 2/4 Gurkha Rifles and the King's Own from Habbaniya, joined by the Morris trucks of the Household Cavalry travelling by road. In the weeks that followed, 10 Indian Division moved rapidly out of the Basra area up both Tigris and Euphrates rivers to Baghdad. The only hindrance earlier was lack of suitable transport, but equipment had flooded into the port during previous weeks and much had also been requisitioned from the civilian population. The Euphrates Brigade (20 Indian Brigade) reached Habbaniya in only two days' hard travelling by water and road after leaving Ur, and the Tigris Brigade (21 Indian Brigade), less two battalions but comprising 1,400 troops and 210 vehicles, reached Kut by requisitioned steamers and hastily converted barges, and was escorted through the ever-shifting silt of the Shatt al-Arab by the Australian HMAS *Yarra* on 17 June, six days after leaving Basra. The following day responsibility for Iraq passed back to GHQ India, with Lieutenant General Quinan in command on the ground, and with Slim in command of the whole of northern Iraq. The impression that both Quinan and Slim were keen to provide was that British forces in Iraq were of considerably greater strength than was in fact the case, reinforcements in the form of 17 and 24 Indian Brigades arriving in Basra on 9 and 16 June respectively.

The advance north was conducted in the face of fading opposition, Slim recalling: 'We had occasional flurries with Iraqi machine-gunners, swooping in and out of the desert in their Ford cars, wide on our flank, at speeds which our armoured cars could not rival. There were a few long-range exchanges with the enemy artillery and we chased his elusive infantry.'[65]   By 18 June the 'occupation' of Iraq was largely complete. Powell's 20 Indian Brigade was in Mosul with a battalion guarding the oilfield at Kirkuk. Slim's headquarters had been established in Baghdad together with a garrison of two infantry battalions and two artillery field regiments. The 2/8 Gurkha Rifles guarded Haditha, Rutba and Falluja, and Weld's 21 Indian Brigade was at Kut. Forming in the Basra area were 25 and 17 Indian Brigades* (each less a battalion) and 19 Medium Battery, Royal Artillery.

In a matter of thirty days the British had initiated and won a war that had been forced on them by a nationalist political clique determined to remove British influence from Iraq and to replace it with that of Germany. That Great Britain needed to fight to preserve its rights in Iraq was understood clearly by the Prime Minister, who saw that to lose control of Iraq would not just deny Britain her precious oil, but allow Germany to dominate the whole of the Middle East, Persian Gulf

* Brigadier R.E. Le Fleming.

and Indian Ocean, threaten Palestine and Egypt from the east, cut off the aerial line of communication to India and menace India itself. The loss of Iraq would have made the retention of the Suez Canal impossible, especially with Rommel knocking at Egypt's western gates. 'The recovery of our position in Iraq might seem a small set-off for the loss of Crete,' commented Eden in his memoirs, 'but its effect upon the Middle East was crucial.'[66]

These threats, when Germany had yet to commit itself to the invasion of the USSR (*Operation Barbarossa*), were very real at the time and justified all the pressure Churchill and the Chiefs of Staff, who unanimously supported the Prime Minister, brought to bear on a reluctant Archibald Wavell. If Wavell's advice had been accepted and negotiations entered into with Rashid Ali, Britain's position would have been fatally undermined across the whole of the Middle East. It would have shown just how weak and close to collapse British power in the region had become and proclaimed that Britain was unable to defend itself against determined nationalist pressure. Churchill's instinct, mirroring that of both Linlithgow and Auchinleck in India, that a decisive blow against Iraq was necessary despite the paucity of resources available to Wavell for the task, was undoubtedly the correct one. The affair showed up several weaknesses in British decision-making. Responsibility for political strategy was not differentiated from military operations, which were themselves poorly co-ordinated between the three Services, a point made by Portal to Tedder on 5 May, it being obvious to him 'that all three Services should make their big efforts in concert and not separately. Unfortunately, 'there appears to be no co-ordinated plan for making the most of our opportunities at this juncture.'[67] The War Cabinet showed itself to be lamentably slow in making urgent decisions: victory in Iraq was ultimately achieved in spite of the vacuum in strategy that allowed decision-making to drag on inconclusively for too long with the result that Wavell and Auchinleck were left to decide strategic priorities themselves. Inevitably, given their quite different responsibilities and perspectives, these priorities clashed.

Three separate factors made up the British success in Iraq. The first was the extraordinary defence of Habbaniya by the plucky impudence of the ill-equipped Training School, flying makeshift aircraft with half-trained crews. This action, supported by the ground-based garrison, undoubtedly turned the war decisively in Britain's favour in the first five days of action. It was the 'stout hearts' of the defenders of Habbaniya – so described by the British Official Historian – that provided Britain with a decisive military success.[68] By taking the initiative into their own hands, the gallant aircrew of RAF Habbaniya and the relative handful of infantrymen guarding the wire not only retrieved the strategic initiative in Iraq for Great Britain but also defeated the Iraqi Air Force and demoralized its army in the process.

Air Marshal Sir Arthur Tedder, Longmore's successor in Cairo, described the battle as 'an RAF epic':

> If the School had been overcome, the Germans would have got a foothold in Iraq. If they had then created a bridgehead behind us, through Vichy-controlled Syria from Greece, our Middle East base could have been nipped out with German forces both to its east and west. Certainly the whole course of the European war would have been changed drastically, if we had not lost it altogether.[69]

Such a view somewhat discounts the part played in the whole Iraqi affair by ground and air forces alike, although undoubtedly true of the siege of Habbaniya itself. Tedder was, of course, merely rehearsing the views of those who briefed him, most notably d'Albiac, who did so on 3 June 1941. Tedder was told that the campaign 'was sorted out by the RAF, 90% by the Flying Training School and 10% by the RAF armoured cars.'[70] Apparently inter-service rivalry remained a dominant theme with d'Albiac and he was reluctant to credit Roberts or Clark with any of the success for the capture of Baghdad.

The second factor in Britain's success was Auchinleck's dogged persistence in promoting the virtues of *Force Sabine* in the face of the equally determined opposition of many in Cairo to any form of military commitment in Iraq. Auchinleck's determination to build up substantial forces in southern Iraq in April in order to send a strong signal to Rashid Ali's regime about Britain's intention to defend its interests in the country, to protect the Abadan refinery, and if necessary to use these forces aggressively, was finally vindicated by events the following month. Much to Auchinleck's chagrin, however, because of the transfer of command to Wavell on 5 May (Northern Iraq) and

8 May (Southern Iraq), 10 Indian Division played but a supporting role in events. India's determination to act, in the face of the overt and determined opposition of Cairo, brought with it enormous dividends, although it needs to be stressed that, until the arrival of Weld's 21 Indian Brigade on 6 May, the only element of *Sabine* in place when hostilities began on 2 May was Powell's 20 Indian Brigade. The division was not complete in Iraq until 30 May. The true weakness of *Operation Sybil* was not appreciated by either Rashid Ali or the Germans, and may well have contributed to the premature collapse of Iraqi resistance. By the end of April the Germans calculated that two Indian Divisions totalling some twenty-eight thousand men and one hundred and sixty warplanes had arrived in Iraq, whereas in actual fact only a single brigade had arrived, bringing with it no transport, tanks or aircraft.[71] The psychological value of the landings vastly outweighed their physical reality.

The third factor in Britain's success was the arrival of Brigadier Kingstone's hastily gathered column in Iraq by 18 May, followed by the remainder of Habforce on 25 May. This force, sent at the insistence of London and in the teeth of opposition from Wavell, provided the troops necessary to conduct the land campaign that followed the collapse of Iraqi resistance at Habbaniya. At the end of the fighting at Habbaniya the odds still appeared to be stacked against Great Britain. *Luftwaffe* reinforcements were soon to arrive, an Iraqi brigade still guarded the Euphrates crossing at Ramadi and at least one brigade defended Falluja. But Habforce doubled the size of Roberts' forces based at Habbaniya and offered the chance of advancing towards Baghdad in the hope that this brazen opportunism might just be enough to panic the Iraqis into surrender. It was.

In Britain's favour two other factors featured heavily in its final victory. The first related to the inability of the Iraqi forces to seize the initiative from the British at an early stage, something they could easily have done and succeeded thereby. Instead, in attempting to use the Habbaniya besiegers as a political tool, Rashid Ali and the Golden Square lost the military initiative as soon as the garrison was able to strike back. Thereafter the Iraqi forces were always on the back foot, despite overwhelmingly superior numbers.

The second lay in the inability of the Germans to exploit the situation in Iraq to their advantage quickly enough. The opportunities open to the Germans, had they acted with more haste, were considerable, but they were too busy in Crete between 15 and 31 May and in preparations for *Barbarossa* to give it the attention it required. Had they acted sooner and more decisively, Germany could quite easily have secured the country without significant military effort, with profound implications for Great Britain's position strategically in the Middle East. As early as 6 May the Iraqi Government urged Germany to intervene to 'save the situation', but Hitler only ordered a strong military mission to Iraq (comprising air force and army specialists led by General Felmy, with the task of advising the Iraqi Army) on 23 May, when he signed Directive No. 30, in time for it to arrive in Aleppo on 31 May. That, of course, was at least two weeks too late. Interestingly, Hitler's Directive showed the true priority of German actions in the Middle East:

> Whether the British can finally be dislodged from their position between the Mediterranean and the Persian Gulf, in conjunction with an offensive against the Suez Canal, and how this can be achieved will be decided only after *Barbarossa*.[72]

Hitler's intervention therefore came too little, too late. By failing to press for the prize aggressively enough in Iraq, Hitler threw away an amazing opportunity to cripple Britain's war effort completely, by denying it its only source of non-American oil and removing the security of her Middle Eastern flank. His failure allowed Britain to fight on.

It remains one of the war's enigmas: why Hitler failed to see the ease with which he could, by attacking Iraq through Syria rather than Crete, rapidly and probably decisively destabilize Britain's position in the Middle East. Perhaps the reason was simply that Hitler was an insufficiently competent strategist. This was the view taken by Major General Ismay, who attributed German failure to seize the magnificent opportunity presented to them to ineptitude:

> It is difficult to understand why the Germans let such a golden opportunity slip through their hands. If they had sent a military mission to Baghdad directly Rashid Ali usurped power, they could have vitalised the Iraqi Army and arranged for their reinforcement by German aircraft and possibly airborne troops. Habbaniya could have

been overwhelmed without much difficulty and the troops at Basrah [sic] compelled to evacuate the country. The control of the pipeline from Iraq to the Mediterranean would have passed out of our hands, and we would have been hard put to it to protect the oil refineries at Abadan in Persia. We were in fact saved from a disaster of some magnitude by the ineptitude of the German High Command.[73]

The *Fliegerführer Irak* was too small and too poorly supported logistically to play a significant role in the campaign and during the last days of fighting Junck's aircraft were grounded owing to a lack of spare parts, the need for repairs and shortage of bombs. Italian aircraft only participated in the final days, and in small numbers, twelve Fiat C.R.42 aircraft arriving in Mosul on 27 May, three being shot down soon afterwards. Even the irrepressible Somerset de Chair was able to capture an unfortunate Italian pilot west of Baghdad on 29 May after his aircraft had been shot down in a dogfight with a Gladiator.[74]

The military risks Britain took during the campaign in time proved to be completely vindicated, as Churchill believed they would be. The campaign was won by the acceptance of huge risks: the weak Habbaniya air force throwing itself bodily against overwhelming odds on the plateau, and succeeding in driving the Iraqis off against all expectation; the marvellous pretension that allowed some 2,000 ill-prepared troops in civilian lorries to cross nearly 500 miles of desert, guided by a single officer in a Chevrolet staff car with a compass; and the outrageous bluff that allowed 1,450 troops to appear to surround and threaten a city with a well-equipped army of some 20,000, enabling the British to win the war through the psychological domination of the enemy rather than exclusively through his physical destruction on the battlefield. Many of these risks were not undertaken willingly, however, and the muted conclusion of the British Official Historian that London's action 'in overriding the man on the spot . . . prevented the situation from becoming far worse' was an understatement.[75] If Wavell's advice had been followed, Britain would have faced a calamity of such proportions from which she might not have managed to recover. Fortunately, this scenario remains merely one of the great 'ifs' of history rather than of history itself.

One of the reasons why such risks could be taken was the remarkable success Great Britain enjoyed in intercepting German communications (through Enigma decrypts at Bletchley Park) and Italian and Japanese diplomatic signals traffic, which kept London well informed of military and political developments in Baghdad, and of the state of German military assistance throughout April and May 1941. On 8 May the Italian diplomatic decrypts had shown that Rashid Ali was still desperately calling for help and, in the days that followed, decrypts of Japanese diplomatic traffic revealed the straits into which Rashid's armed forces had fallen. The newly arrived Japanese ambassador to Baghdad reinforced these messages in a report decrypted on 12 May in which he stated 'that the Iraqi resistance could continue till 15 or 20 May but if British forces advanced from Palestine the Army would collapse sooner and abandon Baghdad.' This intelligence gave more urgency to Churchill's instructions to Wavell to expedite armed intervention, the Prime Minister transmitting the essence of the Japanese decrypt to Wavell on 13 May with instructions to 'burn after reading'.[76]

As the days passed by, these intercepts revealed the precarious state of *Fliegerführer Irak*, the rapid collapse of Iraqi resistance and the dwindling level of support from the Axis Powers. On 24 May the Italian decrypts showed Iraqi frustration at the lateness and inadequacy of Axis support. On 25 May they revealed that fighters of the Italian Air Force were due to arrive on 26 May, although on 25 May it was made clear that no further supplies would arrive by air because of a lack of fuel, a cruel irony for a country awash with oil.* Then, after Rashid Ali had fled Baghdad, the Germans decided, after some prevarication and Hitler's earlier insistence upon a 'last stand', that operations in Iraq were to be suspended and the *Luftwaffe* withdrawn to Syria. On 3 June decrypts indicated that the support base near Athens was being disbanded and that Axis advisers in Iraq regarded further support to anti-British elements to be impossible in practical terms.

What of Wavell? Iraq proved to be one more nail in his coffin as Commander-in-Chief Middle East. Churchill was later to write of the Iraq campaign:

The result was crowned with swift and complete success. Although no one was more pleased and relieved than Wavell himself, the

---

* A number of Italian tri-motor Savoia 79s delivered arms and ammunition to Mosul, however, between 19 and 26 May.

episode could not pass without leaving impressions in his mind and in ours. At the same time General Auchinleck's forthcoming attitude in sending . . . the [10th] Indian Division to Basra so promptly, and the readiness with which Indian reinforcements were supplied, gave us the feeling of a fresh mind and a hitherto untaxed personal energy.[77]

In Churchill's mind the victory that ensued in Iraq – the gamble at long odds that came good in the end – fully vindicated his own attitude and damned Wavell's. This was palpably unfair, but it was how Churchill made up his mind about people. There was nothing like a victory to allow Churchill to assume too much, and nothing like a defeat to allow him to assume the worst. Wavell was stretched in the spring of 1941 in a way few others in the history of British warfare ever have been, and the demands on his scarce resources by enemy action, let alone those from an interfering and even dictatorial Prime Minister trying in London to move the pawns on Wavell's chessboard, were almost intolerable. That said, Wavell eventually did do as he was ordered, and victory was achieved. Churchill, however, had had enough of generals speaking their mind and standing up to him – particularly when virtually all other military opinion supported the Prime Minister – and had determined to seek a replacement for Wavell when the opportune moment came. Auchinleck's positive response to the crisis in Iraq (he at least had troops to spare) warmed him to the Prime Minister, and he became the chosen successor to Wavell. This, however, is another story.

5

Beirut

Vichy French complicity in the use by the *Luftwaffe* of Syrian airfields to support their operations in Iraq came as a considerable shock to those in Cairo who had deluded themselves that Vichy would remain, at worst, passively neutral in the continuing struggle against Germany. Those who had recognized the threat had seen how, through the connivance of Vichy, Syria might become the Trojan Horse by which the Germans could overcome Britain's Middle Eastern citadel.[1] If the Germans could violate it so easily, Vichy neutrality was worth very little and could in actuality become a danger to the whole British position across the Middle East. To those who had held that the Vichy regime would oppose German intervention in Syria rather than welcome it, the events of May 1941 removed the scales of delusion decisively. Suddenly, harsh realities emphasized the strategic significance of Syria to Germany and showed for the first time the scale of Vichy collaboration with the Nazis. Syria provided a direct route from the Mediterranean to the Persian Gulf through Iraq, otherwise inaccessible to Hitler due to the obstinate refusal of Turkey, Germany's First World War ally, to join the Axis grouping. If Syria had come under Axis control the Turkish stance would have been put under great strain, and her neutrality might even have been overturned. But more worryingly, Syria provided a closer and even more direct threat to British control of Palestine and the Suez Canal than Rommel's forces in Libya. If Germany continued the pattern of its dramatic advance across Europe's underbelly, through the Balkans to Greece and then Crete, the obvious next step was to seize Syria, and by doing so it might possibly at one stroke decapitate Britain from her empire.

To Major General Sir Edward Spears, Head of Churchill's Mission to the Free French, the facts were starkly apparent. If the Germans had managed to gain control of the Levant states (Syria and Lebanon):

> we would have inevitably lost the Suez Canal and Egypt, which was within an hour's flight of the Lebanese and Syrian landing grounds. This would have meant the loss of the whole Mediterranean, for our ships could not have held out in Alexandria under air attack from the Levant. The same applied to Cyprus, which could not in any case have become a permanent fleet base. Worse still, our air communications with India and the Far East would have been severed.[2]

Spears considered it only a matter of time, therefore, before the Germans gained the foothold in Syria necessary to achieve this aim. He was not alone in this view. This prospect also worried Churchill, who expressed fears in April and May 1941 that the forthcoming German attack on Crete was merely a feint and that the decisive blow would fall further east. Turkey was an option, but also Syria, where they could 'penetrate and poison' both Iran and Iraq and threaten Palestine.[3] 'Were all the Balkan states, including heroic Greece, to be subjugated one by one, and Turkey, isolated, to be compelled to open for the German legions the road to Palestine, Egypt, Iraq and Persia?'[4]

Eleven months previously the fall of France had prompted Great Britain to think about the implications for the Middle East of the loss of Syria. On 1 July 1940 the War Cabinet's Middle East Committee concluded that such a situation would be disastrous:

> Strategically speaking, the whole British position in the Middle East, including Egypt and Arabia, will probably be untenable unless Syria and the Lebanon are under friendly control or failing that British control.[5]

The very next day, when the French colonial government in Syria and Lebanon accepted the terms of the armistice, London issued the following warning:

His Majesty's Government declare that they could not allow Syria or the Lebanon to be occupied by any hostile Power or to be used as a base for attacks upon those countries in the Middle East which they are pledged to defend, or to become the scene of such disorder as to constitute a danger to these countries.

They therefore hold themselves free to take whatever measures they may in such circumstances consider necessary in their own interests. Any action which they may hereafter be obliged to take in fulfilment of this declaration will be entirely without prejudice to the future status of the territories now under French mandate.[6]

Now, in May 1941, they faced precisely this prospect. The Levant States were never technically French colonies, although they were ruled and treated as such by a France whose national virility was measured in terms of the grandeur of *L'Empire*. France attempted to apply forcibly its *mission civilisatrice* upon a native population largely unwilling to play the part of grateful recipient of France's cultural largesse, and French governments for the most part retained throughout the 1920s and 1930s an obstinate rejection of the nationalistic aspirations of her subject peoples. Her peoples were diverse. Of a population of 3.6 million, the country contained a polyglot mixture of Arab Muslims (both Sunni and Shi'ite), Turks, Turkomans, Kurds, Circassians, Armenians, Iranians, Jews, as well as a wide variety of Christians, including Maronites, Greek and Armenian Orthodox, Melkites and more recently arrived Protestants. Syria was the seat of French power in the Middle East and due to this status Paris maintained tight control over the country, supported by an army that numbered some 120,000 troops in 1939. The credibility of France's mission, however, was undermined by a widespread conviction amongst the populace of the venality and corruption of the regime and the repressive nature of the instruments of government.[7] The principle of 'divide and rule' helped France to keep the lid on popular expressions of nationalist sentiment, although imperious Gallic chauvinism unsurprisingly made French rule universally unwelcome. Spears, one of its bitterest critics after 1941, claimed not without justification that:

it was common knowledge that French rule in Syria was most unpopular, and the proud and ancient Syrian race, which was highly civilized when ours was primitive and savage, was highly dissatisfied with France for not granting the independence to which their culture and standing, as well as their rights under the French mandate, entitled them.[8]

This unpopularity led to regular clashes, the most notable of which was the Druze rebellion between 1924 and 1926, during which French artillery bombarded Druze-occupied Damascus for two days.[9] The mandate was replaced in 1936 by a treaty of friendship and alliance, but although accepted by the Syrian Parliament, it was never ratified by France.

Likewise, French relationships with Great Britain were never strong, soured by imperial rivalry and competing colonial agendas. Britain and France had very different colonial attitudes. The French had secured the mandate for Lebanon in 1920 and had then invaded and conquered Syria. Its possession was based on the maintenance of force. British rule, though not without its problems and ambiguities, was largely pragmatic and concerned with the practicalities of empire – oil, commerce and communications – rather than ideology. The British (except for Palestine, where Britain adopted a divisive pro-Jewish stance) were tolerably accepted by the Arabs, despite the debacle and embarrassment of the Sykes–Picot Agreement. The French repression of nationalist dissent in the Levant contrasted badly with British pragmatism. The stark difference in how Great Britain and France treated their mandates and interests in the Middle East became a major hindrance in establishing any form of mutual understanding between Britain and both Free France and Vichy France in 1941. Likewise the general British attitude towards the Arabs, as developed by local British officers on the ground, was on the whole much more benign than the traditional French view, which held that the Arabs, as receptacles for French culture, had a duty to be thankful for the same. Glubb commented on this contrast:

Wherever the British have penetrated, we meet British officers who believe the Bedouins, the Kurds, the Gurkhas . . . to be the most splendid fellows on earth. The French do not share this passionate interest in other races – they only praise individuals or communities in so far as they have become Gallicized.[10]

Following the fall of France, Churchill entertained hopes that the Vichy regime would be at least accommodating to British strategic interests in the continuing war with Germany, but events soon proved this hope to be a false one. During June 1940 Wavell failed to persuade the ageing French High Commissioner in the Levant to come alongside the British, and Syria capitulated to the triumphant Germans along with the vast extent of her empire. There was much that Great Britain could have done at the time to persuade Frenchmen in the region to join the continuing fight against Germany, but convention, conservatism and timidity got in the way of British policy makers, key among whom was Wavell. Nothing was done to counter the insidious propaganda of capitulation now gushing in violent streams from France, nor was any assistance − practical or psychological − given to the large numbers of Frenchmen disgusted at the collapse of France who were determined to fight on. Wavell by all accounts was unwilling to sponsor or encourage the desertion of officers and men from the army of an erstwhile friend. A great chance thereby was regrettably missed.

Under the terms of the armistice France's army in Syria was reduced to 35,000, a number believed sufficient to maintain internal order, the remainder being disarmed, demobilized and repatriated. Her weapons and equipment were impounded and monitored by an Italian Armistice Commission.

For its part the Vichy regime adopted a neutrality that was initially complaisant towards Germany but which in time became co-operative and even collaborative. This did not mean that the French authorities were actively hostile to Britain, but they were not helpful and sought to diminish British military strength where possible, especially where it impinged on Great Britain's sponsorship of de Gaulle's Free France movement, members of which the Vichy regime branded as traitors and renegades. A significant element within Vichy ranks did nevertheless display violent antagonism towards Great Britain, believing that France's salvation lay in adopting a totalitarianism modelled on that of Nazi Germany. A common and dominant theme in this movement was the idea that France had been betrayed by what Dentz (the Vichy Commander in Syria) was later to describe as 'democratic-masonic politics and judaeo-saxon finance', in which Great Britain was a principal culprit.[11] These characters were convinced of eventual German victory, and sought to arraign themselves as the leaders of a post-war fascist French state. Not all Britons were perspicacious enough to recognize this change in attitude, but the sinking of the French fleet at Mers-el-Kebir (Oran, North Africa) on 3 July 1940 to prevent the vessels falling into German hands, resulting in the deaths of over 1,000 French sailors, together with the abortive attack on Dakar (West Africa) in September, completed the estrangement between Marshal Pétain's Vichy and Great Britain. A state of war between them was created in all but name. An opportunity to invade Syria in 1940 to capitalize on strong anti-German attitudes in the Army of the Levant was also missed, owing largely to Wavell's determined reluctance to take any risks: 'There can be no question of sending British troops to Syria at present', concluded Wavell, and with this decision the second great opportunity during 1940 was missed to drag Syria from the clutches of Vichy.[12]

In the Levant, General Henri Dentz, a rabid Anglophobe and obedient servant of the French state, a man whose loyalty to France was filtered through the prism of considerable military mediocrity, became High Commissioner and Commander-in-Chief in the dying days of 1940, and did what he could to disrupt the British war effort.* Potential Gaullist supporters were shipped back to France in chains in French ships and contraband weapons and equipment made the return journey in the same vessels from Marseille, all under the protection and unrequited courtesies of the Royal Navy, which assumed, wrongly, that Vichy was acting as a neutral party. The problem was that the Vichy French came to see defeat as a virtue, believing that it was far better to embrace the German-dominated future than to continue into defeat with the British. As Spears viewed it, 'Vichy's formula for eradicating the stigma of defeat was to wallow ever deeper in the mire of surrender, relying on a fresh layer of humiliation to hide the unbearable spectacle of the France it had sullied.'[13] This meant that by the spring of 1941 they willingly collaborated with the Germans and did all that they could to undermine British military hegemony in the region. But the three British Commanders-in-Chief in Cairo (General Wavell, Air Vice-Marshal Longmore and Admiral Cunningham)

---

* Dentz had served in Syria during the 1920s, and had commanded the troops who put down the Druze uprising in 1925–6. He had a well-deserved reputation for duplicity. After the war he was tried and condemned for high treason, receiving a sentence of life imprisonment. He died in prison on 13 December 1945.

appeared or chose not to notice this Vichy treachery, much to Spears' profound exasperation:

> Nothing that either de Gaulle or I could say would open the eyes of the Middle Eastern Command to what was going on; to have to admit having been fooled was indeed too much to expect of the Johnny Heads-in-the-Air we had to deal with. On they marched, satisfied and stubborn, certain they could not possibly be mistaken in their assessment of General Dentz, the Vichy Commander in Syria.[14]

Wavell was keen to retain a relatively acquiescent Levant on his northern frontier and so maintained as friendly as possible diplomatic relations with his Vichy neighbour. He reasoned:

> My view was that I wanted a stable and neutral Syria on my northern flank, in view of my general weakness; and that to disrupt it by removing large numbers of the best French officers would be bad policy. It might result in disorder in Syria, which I did not want, and in Vichy sending out officers definitely hostile to the British to replace those we had removed. I did not think the gain of a certain number of French officers without units was worth the risk of this.[15]

This attitude infuriated both de Gaulle and Spears, who failed to see how appeasement of the quietly hostile Vichy regime could ever be in Great Britain's long-term interest, even if in the short term it kept the region subdued. Wavell's view was nevertheless a valid one: he had few resources with which to challenge Vichy hegemony in the Levant even if he had wanted to do so, and leaving it undisturbed made much practical military sense, so long as Vichy or its German masters agreed also to maintain the *status quo*. Thus, from late July 1940 Wavell's policy was not to treat the Vichy Levant as an enemy, but rather as an errant child, and through means of an economic blockade it was hoped that it might be compelled to come into the British fold in due course, or at the very least not fall into the rapidly enlarging German sphere of influence and control.

Wavell's attitude was challenged from September 1940 by the active lobbying of the Free French movement, which pressed loudly for action to recover the Levant for Free France. General Catroux,[*] who had arrived in Cairo in October 1940 as de Gaulle's Middle Eastern representative, had originally hoped that Vichy officers would flock of their own volition to the Free French cause. When this failed to materialize, Catroux became a fervent advocate for British and Free French military intervention to secure the Levant for de Gaulle. From the outset de Gaulle's attitude was that Vichy had to be defeated in the Levant, not merely (or even at all) to prevent German use of the country or to inflict a defeat upon the Germans, but because the honour of France demanded it. Nevertheless his views were accorded little weight in Cairo, and proponents of intervention in Syria were regarded by Wavell as little more than a nuisance. Indeed, from the beginning these calls served only to irritate Wavell who, because of the wide demands on the remainder of his demesne, was entrenched in his policy of non-involvement and non-intervention in the affairs of Vichy Levant. In a series of increasingly bitter debates in Cairo and Palestine during late 1940 and early 1941, de Gaulle called for a reversal of British policy towards Vichy, rather than merely retention of the *status quo*. He did not want necessarily a unilateral British attack on the Levant. Indeed, this prospect roused quite some concern in Free French quarters. De Gaulle's 'Defence Council of the Empire' talked through the problem in London on 3 March 1941. Some did not agree with the idea of a British attempt to overthrow the Vichy regime. De Gaulle's view prevailed, however. This entailed acceptance of any British action with the threefold justification of re-establishing in the Levant the conditions necessary for continuing the fight against the Axis, to safeguard French rights and to help Britain in its struggle.

The best option, of course, was for a Free French-led invasion, with British support if necessary, and it is this which Catroux so assiduously promoted during early 1941. When de Gaulle arrived in Cairo with Spears on 1 April 1941, determined to force the issue of Britain's *laissez-faire* attitude to the Levant, he received a chilly reception. However, by chance de Gaulle had timed his visit well, as during April the likelihood of Syria's being a German strategic target had become newly and starkly apparent to the War Cabinet in London.

---

[*] Formerly Governor-General of French Indo-China and removed by Vichy for his refusal to accept the terms of the armistice with Germany.

Consequently London became supportive during the month of de Gaulle's view.

Thus by the spring of 1941 the Levant had become yet another battleground in the French Civil War, a bitter confrontation between those who clung to the idea that France was represented by the defeated state which had surrendered her to Germany, and which continued to run the country and large swathes of its empire from the small spa town of Vichy in central France, and those – rebels and traitors in the eyes of the former – who flocked to the banner of General de Gaulle's Free France. It was a confrontation that was eventually to lead to the spilling of blood in June and July, although until then in the Middle East at least it was limited to a war of words and of running scuffles between Vichy and Free French sailors in the streets of Alexandria. Pitifully little of the empire rallied initially to de Gaulle's cause, most territories choosing meekly to follow metropolitan France into obedient slavery. Those servicemen who were able to escape to London and Egypt did so, but until 1943 numbers remained too small to make anything other than a political point: militarily they remained insignificant. In the Middle East by early 1941 these forces amounted to six battalions of lightly equipped infantry (with one battery of artillery, twenty light tanks and very little transport) grouped into a single division of two brigades (1 and 13) under the command of General Legentilhomme.* A small number of troops managed to escape from Syria to join the Free French forces but for the most part troops in the Levant – mainly colonial North and West Africans – remained loyal to Vichy.

German interest in Syria increased perceptibly in early 1941. The visit between 26 January and 15 February by Otto von Hentig of the German Foreign Office's Oriental Department, aimed at examining ways in which Germany could be enriched at Great Britain's expense, prompted British fears of closer Franco–German co-operation in the Levant. Whilst von Hentig's visit had deeply embarrassed and antagonized the Levantine French, particularly because of his blatant

---

* One brigade had a Foreign Legion battalion and two Senegalese battalions, the other a battalion of Marine Infantry and two battalions of Senegalese.

courting of Syrian nationalist sentiment and his tactless showing of the German propaganda film *Defeat in the West* to Arab audiences, policy in the region remained firmly in the hands of the Vichy Government ensconced in its hilly sanctuary in the heart of rural France. There remained some hope in British circles that should the Germans force themselves upon the Levant, the local Vichy leaders might oppose the Nazis and throw in their weight with Great Britain. But this was – as Spears always proclaimed – a forlorn hope. Nevertheless, in January 1941 General Catroux approached Dentz by letter to enquire whether he would accept British and Free French help in the event of a German attack on Syria. The approach was rebuffed, Dentz reporting firmly that he would in all cases obey his masters in Vichy.

Meanwhile, Catroux pressed not just for political action in the Levant to destabilize the Vichy regime, but also for Free French military action to remove it completely. His hope was that a largely symbolic invasion would rally to the Cross of Lorraine the large numbers of disaffected troops he and de Gaulle assumed to garrison the Levant. Arab support for a transfer from Vichy to Free French control could be garnered, it was thought, through the promise of limited independence for the Levant on the model Britain had agreed with Egypt. Although talk of invading Syria threatened to upset Wavell's carefully balanced Middle Eastern apple cart, Catroux's ideas received strong support from the Foreign Office in London, which welcomed moves to allow Syrian Arabs a measure of freedom and which went some way to meeting old British promises on Arab unity. Kirkbride and Glubb, for whom Arabism was virtually a divine mission and the French the principal impediments to its achievement, were accordingly instructed by the Foreign Office in February 1941 to begin the process of propagandizing the Druze, virulent opponents of the mandate, as well as to proselytize the Syrian tribes.[16]

But the Foreign Office's plan fell down on various points. The most important was that it did not have the full support of de Gaulle, who was deeply distrustful of any British attempts to undermine the French position politically. It was right in his view to attack the military power of Vichy but not to threaten the legitimacy of France's empire nor to undermine the glory of France. De Gaulle saw in it an underhand attempt by Britain (using Kirkbride and Glubb as the *agents provocateurs*) to wrest from France her Levantine empire and hand it to the British-leaning Hashemite family, led by Abdullah of Transjordan, to whom Lawrence had promised it long ago. From this affair de Gaulle conceived an opinion that a long-term objective of perfidious Albion was to secure for itself the French possessions in the region, a prejudice in which he was to become securely entrenched. For long Wavell had to contend with de Gaulle demanding on the one hand that Britain take decisive military action against Vichy whilst at the same time insisting shrilly that Great Britain's motives were suspect and self-serving. De Gaulle was sensitive to the possibility that in helping Great Britain to defeat Hitler he would unwittingly lose France her empire.[17] In a moment of weakness he admitted to a horrified Spears that his only interest in the region was the 'honour' of France and the continued integrity of her empire. 'You think I am interested in England winning the war?' asked de Gaulle. 'I am not. I am only interested in France's victory.' 'They are the same', retorted Spears. 'Not at all,' de Gaulle responded, 'not at all in my view.'[18] In this commitment to France, de Gaulle's motivations differed little from those of his Vichy foe.[19]

De Gaulle's fears about British ambitions in the Levant were certainly exaggerated, but not entirely unfounded. Whilst it is true, as Churchill was to insist to the House of Commons on 9 September 1941, that Britain did 'not seek to replace or supplant France, or substitute British for French interest in any part of Syria',[20] the seed sown by Kirkbride and Glubb amongst the Arabs in Syria sprouted quickly. As Glubb recalled:

> The Arabs for twenty-five years past had resented the presence of the French in Syria, but the alliance between France and Britain had made it impossible to oust them. Now by a fortunate coincidence, as it appeared to the Arabs, the British and French were on opposite sides. The hour for the redemption of Syria had struck.[21]

But the British propaganda insufficiently distinguished between *false* France (Vichy) and *true* France (Free France) for de Gaulle's liking. The truth was that any offer of independence by de Gaulle was always going to be disingenuous because his ambition was not to free the Levant from France but to strengthen France's hold on her empire, at least in the short term. What he proposed to offer the Arabs at the time was freedom from Vichy, not freedom from France.[22] Great Britain, when its policy was finally decided upon on 21 May 1941, was interested only in removing the threat of Nazi infestation on its Levantine flank, not in taking action to preserve French imperialism. The subtlety of this distinction was one of which Glubb and Kirkbride, now enthusiastically undermining all things French, were understandably unaware.[23]

Catroux's plan, and Kirkbride and Glubb's forays into Syria in pursuit of a strategy that would not only bring about the destruction of the Vichy regime but also unite the Arabs under an anti-French banner, exposed the full force of the confusion that was British 'policy' in the Middle East at the time. The truth was that no single agency of government in London or Cairo exercised a coherent hold on policy for the Middle East. British imperial pragmatism had its downside in the lack of ideological and political rigidity in its approach to affairs of empire, although it did confer an enviable degree of flexibility upon policy makers. The Foreign Office (responsible for relations with Egypt and Iraq) competed with the Colonial Office (responsible for the Palestine mandate and Transjordan), both of which were torn by competing lobbies promoting either the Zionist or the Arab cause. The distance from London gave regional ambassadors considerable liberty in their decision-making, which resulted in the regional tail often wagging the London dog. The competing organs of government in the Middle East added to the dysfunctionality of policy-making. Few agencies talked to each other and the many little empires in Cairo precluded effective understanding and liaison. There was no clarity of responsibility between the military and political structures in the region, between Sir Miles Lampson and Wavell, and no formal liaison, for instance, between Egypt and Palestine. Spears felt keenly for Lampson, 'immense, polite, the essence of diplomatic urbanity' suffering greatly from the fact that Wavell confided nothing in him of his plans.[24]

To complicate matters still further, the conduct of the war gave to Wavell *de facto* political as well as military supremacy in the region, allowing him to influence political issues far outside the normal course of his military remit.[25] Wavell's own personal taciturnity added to the notorious disorganization of the various Middle East headquarters and reduced still further the quality of communication between responsible authorities in the Middle East. Cairo was a confusion of competing fiefdoms and baronies, not just between the three Services but within them as well. It was not well-organized, answered to different masters and was rife with factions. In many ways it resented intrusions on its authority, even from London. The three Commanders-in-Chief ran their own domains and designed their own strategies largely independently of each other, a practice that was to have frustrating consequences operationally. Fighting a 'joint' war (that is, with collaboration between the various elements of government, as well as between the three fighting Services) as well as a 'combined' one (between Great Britain and her various allies) was made immeasurably more difficult, if not impossible, as a result.

Policy as a whole was allowed to drift aimlessly, driven through with imprecision and dominated by the weight of personality. All too often the result was chaos, as Spears scathingly observed:

> the policy of one day was not that of the next, but changed and gyrated according to whether the timid or the bold prevailed in Whitehall. The result at local level was a series of disconnected decisions prompted by the fears and anxieties of minor officials or of soldiers apprehensive of a non-existent Vichy belligerence, haunted by visions of Napoleons in shorts over the border, or of Tallyrands (sic) under coconut trees scheming the overthrow of Britain. And of course the Vichy French were persuaded that the evil British were planning to take advantage of France's defeat to annex the French Empire.[26]

It was only with the appointment of Sir Oliver Lyttelton in July 1941 as permanent representative of the War Cabinet in the Middle East that these anomalies were ironed out through the establishment of a central authority for the prosecution of the war in the region. Wavell was not unaware of these difficulties, asking Churchill on 18 April for the appointment of a political supremo in the Middle East: Lyttelton was Churchill's response. His task, the Prime Minister explained, would be to 'represent the War Cabinet in the Middle East, and his prime duty will be to relieve the High Command of all extraneous burdens, and to settle promptly on the spot, in accordance with the policy of His Majesty's Government, many questions affecting several Departments or authorities which hitherto have required reference home.'[27]

As it turned out, the attempt to unsettle the Vichy regime through surreptitious means at the hands of Kirkbride and Glubb was brought to a halt in March as Wavell, fearful of a collapse in Syria following civil unrest, agreed with Lampson to relax the economic blockade and then struck a commercial treaty with Syria in April. In the view of both men a weakened Levant made it more likely to suffer from German aggrandizement and they sought therefore to strengthen Dentz's position, a decision which of course ran diametrically counter to de Gaulle's warlike ambitions. The struggle for influence in the affairs of the Levant between Wavell (who wanted to maintain the *status quo* with Dentz) and the Foreign Office (who had sponsored the agitation in February) now swung decisively in Wavell's favour, much to the despair of Spears and de Gaulle. Doing any kind of deal with Syria was a mistake, they argued, because Dentz was a stooge of Vichy and Vichy was now a collaborator with the German enemy.

To counter Wavell's view, Spears wrote to Churchill, as was his right by virtue of the terms of his mission, on 11 April, setting out a contrary perspective to that which he regarded as appeasement with Vichy-held Levant. He insisted that nothing Wavell did would prevent Dentz from selling out to the Germans and that risks should be taken to ensure the Levant did not simply become another of Hitler's foreign garrisons, like Bulgaria or Yugoslavia. Spears accordingly asked for a Free French concentration in Palestine on the borders with Syria in order to send a strong signal to Dentz, informing him that Great Britain would not tolerate the Vichy Government allowing the Germans to use Syrian airfields, and might perhaps even provoke an anti-Vichy uprising.

Like Spears, de Gaulle was determined to force the pace on the issue of the Levant and prepared to present the Free French view to Wavell in Cairo on 15 April. At this stage, although he recognized that 'sooner or later we would have to go there', his primary concern was to awaken GHQ Cairo from its pro-Vichy lethargy, and to warn Wavell of the latent danger sitting on his northern flank.[28] Realizing only too clearly the need for subtlety in his approach to Wavell, given earlier rebuffs, his aim was not to demand an invasion *per se*. Unfortunately, by accident or design this strategy was not made clear to Catroux who blurted out at the start of proceedings on the 15th that the only way of dealing with Dentz and his Vichy cronies in the Levant was to mount an immediate Anglo-French invasion. To Spears' amazement

Catroux announced that his plan was to capture Beirut, Damascus and the airfield at Rayak with Free French troops in the belief that they would meet little or no resistance. Furthermore, his plan involved the contribution by Wavell of transport, tanks and aircraft, totalling one mechanized and one infantry division. Catroux's outburst showed, in Spears' opinion, 'that he had grasped neither his chief's doctrine nor the essentials of the problem itself.'[29] Catroux's announcement took the wind completely out of de Gaulle's sails, and ruined any chance he might have had that day to explain his views carefully and dispassionately to Wavell.

Neither Spears nor de Gaulle had envisaged an attack on Syria unless the Vichy regime invited the Germans on to its soil.[30] Both men knew that Wavell would never contemplate the unilateral, unprovoked invasion of Syria without the sort of just cause that a German invasion would provide, and so Wavell's refusal to countenance Catroux's plan did not come as a surprise. When informed of Catroux's plan, Eden, Britain's Foreign Secretary, said that he had no objection in principle to the idea but the Chiefs of Staff noted that Wavell simply did not have the resources available to do what de Gaulle asked. Later that afternoon Wavell saw Spears again. 'He must have been sick and tired of hearing my views on Syria,' Spears recalled, 'but he was very patient, though I am sure I did not make him change his point of view.' Spears nevertheless argued that action needed to be taken now to prevent German use of Vichy aerodromes and that the first step perhaps was the concentration of Free French troops in northern Palestine. But the result was no change. Spears recalled, somewhat bitterly: 'I thought these suggestions appealed to Wavell, but it was clear he would never accept a plan that involved, or might involve, any commitment on his part.'[31]

Was Wavell right to turn down Catroux's plan? To use his precious resources to help what Wavell undoubtedly judged to be de Gaulle's political aspirations when there was a war on was indefensible. But because he could see no strategic reason why Syria should not be allowed to continue to 'wither on the vine', as in his view it threatened no one, Wavell ignored the Vichy wood for the Gaullist trees and failed to recognize the threat that faced the whole of the British position in the Middle and Far East, should the Germans occupy Syria. Such a disaster was certainly possible through the instrumentality of a weak Vichy regime, a fact that Spears did not hesitate to repeat frequently to whomsoever would listen, although the 'ostriches' in GHQ would have none of this Jeremiah-like prophesying and, certain in the infallibility of their judgements, regarded Spears as a trouble maker. Spears recognized this, describing himself as being 'hopelessly out of tune with the vast concourse which was GHQ at Cairo, the 'Chairborne Army'.[32] It needed Dill to make the issue clear to Wavell in a telegram two weeks later, when he stressed: 'if the Germans land in Syria and [Vichy] French can be induced to resist, it would be greatly to our advantage to stiffen them to prevent [German] advance on Palestine or Iraq.'[33] De Gaulle and Spears were fighting a losing cause against Cairo, whose attitude was only to change with the *coup d'état* in Iraq and the receipt of firm direction from London to plan for offensive action. The two men departed for Free French colonies in Africa on 16 April, only returning to Cairo on 3 May.

The calls of de Gaulle, Catroux and Spears for action in Syria coincided with the dawning realization in London that the German threat to Syria was real, and growing, made more acute by the loss of Greece in late April and the outbreak of hostilities in Iraq on 2 May. With the arrival of German aircraft it was suddenly apparent that London's worst fears could soon be realized and that Syria might be next on the German invasion list. In order to test exactly where Dentz stood on the issue of collaboration with Germany, Dill told Wavell on 27 April that the British Consul-General in Beirut had been instructed to warn Dentz of this impending build-up and offer aid to the French if the Germans attacked. If Dentz proved antagonistic to Germany, there was a chance that he would ask Great Britain for help. If this did happen, Wavell was asked to consider how this aid might be provided. He was also asked, the following day, what forces would be required in Palestine to repel an invasion from Syria if the Germans were successful in installing themselves there. The British also wanted to warn Dentz, through the US Government, that Vichy collaboration or participation in a German invasion of Syria would constitute an act of war. Churchill told Roosevelt in a personal telegram:

If the German air force and troop carrier planes get installed in Syria they will soon penetrate and poison both Iraq and Iran and threaten Palestine . . . I feel Hitler may quite easily now gain vast advantages very cheaply and we are so fully engaged that we can do little or nothing to stop him spreading himself.[34]

Wavell replied on 4 May that the only force available at the time to aid Dentz to repel a German invasion was one mechanized cavalry brigade, an artillery regiment and a battalion of infantry. 'This force cannot be expected to deal with the number of troops which the Germans would consider necessary', he wrote, 'and be able to send to Syria, and should not be sent unless French are actively resisting.'[35] Wavell also observed that in his view Dentz was completely subservient to Vichy and thus unlikely to resist German penetration.[36] Dentz, after all, was the man who had signed the instrument surrendering Paris, and so had a poor track record in standing up to Nazi tyranny. Wavell believed that if the Germans did decide to occupy Syria they would meet no resistance from Vichy and that any invasion of Syria needed to be led by British rather than by Free French forces because the 'entry of Free French forces would be bitterly resented' and exacerbate the intensity of the fighting.[37] On this issue Wavell was undoubtedly right, and provided a realistic and pragmatic counter to the excited claims by those in the Free French camp that the Vichy regime would collapse like dominoes at the first hint of an Anglo-French invasion. On the other hand Wavell was energetically marshalling every excuse he could to avoid committing himself to what he considered a nugatory and even counter-productive action in Syria at a time when he was under pressure in Iraq and the Western Desert and the ill-fated Greek adventure was coming to an ignominious end. Finally it was agreed to tell Dentz simply that Britain would help Syria to resist a German attack if it came. On 6 May Wavell replied to Dill's request regarding the forces necessary to defend Palestine from a German advance from Syria. Wavell's view was that it would require at least four divisions, two armoured brigades, two armoured infantry battalions and a cavalry brigade, only half of which would be available, all other things considered, by early July at the earliest.[38]

For his part Dentz asked Vichy for instructions, and was told on 6 May that he was to give German aircraft *en route* to Iraq 'every facility'. Obediently, even enthusiastically, he complied. On 9 May an emissary from Vichy, Jacques Guérard, arrived in Aleppo and on 10 May travelled to Beirut to brief Dentz on the negotiations Darlan* was currently undertaking in Germany. The outcome of successful talks aimed at collaborating closer with Germany included a reduction in the war indemnity, a reduction in the area of France under German occupation, and a large-scale release of prisoners of war. These concessions for metropolitan France went a long way to explain why the Vichy regime in the Levant fought as furiously as it did in 1941. In exchange for French compliance a number of German aircraft in Iraqi colours were to be allowed to transit through Syria to Iraq, and French weapons impounded by the Armistice Commission were to be released and transported to Iraq. Dentz was fearful of the consequences of losing this equipment and asked:

> that the Armistice Commission be requested to supply equivalent arms and ammunition to make up our war reserves, and if possible some . . . anti-tank and . . . anti-aircraft guns, which are seriously deficient in the event of British reaction.[39]

It is clear that he recognized that aiding the Germans could provide Great Britain with sufficient justification for an attack.

With concerted pressure being applied from both de Gaulle and Churchill to overturn the existing policy of non-involvement in the affairs of the Levant, Wavell was forced, much against his will, to convene a conference in Cairo on 5 May to discuss the matter. The previous day, 4 May, Wavell had met briefly with Spears and Catroux, but the meeting was not a happy one, with little commonality of views. Catroux, Spears, Lampson and Longmore attended the conference on 5 May. Catroux stood by the plan he had so incautiously announced on 15 April. Indeed he had told de Gaulle on 2 May that if the Germans entered Syria, and if Dentz did not resist, it was his intention to invade Syria with all the forces he could muster in order to 'rally as many troops as possible' in the Levant to resist the Nazis. Catroux again pressed Wavell to provide two divisions of British troops to support his six weak Free French battalions. Wavell was somewhat nonplussed by

---

* Admiral François Darlan was Marshal Pétain's pro-German deputy from mid-December 1941. Great Britain knew of his negotiations with Berlin through its ability to decode Enigma transcripts.

this demand, as he did not possess two spare divisions, and used the Frenchman's demands and the paucity of HQ Middle East's resources as evidence of Catroux's ignorance of the military realities in the region: argument enough for non-intervention. In Wavell's view, Catroux consistently ignored the fact that the resources available for an operation of this kind did not exist in his command, repeating a heated point he had made the day before to both Catroux and Spears, namely that with the current state of his resources 'intervention in Syria meant dispersal of effort and therefore defeat.'[40] Spears recalled that the meeting was 'extremely depressing', with Wavell asserting 'that the loss of Syria would be better than the risk of . . . intervening with inadequate forces.'[41] Spears' despair mounted when Lampson told him after the meeting that Wavell had confided in him that 'the Iraqi situation was desperate and he was in favour of treating with the rebels', repeating the exasperated sentiment Wavell had blurted out to Spears the previous day that 'he had always been opposed to having anything to do about Iraq.' Spears contented himself with the knowledge that Churchill would agree to no such thing.[42]

Wavell was frustrated that the military extremity in which he found himself did not seem to be recognized by those whom he believed should know better. The facts were clear. He had lost a quarter of his manpower and much equipment, including precious aircraft, armour and artillery in the Greek disaster, and he had been ordered to despatch troops to rescue a hopeless case in Iraq, where in his view diplomacy rather than military force was the appropriate remedy. In addition he was expecting an airborne assault on Crete at any minute and he was committed to an early offensive in the Western Desert. This left him with forces in Palestine amounting to little more than a few regiments of horsed cavalry and Legentilhomme's weak Free French division. Wavell was clearly irritated that Catroux could not see these difficulties and argued that the Frenchman overestimated the kudos amongst Vichy enjoyed by the Free French cause and thus underestimated the military effort that would be necessary to secure the Levant for the Allies.

Spears duly reported Wavell's uncompromising views to the Prime Minister. The Prime Minister's ire was already up over Wavell's reluctance to commit himself to Iraq, and he responded angrily to this latest evidence of Wavell's determined obstinacy against running any further risks. Churchill believed that large political gains could be achieved in Iraq and

Syria from a relatively small investment and was frustrated that Wavell doggedly refused to share his enthusiasm for a political operation against Vichy. With the disastrous end to the Greek debacle concluding only a week before, it is hardly surprising that Wavell remained unsympathetic to such arguments, which he regarded as the trademark call of politicians wielding power without knowledge. Wavell's argument had some validity. Churchill and Spears were politicians (albeit both with distinguished though short military records behind them) with a politician's demand for and expectation of quick action. Wavell by contrast was a career professional soldier, schooled in the difficult disciplines of careful analysis, evaluation and consideration of every relevant factor. It was against his every inclination to rush into ill-considered action, even under enormous pressure of the sort currently being applied by Churchill, de Gaulle, Catroux and Spears. It was clear that he felt propelled into a commitment for which his command was entirely unprepared. Churchill was dismissive of Wavell's fears, however, writing off his approach as low-risk, and comparing Wavell unfavourably, in a letter to his grandson, to merely 'a good chairman of a Tory Association'.[43]

To Churchill, whatever the setbacks of recent weeks, Wavell's attitude was wrong: now was not the time to withdraw into inaction. He told the Chiefs of Staff on 8 May:

> A supreme effort must be made to prevent the Germans getting a footing in Syria, with small forces, and then using Syria as a jumping-off ground for Air domination of Iraq and Persia. It is no use General Wavell being vexed at this disturbance on his eastern flanks. The Catroux Plan should certainly not be excluded.[44]

On the same day the Joint Planning Committee suggested to the Chiefs of Staff that the German airborne forces building up in Greece might be targeted on Syria and that an airborne and seaborne attack on Syria was a possibility. Churchill asserted to the Defence Committee that since military action was required and Britain had no troops herself, she would have to rely on the Free French to do the job. On 9 May Churchill signalled Wavell:

> You will no doubt realize the grievous danger of Syria being captured by a few thousand Germans transported by air. Our

information leads us to believe that Admiral Darlan has probably made some bargain to help the Germans to get in there. In face of your evident feeling of lack of resources we can see no other course open than to furnish General Catroux with the necessary transport and let him and his Free French do their best at the moment they deem suitable, the RAF acting against German landings. Any improvement you can make on this would be welcome.[45]

Churchill's frustration with Wavell began to manifest itself in discussions about his removal, a disgruntlement that quickly became an open secret in London. Dill told Kennedy (the Director of Military Operations) on 6 May that Churchill wanted to sack Wavell: in response Dill told Churchill 'to back him or sack him', which remained his advice throughout.[46] Wavell's reluctance to engage in Iraq in April and early May had infuriated Churchill: now, when he refused to give time to calls for action in Syria, amidst crises in Crete and the Western Desert, it was the last straw for the Prime Minister, and he resolved to remove him.

In the face of the advice he was receiving from Wavell regarding the impossibility of invading Syria and Lebanon with his present resources, Churchill ordered the War Office during the week beginning Sunday 11 May to produce detailed plans for the occupation of Syria. The task irritated Kennedy:

many hours were wasted on this because we did not possess detailed knowledge of the dispositions of the troops in Wavell's command. For some reason he would not ask Wavell, whose business it was, to produce the plan. By the end of the week everyone was worn out by this futile work.[47]

It was clear that Churchill was attempting to marshal his own arguments about what was and what was not possible, so as to be able to make a judgement independent of the advice being given by his own theatre C-in-C, in itself evidence of a breakdown in the trust necessary in such a relationship.

The arguments presented by Catroux and Spears on 5 May failed to move Wavell. His attitude remained unchanged: he did not have the wherewithal to support an invasion with the other pressures facing him and if it were left to the Free French it would end in a fratricidal bloodbath. In a fit of desperation de Gaulle washed his hands of the Levant and ordered Catroux to leave Cairo, an action which de Gaulle reversed only as a result of a direct plea from the Prime Minister. De Gaulle was furious that Wavell's reticence was unnecessarily delaying the concentration of Legentilhomme's division in Palestine, and gave vent to his frustration about the vain delusions the non–interventionists harboured about the true nature of the Vichy/German relationship:

> This delay will result in preventing any action of Free French in Syria in event of that now probable landing of Germans in that country from creating a favourable moral situation in French Army of Levant. To imagine that Dentz would be able to give orders to resist Germans is altogether an illusion. Dentz will not set himself up against Vichy and arrival of Germans in Syria, should that happen, will take place by agreed collaboration between Vichy and Germans.[48]

None of these public histrionics, no matter how valid, persuaded Wavell to move an inch, however. His stance appeared to be vindicated on 18 May when Catroux provided him with intelligence about Vichy's defensive plans that proved in time to be hopelessly optimistic. In his Despatch Wavell recorded:

> He [Catroux] declared that the road to Damascus was open and that it was urgently necessary . . . to send a force into Syria immediately. He was most insistent that I should issue orders to this effect. I insisted on verification of the Free French information before acting on it.[49]

Hard evidence regarding the limited support for the Free French cause within the Levantine garrison came from the testimony of Colonel Philibert Collet, commander of a unit of Circassian cavalry in Hauran province, who on 21/22 May escaped to Palestine with some 350 men to join the Free French forces. He told a story of severe Vichy repression of Gaullists and was lucky to escape with his life, given his well known anti–Vichy inclinations. Wavell was proved right in his suspicion of Catroux's information, although this error in his intelligence did not invalidate his belief that only intervention would serve to prevent a wholesale desertion of Vichy to the Germans in the Levant. In his memoirs written after the war Catroux maintained that Wavell did not understand the dire consequences of a German attack on Syria, believing that German plans were 'neither imminent nor mortal for Egypt'.[50] This was Spears' recollection of the conference on 19 May, when Wavell insisted that 'a German foothold in the Levant would not present an immediate or a mortal danger to Egypt.' Wavell was determined only to intervene if the whole or great majority of Vichy French forces came over to the British side, arguing that his task was to defend Egypt, not to invade the possessions of a neutral power. The evening before, as Spears recollected, Wavell lost his temper with him and Catroux:

> Working himself up into a controlled but red-faced temper, he repeated with dogged obstinacy the points he had so often made before; he would not accept advances by small bodies and would not send into Syria such troops as he had in Palestine; growing crosser and crosser, he declared that he would not be rushed. I noted with feelings akin to despair that Wavell was in fact determined to do nothing. 'The Iraqi revolt must first be quelled, then we can talk about Syria', he said; any excuse to avoid action. It seemed incredible to me that he could not see any danger in the Germans occupying Syria.[51]

However, the seriousness of German plans had become apparent in early May. On 12 May 1941 Mr John Gardner, the British Consul in Damascus, sent a brief message to London reporting that at least eight German planes had been sighted at a Damascus aerodrome that morning, and that thirteen had transited through Syria during the previous two days.[52] Later that day Gardner reported in shocked tones that the French High Commissioner had 'practically admitted' the presence of German planes and asserted that although 'his instructions did not provide for German occupation of Syria . . . if those orders came he would obey them.'[53] Despite the shortage of operational RAF planes in Palestine able to intercept the German aircraft, authority was granted on 14 May to mount attacks on them 'irrespective of possible effect of such action on relations with Vichy and Free French.'[54] Wasting no time, RAF aircraft launched immediate raids on Vichy aerodromes at Palmyra, Rayak and Mezze on 14 and 15 May. An infuriated Dentz countered feebly and unconvincingly on 16 May that German aircraft in Syria were there as a result of forced landings, and not because of any sinister intent. The pattern of activity during the following three weeks showed the hollowness of Dentz's protestations, as upwards of 120 German aircraft used Vichy airfields between mid-May and 6 June.

In the meantime Catroux and Wavell agreed a series of propaganda measures on 13 May to publicize to troops of the French Army in the Levant the German incursions into Syrian territory, in the hope that this information might persuade them to change sides.[55] Unknown to them at the time, the Vichy/Nazi nexus had become much more securely joined, following Darlan's talks with Berlin. Darlan signalled Dentz with the results of these discussions on 14 May:

> Franco-German conversations ended. The Government, under the presidency of the Marshal, have adopted the principle of collaboration with Germany. This collaboration does not imply a declaration of war against Britain, but the orders to resist with force any British attack are confirmed.[56]

In the days that followed, London kept up the pressure on Wavell to consider plans to counter-attack the now expected German occupation of Syria. Wavell laid out his strategic assumptions in a message sent to Churchill on 15 May. He included in it an expectation that, in addition to hard fighting in the Western Desert against Rommel, the Germans would attack Crete as a preliminary for the occupation of Syria, they would continue to support Iraq with air power and foment rebellion in Palestine, and German aircraft in the Dodecanese would mount heavy attacks on the canal area.[57] In his office in Cairo during the morning of Saturday 17 May Wavell gave the problem of the Levant considered thought and concluded that the only way to secure the country would be by a lightning attack on Beirut along the coast, supported strongly by the Royal Navy from the sea so that, in a daring *coup de main* attack, the citizens of Beirut would awake the next morning to find new management in charge. But he was adamant that allowing the Free French to lead such an operation was foolish. His despatch of troops to Iraq left no British troops available and so, *ergo*, an operation into the Levant was a non-starter at the present time. The same night he wrote to Dill:

> The only British force I could make available from Palestine has gone to Iraq, so Syrian commitment would involve using Free French or bringing troops from Egypt. I feel strongly that Free French without strong British support would be ineffective and likely to aggravate situation and that original action must be British, to be followed by Free French if successful . . .

After stressing that operations in Syria could only be mounted by denuding troops then fighting hard in the Western Desert or available for the defence of Egypt, Wavell concluded:

> I am having plans examined for force to Syria but I hope I shall not be landed with Syria unless absolutely essential. Any force I could send now would be painfully reminiscent of Jameson raid and might suffer similar fate.[58]

Wavell's mention of the Boer War, according to Ronald Lewin, touched a raw nerve with the Prime Minister, perhaps by suggesting that Churchill might be willing to oversee a desperate and poorly planned adventure, and reinforced Churchill's determination to replace Wavell when he had the opportunity.[59]

The struggle between Catroux and the interventionists and a doggedly sceptical Wavell reached its nadir on 19 May. Catroux had approached Wavell late on 18 May and demanded immediate action in Syria on the basis of new information from inside Syria that indicated a rapidly improving situation in the country. Not wishing to be rushed precipitately into action he might later regret, Wavell arranged a conference the following day, the day that saw the beginning of the battle for Crete. Those attending included Wavell, Lampson, Catroux, Tedder and Spears, de Gaulle being far away in Brazzaville. Catroux began by telling Wavell that he expected German occupation of Syria soon and that Dentz was preparing to withdraw his troops from Syria into Lebanon, thus making an advance on Damascus with even limited troops a feasible option. He asked that the Free French troops be moved in readiness to Palestine to prepare for operations in Syria.

Wavell remained unconvinced. Catroux's arguments were not new to him, and he articulated his reservations again, reporting them in detail in a letter to Dill later that afternoon. Wavell was certain that he had none of the resources necessary to mount a decisive Anglo-French invasion and that the logistical support required for Catroux's alternative plan of a Free French operation towards Damascus (requiring some 300 trucks and drivers) was also impossible. As Tedder recalled in his diary, 'Wavell took the general line that nothing but a large army would help us there. There was not one available at present and there was therefore nothing to be done.'[60] Wavell was also suspicious of Catroux's new information, and sent his Director of Intelligence to Jerusalem in an attempt to test it. In any case he had made his view abundantly plain in the past: Free French claims that Vichy 'resistance would not be great if we entered immediately with strong forces' were overstated, and that if an invasion of the Levant was to be authorized, a better way could be found for attacking Syria than a conventional advance north towards Damascus.[61]

When the conference concluded, those attending wasted no time in reporting their views of it to their respective ministries and headquarters in London. Lampson, Tedder and Wavell all turned to their signal pads and cipher machines. Lampson was persuaded by Catroux's arguments and reported to the Foreign Office his view that the time for an Anglo-French entry into Syria may well have arrived so as to capitalize on Vichy disarray and the information (soon proved to be false) that Dentz was withdrawing troops from Syria to Lebanon.[62] Tedder was equally convinced, confiding to his diary: 'Personally, I believe that two men and a boy could do *today* what it would require a division to do in a couple of months time.'[63] De Gaulle attempted to reinforce Catroux's confidence by an exhortation from Brazzaville on 20 May: 'Speed will determine the success or failure of the march on Damascus. You must head straight for Damascus, even if only with one lorried battalion. The psychological effect will do the rest.'[64]

Wavell then asked Dill to arbitrate on the Free French request and, although he declared that he was opposed to the idea, was nevertheless prepared to obey if the order was given, so long as it was accompanied by a declaration of independence for the people of the Levant. Wavell was undoubtedly aware of the prevailing pro-intervention attitude in London, and tried as forcefully as he could to present what he regarded to be a balanced contrary view. It is clear from a reading of the signals that travelled back and forth over these difficult days that he did so in a calm and considered manner. He insisted to Dill that he was as aware as the next man of the 'dangers of German intervention in Syria' (which can clearly be seen by his appreciation of 15 May) but that the issue of action depended entirely on resources, and these he simply did not have. To intervene with weak forces would be to invite disaster, a message he was now repeating to whoever would listen, and the Free French belief that Vichy resistance would quickly crumble was a grand delusion. The following day he reinforced his worries about potential action in Syria by warning Dill that an operation in Syria could only be achieved at the expense of the offensive he was planning for the Western Desert.

But the weight of support for intervention in Syria was by now overwhelming, despite Wavell's protestations about inadequate and non-existent resources. He was by now fighting a losing battle. Tedder had made his views clear at the 19 May conference and had written to the Chief of the Air Staff in London, Air Chief Marshal Charles Portal, the same afternoon.[65] He was increasingly concerned at what he regarded to be Wavell's over-trenchant and out-of-touch views. Reporting the outcome of the discussions he told Portal:

> while it was not for me to say what could or could not be done from the army point of view, I felt it necessary to emphasize that the longer it was before action was taken the more dangerous did the situation become from the air point of view. If the enemy was allowed to establish his forces in Syria, the threat to Egypt, particularly the canal and Suez, to Iraq and to our vital oil supplies from Abadan, became gravely increased. Our land communications from Palestine to Baghdad would become precarious since it would be impossible to provide effective air cover . . .
>
> . . . air action alone . . . could clearly not maintain this political effect [bombing of Syrian airfields], and since land action was not possible we had to face the probability of a considerable enemy air force operating from Syria.[66]

Tedder's diagnosis of the problem included a concern both with the quality of Wavell's leadership and with the ostrich-like fixation with Rommel and the Western Desert to the exclusion of all else. To Portal he explained:

> Again I feel whereas the Air Force and to a less extent the Navy have all their units in constant action which lash out in all directions whenever the chance occurs, the Army tends to proceed methodically and unimaginatively along approved text book lines, thereby missing opportunities which can only be seized if one is prepared to take chances.[67]

Tedder recorded Portal's reply:

> To Portal it seemed that the Army regarded German infiltration into Syria and Iraq as an unpleasant subject to be ignored, and reference to it by the Chiefs of Staff was considered an attempt to thrust a puking infant into the unwilling arms of busy men concerned with Africa. The state of German supplies in Libya, the anxiety and uncertainty of Rashid Ali, the possibility of considerable French and Arab sympathy in Syria, indicated valuable prizes which might be won by bold and rapid action which could not be taken by one Service alone.[68]

Tedder's correspondence that day with Portal reinforced repeated warnings from Spears, who had already told Churchill and Eden: 'We are surely not going to allow the Germans to take over Syria by default ... If the only troops available are the Free French, why not use them?'[69] So far as Lampson, Spears and Tedder were concerned, the time to act was now.

The political imperatives supporting action in the Levant were thus growing dramatically and in the process undermining the non-interventionist arguments Wavell had pursued for so long. On 19 May Eden, the Foreign Secretary, wrote to Churchill, adding his considerable weight to the argument:

> If the Germans are able to establish themselves in any strength in Syria and in Iraq, and succeed in organizing a part of the Arabs

against us, Turkey will be effectively surrounded . . . the only way to ensure that Turkey holds fast is to deal at the earliest possible moment with the situation in Syria and Iraq.[70]

The pressure for action in Syria was now unstoppable, the arguments for action being reinforced by the apparent effectiveness of the minimum force deployed in Iraq. On the basis of the premise that Catroux's information was correct, and that Vichy resistance was weakening, Dill warned Wavell in no uncertain terms on the evening of the 19th that it was now London's view that the time for action had arrived. The situation, he reported:

will certainly deteriorate if we do nothing, and we should soon have the Germans in complete control of Syria with all that that entails. In these circumstances it appears to us that there is no option but to improvise the largest force that you can manage without prejudice to the security of the Western Desert, and be prepared to move into Syria at the earliest possible date.[71]

Strangely, Wavell did not take Dill's hint. In his regular situation report to London on the morning of 20 May, Wavell, unaware of the intensity of the telegraphic communications between London and the Middle East during the previous afternoon and focused unsurprisingly on the hard fight now taking place in Crete, noted simply that 'advance into Syria is a major operation which could only be done by taking considerable risks in Western Desert and elsewhere and must take some time to stage.' He must have assumed that his arguments at the 19 May conference – that he did not have the resources necessary for such a venture – had carried the day. He was badly mistaken. At a meeting of the Defence Council at 1 p.m. on 20 May, and after consideration of the advice of Lampson, Spears, de Gaulle, Tedder, Eden and Dill, London's policy was finally agreed: Great Britain would take action in the Levant to forestall any action the Germans might take to use Syria and Lebanon as a base for an attack on British Palestine and Egypt. Churchill drafted the Committee's response, ordering Wavell to activate planning for an invasion:

Catroux's request that Free French troops should be moved at once to frontier opposite Deraa should be granted forthwith and that if situation appears favourable to him [Catroux] he should have authority to advance into Syria.

Defence Committee considered that opportunity is too good to miss and the advance must be regarded as a political coup, in which time is all-important, rather than as a military operation. You should do everything you can to give Catroux not only the lorries and drivers which he requires, but also as much military and air support as possible.

Defence Committee approved immediate issue of Free French declaration of independence of Syria and Lebanon to be backed by His Majesty's Government.[72]

This message took Wavell entirely unawares, despite Dill's unequivocal warning the previous day. Believing that his position had been undermined by special pleading from the Free French camp, he responded furiously:

All reports from trustworthy sources including Arab and Syrian agree that effect of action by Free French alone likely to be failure ...You must trust my judgment in this matter or relieve me of my command. I am not willing to accept that Catroux, de Gaulle or Spears should dictate action that is bound seriously to affect military situation in Middle East.[73]

To Wavell, the instructions that the operation was to be led by the Free French, whom he regarded as characterized by a dangerous combination of military weakness and over-optimism, and with resources that were non-existent, smacked of naivety. But it was apparent in the tone of his response that Wavell underestimated the strength of the support the Levantine adventure had attracted in London, and the poor odour in which he was now held personally by the Prime Minister. Churchill had talked about sacking Wavell for some weeks (at least as early as 6 May) and on the previous afternoon, 19 May, had told Dill that he had resolved to remove Wavell and to replace him with Auchinleck.[74] It is also clear that in a profound sense Wavell had misjudged and overestimated his own role in defining policy. His role was to carry out the military plans necessary to put into practical effect government policy, but his near-plenipotentiary status had served over time to blind him to the necessary distinctions between what London decided politically, and what he was obliged to do militarily to meet the determinants of policy made elsewhere. The lack of effective political–military co-ordination in the Middle East, which was not to be resolved until Lyttelton's appointment in July, was partly to blame for this state of affairs.

Stung by the insinuation that he was effectively undermining Wavell by receiving and listening to contrary reports from the Free French contingent (which was true), and irritated by Wavell's stubborn refusal to be swayed by the emotional rhetoric of intervention, but furious that clear political instructions from London were being disputed, Churchill sent Wavell a long and stern response, received in the early hours of 21 May:

> Nothing in Syria must detract at this moment from winning the battle of Crete, or in the Western Desert . . .
>
> There is no objection to your mingling British troops with Free French who are to enter Syria, but as you have clearly shown you have not the means to mount a regular military operation and as you were instructed yesterday all that can be done at present is to give best possible chances to . . . armed political inroad.
>
> You are wrong in supposing that policy arose out of any representations made by Free French leaders or General Spears. It arises entirely from view taken by those who have the supreme direction of the war and policy in all theatres. Our view is that if Germans can pick up Syria and Iraq with petty forces, tourists and local revolts we must not shrink from running equal small-scale military risks and facing the possible aggravation of political dangers from failure. For this decision we are of course taking full responsibility, and should you find yourself unwilling to give effect to it arrangements will be made to meet any wish you may express to be relieved of your command.[75]

Wavell admitted to Sir Miles Lampson that:

> he had had a rather bad night . . . as he had been pulled out of bed in the small hours to receive two telegrams, the first from our Prime Minister ordering him regardless of anything else to back

the Free French advance into Syria; and the second one from General de Gaulle 'ordering him' to do the same![76]

It is not difficult to sympathize with Wavell: the pressures on him were extraordinary. As Kennedy recalled, looking on from the inner sanctum of the War Office: 'Few Commanders-in-Chief in history have ever had such a row to hoe as Wavell at this moment.'[77] On the day he received this reprimand from Churchill, the German airborne attack on Crete was well underway, the situation in Iraq was still uncertain and in the Western Desert Churchill assumed that a recently arrived consignment of tanks, shipped at great risk and at the personal intervention of Churchill himself, would enable him to mount a rapid and decisive attack against Rommel. But Eden noted in his diary on 21 May:

> Wavell has misunderstood our attitude over Syria. We realise he cannot spare troops from Crete or Western Desert . . . but if the Free French are prepared to chance their arm in something like a Jameson Raid [picking up on Wavell's own observation of 17 May], we are in favour of letting them have a shot, *faute de mieux*. A political more than a military venture.[78]

Bowing to the inevitable, Wavell gave up the fight. He replied to Churchill's letter of 21 May later that same day* in considered tones, making no mention of resignation and explaining his attitude to Free French politicking over the question of Syria. It is clear that he was attempting to make up for his earlier angry outburst, and that he had already decided to bow to the Prime Minister's wishes and plan for the invasion of Syria and Lebanon as he had been instructed:

> Previous experience has made me somewhat sceptical of information on Syria from Free French sources, and Free French plans sometimes takes little account of realities . . . I felt that Free French views were perhaps being given undue weight and that I was being committed to unsound military action on unverified information at time when Crete, Iraq and Western Desert required

---

* Churchill records the date as 22 May, but that of course was when he received and read it.

178

all resources and attention. I was actually doing everything I could to ascertain real situation and preparing to take advantage of opportunity if one existed . . .

This Syrian business is disquieting since German air force established in Syria are closer to the canal and Suez than they would be at Mersa Matruh. The [Vichy] French seem now wholly committed to the Germans. I am moving reinforcements to Palestine [7 Australian Division], after full discussion with Cunningham, Tedder and Blamey,* because we feel we must be prepared for action against Syria, and weak action is useless . . .

Whole position in Middle East is at present governed mainly by air power and bases. Enemy air bases in Greece make our hold of Crete precarious, and enemy air bases in Cyrenaica, Crete, Cyprus, and Syria would make our hold on Egypt difficult. The object of the Army must be to force the enemy in Cyrenaica as far west as possible, to try to keep him from establishing himself in Syria, and to hang on to Crete and Cyprus . . . I know you realise all this and are making every effort to provide requirements, and we are doing our best to secure Middle East. We have some difficult months ahead, but will not lose heart.[79]

Churchill's comment in his *The Second World War* was crafted in masterly understatement: 'Wavell showed by his reply that he fully understood.'[80] Wavell's outburst to the Prime Minister about the influence in London of the Free French lobbyists like de Gaulle and Spears revealed a further problem in the psychology of command in the Middle East at the time. This was the excessive loyalty shown by many subordinates towards their superiors and a general failure to challenge accepted norms and orthodoxies. Around Wavell had developed, because of his almost iconic stature, a cult of obedience that brooked no dissension with his views. In these pre-Monty days the British public trusted Wavell as no other senior military personality, and he was widely regarded as the greatest living British general of the time. This acted to place a psychological barrier between him and the objectivity of his staff. Those unfortunate military minds that succumb to such moral and intellectual numbness perceive their attitude not as

* Commander of the Australian forces, and newly appointed deputy to Wavell.

sycophancy but as loyalty. The result was a weak staff, for whom disagreement within the close confines of the military family savoured of infidelity.[81] As Spears frustratedly let fly in his diary after a difficult meeting on 20 May:

> I have never felt so completely stonewalled or met with a more total incomprehension of the psychological aspects of a problem. To hold different ideas from the Commander-in-Chief is considered to be an extreme act of disloyalty which no one pretending to be an officer and a gentleman should be capable of.[82]

Wavell's change of position was entirely in keeping with his commitment to Dill on 19 May that if he were ordered to do so he would do as he was told. These orders came unequivocally, although unexpectedly, from the Prime Minister and Defence Committee on 21 May and Wavell obeyed with an alacrity that surprised some in London. The irony of this *volte-face* was revealed on 22 May when it transpired that the original information upon which Catroux had based his calls for immediate action in Syria was false, that Dentz was reinforcing the Syrian borders rather than withdrawing and that Vichy troops would almost certainly fight, should Britain and Free France attack.[83]

Indeed, Vichy determination to resist a British attack was hardening. On 21 May Germany and France ratified their agreement regarding co-operation in the Levant, and in view of the military action taken by the RAF against Syria also agreed that France could ship weapons from France to the Levant to strengthen their defences. To maintain secrecy Dentz proposed landing these troops and equipment at Chekka Bay, between Beirut and Tripoli. Ruthless weeding of pro-British or Gaullist officers took place, with many sent back to France in chains. The army commander, General Fougère (replaced on 15 May 1941 by General de Verdilhac) had even embarrassed Dentz by his violent Anglophobia, delivering anti-British addresses to his troops, referring to Britain 'as the historic enemy of France since the time of Joan of Arc' and claiming that '*l'Allemagne . . . désirait loyalement collaborer avec la France.*'[84] At the same time 5,000 Syrian volunteers, offered £10 a month by the Germans, but recruited and trained by the French, were trucked to fight the British in Iraq.[85] In the light of this information

Wavell's original reticence at last seemed entirely vindicated but he now appeared completely to accept the Prime Minister's arguments and began to prepare for war.

Churchill was mollified by Wavell's acquiescence, and wrote to his military Commander-in-Chief two days later:

> It is your views that weigh with us and not those of Free French. You had better have de Gaulle close to you. Let me know if I can help you with him. We cannot have Crete battle spoiled for the sake of Syria. Therefore, inferior methods may be the only ones open at the moment.[86]

6

Damascus

On 25 May, following his placatory visit to meet Auchinleck at Basra to discuss Iraq, Wavell outlined his plan for the Levantine offensive to London, explaining that he had given the task to 'Jumbo' Wilson, the newly appointed GOC Palestine. Dill agreed these plans on 28 May[1] and Wavell issued Wilson with his instructions on 31 May. The forces at Wilson's disposal were severely limited, as apart from the reduced numbers of troops available because of losses in Crete and commitments in both Iraq and the Western Desert, the arsenal was virtually bare of aircraft, tanks, artillery and transport. They comprised five weak infantry brigades: two Australian, one Indian and two Free French. These were 21 and 24 Australian Brigades of Major General John Lavarack's untried 7 Australian Division (the third brigade was in Tobruk), Brigadier Wilfred Lloyd's 5 Indian Brigade (from 4 Indian Division), recently arrived from operations in Eritrea, and Major General Legentilhomme's six infantry battalions in the Free French division. There was pitifully little armour, a fraction of the artillery required and even less anti-tank artillery. For cavalry, horsed remnants of Major General Clark's 1 Cavalry Division were available from Palestine, consisting of British Yeomanry units,* an Armoured Car Squadron of the Royal Dragoons and the impoverished Cavalry Regiment of the 6 Australian Division, equipped with Bren gun

---

* The Cheshire Yeomanry, Scots Greys, North Somerset Yeomanry, Royal Wiltshire Yeomanry, Warwickshire Yeomanry, Staffordshire Yeomanry and Yorkshire Dragoons.

carriers and obsolescent tanks. Finally, an Army Commando Regiment from Cyprus – 'C' Battalion of the Special Service Brigade – was provided for coastal raiding duties. For a major attack of the kind envisaged, these troop levels were pitiful. By contrast, Wavell had calculated that he needed at least eighteen battalions in two fully equipped divisions (i.e. six full-strength infantry brigades each of three battalions), together with their associated artillery and an armoured brigade for the job.

Responsibility for operations in the Vichy Army of the Levant was vested in General de Verdilhac, recently released as a prisoner of war of the Germans and an exceptionally talented soldier. Although Vichy forces in Syria and Lebanon totalled some twenty-nine infantry battalions (eleven of which were locally recruited Syrians, Lebanese and Circassians, many of whom, whatever their loyalty to France, would fight for whoever paid them*), only some twenty battalions, two armoured regiments and assorted colonial cavalry units were available to repulse an invasion from Palestine and Transjordan in June 1941. Facing the Allied troops on the coast were three battalions of mixed French–Senegalese troops of the *24e Régiment Mixte Colonial*. Far to the north and facing off possible Turkish intervention at Homs were the four battalions of the *6e Régiment de la Légion*. The remaining thirteen infantry battalions were colonial *Tirailleurs*, six from Algeria (the *22e* and *29e Algériens*), three from Tunisia (the *16e Tunisiens)*, one Moroccan (*1er Marocains*) and three Senegalese (*17e Sénégalais*). However, in comparison to Wilson's poverty-stricken force, de Verdilhac boasted one hundred and twenty guns in three *Légion* artillery regiments and ninety Renault 35 tanks in two armoured regiments, the *6e* and *7e Chasseurs d'Afrique*. The cavalry units were North African *Spahis*, some in trucks, others on horseback.

For support in the air Tedder was able to rustle together two bomber squadrons (one based in Palestine and the other at RAF Habbaniya) and two-and-a-half squadrons of fighters.† Across the whole theatre of war he had but two hundred and fifty aircraft, of which at least fifty were obsolescent machines. In Syria the Vichy French began the war

---

* Of the 35,000 troops available only some 8,000 were actually French.

† 80 Squadron (Hurricanes), 3 Squadron Royal Australian Air Force (Tomahawks), 'X' Flight (Lysanders), 11 and 84 Squadrons (Blenheims) plus a flight of 208 Squadron (also Hurricanes).

with some ninety-two aircraft but during the engagement acquired a further sixty-six, mostly from North Africa. This paucity of resources alarmed the War Office, who warned Wavell and Tedder on 6 June that more aircraft needed somehow to be made available for the Levantine offensive – *Operation Exporter* – if only for the beginning of the campaign, so as to provide much needed balance to the weakness of the ground forces to be deployed. They suggested that some aircraft allocated to the *Battleaxe* offensive in the Western Desert be stationed in Palestine, so that they could support either operation. 'Loss of position and prestige if Vichy Frenchmen hold Syria for the Axis against us would be serious', the message added, somewhat needlessly.[2] Tedder replied briefly the following day, the day before the operation was launched, ruling out London's suggestion, and confirming that *Exporter* amounted to no more or less than those forces highlighted in his previous report.[3] There the matter ended.

Only at sea were the Allies stronger than the Vichy forces, despite the catastrophic losses off Greece and Crete.* Admiral Cunningham provided a force of eight cruisers and destroyers (increasing to five cruisers and eight destroyers) to bombard Vichy French shore defences and prevent French warships in Beirut from interfering with the advance along the coast.

Wilson decided to advance on three separate fronts, dividing his available forces into three separate columns like the prongs of a fork, with three separate objectives.[4] His idea was to achieve a rapid and decisive advance by these discrete columns against Damascus, Beirut and Rayak, perhaps expecting that the Vichy defenders would feel themselves overwhelmed by attacks on more than one axis of advance. Once Beirut had been captured, the coastal advance would continue north to capture Tripoli.[5]

The first advance would take place along the coast towards Beirut, following the main road north. It was the most obvious line of attack. Although it would be easy to defend with its multitudinous defiles and re-entrants, over which the bridges could easily be blown and every mountain corner defended, it was also the shortest route and Vichy positions could be outflanked from the sea, from where also the Royal

---

* Admiral Cunningham's forces were reduced to two battleships, three cruisers and seventeen destroyers.

Navy could provide gunfire support and the 480-strong Special Service Brigade could launch raids in conjunction with the advancing land forces. Three strong defensive positions guarded the approach to Beirut. The first was at the Litani River, which boasted concrete strong points and gun emplacements. The second covered the town of Sidon fifteen miles to the north, where artillery was hidden in the hills covering the road. The third was at the Damour River, twelve miles south of Beirut, where the northern side is rocky and advantageous to the defender.

The second prong of the fork consisted of an advance between the Lebanon and the Ante-Lebanon ranges, through the rich heart of the Bekaa Valley some twenty-five miles to the east across the Lebanese mountains in a line running due north from Merjayoun to Rayak. The Lebanon range rose steeply from the coastal plain to some 10,000 feet, and was separated from the 8,000-feet-high Ante-Lebanon range – at the southern part of which lay the mighty Mount Hermon, dominating the region at 9,000 feet – by the lush fields and fruit groves of the Bekaa Valley, through which flowed the Litani River. To block the entrance to this key strategic route, General de Verdilhac had placed forces at both Khiam and Merjayoun.

Lavarack was given responsibility for these two avenues of attack. To Brigadier J.E.S. Stevens 21 Australian Brigade,* reinforced with a small number of tanks, armoured cars and horsed cavalry, he gave responsibility for the advance along the coast. Two roads dominated this sector. In addition to the vulnerable coastal road, a further road led from Metulla on the Palestine border through the hills due north to Zahle, the Bekaa Plain and thence to Rayak. The road was good to Merjayoun but thereafter travelled through the narrow gorge of the Litani River. Lavarack gave responsibility for the right hand sector to Brigadier A.R.B. Cox's 25 Australian Brigade.† The two Australian brigades could provide each other with a degree of mutual support, but this would not be possible for the other avenues of advance, where columns would of necessity have to operate largely independently.

Further to the east and in the third prong, Wilson ordered an advance through the relatively open country that lies to the left of the volcanic

* 2/14 Battalion, 2/16 Battalion plus the Cheshire Yeomanry.

† 2/31 Battalion, 2/25 Battalion, 2/33 Battalion plus 'Todforce' (a combined Scots Greys and Staffordshire Yeomanry force in trucks).

expanse of the Jebel Druze and which runs directly from Deraa to the Syrian capital, Damascus. Many desert tracks led to Damascus, which meant that it should be easy to approach. This task was allocated to Lloyd's 5 Indian Brigade,* which would secure the key towns in the south, whilst the Free French Division under Legentilhomme would advance through them to threaten Damascus. Lloyd's first task was to secure intact the railway east of the Jordan as far as Deraa and thereafter to create a defensive line between Deraa, Sheikh Meskine and Ezraa to protect the right flank of the advance from attacks emanating from the Jebel Druze. To reduce this risk, the virulently anti-French Druze were to be cultivated politically, and encouraged to rebel, supported with arms and by irregular troops, one of whom was the explorer Wilfred Thesiger, who had received recent experience in guerrilla work with Orde Wingate in Eritrea. Legentilhomme and Lloyd were to advance on Damascus, first capturing Kissoue, which, eight miles south of the city, commanded the high ground above two principal roads, and was strongly defended.

Protection on the left flank of the right-hand prong would be provided by Colonel Collet and his Circassians, based on Fiq, together with a squadron of *Spahis* in trucks, with a collection of light tanks and armoured cars and two guns. A further group (1 Battalion Royal Fusiliers, less a company) with an Australian artillery battery would cross the Jordan at Jisr Benett Yacoub† to secure Kuneitra, thirteen miles further on.

But it was an extremely poor plan. *Operation Exporter's* main disadvantage was that it provided no single point of main effort, endowed with all the strength that Wilson could muster. Instead, Wilson's limited strength was divided across three separate thrusts, each heading for different targets. By attacking in three fronts in the west at once, he failed to be sufficiently strong at any one place. This immediately nullified the extraordinary expectation that both Beirut and Damascus would be reached, and seized, on Day One of the operation, and seemingly ignored the nature of the terrain, which favoured the defenders in virtually every respect.[6] The plan lacked any pretence of subtlety or intelligence. The possibility of attracting and

---

* 3/1 Punjab Regiment, 4/6 Rajputana Rifles and 1 Battalion The Royal Fusiliers.
† Bridge of the Daughters of Jacob.

then holding French attention around Deraa, whilst then punching hard with the remainder of his strength for Beirut, or vice versa in a dramatic thrust for Damascus, or indeed of driving hard up the middle through the Bekaa Valley, thus splitting Beirut off from Damascus, seemed to be too difficult for Wilson and his planning team. The hapless Military Attaché in Ankara found himself bombarded with incredulous queries about British strategy from Turkish officers who knew Syria better than almost anybody else. 'Why were there no mobile columns? Why were we attacking in almost equal strength on three fronts? Why, above all, had we not concentrated on breaking through in the Bekaa?'[7] He had no answer to these questions. The strategic and tactical impoverishment of the British military mind at work in the planning of *Operation Exporter* provided no answers, only an embarrassing silence.

Inexplicably, Wilson also failed to exploit the forces now available in Iraq to threaten a simultaneous attack on Syria from the south–east and east. These failings prompted Spears to comment caustically that the campaign was only 'useful to the historian as providing the best possible example of how a campaign should not be conducted.'[8] It appears that Wavell delegated responsibility for authorizing Wilson's plan to his Australian deputy, General Blamey, reporting to Churchill on 4 June that Blamey 'thinks plan is good'.[9] The reality was far different, however. The plan was poor and could easily have been improved upon by schoolboys with toy soldiers. As de Verdilhac soon realized, the British plan was in fact childish, but was rescued from failure by the determined valour of many of the British, Australian, Free French and Indian troops engaged, and the failure of de Verdilhac's own forces fully to exploit the opportunities British weakness provided.

Wilson undoubtedly expected that the invasion would be a walk-over. A general belief persisted, which Wilson shared (although not by Wavell), that Vichy forces would only fight briefly, for the sake of their military 'honour', before surrendering. In order to persuade them to surrender, Wilson ordered each advance to be preceded by a shower of leaflets, French-speaking officers were to accompany forward units and to advance under cover of a white flag, berets and soft hats were to be worn instead of steel helmets to show peaceful intent (an order remarked on with some mordancy by the troops) 'and then wait for the magic to happen'.[10] Not everyone in the British camp was as sanguine as Wilson about the ease of the task ahead. On 27 May Kennedy was asked by Dill to prepare briefing notes for the Defence Committee that evening. Dill was deeply depressed at this time, having remarked to Kennedy a few days earlier: 'Do you realize we are fighting for our lives now?' Kennedy agreed, replying that 'if the Germans were to continue to concentrate their efforts on the Middle East, we should soon have to reckon with the possibility of not being able to hold it.'[11] Their advice, therefore, to the Defence Committee was: 'Anything that can be done to occupy Syria, before the Germans are established there, should be done.' There was no choice but to act, and to do so quickly. The whole of the Middle East was at stake.[12]

Wavell, still worried about the prospect of fierce Vichy resistance, warned Churchill on 5 June that success was 'problematical' and that 'the whole enterprise might founder if the French resisted firmly.'[13] He had a ready audience for this kind of despondency in London. Sir Alexander Cadogan, the permanent head of the Foreign Office, asked a joint meeting of military and diplomatic advisers on 4 June: 'Why – a week before your effort in N Africa – do you blunder into a war with Vichy?'[14] Anthony Eden attended this meeting, and recorded:

> We discussed Syria, pros and cons. There was much anxiety. Maybe we are too late for surprise and too early in the sense that our forces are not large. Against this must be set the facts that it must be some time, a month at least, before our forces can be larger; meanwhile French will have time to consolidate, get their breath and German help. Vichy has sold out . . . A useful discussion, the general consensus being in the end in favour of going ahead with what must be a gamble.[15]

Keen to keep the pressure on Wavell and to encourage him to examine every opportunity to maximize the power of his blow against the Levant, Churchill bombarded him relentlessly with requests for information and produced a steady flow of bright ideas for Wavell's consideration. Thus, on 3 June, Wavell received the following:

> Please telegraph exactly what ground and Air forces you are using for 'Exporter.' What are you doing with the Poles? It seems important to use and demonstrate as much Air power as possible

at the very outset, and even the older machines may play their part as they did so well in Iraq.[16]

Wavell patiently explained the structure of the force destined for *Operation Exporter* in a long telegram on the following day, noting that the Polish Brigade was at Mersa Matruh in the Western Desert facing Rommel, that the air forces were limited because of 'heavy losses in Crete' and commenting that the 'Force is not anything like as large as desirable and operation is obviously in nature of a gamble, dependent on attitude of Vichy French.'[17]

French collaboration with Germany over Iraq made London especially fearful regarding Germany gaining access to Iraqi oil through the pipeline to Tripoli. On 30 May Wavell was asked by London to consider the destruction of T1, T2, T3 and T4 to prevent any Iraqi oil leaking into German hands through Syria.[18] This fear was repeated the following week when Cairo was told unequivocally:

1. Defence Committee regard denial of Iraq oil to Germany as of paramount importance. Political or other considerations cannot be allowed to delay immediate action being taken when orders are received from here.
2. Preparations should be pressed on for greatest possible destruction of Kirkuk and Mosul oil fields and pipelines to Tripoli and Haifa. In making preparations no regard need to be had for the future of the fields.[19]

Wavell replied a week later confirming that arrangements for the destruction not only of the pipelines but also of the oil refineries in northern Iraq were in place should they be required.[20] The depth of London's concern about these denial preparations was indicated by the Chiefs of Staff's reply to Wavell on 10 June. This emphasized that the Iraqi refinery at Alwand was to be destroyed in the event that it was likely to become of use to the enemy, as was the Naft Khaneh oilfield, both in northern Iraq. At this juncture it was also admitted that the neighbouring Iranian oilfield of Naft-i-Shah would also need to be destroyed, but that this would be achieved using means other than military force, as an attack would obviously violate Iranian neutrality: 'most secret instructions have already been sent to local officials of the

Anglo-Iranian Oil Company to deal with this problem to the best of their ability in the event of necessity.' The orders were unequivocal: 'In no circumstances must the risk be accepted of any oil resources falling intact into enemy hands.'[21]

The BBC announced the British invasion of Lebanon and Syria on the morning of Sunday 8 June 1941:

> the Vichy Government, in pursuance of their policy of collaboration with the Axis Powers, have placed the air bases in Syria and the Lebanon at the disposal of Germany and Italy and have supplied war material to the rebel forces in Iraq. German infiltration into Syria has begun and the Vichy Government are continuing to take measures whose effect must be to bring Syria and the Lebanon under full German control.
>
> His Majesty's Government could not be expected to tolerate such actions, which go far beyond anything laid down in the terms of the French Armistice and are in flagrant conflict with the recent declaration of Marshal Pétain that honour forbade France to undertake anything against her former allies.
>
> Free French troops have, therefore, with the support of Imperial forces, entered Syria and the Lebanon at an early hour this morning.

On the same day Catroux made his own announcement by radio, declaring himself to his Levantine listeners as France's 'Delegate-General and Plenipotentiary' (rather than simply Dentz's replacement as High Commissioner, as this would have smacked of mandatory succession, which the British were keen to avoid):

> I am abolishing the mandate, and proclaim you free and independent. You are therefore and henceforth sovereign and independent peoples. Your sovereign and independent states will be guaranteed by a treaty which will also define our mutual relations.[22]

Spears revived the idea of independence for the Levantines, which had been first broached in February 1941, on 17 May, when he sent a message to London advocating that Great Britain and Free France make a solemn guarantee of absolute independence for the Levant states. The aim was to drive a wedge between Free France and Vichy and to rally the Arabs to the Allied cause. To de Gaulle, however, such an idea was an effrontery. He rejected the idea of a joint declaration, on the basis that Britain had no right to interfere in French political matters, interpreting British involvement to be sinister evidence of a British plan to seize the Levant for herself. From Great Britain's perspective, it was important to have such a declaration so as to secure the support of the Levantine Arabs, and to gain some form of commitment from de Gaulle about the future status of the mandate in post-Vichy France. Catroux had agreed the statement as early as 20 May. A straightforward, apolitical and uncomplicated soldier possessing none of de Gaulle's political skills, imperial fire, passion and capacity for intrigue, Catroux undoubtedly regarded the long-term survival of the French mandate in the Levant to be meaningless in the circumstances and that the only object of the present was the removal of Dentz's German-leaning regime. Eventually, de Gaulle acquiesced, but time was to show that he never intended to carry out this promise.

Confounding many British expectations, the announcement did nothing but stiffen the resolve of the defenders. The Vichy commanders – Dentz and de Verdilhac – were in no mood to consider precipitate surrender. There were varying motives for this resistance. Some, like Dentz, undoubtedly harboured passionate anti-British sentiments, whereas other professional soldiers were probably motivated less by idealism than by conceptions of military honour, despite the totalitarian barbarism that had invaded their homeland: 'Did the British think that French prestige had sunk so low that the Army of the Levant would surrender without a fight to three brigades and a handful of rebels?'[23] Their duty lay with defending the pride of the French Army. Once Vichy defenders realized just how weak the British attacks actually were, the more determined they became to resist, so as not to be seen to surrender peremptorily and with their soldierly 'honour' intact. Brigadier Freddie de Guingand complained: 'Had we been able to commence with a really powerful punch, it looks as if the French would have capitulated at an early date. As it was, they took heart from the weakness of our attack.'[24] Equally, there were those for whom obedience was paramount: the government in Vichy represented

France, and they would obey her without argument. Followers of de Gaulle, in this perspective, were traitors to France and their appearance alongside the British in the invasion of French mandated territory – as sacred as that of Mother France herself – was an outrage that encouraged resistance. Thus, when the three-pronged British advance began it soon became clear that whilst chivalrous, Wilson's instructions were not martial, costing the leading troops the element of tactical surprise and with it unnecessary casualties – and perversely reinforcing Vichy determination to resist.

Wavell had fought hard to resist a premature advance into Syria, but by 8 June such a long time had elapsed since the first intrusion of *Luftwaffe* forces into the country that by the time the offensive was launched most German troops had in fact left the country (the last leaving on 12 July), all but removing the original justification for intervention. The rationale for war still remained valid, namely the need to prevent German domination of the Levant, but a plausible reason for invasion so as to win over wavering Vichy affections had by now entirely disappeared. Consequently, the British claim to be intervening to repel the German invaders sounded suspiciously hollow: many Vichy troops instead suspected that the devious designs of perfidious Albion were at play, a fact that led them to resist more fervently the British attack when it came.

At the outset of the campaign Churchill found it hard to judge what the Vichy response would be. He wrote to his son Randolph, then serving in Egypt, on 8 June: 'We are waiting with much interest to know what fortunes have attended our entry into Syria. No one can tell which way the Vichy French cat will jump, and how far the consequences of this action will extend.'[25] Despite the publicity, the obvious invasion routes and the widespread speculation in the region as to the imminence of an offensive, the British attack made good progress on 8 June. The first troops to cross the Lebanese border along the coast were a hastily assembled band of Palestinian Jewish volunteers. On 16 February 1941 a group of Jewish agitators had been released from a British prison in Acre. One of these young men, a second-generation immigrant farmer by the name of Moshe Dayan, promptly joined the ranks of his persecutors by volunteering to fight for the British against the Germans and their Vichy collaborators. Formed into a small unit of which he was made the commander, he was charged, when the invasion began, with leading a small party across the Lebanese border to the area of Iskanderun, and seizing by *coup de main* the bridges that carried the main coastal road north to Beirut. With the scantiest of training and a mere thirteen revolvers with fifteen rounds apiece between them, Dayan and his thirty Jewish comrades spent the week before the invasion reconnoitring routes for vehicles through the Syrian hills. Not one of them knew Syria and they had no maps but they were determined above all to prove to their hesitant British overseers that they were worthy of the trust placed in them. They were desperate to do anything to fight back against the forces of fascism that were devouring their people across Europe. During these forays across the border they bumped into smugglers and watchmen but seemed not to raise the suspicions of the Vichy French.

On the night of 7 June, the day before the invasion proper, Dayan's group of thirty enthusiasts crossed the border in the company of a small group of Australians from 21 Australian Brigade, who had arrived in the area only that afternoon.* The whole force boasted one machine gun, a Thompson sub-machine gun, a few rifles, revolvers and grenades. Following a four-hour march through the mountains in the light of a full moon, Dayan's commandos reached and secured the bridges without any alarm being given. He recalled that it was an anti-climax. Moving then to secure a nearby Vichy police station, they found themselves with a stiff fight on their hands. The police station was successfully stormed, but the presence of the raiders attracted every Frenchman in the vicinity and soon a heavy fire-fight ensued, during which the young Dayan was struck in the eye by a fragment of glass from his binoculars, driven in by a Vichy bullet. Australian troops of 2/14 Battalion, having crossed the border later that morning, relieved the beleaguered commandos in the early evening, and the wounded Dayan was evacuated to Haifa by nightfall. He survived, but lost his eye.[26] The raiding party secured Iskanderun and captured two armoured cars, other vehicles, machine and anti-tank guns and thirty-one horses. It turned out that Dayan's commandos had been directed to the wrong place: the bridges that he had meant to capture had in fact already been destroyed by Vichy demolitions.

Troops nevertheless advanced on foot and joined their compatriots at Iskanderun before advancing towards Tyre. The 2/14 Battalion were

* The total force numbered forty-two men.

joined by a mixed force called 'Doncol' composed of the 2/16 Battalion and the Cheshire Yeomanry on horses, who moved through the hills to the east, securing Tibnine. The 2/16 Battalion then approached Tyre from the east, arriving by early afternoon, after which, leaving the troops approaching along the coast road to capture the town, it moved up to the Litani River, where it was stopped by roadblocks and machine guns. Meanwhile, the Cheshire Yeomanry pushed through in hilly country to reach the village of Srifa.

Whilst Dayan's Jewish commandos were fighting for their lives at Iskanderun, 25 Australian Brigade on Lavarack's right flank crossed the frontier near Metulla and made for Merjayoun. Opposition was fierce. In the west 2/33 Battalion was checked at the hill fort of Khiam and 2/31 Battalion failed to secure Merjayoun, an attack on the town failing, under heavy mortar, machine-gun and anti-tank fire, in which two of the three Australian tanks were knocked out.

The right-hand prong, Lloyd's 5 Indian Brigade, advanced from Irbid in the darkness, parties attacking the bridges at Tel Chehab to the west of Deraa and Nassib to the east. The former was taken successfully, but the latter was not, troops of the Transjordanian Frontier Force displaying poor fire-discipline by engaging the bridge with rifle fire in the dark at 400 yards, at which point the French blew the bridge. The defenders at Deraa at first refused to surrender, but did so following a short bombardment by artillery and an assault by 3/1 Punjab. The Rajputana Rifles, after a successful skirmish in which they captured four Vichy armoured cars, mounted a frontal assault over flat ground against the village of Sheikh Meskine at 3 p.m. Against well-sited machine guns the attack did not succeed. The tactics used were dismal, perhaps reflective of the expectation that the Vichy defenders would surrender quickly. The high ground to the west was occupied in preparation for another assault the following day, but during the night the Vichy forces melted away and both Sheikh Meskine and Ezraa were occupied on 9 June.

To the left of Lloyd's Indian Brigade Colonel Collet's group of Circassian cavalry, truck-borne *Spahis* and twelve light tanks took Fiq and then moved on to occupy Naoua before dusk. *Groupement Collet* camped that night close to the Rajputana Rifles.

On the extreme left of Lloyd's brigade the 1 Royal Fusiliers pushed their way to Kuneitra by mid-morning. After some parley with the defenders the Vichy decided to retain their honour by fighting, and despite supporting fire by 25-pounders the battalion was unable to break into the town. However, during that night the Vichy forces evacuated the fort and the Fusiliers occupied it on the morning of 9 June. Thus, after being held up against all expectations on the evening of 8 June, Lloyd's three battalions had all achieved their objectives by midday on 9 June – the Punjabis at Deraa, the Fusiliers at Kuneitra and the Rajputanas at Sheikh Meskine. Rather than fight forward with isolated garrisons, the Vichy commander responsible for the Damascus front, General Delhomme, decided to withdraw his troops to a defence line between Sassa and Kiswe, where he deployed his three *Tirailleur* battalions. Whilst this had the effect of leaving the Jebel Druze vulnerable to British attack, it also provided Lloyd and Legentilhomme with a long right flank and was undoubtedly the correct thing for Delhomme to do.

Most British air activity on 8 June was taken up with dropping leaflets, although the airfields at Rayak and Mezze were attacked, as were oil storage tanks at Beirut. However, at sea the Royal Navy found that the enemy were very aggressive, and lost two Fulmars with others damaged.

After a day of mixed fortunes, during which it became clear that the Vichy defenders intended to stand and fight where they could, Monday 9 June saw a resumption of heavy fighting in all three areas of the advance. An attack by 21 Australian Brigade on the defences along the Litani was due to take place on Monday, but the plan came unstitched from the start. The commando battalion found itself unable to land on 8 June because a heavy surf was running, and was launched instead a day later, but by this time it had lost the essential element of surprise. Two French Colonial battalions occupied concrete pillboxes on the ridge north of the Litani River, which were to be attacked by the commandos from the sea whilst the Australians pushed over the river. The commandos, however, ran into fierce opposition. One group landed short of the Litani amongst the Australians, two landing-craft were lost at sea, their Commanding Officer was killed and the remainder, who managed to reach their first objective, were fought to a standstill. With their Commanding Officer dead, heavy casualties and no remaining ammunition, the remnants were forced to surrender early on 10 June. The commando lost a quarter of its strength and failed to achieve its objective. Beach assaults by raiding parties of this kind were at an early stage in their gestation during the war, and mistakes were common. Some days earlier a force of Palestinian Jews under British command in a gunboat had attempted a raid on the oil refinery at Tripoli, but the Vichy defenders had been alerted by an earlier air attack, and the raiders were never seen again. On this occasion, landing troops into the teeth of a well-defended beach was a serious mistake, especially once surprise had been lost.

Despite the failure and decimation of the commandos, a small group of Australians managed to cross the Litani after heavy fighting on 9 June and reinforcements moved across the river that afternoon. Fighting continued during the night but by dawn on 10 June the French defence of the Litani had been broken and Australian engineers erected a pontoon bridge over the one that the French had demolished.

The two other prongs during Monday 9 June fared better. The French withdrew from the fort at Khiam after a battering by Australian artillery, and further to the right Legentilhomme's Free French division made its way through the Rajputanas at Sheikh Meskine in some 200 requisitioned trucks and buses during that evening to the village of Sanamein, some thirty miles short of the great prize of Damascus.

But the day also saw an ominous sign: Vichy domination of the air, without a single RAF aircraft to be seen in support of the troops on the ground. By some dysfunctional logic the three Services fought separate land, sea and air battles during the campaign. The RAF concentrated not on supporting the ground advance but in attacking 'strategic' targets across Lebanon and Syria such as airfields, barracks and Vichy reinforcements arriving by sea, rather than tactical tasks related to the advance on land. RAF policy for the campaign, designed by D'Albiac and agreed by Tedder in a planning session in Cairo on 3 June, stressed support to the Royal Navy and strategic ground targets within Lebanon and Syria, including oil storage facilities and airfields. This was necessary and important. The Royal Navy could not operate in the Mediterranean without air cover, as a number of tragedies around Crete had shown. Equally, it was important to restrict the ability of the Vichy Air Force to use its bases: this policy was very successful, some 140 sorties destroying 36 aircraft and damaging a further 107.[27] The Vichy air commander, General Jeannequin, later admitted that the RAF attacks on Vichy airfields severely restricted his freedom to act, eventually forcing him to base his aircraft at Aleppo.[28]

This policy, however, had direct and unfortunate consequences and was, on reflection, a mistake. The doctrine of 'strategic' targeting meant that the war could easily have been lost through the defeat of the primary offensive on land even if every fuel dump, airfield and other strategic target had been found and destroyed. It meant also that the land advance – which ultimately would put a stranglehold on Damascus and Beirut – had to be conducted without the same sort of intimate air support the French provided to their own troops. This made the advance very much longer and more difficult than it needed to be. Tedder was aware of the problem. At a regular meeting with the other Commanders-in-Chief on 13 June, meetings which he described frustratingly as 'amiable and vague',[29] Tedder stated what was increasingly obvious to all observers, namely that the three Services were not working together, but planning and fighting independent battles.[30] The extent of the 'jointery' between them extended, as Tedder admitted to Spears, merely to asking Cunningham and Wavell where he should apply his available air effort. The answer that came was to use them in support of the Navy. Spear's judgement that this decision 'was an excellent example of lack of military imagination'[31] applied as equally to Tedder as to Wavell, although Tedder was quick to blame the problem on Wavell's 'inability to understand the principles of air warfare'.[32]

In late June Tedder was able to reinforce *Operation Exporter* with two further squadrons,* but these also tended to be concentrated on 'strategic' tasks in line with D'Albiac's earlier policy. The revolution in the tactical support of ground operations in 1942 and 1943 came too late to assist the long-suffering British, Australian, Free French and Arab foot soldiers in Syria, who only rarely enjoyed the co-operation of aircraft. When it did come, troops were able to compare RAF support unfavourably with the hedge-hopping, aggressive tactics of the Vichy fighters. Major General Clark commented after an attack on 28 June that 'The RAF appeared flying very high and in admirably tidy formation. They then . . . dropped all their bombs at once, turned round and . . . made back immediately to their bases.'[33]

Tuesday 10 June saw the advance continue strongly on the left flank of the offensive. Lavarack's Australians captured 400 prisoners along the

---

* 45 and 260 Squadrons RAF.

coast together with quantities of weapons and equipment, and after attacks by 25 Australian Brigade on villages and positions around Merjayoun on 10 June the Vichy defenders fled. On the right Collet crossed the Aouadj River and captured some prisoners, but otherwise the Free French, surrounded by evident administrative and logistical confusion, spent the day preparing for their attack on the Bourak–Kissoue–Deir Khabie Line, the two defended positions that protected Damascus. The first position, eleven miles south of the capital, extended from Bourak on the right, along the heights of Jebel Madani to Kissoue and then followed the Aouadj River to Deir Khabie. The second, two miles further on, included the Jebel Kelb and Jebel Madani ridges. Silence from the Free French on 10 June in fact covered a further, more insidious problem amongst Legentilhomme's forces. Now that the Vichy forces were demonstrably defending Syria and not capitulating, as they had hoped and expected, a crisis of morale swept through the Free French ranks as the bitter reality became apparent that Frenchmen were killing Frenchmen. The fruit of the crisis was the resignation of Legentilhomme's commander of divisional infantry, a Foreign Legion officer called Colonel Magrin-Verneret,[*] who suddenly and unexpectedly refused to fight, apparently because he was faced with fighting Legion troops opposing him on the Vichy side. This 'resignation' was followed by similar refusals throughout the division, and reduced Legentilhomme's strength by up to a third immediately prior to the key battle before Kissoue.[34]

During the remainder of the week the two left-hand prongs progressed slowly forward, meeting stiffer opposition as each day passed, no single thrust being strong enough to dominate its sector completely. On Wednesday 11 and Thursday 12 June the advance along the Beirut road was led by 6 Australian Division's cavalry regiment. As the Australians moved north they had a hard fight against Foreign Legion troops ensconced in Phoenician-era catacombs in the hills, and over the next few days progress was slow as successive French positions in the hills needed to be systematically reduced, the French mounting regular ambushes and counter-attacks. On 10 June Wavell reported to the War Office that most Vichy prisoners remained 'loyal to Pétain' and, with no obvious smugness, noted that whilst there appeared some

* Alias *Colonel Monclar.*

loyalty to Collet there was very little support either for de Gaulle or Catroux.[35] The news alarmed the nervous Dill in London, who enquired the following day whether or not 'French resistance would . . . collapse if the heaviest possible bombing attack were made on French positions?'[36] Wavell rejected the idea on the basis that it would divert precious resources from the Western Desert. 'Progress in Syria, though slow, is steady and there is no definite hold up', he replied on 13 June.[37]

During these two days of fighting, Dentz showed his true colours. On 11 June the Royal Navy squadron off the coast was perceived by Vichy to be the principal threat and the primary objective for air attack, and on 12 June the French naval commander, Admiral Gouton, asked for the loan of German Stukas as these aircraft were the 'only effective method in present state of our forces . . . [and] would be very well received by all troops.' On the evening of 12 June Dentz agreed, signalling Vichy:

> The constant bombardment by the British fleet, on the one hand, and on the other the rather rapid wastage of my troops, which I cannot replace from my meagre strength, have changed my views concerning the intervention of German aircraft. Request permission for a squadron of German aircraft, intended to intervene against British fleet or for land operations, to use Aleppo airfield.[38]

Early the next day Vichy replied that it was despatching a squadron of French aircraft from France to help attack the British ships, and that use of German aircraft would only be countenanced if they could be used in 'massive' force. Dentz replied saying that he did not have the resources to support a 'massive' deployment of German aircraft, and in any case it might prove a threat to continuing French hegemony in Syria to accept a large commitment of German forces in the country. Nevertheless, the British advance left the possibility of the use of Stukas unresolved and on 17 June the Vichy Minister for Air, General Bergeret, arrived in Beirut to assess the situation. However, by this time Vichy counter-attacks had blunted the weak British attacks, and the need for German support, for the time being at least, dissipated.

The Vichy French fought extremely skilfully during this delaying action to Beirut. They had more and better tanks and complete superiority in the air. In the hills to the east Todforce* was held up at Hasbaya and retired to Merjayoun on 12 June, and a company of 2/33 Battalion sent east to the Mount Hermon foothills on 11 June also retired to Merjayoun. The Cheshire Yeomanry occupied Nabatiye, but the road to the coast had been destroyed, preventing further exploitation in that direction. The Vichy Air Force – in the absence of any RAF defensive air support – attacked 25 Australian Brigade heavily on 12 June, causing a number of casualties.

On the right flank Legentilhomme's offensive against the Damascus defences began on 11 June, with an attack on Jebel Madani, the eastern arm of the main Vichy position. Slow progress was made, but by 12 June it was clear that the Free French were having trouble making headway against Kissoue. Free French Senegalese troops secured Jebel Madani, whilst in a rare moment of support RAF aircraft bombed Vichy positions around Kissoue and Jebel Badrane was occupied. However, all troops displayed a distinct nervousness at the vast preponderance enjoyed by the Vichy in terms of armour. The two-man R35, whilst small was nevertheless fast, manoeuvrable, well-armoured and invulnerable to most of the weapons available to Wilson's troops. Panicked reports of an armoured counter-attack on the right flank, later proved false, nevertheless prompted Wilson, at Irbid with Wavell, to backfill Ezraa with troops of the TJFF and to send up Lloyd's brigade to assist the Kissoue front. Pressure from the air remained incessant, and one air attack on Sanamein left Legentilhomme wounded. On 13 June, therefore, Wilson placed the Free French under Brigadier Lloyd, who retained control until Damascus fell. Brigadier 'Jonah' Jones of the Rajputanas assumed command of the brigade from Lloyd. That the Free French – including both de Gaulle and Catroux – were content, argues the historian Anthony Mockler, that Lloyd take over command of the Free French division at the height of this decisive battle, speaks volumes for the impoverished morale of the Free French by this stage of the battle.[39]

Because of the mountainous terrain and the likelihood of strong Vichy resistance in numerous difficult pockets through the left-hand side of the advance, Wilson and Lavarack agreed to concentrate the

* Part of 25 Australian Brigade, including a combined Scots Greys and Staffordshire Yeomanry force in trucks.

offensive pressure along the coast, reducing the strength of effort in the hills in the direction of Rayak. It was decided that Merjayoun was to be held as a defensive point and the bulk of 25 Australian Brigade transferred to the coast to support the drive to Beirut. Accordingly, a mobile force was ordered to cross to the coast, built around the 2/31 Battalion transported in trucks, together with a machine-gun platoon, the light tanks of the 6 Australian Division's Cavalry Regiment, a battery of the ubiquitous 25-pounders and a detachment of anti-tank guns.

On 13 June the Australians pushed up to Sidon but found the town to be strongly defended. A preliminary bombardment by warships and artillery failed to budge the defenders. On the left infantry attacks by 2/16 Battalion were counter-attacked by tanks. No attack managed to break through the fruit and olive plantations south of Sidon, Vichy troops displaying considerable determination and professionalism in their defence of the picturesque whitewashed town. It helped also that they outnumbered the Australians four battalions to two, and that their aircraft retained complete domination of the sky. Stevens' Australians were later to discover that:

> General Dentz . . . had visited the front here only two days earlier and told the troops that, unless they resisted to the utmost, reprisals were liable to be taken against their kinsmen imprisoned by the Germans. And they were to shoot all British who attempted to parley.[40]

At 7 p.m. on Friday 13 June the mobile group based around 2/31 Battalion moved out of Merjayoun slowly west across the twenty-five miles of steep mountain tracks towards Jezzine, as part of the plan to support Brigadier Stevens' attacks along the coast. The village was secured after heavy fighting by nightfall the following day. On the coast, rather than attempt further frontal attacks against the town, Stevens decided first to dominate the high ground overlooking Sidon to the east, which was occupied by the village of Miye ou Miye. His 2/27 Battalion assaulted the town on Saturday 14 June, although by dusk the French had not been fully driven out. South of Sidon 2/16 Battalion could not get forward, and attacks on them by tanks were only driven off by desperate and sustained Australian anti-tank fire. However, heavy bombardment on the French positions from the sea continued during the day and helped to wear down the defenders.

The road between Jezzine on the right flank and Sidon was now cleared and the bulk of 2/25 Battalion was transferred from Merjayoun to Jezzine. This meant that most of 25 Australian Brigade was now in Jezzine, leaving Merjayoun in a dangerously weakened state, with only 2/33 Battalion and Todforce remaining. On the afternoon of 15 June an attack on Jezzine from the north was repulsed by Australian artillery.

Sunday 15 June was a day of worrisome drama for the faltering Allied advance. By ill fortune it also saw the start of Wavell's luckless *Operation Battleaxe* in the Western Desert, which came to an ignominious end two days later with the loss of ninety-one tanks and the retreat of his forces back to their start-lines in Egypt. But in the Levant the day started well for Wilson's dispersed offensive. The naval bombardment had continued at first light, and 2/27 Battalion proceeded to capture Miye ou Miye. It was then realized that Sidon had been evacuated, and so the town was occupied. The naval bombardment was said to have been very effective, destroying twelve guns and a number of tanks.

Far to the north-east, Lloyd (Legentilhomme had by this stage returned to his headquarters with his wounded arm bandaged, although Lloyd retained command) began the attack on the Kissoue positions in the early morning, the last bastion before Damascus herself. RAF bombers were made available for high-level raids on the French positions over two days. The attack began before dawn. Creeping forward in the darkness and doing away with the double-edged sword of a preliminary artillery bombardment, the Punjabis rushed the village and secured it after a sharp fight. The brigade artillery then concentrated on the Tel Kissoue ridge and at 9 a.m. the Rajputana Rifles, having moved through the Punjabis, assaulted and seized the feature. To the right the Free French then attacked and captured the Jebel Kelb. The day was a complete success for Lloyd, although Collet's group was unable to force its way across difficult basalt country on the extreme right flank, and lost eight tanks to mechanical breakdown and enemy fire, falling back to their start line. Three Vichy counter-attacks were then launched against the Rajputanas on Tel Kissoue, the first two by tanks and the third by a picturesque but futile attack at the gallop by a squadron of *Spahi* horsemen. Accompanied by a Free French officer, Major Bernard Fergusson, from Wavell's staff but attached temporarily to Legentilhomme's divisional headquarters, found to his profound surprise that he was observing the heroic futility of what must have been one of the last charges of its kind in modern warfare:

> there came to our ears the unexpected sound of trumpets. "Cavalry!" said the Frenchman incredulously . . . and stood astonished at what we saw. It had indeed been a cavalry charge, by a squadron of Spahis, which without warning had broken out of the Ghouta and galloped across the open ground towards the lower slopes of the Jebel Madani, the hill on which we stood. By the time we reached our viewpoint the wave had spent itself, and the scene was like that of an old print, with riderless horses and running men making back for the shelter of the Ghouta, and others twitching and kicking on the plain, horses and men alike.[41]

Determined to maintain the momentum of his attacks, Lloyd then ordered the two Indian battalions to advance and seize the remainder of the Jebel Madani. This they were able to do by dawn on the morning of 16 June, the sun rising to show the gleaming minarets of Damascus only nine miles away.

However, despite the successes elsewhere on 15 June, the day also fatefully exposed the weakness of Wilson's right flank. By this stage two of Lloyd's battalions, supported by the remnants of those Free French units who were willing to continue the fight, were close upon Damascus. Far to the rear Lloyd's third battalion, the weakened Royal Fusiliers, were at Kuneitra and a small TJFF force was at Sheikh Meskine and Ezraa. Little of substance protected the long line of communication between the front and rear of Lloyd and Legentilhomme's advance. Kuneitra was especially vulnerable, with few troops available to protect this important nodal point, where roads ran to Sheikh Meskine, Jisr Benett Yacoub and Merjayoun. De Verdilhac had kept most of his armour and the four battalions of the *6e Régiment de la Légion* in reserve ready for this eventuality and in a dramatic counter-stroke hit hard against the weak foundations of Wilson's offensive, the positions at Merjayoun, Kuneitra and Deraa. De Verdilhac had clearly recognized the inherent weakness of Wilson's plan. With three lines of advance, each of equal strength, and increasingly long lines of communication from Palestine, along with strong forces facing them and a dangerously weakened rear, Wilson's offensive was vulnerable to counter-attack.

The first of three co-ordinated attacks began on the afternoon of 15 June against Merjayoun, led by cavalry of the *6ᵉ Chasseurs d'Afrique*. It caught the British and Australians entirely by surprise. By unfortunate coincidence 2/33 Battalion was at the time conducting an operation through the foothills of Mount Hermon in a wide turning movement against Hasbaya, the battalion's commanding officer seeking to exploit what he believed to be the enemy's disarray, but failing in turn to secure his own base. Merjayoun was left defended by a mere company of infantry. At 3 p.m. under cover of an artillery bombardment three battalions of Vichy colonial infantry, supported by armoured cars and tanks, attacked Merjayoun and the village of Ibeles Saki. Ibeles Saki fell first, followed by Khiam. The shock was considerable, both British cavalrymen and Australian infantry falling back, with some evidence of panic, to the cry 'The tanks have broken through!'[42] During the night the remaining defenders were prudently withdrawn from Merjayoun south to the road junction north of Oleaa, and the town fell into Vichy hands.

At the same time de Verdilhac mounted two further counter-attacks that day against British positions at Kuneitra and, far to the right on the edge of the Jebel Druze, at Ezraa. Falling on British weak points he was successful in both. Kuneitra was garrisoned by six hundred Royal Fusiliers (minus a company twenty-five miles to the south at Fiq, but reinforced by a squadron of the newly arrived Royal Dragoons from Egypt). A substantial Vichy force, based on *7ᵉ Chasseurs d'Afrique* and including thirty-five R35 tanks, seven armoured cars and some forty truckloads of troops, drove in the Fusiliers' outposts. At the same time a heavy reconnaissance by two companies of Tunisian *Tirailleurs*, ten armoured cars, two field guns, three anti-tank guns and a few light tanks moved from the Jebel Druze against Ezraa. Defended by but a handful of the TJFF it was taken easily. This placed the Vichy French on the railway and some twenty miles to the rear of the Free French headquarters at Ghabagheb. In the time-honoured tradition of renaming unpronounceable local names, British troops nicknamed this town 'Rhubarb'.

Monday 16 June saw no quick alleviation of British difficulties on the central sector. At Kuneitra some 2,000 Vichy troops attacked the town and after a day of fighting the remainder of the Fusilier battalion, badly outnumbered and out of ammunition, was forced to surrender. After a somewhat pedestrian and unimaginative defence of the town,

470 officers and men fell into de Verdilhac's exultant hands. Dill was horrified when he heard the news, asking Wavell, 'Surely battalion of R[oyal] F[usiliers] have not surrendered to Vichy French[?].[43] Wilson immediately asked for help from Lavarack's 7 Australian Division to recapture the town.

The Vichy French who had captured Ezraa the previous evening made a half-hearted attempt to attack Sheikh Meskine on the vulnerable line of communication between Deraa and Kissoue, but were easily seen off by the assorted TJFF, Indian and Free French defenders.

A rapid reordering of forces was required to stabilize the situation at Merjayoun, but Vichy attacks continued unabated. One, on Jezzine by armoured cars approaching from the east through the hills on a track from the mountain village of Machrhara, was repulsed. Nevertheless, during the day Lavarack's realignment of his troops was successfully completed. At Merjayoun by dawn on 16 June two companies of 2/33 Battalion were in position south of Khiam, and at Oleaa the company of the 2/5 Battalion and the Scots Greys were joined by a company of Australian Pioneers. A probe by two Vichy tanks at mid-morning was repulsed and one tank destroyed. In the afternoon the two companies at Khiam were attacked from both flanks and withdrew to a better position. Later in the afternoon 2/25 Battalion arrived from Jezzine and 2/33 Battalion completed its return from Mount Hermon.

The loss of Merjayoun, Kuneitra and Ezraa posed a considerable threat to Wilson's plans and necessitated a rapid adjustment of forces by Lavarack. With Merjayoun lost, the whole of Palestine lay threatened by a deep Vichy counter-penetration, and no troops remained to prevent an exploitation of this kind. To plug this yawning gap radical decisions had to be made, including calling an immediate halt to Brigadier Stevens' advance on Beirut until the crisis had been resolved. Ordered to defend the crucial Jordan bridge at Jisr Benett Yacoub were 2/3 Machine-Gun Battalion (less two companies), commanded by Lieutenant Colonel Blackburn VC, and the 5 Australian Anti-Tank Battery; 2/33 Battalion was recalled from its operation in Mount Hermon and 2/2 Australian Pioneer Battalion hurried up to guard and prepare for demolition of the bridge over the Litani south-west of Merjayoun in event of a Vichy penetration south.

These worrying setbacks were undoubtedly planned by de Verdilhac to cut off the numerically superior force under Lloyd and

Legentilhomme, at this time preparing to assault the defences at Kissoue, the last obstacle before the great prize of Damascus itself. His brilliant counter-attacks painfully exposed the folly of three separate and simultaneous attacks. Nowhere were the British strong enough to ensure that captured localities on the line of communication were properly secured from counter-attack. The one place where the defenders held on by their fingertips and successfully repelled every attempt to displace them was the Australian defence of Jezzine. Likewise, hopes of mass Vichy defections had not materialized and most of the 800 prisoners taken so far were extremely hostile.

One significant consolation, however, was that despite the strength and success of the Vichy counter-attacks against Merjayoun, Ezraa and Kuneitra, de Verdilhac did not manage to exploit beyond these initial tactical objectives. For a short time the whole of Palestine lay at his mercy, but he took no steps to order any southern advance, allowing Lavarack quickly to contain the threat and organize separate counter-attacks to recover the lost positions. Tactically brilliant, de Verdilhac's counter-attacks were strategically less impressive. The Vichy failure to exploit their initial strategic advantage was perhaps understandable. It would have taken a bold commander to make the decision to thrust deeply into the heart of Palestine, and de Verdilhac's troops were hard pressed across the whole of the southern Levant. Nevertheless a bold thrust could have done untold damage to the British cause politically and militarily, perhaps even destabilizing the British offensive entirely. It is a matter for conjecture as to whether de Verdilhac lacked the courage for such boldness, or whether he even wanted to achieve anything more than to secure local superiority on the battlefield, perhaps desiring to restrict the scope of the current fratricide to the Levant and not widen it further than was necessary.

By the end of the week it was apparent both that Vichy were not going to give up without a fight, and that the forces available were stretched to their limit. Wavell was forced to dig deep into his reserves, and he now ordered up another brigade and an artillery Field Regiment from Egypt. In addition, Habforce was ordered to assemble ready for an advance to Palmyra, although it was not until 18 May that orders were given, following Auchinleck's suggestion, for Slim's 10 Indian Division to move north-west along the Euphrates to threaten Syria's eastern flank.

Well forward on the Kissoue position neither Lloyd nor Legentilhomme allowed the loss of Kuneitra or Ezraa far behind them to distract them from the prize of securing Damascus, and they successfully repelled Vichy counter-attacks during 16 June against the Kissoue positions. The attack on Damascus was due to begin on the night of 18/19 June.

Cut off in the hills at Jezzine and cut out of Merjayoun, the Australian position remained extremely vulnerable during Tuesday 17 June. At Jezzine Brigadier Cox's troops were faced with three-and-a-half Vichy battalions. Soon after daybreak an attack was made on the right flank of Jezzine, now dangerously weak following the reinforcements sent to Merjayoun, although the Australians routed the attacking Senegalese with the bayonet. Cox believed the position to be hopeless. His line of communication was tenuous and constantly under threat from Vichy artillery, and he asked Lavarack for permission to withdraw: Lavarack refused. At the same time the Australians attempted to capture Merjayoun at dawn with an attack by two companies of Pioneers and a company of 2/3 Machine-Gun Battalion, but were counter-attacked in turn by Vichy tanks and repulsed. Meanwhile 2/25 Battalion crossed the Litani gorge to the north-west of Merjayoun and attacked the town. Three platoons managed to get into the town at various points but were forced out by artillery and tanks. The day ended with an artillery duel, the Vichy attacking the Litani bridge and the Australians the fort south of Merjayoun.

Meanwhile, to the east an attempt was made to recapture Kuneitra. As many troops as could be found were committed from across the region. These included 2 Battalion Queen's Regiment (rushed forward from Egypt), a company of 2/3 Machine-Gun Battalion, an anti-tank troop, mounted troops of the Yorkshire Dragoons, two Palestine Police armoured cars and a lone Australian 25-pounder gun from Kissoue. In the early morning of 17 June the empty town was reoccupied, although the Vichy troops with their Royal Fusilier prisoners had managed to withdraw untouched via a track through the hills, unknown to the troops of 5 Indian Brigade who had attempted to block escape routes to the north. At Ezraa a Free French counter-attack failed but later in the day a determined attack by a mixed bag of troops from different units, who by chance had come across each other on the battlefield, stormed the town and retook it after a hard fight. A young Australian-born officer of the 8th Hussars on loan service to the TJFF, Captain 'Shan' Hackett, took command of a confused situation, rallying and leading the attack after the Free French Colonel Genin was shot.* Hackett was wounded in the shoulder but before evacuation he oversaw the capture of nearly 200 Vichy troops from the fort. By this time an unflustered Lloyd, having safely secured Kissoue and the Jebel Madani, arrived to take control of operations. By his presence he calmed and stabilized an otherwise fluid situation. In a welcome change from the norm, Australian Tomahawk fighter aircraft harried the withdrawing Vichy troops, and the route from Deraa to Kissoue was opened again.

In the hills between Sidon and Merjayoun the struggle for Jezzine continued throughout Wednesday 18 June. A company of the defending 2/31 Battalion attempted to counter-attack the Vichy positions but was enfiladed and stopped with many casualties. During the early evening six Vichy bombers, escorted by fighters, attacked the Australian position, killing seventeen and wounding ten. However, that night 2/14 Battalion arrived as reinforcement from the coast.

With the threat to his rear now removed Lloyd's attack on the outskirts of Damascus began in the evening of 18 June. His plan was to cut Damascus off from the west, and the two remaining battalions in his brigade – the Punjabis and Rajputanas – began clearing the road north of Artouz. After fighting through the night the village of Mezze was successfully secured during the early dawn of Thursday 19 June. However, transport carrying anti-tank guns, reserve ammunition, land mines, tools and rations went astray and was unable to follow up into Mezze with the Indians. A Vichy counter-attack against the weak victors in Mezze was mounted almost immediately. The Punjabis and Rajputanas worked hard to turn Mezze into a defended locality but they had neither the equipment nor specialist weapons to do the job properly. Vichy attacks, led by tanks, continued throughout the day,

---

* Hackett was to rise to become a full General and Commander-in-Chief of NATO's Northern Army Group before retirement. He was also the celebrated author of *The Third World War* (1978) and its sequel *The Third World War: The Untold Story* (1983).

battering the defenders hard. As the unfortunate Fusiliers had found at Kuneitra, the imperviousness of the R35 tanks to anything the Indians could throw at them once again proved to be decisive. The remnants of the two Indian battalions found themselves cut off from the rest of Lloyd's force and, in an ever tightening perimeter within the town, were bombarded by tanks and artillery, for which they had no riposte.

The desperate situation now facing the defenders at Mezze was not realized at Lloyd's HQ until messengers managed to get out of the encirclement with the news. An attempt to relieve the town was launched from Kafr Sous, two miles to the south-west, by an ad hoc group of 25-pounders, two companies of 3/1 Punjab and two anti-tank guns on 20 June. Much to Lloyd's disgust his Free French troops refused to budge from their positions. Despite heavy Vichy shelling the rescue force managed to force its way into Mezze, but it was too late to save the gallant defenders, who had been almost wiped out by the Vichy attacks. There were only a handful of survivors. The actions at Kuneitra and Mezze had effectively destroyed 5 Indian Brigade, and Lloyd and Legentilhomme, on 20 June, now faced Damascus with a dramatically reduced force, entirely insufficient to capture the city. The failure of the Free French troops to advance alongside 3/1 Punjab in a twin-pronged attack on Damascus caused the advance to falter, and allowed the devastating armoured counter-attack that all but wiped out the Punjabis at Mezze.

However, the relief force in Mezze was reinforced that evening by the weak 2/3 Battalion* – recently arrived in Egypt from Crete, and which had been hurried forward to support the attack on Damascus – and the Vichy French will to resist was crumbling. Little did de Verdilhac realize (he had now sacked Delhomme) just how weak were the Allied forces facing him. During the day Lloyd and Legentilhomme's troops pressed up around Damascus, although the Free French troops once again displayed a reluctance to lead the way, preferring to advance in trucks behind the machine guns of Blackburn's Australians. To the east Collet moved against the outskirts of Damascus and threatened the route north to Homs. Meanwhile Wavell's injection of reinforcements from Egypt by this stage allowed Wilson to reorganize his forces. Dividing his troops into two parts, he

---

* Commanded by Lieutenant Colonel Lamb, and not to be confused with the 2/3 Machine-Gun Battalion, commanded by Lieutenant Colonel Blackburn VC.

gave Lavarack 16 Infantry Brigade (Brigadier C.E.N. 'Sunny' Lomax) from the 6 British Division to form 1 Australian Corps, with responsibility for the area from the coast to Damascus, whilst Major General J.F. Evetts of the 6 British Division was given command of the Damascus–Kuneitra flank on 19 June.* A frank briefing by Legentilhomme, somewhat embarrassed by his countrymen's newfound reluctance to fight after all the noise that de Gaulle and Catroux had made prior to the offensive, placed Evetts firmly in the picture, as he reported to Lavarack on the morning of 20 June:

> The Free French forces are extremely tired and have little or no desire to go on killing their brother Frenchmen and it is doubtful whether they can be persuaded to advance against even feeble resistance.

Evetts asked Lavarack for the loan of Lomax's brigade, so as to seize Damascus. Without it the capture of the city was at stake. 'My own personal opinion', he urged, 'is that bold swift action is necessary at once if we are to restore the morale of the Free French and ensure their assistance in the future.'[44]

By the evening the RAF attacked transport on the road to Beirut and extreme measures were now considered by Dentz. On 20 June, with Damascus threatened, Dentz signalled to Vichy a renewed call for *Luftwaffe* assistance:

> The fate of the Levant now depends on the immediate introduction of shock troops. They must be moved in large transport aircraft. The German command is prepared to provide the necessary aircraft on condition that the request for them comes from you.[45]

During that night 2/3 Battalion cut the road to Beirut and captured prisoners and vehicles. It was clear that the end of resistance in Damascus was near. The following day the Australians pressed hard, repulsing counter–attacks on the road and capturing forts in the hills above, and the RAF continued to attack Vichy transport on the road to Beirut. Then, the Vichy forces evacuated Damascus and the town fell to

* Major General A.S. Allen took command from Lavarack of 7 Australian Division.

Legentilhomme and Lloyd in the afternoon without a fight. The intervention of 16 Brigade was not, in the end, required, and the city surrendered to a combination of Lloyd's boldness and Vichy fears.

Meanwhile, to the south attacks during 19 June to recover Merjayoun continued to be repulsed. Troops of the 2/25 Battalion managed to break into Merjayoun but the fighting was hard and hand-to-hand and Vichy armour intervened, with the result that by nightfall the forward detachments of troops were withdrawn back to the Litani River.

With possibly well-timed irony, Blackburn's Australians were determined to ensure that they, and not Legentilhomme's timid Gaullists, received the honour of first entering Damascus. Bernard Fergusson was waiting with General Legentilhomme at the outskirts of the city for suitable cars to arrive to allow them to enter so as formally to receive its surrender:

> At 3 p.m. the cars arrived, and we were about to get into them when there was a clamour of noise from the south, and lorry after lorry of yelling Australians drove past, covering us all with dust. Legentilhomme, livid, made one attempt to stop them, but had to jump clear.

Later, in the cheering crowds in Damascus, Fergusson's hand was pumped by Blackburn, wearing a row of medal ribbons including the Victoria Cross, exclaiming, 'I was first!'[46]

In Damascus, to which de Gaulle now hurried, Evetts established his headquarters. Despite both Legentilhomme and Lloyd chomping at the bit, the victors settled down to consolidate their gains and establish Damascus as a base for further operations, but in so doing lost the momentum of their attack and a chance to pursue the retreating French through the Barada Gorge into the Bekaa Valley, and north towards Homs. The three days of caution and consolidation that followed allowed the offensive to falter, providing an opportunity for de Verdilhac to re-establish control and turn the mountain approaches to the Bekaa into defensive positions as formidable as any seen in the history of war. As Lieutenant Colonel Blackburn VC grimly remarked, 'a single battalion adequately munitioned could hold out against the whole world.'[47]

7

Deir-ez-Zor

Saturday 21 June 1941 was a momentous day not simply because of the fall of Damascus, great though that was to Lloyd and Legentilhomme's troops. It was also the day when Hitler's troops made their final preparations for the invasion of Russia in the early hours of the following morning and when Major General George Clark's Habforce, buoyed by their recent victory in Iraq, entered Syria. Pessimism in London about the outcome of the war in the Middle East, despite the capture of Baghdad, was still running high. With Wavell's offensive in the Western Desert having collapsed with heavy loss, Dill remarked despondently to Kennedy on the day Damascus fell: 'I suppose you realize we shall lose the Middle East?'[1] The orders for Clark to advance into Syria, with his first objective the oasis of Palmyra, site of the ancient city of Zenobia, where the desert of eastern Syria meets the mountains, had been long in coming. Arguably, they had been too long, as Damascus surrendered on the very day that Clark's vehicles, dust streaming behind them like billows of smoke, headed deep into the Syrian Desert on the long journey north. The strategic advantages of a right hook from the mountains in the south-east and the desert to the east, complementing the attacks in the west, seemed self-evident to many observers. Glubb, amongst others, had argued the need for such an operation in the event of an invasion, recommending that an advance along the coast to Beirut, and from Deraa to Damascus, be joined by an attack on Damascus from the west, with an advance through the Druze Mountains.

Glubb was bewildered to find, however, that when Wilson prepared his final plans, the inclusion of a flanking attack from the east had been ignored.[2] It was only on 13 June that Clark received orders to send Habforce into Syria. Its point of entry was to be the H3 pumping station on the Haifa pipeline. It took a further eight days to get troops moved from Habbaniya across the start line, by which time the potential impact of their advance on the Vichy defence of Syria had been significantly lessened. Spears regarded the failure to launch an attack from the east at the outset to be a profound mistake. 'Why a wide outflanking movement was not being undertaken baffled understanding', he recorded, attributing this failure to what he regarded as Wilson's incompetence as a commander, a subject on which his memoirs are remarkably caustic.[3] 'As for wisdom,' his sharp pen noted, 'military historians may discover in his decisions a sagacity which my own shortcomings no doubt prevented me from detecting.'[4] Spears' criticism of Wilson's failure to include in his plan an attack from the direction of Iraq is exaggerated but does contain an element of truth. If an attack from the eastern desert had been launched simultaneously with those in the west, it might have had an immediate impact on the Vichy defences, and forced Dentz to deploy troops to the desert who were otherwise available to beat back the attacks from Palestine. It was certainly an attack which de Verdilhac expected and feared, but much to his surprise did not arise until the end of the campaign.

Habforce's objective was to penetrate deep into Syria through Palmyra to seize Homs, thus cutting the road and railway between Damascus and Aleppo. Finally, and to Glubb's delight, orders were received for the Arab Legion to join the rested Habforce at H3 ready for the long-awaited advance into Syria. 'Red in the face and hearty,' Glubb recalled, 'Brigadier Kingstone roared: "Hullo, Pasha! Back again! I thought we'd got rid of you!" But this time he did not mean it.'[5] Glubb had 350 men, arranged into nine troops, together with three of their home-made armoured cars. For the Arabs, this was a war of liberation. The Emir Abdullah himself came to Mafraq to send off his troops, leaning on a stick and telling Glubb's men excitedly amidst swirling robes and cloak 'that the moment for the freeing of Syria had come and that he relied on them to seize this golden hour in the history of the Arabs!'[6] The journalist Godfrey Lias, who knew the Arab Legion well, recorded that volunteers, many with ancient rifles used under Lawrence and Feisal, flocked to the cause, all 'fired with the same double motive: helping the British drive the French into the sea in the interests of Arab unity and the thrill of battle and plunder.'[7] Palmyra, 150 miles north-west from H3, once captured, was to provide the base from which Kingstone was to strike north-west at the Vichy line of communications near Homs. The Kirkuk–Tripoli pipeline ran east to west across the desert skirting the southern edge of the town. The Syrian vastness was garrisoned by three Light Desert Companies, mobile forces equipped with armoured cars and trucks, together with units of local troops and companies of the Foreign Legion. The fort at Seba' Biyar ('Seven Wells') contained part of the French 1st Light Desert Company (*1ère Compagnie Légère du Désert*), the 2nd was based far to the east at Deir-ez-Zor on the Upper Euphrates, and the 3rd, together with two companies of the Foreign Legion, totalling some five hundred men, garrisoned the oasis at Palmyra

Dividing into three columns, two from Kingstone's 4 Cavalry Brigade to attack Palmyra from the east and south-west, together with a strong headquarters column, Habforce left H3 on the morning of 21 June. Kingstone was to strike against Palmyra from the east, leaving the H3–Palmyra track at the Juffa oasis, some twenty-five miles south-east of Palmyra, and turning north to meet the pipeline at T3, before turning left against Palmyra in what was hoped to be a surprise attack from the east. Simultaneously the Royal Wiltshire Yeomanry was to attack the oasis from the south and west to capture rocky ridges ('Yellow Ridge') and an old fort called the 'Château'. The Household Cavalry Regiment, meanwhile, was to advance from Habbaniya and assemble at the pumping station at T1, prior to advancing on Palmyra along the route of the pipeline. The weakness of air support became immediately apparent as the day progressed. Bowling along the flat desert floor, the widely dispersed vehicles threw up huge sand clouds denoting their presence, and attracting to them like bees to a honey pot the predatory aircraft of the Vichy Air Force. It was only a matter of time before they were discovered and the weakness of their force exposed. Glubb's men overran a small enemy outpost at Juffa, and the alarm went up, despite the legionnaires' smashing of the Vichy French radio. As the leading elements of Kingstone's brigade prepared to attack the Vichy defences at T3, disconcertingly strong with concrete bunkers, barbed wire and clear arcs of fire from their machine guns over acres of open desert, formations of silver bombers emerged from the sun haze in the direction of Palmyra and proceeded to bomb the attackers from the air.

The British had no effective means of retaliation apart from rifles and light machine guns, and no means of protection except for hurriedly dug shell-scrapes in the ground. Vichy French control of the air allowed them to attack British ground forces at will during the campaign, and became a bitter characteristic of the fighting. Glubb, visiting Kingstone on the morning of 22 June, and blissfully unaware of the momentous events then unfolding in Eastern Europe, watched a flight of six French bombers from Palmyra attack slowly, almost lazily, wheeling in formation over the British vehicles spread across the sand and carefully levelling off for repeated bombing runs over a period of some twenty minutes. They attacked with impunity, no RAF fighters being available to fight them off.

> I sat down in the mouth of a rat-hole, which seemed to be the only break in the flat surface of the desert . . . I lay on my back and watched the first three aircraft coming straight at us. When they seemed to be about two hundred yards short of us, I saw the bombs leave the aircraft. They looked as if they must fall straight on me. I wriggled myself as much as possible into the mouth of my rat-hole, but without much success. Suddenly there was a deafening crash behind me. Krump-krump-krump-krump went the burst in quick succession.[8]

The result, he records, was much noise, dust and smoke, and a severely injured officer. It was in one of these raids in the desert outside Palmyra that Captain Somerset de Chair's romantic perambulations as a military tourist came to an abrupt stop. He, too, saw the first flight of French Potez 63 bombers flying towards them across the bright blue sky.

> They were not too high up for me to distinguish at a glance the blue, white and red circles under the wings and the twin engines, which made me take them for our familiar Blenheims. Even as I watched I saw three bright yellow eggs begin to fall against the blue and my mind, slowly somersaulting to the horrid truth, warned me that there was something wrong with the picture. I threw myself down on the hard ground and the bombs burst

seventy-five yards away, blowing the forearm off an officer of the new Australian anti-tank troop.[9]

Lucky that time, he was less fortunate shortly afterwards when, forgetting every rule about dispersing from vehicles when under air attack, de Chair stayed too close to his beloved Chevrolet, and was hit in the leg from part of a cannon shell that went on to wreck the car, fired from a low-flying De Woitine D.520 fighter, an aircraft similar to the familiar British Hurricane. The French attacks on that and the following days were sustained and powerful. No column was exempt from their merciless pounding, and casualties were high, both in men and vehicles. One troop of the Royal Wiltshire Yeomanry, for example, had lost thirteen of its seventeen vehicles, including the precious water-truck, to air attack by the end of 22 June. Even de Chair, now lying wounded in the back of an ambulance, was not yet free from danger, being wounded again, along with other unfortunates, when it was struck by machine-gun fire after another strafing attack by one of the dreaded De Woitines. 'The white circle, with its brilliant red cross, stared reproachfully at the sky,' he wrote, reflecting on the bitterness of this campaign, 'the emblem . . . clearly visible at 200 yards when the pilot fired his burst.'[10] After many adventures he was evacuated to Palestine, his war over and his career as a poet, author and Member of Parliament about to resume.

The Royal Warwickshire's failure to penetrate the defences at T3 was mitigated in part by a precarious hold the Royal Wiltshire Yeomanry managed to obtain on a portion of Yellow Ridge. But they were unable to move further forward, and came under an unremitting assault in the following days from air, artillery and machine-gun attack. Kingstone's failure to seize Palmyra by a *coup de main* on 23 June led now to a drawn out siege, but his weak force, battered daily from the air, could not manage to break into the heavily defended town. Churchill characteristically told the House of Commons that a 'ring of steel' was being placed around Palmyra, but this was far from the truth. Vichy aircraft tore into the defenceless attackers day after day, so that even the imperturbable Glubb began to ask himself whether the invasion of Syria was going to be 'another fiasco, like the recent expedition to Greece?'[11] He did not, however, express these doubts to his legionnaires, all of whom believed that, despite current vicissitudes,

Great Britain would in the end vanquish her enemies. Nor did they doubt that they – the Arab Legion – would also emerge victorious from this war under their leader, 'Abu Haneik'. Had they not shown what they were capable of whilst rescuing their brothers in Iraq? They sang their battle song:

> We'll not disgrace our corps
> Nor yet the arms we bear.
> Our foes are sick with fear.
> Pursue them to the death!
> Abu Haneik! Abu Haneik! Abu Haneik![12]

Few Britons in the Middle East at the time had the faith of Glubb's loyal Arabs.

The stalemate at Palmyra seemed destined to continue indefinitely and inconclusively, in part because of the absence of any British aircraft to support ground operations. The initiative had been lost, and Clark seemed unable to escape from the besieger's quandary: he was far too weak to be able to break in but neither did he have the resources for a prolonged siege. Nor did he think of bypassing Palmyra completely and bottling the defenders in with a scratch force whilst he drove on hard for Homs. This was what de Verdilhac expected him to do, but the Vichy commander sorely overestimated the imagination and ingenuity of the general run of commanders on the British side in the campaign. Clark was perhaps concerned about increasing the vulnerability of his vehicle-borne troops by moving across the desert in daylight. So he stayed put, attempting to weather the storm of Vichy air attacks during the day in trenches dug hastily in the desert sand but making no effort to worm his way into Palmyra in either daylight or darkness. The heat and pressure proved too much for Kingstone, who collapsed and was evacuated on 24 June. Habforce was going nowhere fast.

In the meantime Vichy raiding parties had begun damaging skirmishes against the long and ill-defended line of communication between Juffa and H3 and de Verdilhac withdrew what reserve he had into Homs. Glubb judged that these attacks originated from one or more locations deep in the desert. The first possibility was the Vichy-held fort of Seba' Biyar situated south-west of Palmyra and the second was from the village of Sukhna, which guarded the only access through the mountains some thirty miles north-east of Palmyra. If it could be captured, Seba' Biyar would provide an added advantage to Habforce, as it would mean a drastic reduction in the length of the line of communication to Transjordan and Palestine, as H4 could be used as the starting point rather than H3. It was therefore an objective of some considerable strategic import. So too was Sukhna. It was more than possible that the Vichy Light Desert Company patrols were mounting attacks through Sukhna from as far away as Deir-ez-Zor on the Upper Euphrates. After being briefed by Glubb on 26 June, Clark agreed that the Arab Legion should seize Seba' Biyar and then turn to the north-east to secure and garrison Sukhna to prevent French raiders using the town to gain access to the desert areas crucial to the British operation at Palmyra. It was Glubb's initiative that led directly to a change in Habforce's fortunes.

The blood-curdling screeches of the ringlet-haired legionnaires at Seba' Biyar on the morning of 28 June 1941 were too much for the tiny Vichy garrison and, to the chagrin of the Arabs intent on loot and glory, surrendered with alacrity. Turning around and retracing their steps, Glubb's Arabs reached the prominent gap in the mountains at Sukhna on the evening of 29 June. Pressing through the gap the following day, they conducted a wide sweep of the desert in an attempt to locate traces of the marauders who were troubling the weak British right flank. Later that day Clark sent up a squadron of the Household Cavalry to Sukhna to support Glubb's desert forays.

Then, on the morning of Tuesday 1 July 1941, Glubb finally found his elusive enemy: a convoy of eighteen trucks and armoured cars of *2e Compagnie Légère du Désert* proceeding unsuspectingly along the road that led from Deir-ez-Zor sixty miles across the desert to the east. A sharp initial encounter was followed by a hair-raising chase across the desert between the fleeing Vichy vehicles racing at top speed back in the direction whence they had come, and the cheering, exultant and wild-eyed legionnaires swaying dangerously in their vehicles, scenting victory at long last. Glubb, driving a car across the desert floor, had difficulty controlling it at speed, as the back was filled with shouting soldiers, and more filled the running boards, some of them tribal volunteers along for the glory of fighting the hated French. He recalled:

> One of these was in a paroxysm of excitement, shouting his war-cries. Every now and then he thrust a tousled head in at the

window and bellowed exhortations in my ear. At intervals he fired a rusty rifle into space at no particular target.[13]

The chase was fruitful, the French finally giving up and surrendering, but not before one French officer had stepped aside from his now halted armoured car and, the humiliation too great, blew out his brains with his revolver.

The Sukhna battle had far greater consequences for the desert war than the eighty prisoners, six armoured cars, four trucks and twelve machine guns captured by the Legion suggested. It meant the destruction of the 2nd Desert Light Company, which left only the remnants of the 1st, now locked up inside the besieged Palmyra, clearing the Syrian desert completely of the enemy. When news reached the defenders of Palmyra that they were now alone, morale fell and their surrender was hastened.

In the meantime, to the great relief of the troops huddled in trenches in the desert avoiding the daily attentions of the Vichy Air Force, Australian Tomahawk fighters made a belated appearance in the skies above Palmyra on 26 June, quickly sending six Vichy Glen Martin bombers into the sand, to the delight of those watching.* Infiltration attacks began to be mounted on successive nights by troops of 1 Essex against the Château, which was captured on 28 June, and the Royal Wiltshire Yeomanry secured the remainder of Yellow Ridge on the same day. But the Vichy defence of Palmyra was vigorous. The Royal Wiltshires were forcibly ejected from Yellow Ridge on 29 June, although an attack by artillery and 1 Essex managed to recover it the following day. Whilst the ring was slowly tightening around Palmyra, Clark's strategic objective – an advance to threaten Homs – was now long forgotten. It was to take news of Glubb's success on the Sukhna road to demoralize the garrison, and persuade it to surrender, which it did so, begrudgingly, on the morning of 3 July 1941. One hundred and sixty-five officers and men stepped into British captivity, including some eighty-seven German and Russian Legionaries, who were unaware that their two countries were now at war.

* The Glen Martin was an American aircraft delivered to France prior to the German invasion in 1940. Other accounts have it that this action took place on 28 June, rather than the 26th as Glubb records.

While Habforce was besieging Palmyra and acting as targets for the Vichy Air Force, Slim's 10 Indian Division began its own advance into Syria from Iraq. With Wilson's advance into Syria being set back at Merjayoun, Kuneitra and Ezraa on 15 June, Wavell issued orders on 18 June to apply pressure on the Syrian eastern flank through the capture of the town of Deir-ez-Zor on the Upper Euphrates and thereafter to advance on Aleppo. Auchinleck had suggested the occupation by Indian forces from Iraq of north-east Syria as early as 7 June (a point repeated by Dill to Wavell on 10 June), but the suggestion had not been taken up because of pressure on Habforce in Iraq and the shortage, Wavell claimed in response, of suitable transport.[14] General Quinan on 19 June accordingly ordered Slim – whose division was still only just arriving in northern Iraq – to take two brigades of his division along the Euphrates so as to enter Syria through the back door and to threaten Aleppo.

Deir-ez-Zor, the capital of eastern Syria and a historic crossing of the Euphrates for many hundreds, if not thousands, of years, saw desert tracks from across Asia Minor converge on the only bridge for many hundred of miles to cross the river. Theoretically, the opportunities for an attack on eastern Syria in the direction of Aleppo were boundless, but Slim's greatest difficulty was logistics. The considerable distances combined with a lack of adequate transport for his division and the difficulties of maintaining a long line of communication for his petrol and supplies, particularly in the face of regular attacks by insurgents, made any long-range penetration with substantial forces a significant challenge. These pressures led to some wag christening the forthcoming campaign *Operation Deficient*: thanks to its pertinence, the name stuck.

Because of the attacks on his supply lines and the need to protect them while he advanced, Slim decided to proceed with one brigade forward – 21 Indian Brigade – whilst 25 Indian Brigade protected his communications.* Establishing a base first at the straggling riverside village of Haditha, part-way between Habbaniya and the French border, he stocked it with supplies for fifteen days, and then placed his advanced headquarters at T1. So as to achieve the maximum amount of

---

* For *Operation Deficient* Brigadier Weld's brigade contained 2/4 Gurkha Rifles, 4/13 Frontier Force Rifles and 2/10 Gurkha Rifles, together with 13 Lancers and 157 Regiment Royal Artillery.

surprise for an operation which the Vichy French had long anticipated, Slim launched his advance at the end of the month, with the aim of executing a rapid approach march to Deir-ez-Zor, rather than one that was laborious and protracted. On 28 June two companies of 2/4 Gurkhas, the battalion of which Jack Masters was adjutant, captured the frontier post at Abu Kemal, but the French had by that time fled. By stripping Iraq Command bare, Slim gathered some three hundred 3-ton trucks to assist in his advance up the Euphrates. In total Weld's 21 Indian Brigade had around eight hundred vehicles: the plan was to advance with these some two hundred miles in two days. In support Slim was also allocated four Gladiators and four Hurricanes, all based at T1. Unfortunately, the pilots were new to fighter aircraft and none had experience of air-to-air combat.

The advance through Haditha, TI and Abu Kemal was extremely difficult in the intense heat and dust. Jack Masters recalled the difficulties of the approach march. His battalion had already suffered heatstroke casualties, and during this journey he felt its dangerous tentacles entwining him:

> The dust billowed up now and I began to choke. My thirst increased until I could not identify the seat of it, for it was all over my body. Swaying in the front of the truck, waves of heat crawling inside me, I held desperately to the discipline that would not allow us to touch our water-bottles until a fresh supply was at hand . . . The wind blew steadily into our faces, at forty miles an hour and 140 degrees. The sweeping desert blurred and I thought, What a way to die.[15]

Fortunately for Masters and the troops suffering with him the distribution at a vehicle halt of water melons, which grew in abundance along the Euphrates, brought considerable relief.

The information Slim had received suggested that Deir-ez-Zor was well defended, by machine-gun posts and concrete gun emplacements, especially to the south and west of the town. The garrison was said to comprise between two and four thousand troops, with up to four batteries of artillery, a desert company, Foreign Legionnaires and armoured cars. This was not a place that would fall to a conventional attack. Even if he did have a preponderance of troops, Slim was not predisposed to tactics that would have entailed a conventional forward-facing attack, from a direction the enemy would expect. Indeed, with the limited troops available to him, he was convinced that only a quick surprise attack would have any chance of success. A plan was hatched with Brigadier Weld. Weld would take his brigade up from the south in a conventional approach to Deir-ez-Zor whilst from T1 a motorized column comprising 13 Lancers, 10 Indian Division's armoured car regiment, together with a section of field guns and 4/13 Frontier Force Rifles in trucks, would navigate their way across the desert, cross the Palmyra track far to the west of Deir-ez-Zor and then attack the town from the direction of Aleppo. In the process it was hoped that the defenders would be surprised and dislocated. The plan was that, once this motorized column entered the town from the north, Weld's two battalions of Gurkhas would launch an attack from the south. The combination of pressure from the front and a surprise attack in the rear, Slim hoped, would be enough to rattle the defenders into a premature surrender. The attack was planned for 2 July.

Slim admits that the plan was full of risks but, as the title of the chapter of his *Unofficial History* in which he describes the affair expresses clearly, Slim was certain that 'it pays to be bold'.[16] The eighty-mile approach for the motorized column could easily have been discovered from the air, and navigation in the desert was notoriously difficult, even for those with experience of desert travel. Colonel Ouvry Roberts, back with the division following his adventures at Habbaniya and Falluja, comments that the greatest danger was the dust storms, in which:

> it was literally impossible to see anything . . . There were no roads and no road signs, you just had to follow the tracks in the sand. If you lost these tracks there was no way of telling whether you were right of them or left of them — very frightening. Many vehicle drivers have guessed wrong, got completely lost and died of starvation and thirst.[17]

Weld began his advance on 1 July and made good progress, although attacked a number of times from the air. The weakness of the column's air defences and the paucity of supporting aircraft made the division, like that of Habforce in the desert outside Palmyra, desperately vulnerable to the unrelenting assaults by Vichy bombers flying all the way from Aleppo, attacking with what Masters described as 'increasing insolence and exactitude'.[18] The traditional complaint of the infantryman about the fighter pilot – 'sitting in comfortable quarters with iced drinks and pretty girls and you are driving into a sandstorm, half crazy with thirst, suffering from a crick in the neck' – was somewhat assuaged the following day when Masters watched two of Slim's precious Hurricanes, taking on nine Glen Martins at 8,000 feet, being shot down, their burning carcases plunging on fire into the sand.[19] Within days the remaining two Hurricanes were also shot down. Without the modicum of protection provided by the Hurricanes, Masters knew that they were sitting ducks. The sheer terror and enormity of attack from the air by troops only able to retaliate with rifles and Bren guns was almost overwhelming. Masters recalled a typical attack.

> French Morane fighters, tearing in at 300 miles an hour, twenty feet above the desert, six of them in line ahead. All round the whistles went, men dived for cover. The lead plane opened fire when almost directly over me and I heard a multi-gun fighter, close to, for the first time . . . The sound of this weapon firing at you is a single enormously loud CRRRRRRRUMP, and in those two seconds three hundred bullets have crashed by.[20]

Very early the next morning Slim discovered that his plan had gone awry, and that for some reason Weld had recalled the desert column to join the rest of his brigade alongside the Euphrates. In his account Slim was careful not to criticize Weld, but he immediately took charge, driving across the desert in the darkness from T1 to reach Weld's position and reverse the decision. It transpired that the motorized column had been badly dispersed by a sand storm in the desert and attacked from the air, and had consumed far more fuel than it carried, making it doubtful that it would reach the rear of Deir-ez-Zor as planned. It would certainly not be able to do so by 2 July, when it was due to launch its attack in conjunction with an attack on the town from the direction of the Euphrates. Weld accordingly had aborted the attack by the column and ordered it to join him on the Euphrates. By this time Weld's force was within artillery range of his objective, and was daily attacked from the air, his own puny air component having been dissipated already through air action.

Weld's alternative plan – to attack with a smaller column from the direction of the Palmyra road to the west of the town – was rejected by Slim, whose battlefield trademark was not to do the obvious and to take every manageable operational risk where he considered it prudent to do so. A frontal attack from the south-east along the Euphrates was the most obvious direction of attack, one for which the French would have prepared most thoroughly, and was thus the approach that Slim eschewed. If he had a choice at all, it would be to mount an attack in a manner and a direction in which the French would be most disadvantaged. In a country awash with oil, Slim's greatest need this day was for petrol, without which his division would be immobile and unable to continue with his original plan. Examining his rapidly diminishing options, Slim determined that the one most likely to succeed was also the riskiest. Siphoning petrol from all vehicles not required for the operation, Slim managed to provide just enough fuel to enable his desert column to make a second attempt to navigate to the rear of Deir-ez-Zor. Complaining bitterly, the Gurkhas emptied their fuel tanks. 'If the attack failed we would all be stranded. My God,' thought Masters, 'what a decision to have to take!'[21] Late that night the column departed for its second attempt, replenished with petrol scavenged from vehicles across the breadth of northern Iraq and brought in that day to Weld and Slim's location on the Euphrates. Listening, as Slim described it, to his hopes rather than to his fears, and putting aside the many nagging doubts as to the probability for success, Slim ordered the advance to begin.

According to Ouvry Roberts, Weld's action in pulling back the desert column nearly destroyed Slim's plan altogether. Characteristically, however, Slim rescued the plan by his direct intervention, although nowhere in his *Unofficial History* does he state or imply criticism of Weld. 'I can never remember Slim writing or saying a detrimental word about anyone', Roberts recalled; 'if he had nothing good to say, he just said nothing. The only person he blamed was himself.' Slim's career would take him, by October 1943, to command the army that was destined to defeat the Japanese in both eastern India and Burma. His quickness, strength of character, ability and easy leadership struck Roberts immediately: 'Slim was, in my opinion, the finest British General of World War II . . . He was also the most humble.'[22]

Early the next morning, Slim was in a position to observe the Gurkhas and artillery of Weld's brigade making last-minute preparations for the attack, whilst Vichy bombers continued their ceaseless bombardment from the air, judiciously flying just outside small-arms range. Nervously he waited whilst the sun came up. The Euphrates glided silently past with no sign that the desert column had made it to the rear of the town as planned. Then, late in the morning, came the news that the column had successfully navigated its way through the desert during the night and was now advancing along the Aleppo road. Weld immediately ordered his own offensive to begin, his old 18-pounders crashing out and covering the advance on foot of his two Gurkha battalions. The force of this asssault, when combined with the surprise generated by the motorized attack from the rear, did precisely what Slim had hoped, and caused the defence of the town quickly to collapse. Nevertheless, sporadic fighting continued during the day and the Vichy Air Force from Aleppo retained complete control of the air. The absence from the town of the *2ᵉ Compagnie Légère du Désert*, at the time skirmishing with Glubb's Arabs on the Palmyra road, substantially diminished the strength of the defences. Making his way into the town as the final defence crumbled, Slim found himself, with his *aide-de-camp*, entering what he took to be the municipal offices, and coming face to face with the reality of the dilemma Great Britain faced regarding the promise of independence from France:

> At the main door were waiting two or three Syrian functionaries who, with almost overpowering politeness, led us upstairs into a large and airy room. I was greeted by a distinguished-looking Syrian in European dress who introduced himself as the deputy-governor. The governor, he explained, had also been the French commander, now in flight. The deputy-governor welcomed us, the British, as deliverers, and trusted the French would never return. I made no comment on this nor did I confide in him that I thought General de Gaulle might have different views.[23]

Deir-ez-Zor proved to be a veritable treasure-trove for 10 Indian Division, providing huge stockpiles of petrol, some eighty lorries and large quantities of arms and ammunition, which Vichy counter-attacks later that day by bombers flying from Aleppo failed to destroy. The petrol fuelled Slim's advance along the Euphrates, first the seventy miles to Raqqa two days later, and then as the 2/4 Gurkhas stayed close on the heels of the retreating French for two hundred more miles towards Aleppo, hastening in the process Dentz's acceptance of the inevitability of defeat. At the same time, a battalion from Douglas Gracey's 17 Indian Brigade, which had moved north from Basra and concentrated at Mosul by 28 June, rapidly cleared the area known as the *Bec du Canard*, prominent within which was Tel Kotchek, in north-east Syria.

From the moment the first dust clouds were thrown up by the advancing units of Habforce at H3 on 21 June and the first move north-west along the route of the Euphrates was made by Slim's division, it took a mere two weeks for the whole of eastern Syria to fall under British control, giving credence to the views of those who believed that, had these attacks been co-ordinated with those in the west, a greater overall effect would have been obtained much earlier than that which occurred. Spears claimed that 'Tedder was as puzzled as I was by the fact that Jumbo Wilson did not turn the flank of the Vichy forces from the East. It was wide open, and a thrust from the direction of Palmyra would have compelled either the evacuation or surrender of Damascus', although Spear's claim that the oasis was garrisoned by not more than twenty legionnaires was hopelessly inaccurate.[24]

Dentz stubbornly fought on in the mountain passes between Damascus and Beirut, and along the coast south of Beirut until 11 July, although he had put out peace feelers as early as 18 June, acknowledging reluctantly the inevitability of defeat. Despite the certainty of Allied victory, the intensity of the fighting increased markedly in the remaining two weeks of the campaign. It was the last gasp of a dying man: Dentz and de Verdilhac determined to assuage their honour by sustained and bitter resistance, unwilling to grant to the renegade Gaullists an easy passage. Not an inch was to be squandered without making the Allies pay. Hard, bitter and bloody fighting now developed on the coastal flank before Beirut, in the mountains that guarded the eastern route to the capital from Damascus and the Syrian desert, as well as the southern door to the Bekaa Valley at Merjayoun. Lavarack quite sensibly concentrated his forces to secure Merjayoun before he built up his forces for the advance along the coast towards Beirut, and after two days of hard fighting de Verdilhac withdrew from both Merjayoun and Ibeles Saki on 24 June. On the same day attempts were begun slowly to break the Vichy hold on the mountain passes to the west of Damascus. These, however, were defended with considerable tenacity and, despite substantial effort, attempts over the ensuing days to break through into the Bekaa Valley were to no avail. With no prospect of success, Evetts withdrew his troops on the evening of 27 June and placed his forces in defensive positions west of the city until a second attempt was made to take the Jebel Mazar on 10 and 11 July. This hard-fought fight struggled to make an obvious impression on the Vichy defenders but, just as Evetts again ordered his troops to withdraw from the slaughter, de Verdilhac also began to withdraw, a process interrupted by the cessation of hostilities on 12 July. Whilst this struggle was taking place, mobile Free French units were redeeming themselves in aggressive action on the road to Homs.

On the coast the defences at the Damour River proved a difficult proposition for Lavarack's Australians. The delay whilst Merjayoun was being dealt with allowed reinforcements to build up for the assault on the Vichy positions. Evetts' failure to penetrate across the Anti-Lebanon Mountains and his decision to adopt a defensive posture at the end of June allowed him to take responsibility for the Merjayoun area, which in turn permitted Lavarack to transfer more of his Australians to the coast. Evetts was at this time also reinforced by the newly arrived 23rd British Brigade from his division.[*] Determined pressure eventually overcame the French defences and Damour fell into jubilant Australian hands on 9 July.

An armistice was signed between the two parties at Acre on 14 July, Bastille Day, which drew hostilities in the Levant to a close. However, the British treatment of Vichy during the period leading up to the armistice was unwittingly naive, and created the ingredients for yet another war, this time one of words and emotion between Great Britain and Free France, subtly fostered and encouraged by the vanquished Vichy leaders. The primary factor that precipitated this war was the unintended arrogance of Wilson's treatment of Free France

---

[*] Comprising 1 Battalion The Durham Light Infantry, 4 Battalion The Border Regiment and a Czechoslovak Battalion.

during the negotiations and subsequent armistice, which stoked the fires of de Gaulle's misgivings about British intentions. Throughout, Great Britain's purpose in *Operation Exporter* was to deny Germany a foothold in Syria, so preventing the opening up of Iraq (and thus Iran) and Palestine to the threat of German invasion, not to overthrow the Vichy regime or to defeat its armies *per se*. Its objective therefore was precautionary. For de Gaulle, however, the rationale was entirely different, being associated with the recovery of French honour and the retention of the integrity of its empire against the concerted depredations of those amongst the British who, to de Gaulle's mind, were bent on its destruction.

In his haste to end hostilities, Wilson seems not to have considered the intricate and delicate political relationship between Great Britain and Free France. Instead, he concluded a treaty with the Vichy enemy without allowing Free France a meaningful role in negotiations, treating Vichy with more consideration than the cause of Free France itself, relegating it to a position of insignificance and in the process creating a rift between de Gaulle and his British allies.

For his part, Dentz was desperate not to have to suffer the humiliation of surrendering to de Gaulle. Wilson's bungling allowed him to retain his spurious honour at the expense of Britain's allies. The affair showed clearly that despite the claims of one of his biographers, Wilson was not an astute diplomat.[25] Thus, Vichy surrendered to Great Britain, not to Free France. As news of the armistice filtered through to Cairo, the terms agreed with Dentz caused immediate consternation, recalled Spears, to 'all but the military. Jumbo Wilson's attitude seemed to some of those closest to the Minister of State [Lyttelton] (and I thought the Embassy also) to be incomprehensible.'[26] These terms placed Free France at a significant political disadvantage *apropos* Great Britain: large numbers of Vichy troops were to be allowed to embark with their weapons and equipment to France, there in all probability to be deployed against Great Britain again in North Africa, which remained under Vichy control. The local auxiliaries were handed over to Great Britain, there was no mention of the mandate and Wilson agreed a secret protocol that allowed for the repatriation of Vichy troops to France, thereby denying de Gaulle the ability to recruit freely. As it was, only 5,600 soldiers and 400 officials joined the Free French cause. Smugly content with a straightforward and seemingly amicable military settlement, Wilson – a simple and uncomplicated soldier described by one historian as a 'breezy pragmatist'[27] – remained ignorant of the political disaster he had caused.

On Monday 21 July de Gaulle let loose in fury at the unfortunate Lyttelton, refusing to accept the armistice terms on the basis that they were made without his approval and handing him a written ultimatum stating that with effect from 24 July all Free French troops would cease to be under British command. Lyttelton refused to accept the note but a serious rift remained. Plans were even made for de Gaulle to be arrested if he took the step he threatened, but tempers diminished in the ensuing days and all parties moved back from the prospect of a dangerous and potentially catastrophic fissure between the Allies. De Gaulle saw in the debacle not Wilson's soldierly plodding but a political stitch-up by the British at the highest level, conspiring to 'replace France at Damascus and Beirut'.[28] In this he was mistaken, his passion blinding him to the truth that it was the tyranny of distance, poor command and control, and incompetence which were the real culprits, rather than grand and devious political design. To de Gaulle's suspicious mind, however, it seemed that the dastardly British had managed to get their hands on the Levant, despite his best efforts.

It is not surprising that de Gaulle was suspicious, as both he and Spears had drafted a series of notes relating to the expected armistice terms as early as 13 June, copying them to both Wavell and Churchill. These notes covered a range of areas that in the event Wilson had entirely ignored.[29] It was to take the combined efforts of Spears, Lyttelton and Eden to plaster over the crisis during the following days with a set of protocols that interpreted Wilson's armistice terms much more decidedly in favour of Free France. But the harm had been done, and relations in the Levant between its new rulers and Great Britain were never fully repaired.*

Was *Operation Exporter* worth the blood and treasure expended in June and July 1941? The campaign cost the Allies 4,600 killed and wounded

---

* This story is told well, and briefly, in chapter six of François Kersaudy's *Churchill and de Gaulle* (London: Collins, 1981), and somewhat less objectively in de Gaulle's own war memoirs, *The Call to Honour*, also chapter six.

and the Vichy French some 6,500. On the basis of the evidence that faced Churchill and the War Cabinet in 1941, there is no doubt that it was a clear and unequivocal strategic necessity for Great Britain. *Luftwaffe* support to Iraq in May had revealed the vulnerability of Great Britain's grasp on its northern flank, and the pattern of German activity, both military and political, reinforced fears that Syria was threatened and, with it, Palestine and the Suez Canal. Until 21 May 1941 Wavell had been a lone voice against every other rational indicator which showed only too clearly the thrust of the German advance towards the Middle East in general (through the Balkans and Greece) and Syria and Iraq in particular, and the consequences that this would have for the British position – both politically and militarily – in the Middle East. As Spears repeatedly and correctly insisted, the basic problem in the dispute between London and Cairo in the weeks leading up to Wavell's enforced acquiescence on 21 May was 'Wavell's failure to realize the absolute necessity of undertaking the Syrian campaign', a necessity as clear as the light of day to virtually every other interested party in the region at the time.[30]

Harold Raugh argues a contrary view. He considers that the invasion of Syria and Lebanon was futile because the threat of German intervention had dissipated by the time it was launched, and does not believe that the collaboration of Vichy in the Levant was sufficient to justify the action. It is true that clear information that the Germans were evacuating from Syria was ignored by both Cairo and London, and that Germany was obviously concentrating forces for an attack on Russia.[31] But German plans to invade Russia by no means indicated that they had given up plans to attack Syria, even in the short term. British strategists regarded the idea of a German invasion of Russia as an enormous folly: Sir Alexander Cadogan, the permanent head of the Foreign Office, commented on 31 May that even though the signs looked as though Germany was prepared to attack Russia he was certain that they would not, as 'they're not such fools [as the British General Staff]'.[32] Equally, most observers, even when Britain knew for certain on 12 June that the attack would take place (four days *after* the start of *Operation Exporter*), did not consider that *Barbarossa* would completely shut the door on German ambitions in the region. The logical strategy in Cadogan's eyes was for Germany to seize Turkey or Syria so as to drive on Iraq and Iran (and thus secure Britain's oil) and then to punch down through Palestine to grab the Suez Canal.[33] Fortunately for Great Britain, Hitler was no strategist, although amongst his advisers Raeder and Goering recommended this plan.

Raugh concludes that the facts relating to the German withdrawal from Syria in early June:

> indicate clearly that Wavell was correct in his reluctance to advance into that country which, bereft of Axis support, could have been ignored, and would have eventually succumbed because of its relative isolation and impotence. Wavell's assessment that Free French political intrigue, combined with the Prime Minister's insatiable desire for offensive action, had served as the impetus for the Syrian campaign, was probably correct.[34]

Yet Raugh's argument does not accord with Wavell's own conclusions. As early as 15 May, as can be evidenced from the appreciation he sent to Dill on that date, Wavell had recognized that a threat to Palestine and the Canal from a German attack from Syria was very real and dangerous. After this date Wavell did not deny the facts of the threat, but merely expressed concern about the level of resources he had available to deal with it. After the ultimatum from Churchill six days later on 21 May, Wavell knuckled down and prepared to deal with the Syrian crisis as best he could. Had British intelligence been better than it was, Syria could have been left to 'wither on the vine' as Wavell wanted, and the demands by the Free French for action effectively resisted. Not dealing decisively with a threat from Vichy-held Syria, however, would not have been a sensible long-term policy for London, because although the Germans were not able to operate in 1941 on a large-scale in the Middle East, they had not rejected it entirely as an option. Raugh's conclusion is also analysis by hindsight. We only know that Syria posed a negligible threat *after* the event. At the time, the Vichy policy of collaboration made Syria a latent threat to British interest in the Middle East, and to this fact Wavell reluctantly acceded.

Fears of a continuing German interest in the region were well founded. Whilst it was known in early June that Germany was preparing to attack Russia, and that this would become the short-term focus of German ambitions, it was also widely believed that Russia would fall quickly, which would then leave both Turkey and Syria at threat from the north. On 30 June German Military Directive 32 was drafted, which shows that, despite *Barbarossa*, Germany still had ambitions in the region:

> [the] continuation of the struggle against the British position in the Mediterranean and the Middle East by means of a concentric attack which is to be launched from Libya through Egypt, from Bulgaria through Turkey, and possibly from Transcaucasia through Iran.

On 24 July 1941 Field Marshal von Brauchitsch, the Commander-in-Chief of the German Army, submitted a detailed plan for these operations, entailing a force of five armoured divisions, three motorized divisions and twelve infantry divisions.[35] Wilfred Thesiger, who served with a squadron of mounted Druze fighters during the short campaign, recalled in late 1941 the still persistent fear of a German plan to invade Syria by way of the Caucasus and Turkey, so much so that he was instructed to arrange stay-behind guerrilla parties to resist a German occupation, should it come.[36] It was only Russian resistance and the US entry into the war in December 1941 that allowed these contingency plans to be shelved.

The latent threat of German occupation of the Levant States, together with Vichy willingness to collaborate with the Axis Powers, was sufficient justification for an attack. Moreover, German activities in Syria in May 1941 gave perfect evidence of what they would and could do. Leaving a sore to fester was poor strategy, as was an attitude that saw only imminent battle (in the Western Desert) to be the pre-eminent danger. Wavell's determined refusal to accept the strategic imperatives as they appeared at the time can only be an indication of a serious flaw in his generalship. We have noticed already his focus on the military at the expense of the political, and London had some considerable responsibility for the tortuous and even unworkable command and control relationships in place at the time. In May and June 1941 the simple strategic reality as it pertained to the Levant was that summarized by Spears in a message to Churchill on 22 May, namely that the 'unchangeable constant is the extreme danger of the occupation of Syria by Germans.'[37] This Wavell saw, but failed to act upon until forced to do so, against his will. Churchill understood *why*

Wavell refused to act, but he did not consider lack of resources sufficient excuse for inaction. 'There is always much to be said for not attempting more than you can do and for making a certainty of what you try,' Churchill recorded. 'But this principle, like others in life and war, has its exceptions.'[38] To his mind, both Syria and Iraq were clearly so.

Wavell has come in for criticism on another count. According to both Dill and Kennedy, Wavell blundered in attempting to conduct a campaign in Syria simultaneously with an offensive in the Western Desert, making no attempt at phasing the two so that he could switch resources from one to the other and reduce the inherent weaknesses of conducting both at the same time. Dill wrote to Auchinleck on 26 June to explain the problems that Wavell faced as C-in-C and which Auchinleck was now to inherit:

> It was most desirable to clear the Germans back in Libya at the earliest possible moment, so that the Navy might be able to get the air protection necessary to enable it to attack the enemy's communications with Tripoli and also maintain Malta.
>
> It was also highly desirable to act rapidly in Syria to forestall the Germans.
>
> From Whitehall, great pressure was applied to Wavell to induce him to act rapidly, and, under this pressure, he advanced into Syria with much less strength than was desirable, and in the Western Desert he attacked before in fact he was fully prepared. The fault was not Wavell's except in so far as he did not resist the pressure from Whitehall with sufficient vigour.[39]

Kennedy likewise accepted the argument that both issues needed to be resolved, but that executing them at the same time was an 'error of judgement' that led to both operations suffering from the very dispersion of forces of which Wavell was afraid.[40] On 17 June General Alan Brooke attended a meeting with Churchill as one of the Prime Minister's Commanders-in-Chief.* When Churchill commented that they were planning a large-scale operation in Libya, Brooke was horrified. He confided to his diary:

* Alan Brooke replaced Dill as CIGS on 25 December 1941.

How can we undertake offensive operations on two fronts in the Middle East when we have not got sufficient for one? From the moment we decided to go into Syria we should have to put all our strength on that front to complete the operation with the least possible delay. If the operation is not pressed through quickly it may well lead to further complications.[41]

Kennedy argues that Dill had given Wavell a strong hint that it would be wise to postpone the desert offensive and to make sure of Syria first, but he elected not to do so, with the result that both operations suffered for lack of punch.[42] In a briefing note prepared for Dill on 26 June Kennedy wrote:

In a retrospect over the last few months, even making allowance for the great difficulties with which Wavell has had to contend, it is clear that grave errors have been committed both in London and the Middle East . . .

The pressure exerted by London upon the Commanders-in-Chief in the Middle East has been far too great. There has been a constant flow of directives and suggestions regarding both major and minor policy . . .

It seems to me, however, that the gravest mistake has been committed in the Middle East. This mistake . . . consists in the acquiescence by the Commanders-in-Chief in practically every suggestion which was put to them. On occasion they have expressed disagreement, but their disagreement has never been insisted upon.

It is probably true to say that every commander in the field has been subjected to pressure by his government to adopt this or that strategy. But the great commander, in this situation, must display, and in history he has always displayed, a considerable degree of toughness or stubbornness in resisting propositions which he believes to be unsound. [Consequently] much of the blame for the present situation must be laid upon the shoulders of the Commanders-in-Chief, and of Wavell in particular.[43]

This criticism seems unjust, as it is clear from the record that Wavell was ordered in no uncertain terms to mount both offensives. Churchill gave firm instructions to Wavell on 21 May and insisted that if he were unable to effect these plans he would be relieved. Wavell had no choice but to act to remove this threat to his northern flank. But, as Kennedy insists, it is also true that Wavell did have the choice about phasing and dates, and he could have managed his forces more intelligently so as to maintain real strength for each offensive, instead of violating the elementary principle of concentration.

It is clear that the invasion of Syria and Lebanon was not cleverly planned, and that *Operation Exporter* suffered from a plethora of unfortunate mistakes at the hands of its senior commanders. Fortunately it was rescued, as is often the case, by the courage and fortitude of the fighting troops. The first problem was that it was too late: to have made real political capital, it should have taken place in mid-May rather than a month later so as to exploit the unequivocal evidence of German involvement in Syria. Many post action reports spoke of the French claim that, had Great Britain marched into Syria within a week of the arrival of German aircraft, the British advance would have been unopposed.[44] Second, Wilson's three-pronged assault dissipated the force that should have been concentrated at one point, in' clear violation of the principle of concentration of force, exacerbating dire British numerical weakness. This was partly the result of over-optimistic expectations about how quickly the Vichy regime would fall, but it was also an elementary failure in military planning (and one that worried Lavarack immensely), for which Wilson and Blamey bear the greatest responsibility. Third, if we accept the criticism made by Dill, Brooke and Kennedy, Wavell made the mistake of conducting his offensives in the Western Desert and the Levant simultaneously, and not phasing them. Fourth, no attempt was made to exploit the wide-open weakness of Dentz's eastern flank until much later in the campaign, and both Clark's Habforce and Slim's 10 Indian Division showed how much could have been achieved with an earlier and more co-ordinated deployment from the south-east and east.

The problem of Iraq had been forced upon Great Britain at the last minute because of its inability to forestall the crisis in the months and years before, if that were possible, by political action. Nevertheless, when threatened, strong military action was required and, when applied pre-emptively, succeeded against all expectations in restoring a British position that had been grievously imperilled by the odd mixture of Arab nationalism and Nazi opportunism. In Syria the same logic held true. Vichy-controlled Syria remained a latent threat to the security of British interests in the Middle East, but became a real threat when the regime began to collaborate with their erstwhile enemies to defeat their one-time friends and allies. With the world so turned upside down, Britain had to act; and she did so, if not decisively, then at least successfully. In so doing, as Churchill with some relief explained, it 'greatly improved our strategical position in the Middle East. It closed the door to any further attempt at enemy penetration eastwards from the Mediterranean, moved our defence of the Suez Canal northwards by 250 miles, and relieved Turkey of anxiety for her southern frontier.'[45]

The final word on the *Affaire Levantine* – or at least the end of military hostilities in July 1941, for the political struggle for control of Syria and Lebanon was to run until the French were ejected in 1946 – can be left to Churchill, who told the House of Commons in his least triumphalist tone on 15 July:

> If anyone had predicted two months ago, when Iraq was in revolt and our people were hanging on by their eyelids at Habbaniya and our Ambassador was imprisoned in his Embassy at Baghdad, and when all Syria and Iraq began to overrun with German Tourists, and were in the hands of forces controlled indirectly but nonetheless powerfully by German authority – if anyone had predicted that we should already, by the middle of July, have cleaned up the whole of the Levant and have re-established our authority there for the time being, such a prophet would have been considered most imprudent.[46]

Churchill's relief on a successful outcome was palpable. *Operation Exporter* was a close-run thing and could easily have turned into yet another disaster for British arms and a further crisis for the British strategic position in the Middle East: indeed, even for Britain's ongoing ability to continue resisting Nazi tyranny altogether. If the gamble to seize Syria had been lost, Germany might not have exploited this disaster to attack the Suez Canal through Palestine or to seize control of Iraqi oil (although it is clear that German policy makers still regarded this as a serious possibility). But if Germany had taken this action, the war would have turned very much worse for Great Britain, and might even have ended there and then completely if American oil was threatened or cut off in any way. As it was, first Iraq and then Syria were secured, both by the closest of margins. Both gambles had been close-run things, but had eventually, and against the expectations of many, paid off.

As the Indian Official Historian presciently observed, the invasion and occupation of Syria was made possible only, in an unintended way, by the use of firm action in Iraq, although this was unknown of course to policy makers at the time. Iraq then acted as a pivot in a series of schemes during the coming months to defend the Middle East from Axis attack through either Turkey or the Caucasus.[47] The primary threat to the British position in the Middle East now lay to the east, in Iran. It was to this that London now turned.

8

Tehran

By June 1941 Iran* had been governed for fifteen years by Reza Khan Pahlevi, the Shah-in-Shah,† an ex-colonel of the Russian-trained Cossack Division of the Iranian Army who had seized power in a *coup d'état* in 1921 before assuming the throne in 1926. Iran had, under his tutelage, attempted to make the transition from an agrarian to a modern industrialized economy. However, the Shah – conservative, introspective, illiterate and dictatorial – was distrustful of foreigners, a not entirely unexpected characteristic for the king of a country that had been repeatedly fought over by competing European imperial powers for centuries, and the immaturity of his dealings with foreign powers contributed significantly to his downfall in 1941. He attempted to protect Iran from Great Power entanglement whilst at the same time trying to provide the investment necessary for the modernization of his country's infrastructure. This juggling act proved impossible to sustain, in the main because of the stark realities of Iran's geo-strategic position. The fact that longitudinally it straddled the divide between the Middle East and Asia and latitudinally that between the Persia Gulf and Caspian Sea, as well as possessing vast riches of oil, made it impossible for a warring Europe to ignore.

* Iran was officially known as such since 1935, although the term 'Persia' was still widely used outside the country, not least of all by Winston Churchill, who insisted on its use.
† King of kings. He assumed the title of Reza Shah Pahlevi.

The late nineteenth century had witnessed the growing involvement and influence of European powers in Iranian affairs, as part of the 'Great Game'. The government of the country was weak and divided and the European powers exploited this disarray for their own ends. During the First World War, despite declaring her strict neutrality, Russia entered from the north and the Caspian Sea, Germans and Turks entered from Iraq and the British entered from India.

Russia's (pre-1917) interest in Iran had been to gain access to a warm-water port. Great Britain's counter-interest had been, until the early years of the twentieth century, to deny Russia this goal, as it threatened Britain's hegemony all the way from the Persian Gulf to India. Then, from the first decade of the new century, Great Britain's interest narrowed to focus almost exclusively on black gold. From before the First World War the British Government was concerned to secure oil rights in Iran, to fuel the conversion of the Royal Navy from coal. It obtained a controlling interest in the Anglo-Persian Oil Company (APOC) and built a huge refinery, for many years the largest in the world, on the Shatt al-Arab at Abadan. Many of the APOC oil fields lay in the province of Khuzestan, and others were in the west around Kermanshah. The APOC was important to Iran, as it earned royalties from the company. In 1939–40 these constituted 11.5 per cent of total Iranian revenue.[1]

Iran was bordered to the north by the Soviet Union, to the west by Turkey and Iraq, and to the east by India and Afghanistan. A large country – with a length of some 1,400 miles and a breadth of 900 – it is mountainous for half its size, one-eighth cultivable and the remainder desert. It is a country of climatic and topographical extremes. The northern part forms a massive plateau, some 3,000 to 5,000 feet above sea level with mountain ranges in the north and west, and a vast desert in the east some 200 miles wide and 800 miles deep. The north sees snow for three or four months of winter across the expanse of the plateau, whilst along the Persian Gulf the summer temperatures compete with those of Iraq for intensity and magnitude: 130 degrees Fahrenheit in the shade being the daytime norm.

Once in power, Pahlevi proceeded ruthlessly to consolidate his position. He built up his army with the help of a French military mission, religious fervency was discouraged and the modernization of the country's infrastructure, financed by taxes, gained a new impetus.

During the late 1920s Iran was thus largely able to go its own way, without the interference of outsiders. Russia was too concerned with her own Stalinist agenda, Germany was in domestic political turmoil, and Great Britain was content to encourage the growth of a strong Iran. However, the 1930s saw a dramatic shift in Iran's international allegiances in favour of Germany, which was prepared to provide Iran with the credit it needed to sustain the Shah's ambitious modernization programme. By the end of the decade Germany was by far the largest external investor in the country. Iranian goods flowed to German markets and large numbers of German technicians moved to Iran. By the mid-1930s Germans were dominant in many parts of the economy. By 1941 two-thirds of Iran's trade was with Germany. German engineers completed the construction of the trans-Iranian railway, which traversed the country from the Persian Gulf to the Soviet border 900 miles to the north. The Nazi regime did much to propagandize Iran and in November 1939 Berlin appointed the ardent Nazi, SS-Oberführer Erwin Ettel, as its ambassador to Tehran.

Trade relations had fallen off with the Soviet Union for political reasons in 1939.[2] The relationship with Great Britain had deteriorated during the 1930s, landing and flying rights for Imperial Airways aircraft were withdrawn in 1932 and the APOC was forced to renegotiate its concession. By 1941 Great Britain received a mere 8 per cent of Iran's exports and provided 9 per cent of her imports. Despite the declining influence of Great Britain in Iran, the country remained of enormous strategic significance to her. There were two reasons for this. The first was the security of her precious oil, especially that of the massive APOC refinery at Abadan. The vulnerability of the Iranian oil fields to Axis action had been demonstrated by an ambitious aerial attack on Bahrain by Italian bombers in October 1940, flying from Eritrea across Arabia. The bombs missed their targets but they provided an indication of what could be achieved by a resourceful and determined opponent. Without Iranian oil, the British strategic situation would be parlous indeed. The second was the security of the imperial communications along and through the Iranian and Arabian littorals. If an enemy were to secure aerial access to the Persian Gulf, the whole of Great Britain's freedom of action in those waters would be put in jeopardy, as would the aerial link between Cairo and New Delhi, which passed directly through the region. At the very least a number of strategically placed

Iranian airfields running along the Iranian littoral would need to be secured against enemy use.[3]

Until early 1941 the clear enemy to Great Britain's interests in the region was the USSR, Britain's traditional rival in Iran. Moscow's three-fold strategic aspiration – eradicating British influence in the country, separating Great Britain from the source of her Middle Eastern oil, and achieving the age-old Russian goal of securing a warm-water port – could be brought about through an invasion of Iran.

London was right to be concerned about Soviet intentions. On 23 August 1939, a week before the onset of war, the USSR and Germany concluded a non-aggression treaty, known thereafter by the names of its two signatories – Ribbentrop and Molotov. This marriage of convenience added a new seriousness to the old geo-strategic 'game' between the two competing empires in Central Asia, as it allowed Stalin the freedom to contemplate territorial aggrandizement in Asia without the fear of a military confrontation with Germany.

Despite Germany's close trade ties with Iran, Hitler did not have what Churchill assumed to be an 'Oriental Plan'.[4] Germany had no strategy for the Middle East beyond the vague intention to cause Great Britain mischief wherever and with whatever means it could. North Africa and the USSR absorbed her attention once Greece had capitulated and Crete had fallen. Hitler's strategy for direct German involvement in the Middle East in 1939 and 1940, therefore, was small-scale and opportunistic, rather than detailed and strategic. Iraq was one example of this policy of muted engagement. The consequence of Germany's policy (or lack of one) was a dramatic increase in the influence of the Soviet Union in Central and Southern Asia, a development greeted with consternation by both Turkey and Iran. Moscow's hostility to Iran in the late summer of 1940 was thinly disguised. Soviet troop build-ups in the Transcaucasus began within weeks of the outset of war.[5] The options for Tehran were clear: be courted by Moscow in a one-way relationship where it would become little more than a vassal state of its aggressive neighbour, or be invaded. Unwilling to accede to either option, in January 1940 the Iranians began to strengthen their northern fortifications and initiated secret approaches to Great Britain, seeking increased military liaison, co-operation and equipment.[6] This path had already successfully been taken by Turkey. That Iran felt compelled to approach Great Britain for succour in its hour of need is indicative of the enormity of the threat it believed it faced from the USSR.

Iranian fears coincided precisely with those of Great Britain. The problem for Great Britain was one of over-extension. It simply did not have the military resources to confront aggression simultaneously across the length and breadth of its global interests. When the USSR invaded eastern Poland on 17 September 1939, as part of the carve-up agreed by the Ribbentrop–Molotov Pact, Great Britain decided not to declare war on the USSR – as it had done to Germany on 3 September following the German invasion of western Poland – because it feared that the USSR might use this as a pretext for an invasion of Iran. These fears were reinforced by intelligence reports in October 1939 that the Soviets were reinforcing their garrisons along the Iranian and Turkish borders.

Consequently, GHQ India was asked to compile a plan to counter Soviet moves in the region – and the *Herring/Trout* (*Sybil/Sabine*) family was born, which envisaged the despatch of initially a single Indian brigade to Basra to be followed, if a Soviet land-based offensive developed, by a further two full divisions.* At the same time Wavell in Cairo carried out his own analysis of the threat from the USSR, and concluded that the immediate threat was to the oil fields – the Abadan refinery in particular – and was posed by Soviet aircraft flying from the Caucasus. He suggested that a suitable response to such an attack would be for British and French aircraft to strike at the Soviet oil fields, such as Baku, Grozny and Batum, in reply. This conclusion was accepted by the Chiefs of Staff in December 1939. Wavell was ordered to make preparations to secure the British air bases in the region, which provided the only means of ensuring a counter-strike capability against the Soviet oil fields in the event of war breaking out between the two countries.[7]

Tehran's secret approach to London for the joint co-ordination of war plans against the possibility of Soviet attack met with failure, however. The Chiefs of Staff were reluctantly forced to reject these proposals because of the undesirability at the time of 'mortgaging' the limited British military capability in the Middle East to Iran. There were just not enough troops or aircraft to go around. London, as has been seen, was also fearful of precipitating a Soviet counter-action.[8] Iran would have to remain neutral for the time being. On 19 February

---

* See page 40.

1940, however, London did agree that a Soviet invasion of either Iran or Afghanistan would be sufficient cause to declare war and it continued to plan for such an eventuality.

Until January 1940 British concerns had been entirely defensive, with counter-strike options considered against the Caucasian oil fields only as a consequence of initial Soviet action. However, Edouard Daladier, the French Prime Minister, began to advocate the use of pre-emptive strikes against these oil fields with long-range bombers flying from French bases in Syria, British bases in Iraq, as well as airfields in Iran and Turkey, with the aim of preventing Soviet petroleum from reaching Germany and fuelling the Nazi war machine. In the event, the same worries about precipitating war with the Soviet Union that had swayed the Chiefs of Staff in September 1939 over the issue of eastern Poland persuaded them again in March 1940 not to participate in these plans.[9] Planning, however, for potential attacks against the Soviet oil fields continued without interruption, including reconnaissance overflights of Baku by British aircraft. The Soviets responded with ineffective long-range anti-aircraft fire.[10]

Anglo-French interest in the region persuaded the Soviet Union that Great Britain at least had offensive aspirations in Iran, causing it to continue the movement of large numbers of Soviet troops and aircraft to the area that it had begun in October 1939. The numbers of aircraft deployed, for instance, increased from 40 in 1939 to 400 over a year later, and troops and tanks totalled some 200,000 and 1,000 respectively, an increase of 50 per cent over pre-war figures. By late March 1940 Soviet forces in the Caucasus totalled eleven infantry divisions, one armoured division, three cavalry divisions and three independent light armoured regiments.[11] During the desperate summer of 1940 London fully expected the USSR to take advantage of Britain's military embarrassment in Western Europe by invading Iran.

These fears were reinforced in June 1940 when Stalin seized the Baltic states of Estonia, Latvia and Lithuania, followed by eastern Romania. His attentions then turned southward to Iran and Turkey again. The first step in Stalin's plan was to force through transit rights in Iran and to insist on the elimination of what remained of British influence, and in June and July pressure against both Iran and Turkey was stepped up, creating a common assumption amongst decision-makers in London and Tehran that Stalin was creating a pretext for an invasion. In mid-July London was convinced that Soviet action was imminent, and authorized the immediate preparation of 9 Indian Infantry Brigade – the vanguard of *Force Herring* – for despatch to Basra.

However, as the lead brigade was setting sail from Bombay for Basra, Wavell intervened, suggesting that the move of British troops to Iraq could be construed by the Soviets as a hostile act, and might provide them with the *casus belli* for which they had been seeking. If the Soviets did invade, Wavell did not have the wherewithal to defend the oil fields and refineries. So, for the third time in eleven months Great Britain stepped back from the brink of a confrontation with the Soviet Union, fearing that it did not have the military resources necessary to win an argument if it came to war. New Delhi agreed, and the whole of 5 Indian Division was sent instead to North Africa.

Stalin's appetite for war against Great Britain in Iran in actual fact reduced during the second half of the year. He was impressed that Britain did not fall to the *Luftwaffe* onslaught during the long hot summer of 1940. He was also fearful of the prospect of devastating Allied air strikes against his vulnerable oil fields, a worry reinforced by the persistent overflight of unmarked Allied aircraft during the spring. The German capture of French plans in July 1940, and their sharing of this intelligence with Moscow, persuaded Stalin of the viability of such an attack. For its part too, Iran, under the Shah's dogged leadership, refused to kowtow to Soviet demands, and heavy-handed Soviet diplomacy had already chased Turkey into a treaty with Great Britain. Stalin appeared to allow the Iranian situation to wait out the winter before new measures could be considered in the spring of 1941.

For his part, Hitler continued to press the Soviet Union to involve itself in the Middle East, and offered up Iran as part of the spoils resulting from the soon-expected demise of the British Empire.[12] Discussions between Ribbentrop and Molotov took place in Berlin in November 1940. Hints of the nature of these talks made Iran increasingly nervous of Soviet and Nazi intentions. Hitler in fact offered Stalin all the territory that lay between Europe and the Indian Ocean. On 25 November, Stalin accepted Hitler's offer and Soviet military preparations to invade Iran were accelerated. Moscow's reaction to Berlin's offer, however, precipitated a falling-out amongst thieves that was ultimately to allow Iran off the hook, at least for the time being. In his response to Hitler,

Stalin also claimed Finland and the Dardanelles, claims that so infuriated the Führer that he ordered planning to begin in the German High Command for *Operation Barbarossa*, the invasion of the Soviet Union. Work on this ambitious endeavour, last attempted so disastrously by Napoleon, was initiated on 18 December 1940.[13]

As the curtain fell in the final stages of the drama in Iraq during late May, London pushed hard for Wavell to seize Mosul at the earliest opportunity. The town had an airfield within striking distance of the Baku oil fields. London believed that Stalin would give in to German pressure to act against British interests in the Middle East, which was how some in London were interpreting the now obvious build-up of German forces along the Third Reich's eastern border. The Chiefs of Staff told Wavell on 31 May 1941:

> We have had firm indication that Germans are now concentrating large army and air forces against Russia. Under this threat they will probably demand concessions most injurious to us. Russian resistance may be strongly influenced if they think that should they submit to Germans we shall attack Baku oil. If we are to use this threat to exert pressure on Russians we must control Mosul before Russians and/or Germans can forestall us. Most energetic action should therefore be taken to get control in Mosul. Can you devise method to achieve this? Small airborne force might suffice.[14]

Seizing Mosul airfield, it was believed, would provide a deterrent to Soviet ambitions, as it would enable Great Britain to strike back against Baku if Moscow ever attempted to attack British interests in the region by air. All the indications were that Soviet action against Iran was imminent. Between May and June 1941 the Soviet Transcaucasus Military District conducted detailed field exercises in preparation for an invasion of Iran. At the same time substantial reinforcements – the whole of the 16th Army from the Transbaikal Military District in fact – were despatched to the region from Siberia. As it turned out, they were re-directed *en route* to Kiev, never reaching their intended destination, but their original purpose was to support an offensive against Iran.[15]

In early 1941 a new worry presented itself to London. This was the fear that both Germany and the USSR might work in concert to attack the British in the Middle East, with thrusts by Germany through

Turkey or Syria into Iraq, and by the USSR into Iran through the Caucasus. This fear of an external attack added to a growing worry about the possible consequences of internal Nazi influence in Iran. If Iran's long-standing economic friendship with Germany were translated into political acquiescence, Iran's neutrality would be subverted. The result, if Iran became strongly pro-German, would be to split British interests in the region in two, between Palestine and Iraq in the west and India to the east. Second, a German-leaning Iran would undoubtedly attempt to prevent Great Britain's access to its oil. The battle of the Atlantic was placing a new pressure on Iranian and Iraqi oil, given the submarine threat to tankers crossing the Atlantic from the New World.[16] A Nazi-friendly Iran would also threaten India and the vital lines of communication between the Middle and the Far East. The issue of imperial communications was closely linked to the security of India, and the protection of India from Russian expansion towards the Persian Gulf had always been a key motivation of the 'Great Game' and was deeply ingrained in the psyche of the Raj.

In New Delhi, Auchinleck articulated these fears, and his solution for countering them, in an appreciation he sent to Wavell in Cairo on 21 February 1941. Auchinleck's view was that the deployment of up to three divisions of Indian and British troops was the minimum requirement to secure Iraq, and to prevent Germany from attacking Iran through Turkey or Iraq, with or without Soviet help.[17] In Iran, nervousness about Soviet ambitions continued to bubble at the surface of political life. With London unable to help through lack of resources, and unwilling to ally itself to Iran for fear of the Soviet reaction, Iran was thrown on to its own resources, and feverishly prepared defensive fortifications and demolitions in the north. All the while, Soviet plans and exercises based upon a decisive thrust into Iran continued through March and April 1941.

Speculation was rife throughout the region of an impending Soviet invasion, so much so that even the precocious Captain Somerset de Chair was informed in Baghdad on the strongest authority that a Soviet move against Iran was imminent. This prospect, of course, seemed to be cancelled out by the even stronger speculation that the Soviet Union was herself about to be invaded by Germany 'within a week'. Baghdad, a hotbed of intelligence, rumour and gossip, some well founded and some not, nevertheless had a surprisingly accurate finger on the pulse of the dramatic events about to engulf the whole of Eastern Europe.[18] Needless to say, de Chair's regimental colleagues scoffed at his prognostications, but his sources proved to be remarkably prescient.

London had for some weeks been in receipt of secret signals intelligence from Ultra decrypts reporting vast movements of German forces to the east. London's theory was that this build-up was posturing designed to secure political concessions from Stalin. On 2 June Anthony Eden, the Foreign Secretary, met the Soviet Ambassador to Great Britain, Ivan Maisky, in Eden's office in Whitehall.* Warning Maisky not to succumb to German pressure to invade Iran, Eden insisted that Great Britain would defend its position in the Middle East vigorously, pointing to the action taken in Iraq as evidence of Great Britain's determination in this regard.[19] Despite Eden's strong words, however, Great Britain did not have the military resources to stand in the way of a Soviet offensive into Iran, were it to arise. Nevertheless, in this and in subsequent meetings in the days following, Eden repeated this message as forcefully as he could. Maisky, in turn, was unable to provide a clear explanation of his government's plans for Iran and Iraq, and therefore could not alleviate Eden's fears about the prospect of Soviet aggrandizement at Great Britain's expense – as was clearly being urged by Germany – in the Middle East.

The primary political motivations for the Shah were the neutrality and sovereignty of his country. His antipathy to uninvited foreign involvement was profound. He feared a repetition of the alliance between Russia and Great Britain which, during the First World War, had led to the occupation of southern Persia by the British and that of the north-west by Russia. The political situation in Iran was peculiarly coloured by the Shah's character. Dogmatic and dictatorial, he had created an environment where his staff were reluctant to proffer advice that they knew would be at odds with his position. The Shah could not read, and was dependent upon his advisers for verbal information. Such was the fury of his temper and the obstinacy of his

* Maisky served as Soviet Ambassador to Great Britain for eleven years until 1943. He was well liked by Churchill and had many friends in the West, although was kept poorly briefed by Moscow.

views – whatever the facts of a situation – that his political and diplomatic staff became little more than a sycophantic band, unwilling to give their chief unpalatable news. Throughout the period between July and September 1941 he never fully understood Great Britain's determination to destroy the sources of German intrigue in Iran, nor was he able to control such intrigue, given the pro-German nature of his own police, military and civil service. Both failings were to contribute to his downfall.

One of the weaknesses of European diplomacy at the time was a failure to appreciate the isolationism of the Iranian State, and also of the insularity of the Shah-in-Shah. The Shah was unwilling to be bullied by any foreigners – German, British, Soviet or American alike – and this factor played strongly in his decision-making. Berlin, for example, assumed that the Iranian Government would naturally support the Iraqi rebels because they, like Iran, lay within the broad expanse of German influence and likewise had displayed hostility towards British interests in the past. But this was to define Iranian foreign policy too narrowly. It took no account of Iranian suspicions about the nature of German support for Soviet plans to invade Iran, or indeed of foreigners generally. Iranian dependence on Germany for technical support and its willingness to create and develop relationships with the Third Reich across a range of economic and cultural activities did not mean that all of Iran's political or diplomatic loyalties flowed in the same direction. Far from it. Germany's economic interest in Iran, and the general favour shown to Germany by many Iranians, did not equate to acquiescence by the Shah in any involvement or influence by Germany in Iran's sovereign affairs, or indeed any diminution of Iran's sovereign national prerogatives. Iran's relationship with Germany was a practical and pragmatic friendship forged in times of peace and built on a foundation of expediency, and was increasingly strained as a result of war. Courting Nazi Germany for economic ends, however, was a dangerous game for the Shah to play. Berlin attempted to put pressure on the Shah to support the Iraqi regime in its fight against the British, but throughout May Iran maintained a defiant neutrality and refused to be dragged into quarrels not of its own making. The Shah had not welcomed Rashid Ali's coup and the consequent unrest in Iraq in April 1941. He even suggested to his Supreme War Council that Iran despatch two divisions to crush the revolt, although he was eventually persuaded against this idea.[20]

For its part London assumed that Iran, if not necessarily a willing participant in anti-Allied activities, was at the very least a stool pigeon for Axis intrigue. German interests were closely controlled from Tehran by Ettel, and Great Britain had evidence that he had a number of espionage agents on his payroll. Indeed, the Iraqi *putsch* in April 1941 was financed and organized from the German Legation in Tehran. Dr Grobba, the German Ambassador, had made Tehran his headquarters until Rashid Ali's coup had allowed him to return to Baghdad, and it was to Tehran that the Iraqi fugitives fled when their adventure collapsed at the end of May. None of this, however, made it axiomatic that Iran would blindly follow the diktats of Berlin in respect of her foreign, let alone domestic, policy. But the equation of the two ideas served British political purposes in terms of its developing *casus belli*.

Privately, Tehran was fearful that Germany would use any pretext to accuse it of favouring London. The only way Iran could withstand such pressure was by an alliance with Great Britain, or even the United States. Sir Reader Bullard, Great Britain's ambassador to Iran, informed London that the Iranians would stand up to German bullying if Great Britain were able to provide military support to Iran, Bullard assuring the Iranian Foreign Ministry that Great Britain would 'assist the Iranian Government within the limits of military necessity.'[21]

Given the importance to her of Iranian oil, and so of not upsetting Iran so much that this oil was denied to her, Great Britain was initially very keen to respect Iranian neutrality. When Major General Fraser was preparing to mount *Operation Sabine* in April, he was ordered to ensure that he did not infringe Iran's neutrality. Within a month, however, the exigencies of war placed this neutrality under threat. The onset of war in 1939 had resulted in the stranding at the Iranian port of Bandar-i Shahpur of eight Axis vessels, three Italian and five German. If scuttled in the middle of the main channel leading into the Shatt al-Arab waterway, the Rooka Channel, these vessels could effectively close the waterway, preventing oil from leaving by ship through the Persian Gulf.[22] British fears of the threat posed by these vessels were well founded, as the Turks had successfully blocked the Rooka Channel during the First World War through the sinking of a German steamer. Intervening to prevent these ships leaving port and scuttling themselves in the entrance to the channel would, however, interfere with Iranian sovereignty and constitute a dramatic escalation of the war.

On 11 May the Foreign Office asked the Admiralty to take steps to ensure that the vessels did not escape. The legitimate demands of Iranian sovereignty were not considered by London to override or negate the equally legitimate requirements of British security. Indeed, on 16 May the German ships were ordered by Berlin to try to break out and scuttle themselves in the channel. Fortunately for Great Britain, they were unable to escape the British naval blockade.

The onset of *Operation Barbarossa* on 22 June 1941 triggered new fears in London regarding Germany's strategic ambitions in Central Asia and the Middle East. British concerns about the security of Iran grew rapidly with the dramatic advances made by the *Wehrmacht* in the east, in the expectation that within months, if not weeks, the Germans would have penetrated the Caucasus and be in a position to threaten Iran from the north. In fact, many expected the Soviet Union to collapse quickly, and for the German legions to be hammering on Iran's northern door by mid-August. The large numbers of German technicians and 'tourists' in the country posed a grave threat in British eyes to the security of the country and made it far more susceptible to external pressure.

New Delhi had assumed responsibility for the defence of British interests in Iraq and Iran on 18 June. A team was hurriedly despatched from India to evaluate the requirements for the defence of the oil fields and the security of the Iranian and Arabian littorals. This recommended the seizure of the ports and airfields at Bushire and Bandar Abbas. In enemy hands, these locations would make operations in the Persian Gulf, and the safety of the oil refineries at Bahrain, especially difficult, if not impossible.[23] There was a very real fear of attempts by in-country Germans to sabotage the oil fields. A summary of GHQ India's conclusions was telegraphed to the Chiefs of Staff in London on 21 June 1941 coincidentally (and unknown to New Delhi) with the eve of the launch of *Barbarossa*. New Delhi told London that the threat was of the Germans seizing airfields in northern Iran, from where they could launch bombing attacks against British strategic sites – the oil fields and ports – across the region.[24]

The question now was how to prevent Iran falling prey to German aggression. Efforts were made immediately to place pressure on the Iranian Government to reduce the influence of Germany in the country, something that New Delhi began to press for soon after *Barbarossa* started, Linlithgow representing forcefully to Leopold Amery, the Secretary of State for India, the view that this malign influence posed a 'dangerous threat to India's security'.[25]

London believed Germany already to hold a position of some strength in Iran, due to the large numbers of German nationals residing there and to Iran's apparent political leanings towards Germany. The Germans had extensive networks of agents in Iran, spying on both the Soviet military structures to the north and on British oil interests in the west and south, and the size of the German expatriate population – some 2,000[*] men, women and children – gave rise for concern. Many, it was feared, could easily act as a fifth column inside the country to support German moves against British interests in Iran, either by sabotaging oil installations, supporting a *coup d'état* and acting as anti-British propagandists or by directly supporting the Iranian Armed Forces in operations against the British. This fear was greatly exacerbated in April and May by German involvement in the war in Iraq. The danger posed by small groups of Nazi agents was only too evident: German successes in the Balkans had been accompanied by significant fifth columnist activity.[26] If Iran fell under direct German control, or became virulently hostile to British interests in the region, it could easily lead to great danger to Great Britain, not just because of the loss of oil it would entail, but also because of the damage it would inevitably cause to imperial communications to and from India. Major General John Kennedy, the Director of Military Operations, wrote on 21 July 1941:

* This was the highest estimate of German nationals in Iran made by the British Embassy in Tehran. However, because of a transmission error in a report from Bullard, London erroneously reported the figure to be 3,000. In fact, on 9 July 1941 there were 690 Germans employed in Iran, most of them in Tehran, with an additional 'several hundred' employed in the German Legation. Their families swelled the total number of German nationals in the country to between 1,500 and 2,000. For those who had access to their own sources, not least of all the Iranian Government, the accusation that there were '3,000' Germans in Iran appeared absurdly inflated and led to charges that Great Britain was artificially creating a justification for war.

The situation in Iran is not too happy. A large number of German agents are established in the country. We are now in communication both with India and the Middle East as to action which might be taken in the diplomatic, and possibly in the military, sphere to secure their expulsion and establish ourselves in a controlling position. If the Germans were to appear in force in Iran by way of Russia, our whole position in Iraq would be threatened and our communications in the Persian Gulf might be cut.[27]

It was immediately clear to London that if the USSR collapsed under the weight of the German onslaught, as many were predicting in the weeks following the invasion, Germany and Nazism would reign supreme across most of Europe, as well as threatening much of Central Asia. To the surprise of both countries, Great Britain and the USSR suddenly found themselves allies of a kind. Despite the cruelties of communism and Churchill's own very public stance on this subject in the past, he knew that he was confronted now with an option of two evils. He chose the lesser one. Winston Churchill told the British public through the BBC Home Service on the evening of 22 June, the very day on which Hitler launched his eastern *blitzkrieg*:

No one has been a more consistent opponent of Communism than I have for the last twenty-five years. I will unsay no word that I have spoken about it. But all this fades away before the spectacle which is now unfolding. The past, with its crimes, its follies, and its tragedies, flashes away . . . We have but one aim and one single, irrevocable purpose. We are resolved to destroy Hitler and every vestige of the Nazi regime . . . *Any man or state who fights on against Nazidom will have our aid. Any man or state who marches with Hitler is our foe* . . . It follows therefore that we shall give whatever help we can to Russia and the Russian people . . . The Russian danger is, therefore, our danger, and the danger of the United States.[28] [my italics]

In a country which had grown to consider the USSR and Nazi Germany as the contemporary equivalent of the 'axis of evil', accepting the Soviet Union as an equal partner in a new moral crusade took some explaining. But in the early days of this enforced relationship between the two nations, the overwhelming threat posed by Germany to both countries served to remove for a time the political, economic and ideological animosities that had fuelled previous relationships. The urgent need to secure Iran from German influence or intervention was so great that the old political certainties were displaced at a stroke.

The old enmities had now to die away and be replaced by pragmatic relationships based on new – and unexpectedly new – shared interests, not the least of which was a common enemy. Accordingly, the Soviet Union and Great Britain signed the Anglo-Soviet Agreement for Mutual Assistance on 12 July.

On 26 June the Soviet ambassador to Tehran delivered a note to the Iranian Government protesting at the large numbers of German 'agents' apparent in the country, and warned that a pro-German *coup d'état* was a certainty.[29] Eden did likewise to the Iranian Ambassador to London, Mohammad Moggadam, on 30 June. On 1 July in a meeting in Tehran with the Iranian Prime Minister, Bullard demanded the expulsion of four-fifths of the German population, and the immobilization of German ships currently sitting at Bandar-i Shahpur. On 9 July Lord Linlithgow wrote to Amery: 'In our view positive policy to secure elimination of enemy centres in Iran is a matter of most vital importance.'[30] For its part, the Iranian Government listened politely, but did nothing to allay British fears. News of *Operation Barbarossa* was enthusiastically received by most Iranians, certain that swift German victories would follow, leading to an end to the unwanted attentions of their northern neighbour. The prospect that their own security and sovereignty were threatened equally by Nazi aggrandizement occurred to few.

Auchinleck, now in Cairo as Commander-in-Chief instead of Wavell, on 7 July sent an appreciation to the Chiefs of Staff of the threat facing the region from an unchecked German advance through the Caucasus. He suggested the construction of defensive zones in the areas around Baghdad in Iraq and Tripoli–Homs in Syria. This would allow a German advance substantial penetration of the region, but at the risk, Auchinleck believed, of a serious over-extension of their supply lines. Meanwhile, the War Office had concluded separately that the likely initial target of Axis aggression would be Iraq, and that an offensive against the country would come by way of Anatolia in

Turkey. An attack from Caucasia would undoubtedly be aimed at Iran, but London concluded that it could not be expected until April 1942 at the earliest.

To Wavell, newly ensconced in the Indian capital, New Delhi, as the C-in-C India following his sacking from the Middle East, Auchinleck's plans sounded unduly pessimistic. He did not accept that the Soviets would suffer an early collapse and that Turkey would comply readily to Axis demands to open up their country to the transit of armies intent on invading Iraq, nor that the Germans would manage to penetrate the vastness of the Russian interior to the extent or at the speed at which some of the observers were predicting in Whitehall. Unlike Auchinleck, he argued that the main defence of the Persian Gulf area must, if possible, be in Anatolia and northern Iraq, on the basis that if the Axis forces were able to secure the north then this would be sufficient to provide them with the airfields they needed to launch attacks down to and including the strategically vital oil fields and the seaborne lines of communication through the Persian Gulf. Wavell's argument was subsequently accepted by London as the basis for future planning. The original plans to secure the Iranian oil fields were re-examined with a new urgency.

This spate of planning suffered from the difficulties attendant upon keeping secrets in Cairo. No sooner had the work begun than it was leaked across the Middle East and into the hands of Tehran and Berlin. The culprit was Egypt's King Farouk. Nervously aware of Rommel's armour pushing on his western border and fearful of his own future should the British defence collapse, he fed information on 29 June to the Shah about British plans to occupy the oil fields in the event of German air attack. By 2 July, Ettel had passed this intelligence back to Berlin.[31]

When Wavell was appointed to his new role as C-in-C India, Amery took it on himself to impress upon his new military chief India's collective view about the threat posed to India by a German-occupied Iran. Amery had initially questioned Wavell's suitability for the role, given his low stock with Churchill following his reluctance to toe the Prime Minister's line over Iraq and his growing reputation for caution. Amery began his offensive long before Wavell had even managed to get his feet under the table in New Delhi. His initial tack was to emphasize Germany's need for oil, an issue of which, as his appreciation in 1940

amply illustrates, Wavell was only too well aware.* Welcoming Wavell
to his new appointment, Amery wrote:

> As I read the situation, that war [with the USSR] has been forced
> upon Germany largely because she must get oil and other supplies
> next year if she is to carry on. She had hoped to get that by a
> victorious spring campaign in the Eastern Mediterranean. We are
> so apt to make much of our set-backs in detail that we forget that
> from the German point of view you handsomely defeated them
> . . . So now their second string is Baku and Transcaucasia, to be
> secured either by cession from a quickly defeated Russia, or by a
> separate expedition after the Russian armies have been pushed
> back sufficiently in Europe. Once there they will be pretty close
> to your troops in Iraq and ready for every kind of mischief in Iran
> and Afghanistan. All that means, I imagine, pretty close co-
> operation between ourselves and the Russians, and no one is
> better qualified than you to handle that.[32]

To his surprise, Amery did not have to persuade Wavell at all. In contrast to
the stridency of his earlier opposition to intervention in Iraq, Wavell saw
clearly the threat posed by an unchecked German advance through
Anatolia or the Caucasus. Writing to General Sir John Dill on 17 July, he
urged immediate action to protect India's security. To him the issue was
clear: a pro-Axis fifth column had very nearly achieved great things in Iraq,
and something equally dangerous could easily take place in Iran. In Iraq,
German support to Rashid Ali had been nascent and improperly formed,
yet the threat had proved to be dramatic. How much more, he reasoned,
was the threat to British interests in Iran, where the Germans had long-
established relationships, agents and propaganda? London needed to take
strong action – politically and militarily if need be – to nullify this threat.
The apparent slowness of politicians in London to appreciate the danger
by accepting the lessons of Iraq, however, as he had done, was dangerous
and irresponsible. In unusually strong language he told Dill:

> The complaisant attitude it is proposed to adopt over Iran appears
> to me incomprehensible. It is essential to the defence of India that

* See page 5.

the Germans should be cleared out of Iran now, repeat now. Failure to do so will lead to a repetition of events which in Iraq were only just countered in time. It is essential we should join hands with Russia through Iran and *if the present Government is not willing to facilitate this it must be made to give way to one which will* [my italics]. To this end the strongest possible pressure should be applied forthwith while issue of Russo–German struggle is still in doubt.[33]

Wavell's anxiety had nothing to do with oil, and everything to do with the security of his new charge. Whilst he admitted to his diary in early August 1941 that he thought the chances of the Germans advancing so far that they could end up knocking on India's northern or north-western door to be remote, he fought hard to defend its security prerogatives.[34] In a note to the Foreign Office on 19 July he argued that failure to place effective pressure on Iran would 'allow German penetration supported by air forces and finally mobile troops right up to the frontiers of India with [the] connivance and active support of Iranian and Afghan governments.'[35]

Wavell's alarm about apparent inaction in London was articulated at the height of a debate that raged in Whitehall during late June and July about whether or not to use force against Iran. Wavell was in fact repeating forceful representations made by Linlithgow to Amery on 9 and 16 July, in which the Viceroy had protested:

in the strongest terms against the apparent failure in spite of assurances given in your telegram No 8169 of 15 July even to take into account our considered representations regarding policy in a country where we are most directly interested, and from which [a] most dangerous threat to India's security may well develop.[36]

The Foreign Office and War Office were divided, only the India Office being resolute supporters from the outset of military action. Churchill's view was that Great Britain should 'adopt a firm attitude' towards the Persian Government, although significant voices in the Cabinet opposed the use of force to secure Great Britain's demands.

Amery had tried to persuade Anthony Eden on 27 June to consider joint military action with the Soviet Union against Iran in order to protect British interests in India, but the Foreign Secretary remained unconvinced of the need for military intervention. Eden was supported by Bullard, who reported in some anguish to London that the talk of military action against Iran would violate every principle of neutrality and would not be justified in terms of the relatively small number of Germans in the country. But Sir Stafford Cripps, Britain's ambassador to Moscow, urged the opposite view on 14 July, noting that Great Britain had already been prepared to overcome its attitude to neutrality in the case of Norway the previous year and that delay in acting decisively in Iran might lead to the opportunity of the moment for joint action with the Soviet Union being lost. Eden was concerned that Cripps' proposals went a step further than was either appropriate or necessary at the time. Instead, whilst the War Office feverishly planned for military action, Eden agreed merely to apply first diplomatic and then economic pressure against Tehran. In an internal memorandum on 19 July discussing Wavell's telegraph of the same day, Eden made it clear that his position was driven not by a policy of appeasement but rather to ensure that if the threat of force was used against Iran, it should be done only if 'forces are available to give effect to that threat'.[37] Cripps did not give up, however, and asked again on 17 July that 'maximum pressure, economic and military if necessary . . . be applied before the opportunity passes as it may do with a German advance into the Caucasus.'[38]

As July drew to a close it was clear that Eden was wavering in his opposition to military action in Iran. The doubt in his mind was prompted by his increasing scepticism about the effectiveness of either economic or political pressure against a country so determined to protect its national prerogatives. He confided on 20 July to Maisky, the Soviet ambassador to Great Britain, that it looked unlikely that economic or political pressure would serve to move the Shah into agreeing to Anglo-Soviet demands to expel German nationals from the country. Military action might be the only real option, and should be something that both Moscow and London could examine together.[39] (In fact, a week earlier, on 11 July 1941, the Cabinet had asked the Chiefs of Staff to consider a joint Anglo-Russian operation in the event that Iran failed to expel the German advisers in Tehran.) The previous day, 19 July, Bullard and the Soviet ambassador to Tehran, Smirnov, had pressed their case against the alleged German *agents provocateurs* in a strongly worded demand to the Iranian Government, telling Tehran that the large numbers of Germans in the country threatened to compromise the country's neutrality by mounting action against British and Soviet interests, and that neither country would allow their security interests in Iran to be prejudiced.

The view of the Chiefs of Staff on 18 July was that a combined invasion of Iran by both Great Britain and the Soviet Union would overwhelm the Iranians. British forces could attack into the west and south-west from Iraq, whilst the Soviets moved down from the north, with the primary British objective being to secure the strategic oil fields. The Iranian Armed Forces would be too weak to resist this type of twin-pronged attack. The Iranian Army was a conscript-based organization which suffered from low morale, and had a poor reputation for planning. It comprised nine mixed divisions, five independent brigades and independent regiments, together with an independent mechanized brigade consisting of anti-aircraft, tank and mechanized infantry regiments, totalling 126,000 soldiers and 100 Czecho-Moravska 7.5-ton and 3.5-ton tanks, the latter of which the Indian Official Historian remarked only came out, highly polished, for ceremonial parades.[40] The Air Force contained some 200 mainly British aircraft, including 25 fighters, 100 general-purpose aircraft and 75 training aircraft. The Navy had a coastal focus only, consisting of two 950-ton gunboats (4-inch guns) and five sloops of 350 tons (3-inch guns). An internal armed gendarmerie of seven mixed regiments and fifteen mixed battalions was responsible for maintaining internal and external borders.

The problem for the British, yet again, was the acute lack of resources necessary to mount an overwhelming and decisive attack on Iran. Any troops required could only come from those garrisoning Iraq and these forces would themselves have to be back-filled from the already hard-pressed Middle East.[41] This was now the critical issue facing London, as Churchill told Wavell on 21 July.[42] Indeed, the lack of troops in Iraq undoubtedly reinforced the need to achieve diplomatic rather than military coercion in Iran.[43] On the following day Eden told Churchill that diplomatic pressure on Iran should only begin once Great Britain was in a position to follow up its threats by the use of force. With those forces still not available, the credibility of any attempts at diplomatic coercion would be minimized and, indeed,

Iran could take pre-emptive steps to ensure the security of the oil fields.[44] Nevertheless, Eden was convinced that some form of action was required, arguing that if the Soviets were too badly beaten on the Eastern Front to be able to commit themselves to military action in Iran, then the victorious Germans would be able to place unbearable pressure on the Iranians to expel the British altogether. Action, of one kind or another, was therefore inevitable.

Diplomatic action and threats of economic pressure had failed so far to move the Shah, and so on 22 July Wavell ordered Quinan to be prepared to secure the oil refinery at Abadan, and to occupy Naft-i-Shah and the Khuzestan oil fields. On 24 July Quinan was told that London had agreed a plan for joint Anglo-Soviet diplomatic pressure 'backed by a show of force'. The plan was to present a joint Anglo-Soviet note to the Iranian Government on 12 August. Quinan was ordered 'to complete the preliminary concentration of a striking force near the Iranian frontier in the Basra area.' But within two days of these orders, efforts to apply economic leverage were recognized to be unviable, and agreement was established – for the first time since the issue of Iran arose – that only the prospect of co-ordinated military action by both London and Moscow would have any chance of success against an intransigent Shah, conscious only of his country's sovereignty, neutrality and national prerogatives. On 25 July, therefore, Dill told Wavell to prepare to take military action in Iran in support of diplomatic pressure mounted simultaneously by both the USSR and Great Britain. He was to concentrate an Indian infantry division, a mechanized cavalry brigade and two Indian armoured regiments against the Abadan and Khuzestan oil fields. Four bomber squadrons were to be made available by the RAF for operations against military objectives in Tehran, whilst a fighter squadron was to be deployed to protect the southern oil installations. What small naval forces existed in the Persian Gulf would also be deployed to assist, particularly in the capture of the important port of Bandar-i Shahpur.

Bullard received a non-committal response from the Iranian Prime Minister when once again the British ambassador forcefully pressed his government's demands on 27 July. This form of diplomatic pressure did not have the desired impact on the Shah. Fiercely independent, he could not see how any number of Germans in his country could pose the sort of threat that the Allies claimed. He also had trouble believing that Great Britain would allow its arch-imperial rival, the USSR, any opportunity to enter Iran, let alone support the USSR in doing so, little realizing how dramatically old rivalries (for both powers) had become subverted by harsh new realities. As a result the Shah discounted Allied threats as mere posturing. There is also doubt whether in the sycophantic world of the Pahlevi dictatorship the Shah was actually briefed accurately by his subordinates about the seriousness of the threat against him.[45] Iran replied that the expulsion of four-fifths of the Germans in the country would run counter to the Iranian national interest, but that in any case measures were being undertaken to reduce the numbers of Germans. Limited military preparations were nevertheless made by Iran, the most significant of which was the despatching of Major General Moggadam's *12th Division* to block the mountain passes west of Kermanshah. At the same time German pressure not to accede to Anglo-Soviet demands remained strong. Ettel informed the Iranian Government on 6 August that any action taken by Tehran to meet Allied demands would be regarded by Berlin as 'an unfriendly act and would force his government to break off diplomatic relations.'[46] The result, as Freya Stark described it, was that Persia had become mesmerized into inaction by a fear of Nazi threats but unable by itself to take charge of events. This situation was evident to Stark even during her brief visit to Tehran before the Iraqi imbroglio. 'The general feeling in the country is that of a rabbit hypnotized by a snake,' she wrote in her diary on 28 April, '– we are not masters of events and things have gone beyond ordinary methods.'[47]

Iran's unwillingness to bow to British pressure confirmed the determination of both Great Britain and the USSR to take military action to secure their joint interests in the country. One final combined ultimatum was to be delivered to the Iranian Government, following which joint military action would be taken. On 30 July Wavell was told that this ultimatum would be delivered to the Shah on 12 August.

On 31 July Churchill presided over a meeting of the Chiefs of Staff. Eden and Auchinleck, visiting from Cairo, also attended. Churchill insisted on tough action. Eden, however, remained to be convinced of the need to use force to ensure Iranian compliance. On 1 August he told the Cabinet that he believed that estimates of German influence in Iran had been greatly overplayed, not least of all because they had failed to persuade the Shah to support Rashid Ali's war against Great Britain in Iraq.[48] But the issue, as Sir Horace Seymour of the Foreign Office had pointed out to Eden on 26 July, was not merely confined to the malign presence of German fifth columnists in Iran. Even if this influence was negated in some way it would still not provide adequate security for Great Britain's oil, for which drastic measures, in event of a German breakthrough in the Caucasus, would still be required:

> If the Russians lose control of the Caucasus, the threat to the oil becomes immediate, and this is not the case whether the Germans . . . in Iran have been expelled or not. It follows that our own object, as distinct from that of the Russians, will not be accomplished simply by the removal of the Germans from Iran. It also seems to follow that . . . it will at some stage be necessary for us to take over the protection of the oil fields.[49]

The path was now clearly set for a showdown. As Churchill contemplated this near certainty, he appointed a separate committee under Sir John Anderson, the Lord President of the Council, to look at all the options available to him, and to measure the consequences for Great Britain of taking military action to force Iranian compliance with Allied wishes. Anderson convened his special committee on 4 August and endorsed the logic that was leading Great Britain towards military intervention. The committee recommended, however, that instead of a final ultimatum to the Shah, a 'firm but friendly' note should be given, and that Great Britain should offer to double the oil royalties the APOC paid Iran, should the Shah accede to Anglo–Soviet demands.[50] If he ignored this note, it was argued, military action would then be justified. Major General John Kennedy, a member of Anderson's committee, recalled the special imperative driving British policy towards Iran:

> we were anxious to get the German 'technicians' out of Persia, and we wanted to get control of that country in case the Russian front broke up in the South: in which event German armies would soon reach the Caucasus and, perhaps, the eastern side of the Caspian. If this happened, Persia would then become the essential bastion of our right flank in the Middle East, and an outpost for the

defence of India; moreover, it was necessary to be sure of Persia if we were to continue to draw the vital supplies of oil from the Gulf.[51]

Diplomacy, as Kennedy asserted, was the primary vehicle for achieving this goal. Indeed, he insisted throughout that diplomacy was by far the better way: 'At these meetings I urged the advantages of avoiding the use of force, and I felt strongly that the diplomatists should be able to accomplish what we wanted without it.'[52] But such hopes, reasonable in theory, were not achievable in practice. Iran was unable or unwilling to understand the urgency of Great Britain's security needs, too certain in its determination to remain neutral and too fearful of German counter-reaction, should it agree to British demands, to consider that it might thereby suffer the indignity of invasion. Eden's natural reluctance to use force was only slowly overcome, by virtue of the gradual exhaustion of other options. 'When this pressure failed,' Eden recorded, 'I reluctantly agreed to the forces of the two countries [Britain and the USSR] entering Iran from south and north.'[53] Kennedy recorded: 'my views about diplomatic action were over-ruled, the Foreign Office and their Ambassador declared themselves impotent, and our troops marched.'[54]

As August arrived, a further justification for intervention in Iran began to emerge. The urgent necessity of supplying Stalin with materiel to prevent a Soviet collapse became quickly apparent to both London and Washington. Given its location, a compliant Iran could play a significant role in acting as a conduit for supplies from the USA through the back door, especially with the difficulties associated with the two other routes, by North and Arctic Seas to Murmansk, and across the Eurasian land mass from Vladivostok. On Maisky's advice, Roosevelt despatched Harry Hopkins on a perilous journey from London to Moscow in late July via Archangel with the task of convincing Stalin of the USA's willingness to provide supplies for the USSR, and to ascertain the Soviet Union's resource requirements. On his return journey Hopkins briefed Churchill, on 4 August, on the results of his discussions, one of which was Stalin's suggestion that US supplies could reach the USSR through Iran. The possibility of using Iran to ship military supplies to the USSR came to Churchill therefore at an opportune time, coinciding with Sir John Anderson's recommendations to use military force if the Shah refused to accede to Great Britain's demands. It meant that the violation of Iranian territory could now have an additional, if consequential, justification. By the time the invasion was launched in late August, this motivation had become a major justification (though not the public explanation) for war, overriding almost all others.

Like Great Britain, the USA was forced to undergo a radical change in its own public position following the German invasion of the USSR on 22 June 1941. It was not easy, given widespread public antipathy towards a country regarded by many Americans as nothing more than a 'godless tyranny'. Nevertheless, the State Department had for some months been considering national policy options for the USA, should Germany launch an attack on the USSR. The first public utterance by an American official reflecting on the new strategic situation was made on 23 June 1941 by the Acting Secretary of State, Sumner Welles, who observed that 'Hitler's armies are today the chief dangers of the Americas.'[55] For several months, certainly until October 1941, the public and private manifestations of the USA's policy regarding aid to the USSR were very different, in the main to allow a groundswell of public sympathy to build up across the USA that would make a *post factum* announcement of the delivery of aid more politically palatable.

The USSR stood at the time outside the limits of the Lend–Lease Act,* which enabled US supplies to be provided on advantageous terms to Great Britain, and American public opinion was resolutely anti-Soviet, especially following Stalin's invasion of Finland. The delicate subject of American aid to the USSR, an erstwhile enemy of free world democracy, was therefore one that until October 1941 was kept hidden from public gaze. Where it had to be justified, it went under the explanation of support to Great Britain in the latter's attempts to secure Iran from the Nazis. Lend–Lease was conceived on the notion that the enemies of freedom were America's enemies, despite the fact that the

---

* The US Congress passed the Lend–Lease Act on 11 March 1941, giving Roosevelt authority to provide warlike material to countries upon whose defence the USA's security was thought to depend. Of the $50 billion provided by Lend–Lease between 1941 and 1945, Great Britain received $31 billion. It was required at the end of the war to repay a mere £650 million. The USSR was declared eligible for lend–lease aid on 7 November 1941.

United States itself was not a co-belligerent. It served effectively to bring the USA into the war in the summer and autumn of 1941, despite its official neutrality. President Roosevelt told Welles on 9 July of his intention to establish a lifeline to the USSR, and the State Department was set to work to establish the mechanisms that would enable this to occur. During the following week a committee to advise on this sensitive subject was created, involving the Soviet ambassador, the chairman of the British Supply Council in North America* and Harry Hopkins. A Soviet Military Mission arrived in Washington on 23 July. The *modus operandi* arrived at, following negotiations in August, was that the USSR could be supplied with equipment initially contracted to be delivered to Great Britain, if the latter agreed. As Churchill had already agreed that it was in Great Britain's interests that the USSR be helped to resist the German invasion, and although lend-lease equipment allocated for the USSR came off the quantities initially designated for Great Britain, this arrangement worked well.

Roosevelt and Churchill sent a joint declaration to Stalin committing their countries to assisting the USSR, on 5 August 1941.[56] In Churchill's mind at least, his decision to use Iran for this purpose was already made up. 'Without waiting for the acceptance by the Iranian Government of the terms submitted to it in the identical notes of 30 August, the British Government promptly charged the United Kingdom Commercial Corporation with procurement of commodities for the USSR and their delivery through the Persian corridor.'[57] By September Quinan had been formally tasked with taking 'steps to develop such road, rail and river communications as are necessary to ensure . . . the maximum possible delivery of supplies to Russia.'[58]

Iranian intransigence combined with the urgency of the German threat to the Caucasus, and the need to prevent the collapse of the Soviet Union by providing a blood transfusion to it directly from Detroit, made the prospect of an Anglo–Soviet invasion increasingly certain. However, such action raised the difficult prospect of violating Iran's sovereignty and neutrality.† They were significant moral and legal

* E.P. Taylor.
† Iran had declared her neutrality on 4 September 1939.

obstacles to Great Britain's freedom of action. Nevertheless, Churchill was certain of the logic of the moral expediency which underpinned his determination to act. He concluded that combined together, the presence of German nationals inside Iran as well as the prospect of a Soviet collapse, created an argument of sufficient strength to override the legal and moral constraints provided by the norms of civilized international behaviour, norms that upheld the convention against military intervention in the sovereign affairs of another state and which the free world, with Great Britain in the vanguard, were fighting hard to preserve. The moral difficulties of preaching the principles of inviolate sovereignty whilst practising something else were profound. Winston Churchill observed after the event that 'I was not without anxiety about embarking on a Persian war, but the arguments for it were compulsive.'[59] His argument was first articulated in a memorandum considering the use of force against Norway in December 1939:

> We have taken up arms in accordance with the Covenant of the League in order to aid the victims of German aggression. No technical infringement of international law, so long as it is unaccompanied by inhumanity of any kind, can deprive us of the good wishes of neutral countries . . . The final tribunal is our own conscience. We are fighting to re-establish the reign of law and to protect the liberties of small countries. Our defeat would mean an age of barbaric violence, and would be fatal, not only to ourselves, but to the independent life of every small country in Europe. Acting in the name of the Covenant, and as virtual mandatories of the League and all it stands for, we have a right, and indeed are bound in duty, to abrogate for a space some of the conventions of the very laws we seek to consolidate and reaffirm. Small nations must not tie our hands when we are fighting for their rights and freedom. The letter of the law must not in supreme emergency obstruct those who are charged with its protection and enforcement. It would not be right or rational that the aggressor Power should gain one set of advantages by tearing up all laws, and another set by sheltering behind the innate respect for law of its opponents. Humanity, rather than legality, must be our guide. Of all this history must be the judge. We now face events.[60]

London and Moscow's plans for joint action against Iran evoked considerable concern in Turkey. Aligned by a recent treaty to Great Britain, Turkey was nervous about the motivations of its northern neighbour, having successfully resisted Soviet bullying in June and July over Soviet claims to the Dardanelles. It now appeared to Turkey that her primary ally – Great Britain – was selling her soul to consort with the devil over Iran. Sir John Anderson's committee belatedly recognized this fear when it reported its findings on 8 August, recommending that the delivery of the 'firm but friendly' note to Tehran – planned for 12 August – be delayed until the British ambassador in Ankara had been given the opportunity to explain the rationale for Anglo-Soviet plans and to allay, if possible, Turkish fears and suspicions.[61] These suspicions were never entirely alleviated; the Turkish Government remaining unconvinced of the British justification for action, believing that it was a cover for a more serious design.[62] London was nonplussed by Turkish fears, believing that a secure and pro-British Iran would serve to protect Turkey from any potential German threat emanating from the Caucasus.[63] Turkey was eventually mollified by assurances from both London and Moscow that both countries would respect Iranian sovereignty and independence.[64] The delivery of the final note to Tehran was now timed for 16 August, and was to include a statement affirming Great Britain's intentions to 'proceed to other measures' should the Iranian Government not act decisively to meet Great Britain's wishes, and to do so by the end of August.

Churchill had the opportunity personally to brief Roosevelt on the battleship HMS *Prince of Wales* in Placentia Bay off Newfoundland on 11 August.[65] Churchill telegraphed Eden (who had remained in London) with the American leader's response on 15 August: 'I told the President about our plans in Persia and he seemed quite content with them.'[66]

The existing division within the British Government towards the issue of intervention in Iran did not dissipate entirely during August, leaving a residue of unresolved debate right up to the invasion. Agreement as to the necessity for military action was by no means universal, and arguments for it far from unequivocal. Although Eden remained uneasy about the concept of military action, he had by this time been convinced of its necessity by the apparent failure of diplomatic and economic pressure. His ambassador in Iran, however, continued to report that the rationale for Allied intervention – the threat posed by German nationals in the country – had been overstated, and was being weakened by gradual Iranian acquiescence, under British and Soviet pressure. Bullard reported on 8 and 9 August that the Iranian authorities were taking steps to comply with British wishes, and stated his belief that the Germans in Iran were under so much surveillance that it was unlikely that they would be able to carry off a *coup d'état* even if they wished to.[67] Amery reported Bullard's views to Linlithgow on 11 August and remarked that the situation in Iran appeared to be under control. Linlithgow reacted furiously to this news, fearful that a weak-willed Foreign Office would back away from the necessity of using force to secure Great Britain's legitimate interests in Iran, not least of which was the security of India. In a note to Amery he stated his hope that 'local complacency [i.e. Bullard] will not be permitted to divert H.M.G. from pressing home their demands in Persia.'[68]

On 13 August Eden met Maisky and agreed the wording of the respective diplomatic 'Notes to Tehran', which Bullard and Smirnov delivered to the Iranian Prime Minister on 16 August. It read:

> The Imperial Iranian Government on many occasions have affirmed their desire to maintain an attitude of most scrupulous neutrality; the British Government fully endorse this policy; they have no designs against Iran's political independence; their sincere desire is to maintain the policy of friendship and co-operation; as long ago as January last they brought to the notice of the Iranian authorities their grave concern in regard to excessively large numbers of German nationals who have been permitted to reside in Iran; since that date they have repeatedly warned the Iranian Government of the potential dangers arising from activities of these Germans and asked for effecting a drastic reduction in their numbers; towards the end of July they instructed their representative at Tehran again to impress upon the Iranian Government the utmost gravity and urgency of the matter; the Iranian Government appear to recognise in principle the wisdom of our advice, but the number of Germans who have left the country is very small; they now wish to repeat in most formal and

emphatic manner their recommendation that Germans remaining in Iran should be required to leave the country without any further delay; if Iran should wish to retain temporarily a few German technicians employed in connection with Iran's industrialization projects, a complete list showing their names and exact nature of their work should be communicated to their representatives at Tehran; they can endeavour to find suitably qualified British or neutral experts to replace German technicians; as regards the remaining Germans they should be kept closely informed of dates of their departure; no further Germans should be permitted to arrive in Iran; none of the German technicians to be retained should be employed on work connected with Iran-Syria communications, e.g. railways, roads, telephones, telegraphs and wireless; the German technicians to be retained should be kept under strict surveillance and their movements should be restricted; the activities of refugees who fled from Iraq should be strictly controlled.[69]

An informal, verbal response was delivered to Bullard by the Acting Minister of Foreign Affairs two days later. He told Bullard that Iran agreed to the joint demand but that they insisted on the right to do so 'in accordance with our own programme', indicating that thirty Germans had left in the previous three weeks, and that more would follow. Two days later, on 20 August, Bullard was informed that one hundred Germans would leave within a week, at least another hundred within the month and that thereafter schemes would be put forward by various ministries to reduce the number of Germans needed to support Iranian industry. No names would be furnished but remaining Germans would be closely watched.

On 21 August the formal Iranian reply – in Farsi – was delivered to both Soviet and British ambassadors. It robustly reiterated Iran's sovereign right to govern regardless of foreign interference. Whilst it agreed to take steps to reduce the numbers of Germans in the country it stoutly defended its prerogative to make its own decisions:

determination of superintendence and other minor matters of detail were the affairs of the Imperial Government who would take whatever steps they considered necessary; in respect of nationals of other states the Imperial Government could not take steps incompatible with their engagements and contrary to their treaties and which would lead to abandonment of their neutral course; they were ready to carry out any plan that they might consider necessary for the safety of their country and protection of the legitimate rights of their neighbours, but they could not accept any proposal which was contrary to their policy of neutrality, or to their rights of sovereignty.[70]

It was clear from this response that Iran was not prepared to give in to what it perceived to be bullying or to accept the legitimacy of Great Britain's concerns. Bullard, on instructions from London, replied that these efforts were not sufficient and did not meet the full rigour of Great Britain's requirements, confirming the conclusion of both countries that Tehran would make none of the concessions demanded, and initiating the final timetable for war. Bullard had already been told of secret discussions between Ettel and the Iranian Prime Minister which indicated that Iran would not back down, and indeed was talking to Germany about possible counter-action in the event of invasion.[71]

The reality of Iranian decision-making was forcefully impressed on Bullard, who with Smirnov was then invited to an audience with the Shah on the afternoon of 25 August. Bullard recalled:

> The shah looked old and rather feeble. We both gained impression that he was taken aback by invasion, because he had supposed that everything was doing nicely, and we saw clearly that he had not been kept fully informed by his Ministers . . . We spent much time in giving him information about the German menace in Iran and much of it seemed to be new to him . . . Shah asked whether Great Britain and Soviet Union were at war with Iran.[72]

Eden and Maisky had already agreed that in the absence of a capitulation both parties would take military action against Iran, a decision ratified by Churchill, on HMS *Prince of Wales*, in the mid-Atlantic, on 19 August.[73] Whilst it was clear that these diplomatic notes were unwelcome to Tehran it was also clear that the Shah believed that he had the most to gain from prevarication. He was terrified of upsetting Berlin, and there was every indication that both the British and the Soviets were being bettered on the battlefield by the Germans: every day brought further respite from Allied demands, or so he thought. At the time the Germans were making dramatic headway against the collapsing Soviet armies in southern Russia, and it was easy for the Iranians to believe Ettel's urgings that the *Wehrmacht* was unstoppable and there was no need to bow to British and Soviet pressure.

The speed of the German advance in eastern Europe was nervously observed in London, and the implications endlessly played out in the corridors of power. Such was Churchill's concern that on 20 August he asked Stalin to give consideration to destroying the Soviet oil fields to prevent them falling into German hands.[74] Fear of a German military thrust through Anatolia and into Syria, Iraq and Iran, facilitated by a Russian collapse, exercised London more keenly, noted John Connell, than did the prospect of Japanese aggression in south-east Asia.[75]

As Bullard was meeting the Acting Foreign Minister in Tehran, Eden and Maisky met in London and agreed that they should put their invasion plans into effect on 22 August. Wavell was instructed to prepare for invasion early on that morning. Maisky was somewhat ahead of his own armed forces, however, and a further delay of three days had to be added to enable the Soviet invasion forces time to complete their final preparations. Only on 21 August, with hours to go before the invasion, was it postponed until 4.10 a.m. on 25 August.[76] Whilst this merely meant a stand-down for the troops on the ground, forces already at sea in the ships of the Persian Gulf flotilla found that they had to endure an extra stiflingly hot three days cooped up on board before they could disembark.

The delay in the invasion date forfeited the element of surprise, allowing the Iranians to reinforce troops in Khuzestan. The Shah ominously and melodramatically warned the newly commissioned officers of his military academy to be ready for war. British intelligence reported that reinforcements were making their way to the border areas and two divisions – the *5th Kurdistan* and the *12th Kermanshah Division* – together with a composite brigade from Tehran and a weak brigade from the *13th Division* currently *en route* from Isfahan, blocked the mountain passes. The expectation was that up to 10,000 troops covered the route through the mountains.

This delay also afforded an opportunity further for London to brief Washington. This was important, as despite Roosevelt's sympathy for Great Britain and his stated willingness to support the USSR in her new-found extremity, an invasion of a neutral state by an ally of sorts was a hugely risky undertaking. Great Britain could not afford to lose the goodwill of the government in Washington, nor of its public standing in the USA as the victim of Axis aggression amongst the American public at large, through the ill-considered use of force. The problem was that by mid-August the public justification for invasion – the presence of a Nazi fifth column in Iran – was looking increasingly tenuous. It certainly had not persuaded either the Turks or the Iranians, and it puzzled many in the USA. Accordingly, a note was presented to the US ambassador in London outlining and defending the rationale for military action. Great Britain recognized fully, Eden told the US ambassador, the weak moral and legal grounds for its proposed action, but insisted that the presence in Iran of large numbers of German nationals acted as a very real threat to both Iran and Great Britain.[77] Eden stressed that Great Britain neither had designs on Iranian independence nor disputed her neutrality. Rather, the exigencies of a war in which the bitter precedent of Nazi action showed all too clearly the importance to Germany of fifth columns in prospective victim states led Great Britain to take in Iran what would ordinarily be unthinkable action.

The importance of Iran to the emerging idea of supplying the USSR via the Persian Gulf was not discussed: the issue remained too sensitive for public consumption. However, even by late August 1941 it was not considered prudent, especially for the USA, to be seen to be supporting the violation of the sovereignty of a small, neutral state, in the interests of wider, pragmatic strategic goals, especially those that intended to help the one country – the Soviet Union – seen by many in the West as the epitome of evil. Roosevelt, therefore, denied all knowledge of British intentions and allowed Britain to invade on the public pretext of the threat posed by German fifth columnists. Iran's neutrality and sovereignty became a victim to the strategic necessities of the Great Powers. Military intervention had to have at its heart an actual, physical threat posed by a real enemy (Germany), whether this was real or imagined. It would have been wholly unacceptable, despite the growing weakness of Great Britain's arguments that these German nationals did in fact entail a very real threat to her security, to exchange this rationale for the wholly pragmatic one of supplying with arms the erstwhile enemy of the West.

The Iranians, for their part, worked hard to persuade the United States to support their sovereignty and neutrality unambiguously. The

United States had not been entirely persuaded of Great Britain's 'German fifth column' argument, and a debate developed in Washington in the fortnight before the intervention that mirrored in many respects the debate in British circles. Many in the State Department were as unconvinced of British arguments regarding Nazi fifth columnists in Iran as the Turks, and Cordell Hull, the Secretary of State, demanded greater clarity from London about its plans.[78] It was obvious during this debate that the issue of support to the USSR had not been widely discussed amongst US policy makers, even at a very senior level, and remained the preserve of Roosevelt and Churchill, and their closest advisers. Roosevelt, under intense Iranian diplomatic pressure, denied all knowledge of British intentions, despite being briefed by Churchill the previous week.[79]

On 23 August the War Office telegraphed fresh orders to Wavell, clarifying the purpose of the invasion. For the first time what had previously (and only recently) been regarded as a benefit of invasion, namely the opening up of communications to the Soviet Union from the Persian Gulf, had become part of its *raison d'être*. However, the sensitivities of going to war in a neutral and relatively friendly country (Iran) in order to support an erstwhile enemy (the USSR) on behalf of a country not currently at war and publicly disowning knowledge of British intentions (the USA), rather than simply to secure Great Britain's sources of Middle Eastern oil, were simply too great to be discussed publicly. The orders Wavell received were as follows:

> ONE. His Majesty's first object in Persia is by military action to bring pressure to bear on the Persian Government to expel German nationals and later with Russian help to control communications. *Question of communications is not, repeat not, to be publicly mentioned at present.* [my italics]
> TWO. For the first object your forces will occupy and hold the oil producing areas in Khuzestan and Naft-i-Shah.
> THREE. Further military operations must depend on the attitude of the Persian Government when the oil bearing areas have been occupied and whether they agree to use of their railway.

FOUR. The plan and objective of the Russian forces are as yet undisclosed. Urgent enquiry has been made and reply will be cabled to you in near future.

FIVE. It will then be necessary to agree with Russians limits of areas in which their forces and yours will operate.[80]

The ulterior motives for the invasion were to be kept from public view, but it was clear that the principal purpose was to secure the oil fields and to force Iran into agreement over transit rights. The public reason for war was that Great Britain went into Iran 'to uproot German influence and forestall enemy action.'[81] However, it is obvious that by mid-August this reason was no longer the primary motivation or imperative for invasion. It was rather, as Churchill perhaps unwittingly admitted after the war, to bring succour to the Soviet Union. By late August no one really believed that a handful of German nationals were the primary reason for invasion. No one doubted that they could be dangerous saboteurs, or fifth column catalysts for external invasion, or perhaps even agents for a pro-Nazi *coup d'état* (as had occurred in Iraq in April). However, by that time these had become excuses, rather than justifications, for war.

As time went on and greater events in the war eclipsed those of 1941, the fact that the *exigencies* of war had overridden the *principles* of international conduct in the decision to invade Iran, was forgotten. With no attempt to preserve at least the facade of a legitimate *casus belli*, Churchill remarked in passing in *The Grand Alliance* that 'Our main object in proposing the joint Anglo-Russian campaign in Persia had been to open up the communications from the Persian Gulf to the Caspian Sea.'[82] This was hardly a proper justification for war. In any case, Churchill's assertion was not true. By late August it had become the primary justification for military intervention, but even at the start of the month London's main concern remained that of the presence in the country of large numbers of what were assumed to be German agents, who threatened the integrity of a range of British security interests in the country. The fact is, however, that the possibility that Iran could be used fruitfully as a means of supporting the USSR in its moment of crisis did not come to Churchill until 4 August at the earliest, when Hopkins briefed him on his recent meeting with Stalin. Eden's memoirs reflect the same motivation, equating the presence of German nationals not with a latent danger to the country's stability or to the threat posed by a fifth column, but by the danger afforded to the trans–Iranian railway.

> German agents had been active there for some time, but now that the Soviets were under Nazi attack, the railway across the country became of capital importance as the only practicable land route from the Persian Gulf for the despatch of supplies to Russia . . . The Iranian route could not be secure while Nazi agents were free to subvert and sabotage.[83]

On 23 August the Soviet Transcaucasus front was activated and prepared for invasion.

Eden instructed Bullard to deliver a note explaining Great Britain's decision to invade early on the morning of 25 August. It read:

> It is regretted that the Iranian Government have not seen fit to return a satisfactory reply to the memorandum of 16 August. It is evident that the Iranian Government attaches greater importance to retaining these German nationals in Iran than they attach to meeting the wishes of His Majesty's Government in a matter which is becoming one of increasing urgency as a result of the developments in the war situation. The Iranian Government must bear full responsibility for the consequences of their decision. In these circumstances, His Majesty's Government now feel themselves obliged to take appropriate measures to safeguard their own vital interests and to deal with the menace arising from the potential activities of the Germans in Iran. The Iranian Government may be assured that these measures will in no way be directed against the Iranian people. Any military measures which British forces may be obliged to take are of a temporary nature and are directed solely against the Axis powers.[84]

Bullard and Smirnov delivered their notes in the very early hours of 25 August. As they did so British and Soviet troops crossed Iran's borders.

The extent of the agreement between Great Britain and the USSR to move into Iran was limited to a general apportionment of broad areas of responsibility between both sides. The *ad hoc* nature of the preparations for this invasion, especially the complete absence of joint planning between the Soviet Union and Great Britain, was perhaps, in the circumstances of the time, understandable. The admission that London had no idea what Soviet operational plans were, apart from Eden's agreement with Maisky that Great Britain would attack from the west and south-west and the Soviets from the north, indicates just how little Great Britain knew about the USSR, and the complete lack of information about Soviet forces, plans or intentions. Indeed, the Soviets in 1941 were as alien to the troops of the British Empire as Lilliputian pygmies were to Gulliver. Neither country knew how to talk to each other outside of the rarefied diplomatic relationships that existed, let alone engage in the detailed dialogue necessary to mount a combined military operation. Maisky himself knew very little in fact of what Moscow was contemplating. When Kennedy and Dill asked him on 20 August what the Russian plan was for operations in Iran, the embarrassed ambassador could provide no answer.[85]

In fact, the Soviet advance comprised two strong armoured columns, commanded by General Novikov. One column would advance along the Caspian Sea to Kazvin, whilst the other advanced on Kazvin from the west through Tabriz. Both columns would then advance from Kazvin on Tehran. The British plan, submitted by Quinan to Wavell on 8 August, was to secure the vital oil fields and refineries at Abadan and at Khanakin before striking out for Tehran in two columns. The plan was given the name *Operation Countenance*. A plan was also prepared – *Operation Dover* – to seize Abadan by *coup de main* should it be necessary before the larger operation was undertaken. In the south-west, Major General Harvey's 8 Indian Division would capture the Abadan refinery, then seize Khurramshahr and Ahwaz, and simultaneously the Haft Khel oil fields. At the same time an infantry force, embarked by ship, would capture the port of Bandar-i Shahpur. In the north-west Brigadier Aizlewood's 2 Armoured Brigade would cross the Iranian border at Khanakin, before striking out over the Pai Tak Pass and the 6,000-foot high mountains that run from north-west to south-east along the frontier. Once over the mountains the advance would follow the road through Kermanshah, Hamadan and Kazvin on the 600-mile journey to Tehran. This force would be responsible for the simultaneous seizure of Naft-i-Shah and Qasr-i-Shirin, followed by an advance to Gilan and Shahabad, preparatory to a general march on Kermanshah.

Quinan, however, was plagued with the perennial problems that discomfited British commanders in the Middle East during 1941: a serious shortage of troops, armoured vehicles, aircraft and shipping. Indeed, on 28 July, because of the time it would take to ship Indian forces to Basra, Wavell suggested to London that military action be delayed until 26 August. Yet again an operation of strategic magnitude would need to be conducted on a shoe-string. There was insufficient shipping to consider simultaneous landings at vital points along the Iranian littoral, with the result that naval operations would need to be sequential. This would have a significant impact on the opportunities for surprise. Likewise, the build-up of land forces was slow. Major General Harvey's 8 Indian Division was weak and not yet acclimatized to the fierceness of the summer heat. When he received his warning order on 29 July he had but a single weak infantry brigade (18 Indian Infantry Brigade), 11 Field Regiment Royal Artillery and a single engineer company. A major part of 18 Indian Brigade did not begin to arrive in Basra until 5 August, and units had to be brought up to strength by stripping out troops from units across Iraq. The brigade was not complete until 12 August.[86] So, by mid-August, by some miracle, Harvey now had under his command 18, 24 and 25 Indian Infantry Brigades. That the division was complete at all in time for *Operation Countenance* was a remarkable feat in a year of extraordinary logistical and organizational achievements by the Indian Army.

Despite these deficiencies there was no talk of calling off military action. The strategic imperative was as clear as that which had forced the ill-defended air station at Habbaniya to strike out at the Iraqi units besieging it in early May, and which had driven weak and *ad hoc* British formations into Syria in June. Commanders had no choice but to apply their plans as ingeniously as they could, take risks, and stretch and reuse every resource to maximize its effectiveness on the battlefield.

In his analysis of the campaign Richard Stewart points out what he believes to be the differing approaches to the operation taken by the British and Soviets. The British, he argues, were confident of out-manoeuvring the Iranians with substantially inferior numbers (19,000 men and 50 light armoured vehicles compared to 30,000 Iranian infantry and 16 tanks). The British operation in Iran was designed therefore to persuade the Iranians that they were beaten, rather than to force them to stand and fight. There is no evidence for this in the plans for *Operation Countenance*, however. Quinan's plan was one dictated by expediency: he did not have the troops or equipment necessary for anything more than the seizure of the oil fields and a demonstration into the heart of the country in the hope of precipitating an Iranian collapse. Furthermore, the immediate strategic objectives for the invading force – Abadan in the south and the Pai Tak Pass in the north-west – were so obvious as to preclude any opportunity for surprise.

Undoubtedly, had more troops been available they would have been used, although efforts were made, such as the use of leaflet drops, to maximize the psychological effectiveness of the force arrayed against Iran. The British plan was not built on the opportunities presented for 'out-manoeuvring' the Iranians, but rather on the twin necessities of seizing the oil fields (in spite of the complete loss of surprise that had been engendered by delays to the start of the campaign) and trusting to hope that the Iranian defences would collapse quickly when confronted with the reality of invasion. That the Iranians did in fact collapse quickly was brought about not so much as by strategic design, nor by the profundity of British tactics, but as a result of the profound weaknesses of the Iranian defences. The British attacked where the Iranians expected them to do, in far weaker strength, but the disarray of the Iranian defences was acute. For their part the Soviets were sceptical about British plans, certain that the number of troops deployed was entirely insufficient for the task.[87] By contrast, the Soviet Union deployed a massive superiority in numbers, with the aim of simply steam-rolling through any opposition – some 40,000 troops and 1,000 tanks.[88] Maisky told Kennedy on 24 August that the Soviet force comprised three infantry divisions, two tank divisions and two cavalry brigades.[89]

The start of what was to become a four-day war for the conquest of Iran, one of the fastest capitulations in history, began at 4.10 a.m. on the morning of 25 August 1941. The two battalions of Brigadier Le Fleming's 24 Indian Brigade* moved quietly in the pre-dawn darkness along the Shatt al-Arab from Basra in an assortment of craft and

* 2/6 Rajputana Rifles, 1 Kumaon Rifles and 3 Field Regiment Royal Artillery.

launched a surprise attack against the port, town and refinery at Abadan. The ground operation was supported by four RAF squadrons. Whilst initial surprise was achieved, and the Iranian guard sloop *Palang* was sunk at its moorings by shellfire from HMS *Shoreham*, sporadic but spirited opposition meant that it took the whole day for the remaining machine-gun posts and snipers to be eradicated. By the close of the day the refinery had been secured and a concentration of troops to the north at the Bahmanshir ferry dispersed. With the exception of some determined bands of fighters, for the most part the Iranians surrendered, fled or melted in with the civilian population, discarding their uniforms and equipment, on that and ensuing days.

Whilst the assault was underway against Abadan, three separate attacks were being launched by the remainder of Harvey's 18 Indian Division. First, Brigadier Lochner's 18 Indian Brigade* moved from its forming-up area at Tanuma opposite Basra to attack the river town of Khurramshahr. The town lay just to the east of the border with Iraq and was well defended with substantial earth defences and ditches. In addition to army units in the area, some 1,000–1,500 sailors of the Iran Navy were garrisoned in the town. However, an imaginative attack by boat up the Karun River in conjunction with a wide outflanking movement to the rear in the darkness brought about the town's rapid collapse during the day with few casualties.

Second, Brigadier Mountain's reinforced 25 Indian Brigade† advanced north-east from Tanuma along the line of the border to attack and secure the Iranian fort at Qasr Shaikh. Seizing the fort would help to protect the left flank of 18 Indian Brigade as well as to prepare for the move of the whole division against Ahwaz once Abadan and Khurramshahr had been secured. After strong resistance for half a day the Iranian battalion surrendered, having suffered thirty-eight dead. Two hundred soldiers were taken prisoner.

Third, along the Gulf coast at Bandar-i Shahpur two companies of 3/10 Baluch, carried in a mixture of ships and dhows, and led by the Australian armed merchant cruiser HMAS *Kanimbla*, crept into the

---

* 1/2 and 2/3 Gurkhas plus the 5/5 Mahratta Light Infantry from 24 Indian Brigade, a squadron of 10 Guides Cavalry (in armoured wheeled carriers) and a battery of field artillery.

† 13th Lancers, two Sikh battalions, a Mahratta battalion and three Jat battalions.

harbour at first light on 25 August in an attempt to seize or disable the eight German and Italian ships lying in mid-stream. With the exception of one ship, which the crew managed to scuttle, the other vessels fell into the hands of enthusiastic 'cutting out' teams of Australian sailors and Indian soldiers. Once ashore, the Baluchis captured the town with little further ado. Whilst this was underway, an airborne landing was carried out on the oil field at Haft Khel. A company of 3/10 Baluch, transported by six Valentias flying out of Shaibah, with orders to protect the oil fields and to provide escorts for British civilians, completed their task successfully, despite two of the aircraft crashing on landing.

By the end of the second day of fighting the strategically vital Abadan and Khurramshahr areas, together with Qasr Shaikh had been secured, and preparations were now made to advance along the route of the oil pipeline north-east to Ahwaz. By now, of course, surprise had been lost, and a reconnaissance by the 13 Lancers on 27 August indicated that the Iranian defences in the area of Ahwaz were substantial, comprising tanks, artillery and anti-tank weapons. Harvey decided to attack in two prongs. Whilst the 18 Indian Brigade was to approach along the eastern bank of the Karun River and emerge on the eastern and north-eastern extremities of the town, 25 Indian Brigade was to advance along the west bank of the river and attack from the west. Kept in reserve was 24 Indian Brigade, ready for any eventuality on either flank. The heaviest opposition was expected to the west of the town, so the divisional artillery (11 Field Regiment Royal Artillery) was concentrated to support 25 Indian Brigade.

Far to the north, Aizlewood's brigade prepared at Khanakin for the ambitious advance into Iran through the Pai Tak Pass. Aizlewood's 2 Indian Armoured Brigade* had been reinforced by stripping out units across Iraq, and an *ad hoc* formation designated 'Hazelforce' was created. Habforce, now grandly, if inappropriately, re-designated '9 Armoured Brigade'† and under

---

* 14/20 Hussars, 15 Field Regiment Royal Artillery, 1/5 Gurkha Rifles (loaned from 17 Indian Brigade), 2/7 Gurkha Rifles (loaned from 20 Indian Brigade) and 32 Field Squadron Sappers and Miners.

† Household Cavalry Regiment, Warwickshire Yeomanry, Wiltshire Yeomanry and 2 Field Squadron Royal Engineers.

a new commander, Brigadier Tiarks, was recalled from Syria. It still boasted only 15-hundredweight trucks and had no armour of any kind. The 14/20 Hussars, noted Slim, still had their 'gallant but decrepit and slightly ridiculous old Mark VII tanks, whose only armament was a single Vickers machine-gun apiece and whose armour almost anything could pierce.'[90] Nervous about the obvious weakness of this force, Quinan decided on 23 August to reinforce Aizlewood and bring his force up to divisional strength, giving responsibility for the advance to Slim's 10 Indian Division. This had the effect of adding Slim's divisional headquarters to the invasion force as well as a further two infantry battalions from Brigadier Weld's 21 Indian Brigade, together with substantially more artillery – 157 Field Regiment Royal Artillery and 19 Medium Battery Royal Artillery. In addition two bomber and one Blenheim squadrons based at Habbaniya were allocated to the northern operation.*

Slim, who had just returned to Iraq to rejoin his division after being recalled from a brief visit to Jerusalem, arrived in Khanakin on the evening of 24 August. He recalled that his only previous recollection of the town related rather incongruously to a rude soldier's ditty from his Mesopotamian days, which ran:

The Khaimaqam of Khanaquin,
Is versed in every kind of sin;
For all the grosser forms of lust,
He makes a gorgeous bundobust.[91]

With the operation due to begin the next morning and no time to work through the details of the plan, Slim, after listening to Aizlewood's plan, decided to accept it in its entirety. The whole affair was, in Slim's words, 'hastily improvised'.[92] Aizlewood's plan was to advance in three columns on Monday 25 August 1941, capturing the oil fields at Naft-i-Shah, Gilan and Sar-i-Pul Zuhab, forty miles from the frontier, on the first day. The Pai Tak Pass lay a further twelve miles on. Well defended, the pass could hold off an attacking army with ease. 'Viewed from below', recalled Slim, 'it was a most formidable and threatening obstacle . . . It looked as if a handful of men could hold it against an army many times the size of mine.'[93] Its great strategic weakness, however, was the

---

* 11 Squadron (Bombers), 14 Squadron (Bombers) and 45 Squadron (Blenheims).

route around it to the south that ran through Gilan and thence to Shahabad, allowing the mountain pass to be completely bypassed. The pass was to be attacked first from the air during the early morning of 27 August, after which it was to be taken by ground assault by the two battalions of 21 Indian Brigade, whilst the remainder of the division moved along the route to the south that ran through Gilan.

The oil fields at Naft-i-Shah were captured quickly, with little opposition, few casualties and exactly to plan. Other border positions were quickly captured without significant opposition. Fierce resistance was encountered, however, outside the town of Qasr-i-Shirin. A heavy fire-fight developed for some five hours whilst 1/5 Gurkhas and 14/20 Hussars in trucks and light armour encircled the town. With exit routes cut off, the Iranians surrendered at 10 a.m., after a display of martial ardour that whilst spirited was ineffective, one Gurkha alone being injured in the arm.

By the late afternoon of 25 August, following the capture of Qasr-i-Shirin, 1/5 Gurkhas had established defensive positions at the village of Sar-i-Pul Zuhab, some five miles west of the pass. Whilst the advance was underway, a column consisting of a squadron of the 14/20 Hussars, the Warwickshire Yeomanry, a battery of 15 Field Regiment and a troop of engineers, made directly for Gilan. Iranian defensive positions made a show of defending themselves before withdrawing, and on 26 August the column met up with 1/5 Gurkhas, which had moved south to Gilan from their bivouac in the mountains to the north.

With Weld's 21 Indian Brigade facing off the defenders at the Pai Tak Pass and preparing for the difficult task of mounting an assault amidst the rocks and crags of the pass, the rest of the division – 2 and 9 Armoured Brigades – moved along the route through Gilan that had been opened up by the Hussar's column. This complete force, leaving Khanakin on the morning of 26 August, made steady progress, unhindered by Iranian defences, occupying the key strategic town of Shahabad by the afternoon of 27 August. Local civilians, well disposed towards the 'invaders', told the Indian and British troops that the Iranian defenders had been short of food and so were in no mood to stand and fight. Colonel Ouvry Roberts recalled meeting the provincial Governor at Qasr-i-Shirin who proved 'to be a charming old man who had no love for the Germans or the Russians.'[94] The British (or Indians), it appeared, were just about acceptable, although the only language they could converse in was French. Slim recorded the same of the citizens of Kermanshah, who, though delighted that the fighting was over, were terrified of the Russians, and with rumours of the Soviet advance in the north, greeted the British with some relief. It was just as well. Slim's invading forces enjoyed only limited means and were pursuing a stratagem that consisted of little more than colossal bluff. Determined defenders could have denied the advancing columns access to western Iran, and punished them so heavily that exploitation through to Tehran would have been impossible.

The capture of Shahabad without a fight now provided Slim with the opportunity to squeeze the Pai Tak Pass from both east and west. On 26 August 21 Indian Brigade advanced up the mountain road and reconnoitred the Iranian positions, which comprised some 400 men with anti-tank artillery and machine guns. At the outset, however, there was no sign of Iranian defences, and the advancing troops began to wonder whether their intelligence, recording 'several thousand Iranians' defending the mountain pass, was accurate. Slim and Aizlewood, throwing caution to the wind in succumbing to that 'irresistible urge to look around the corner' drove far ahead of the troops. Sitting upright in their open-topped staff car, they cautiously made their way to the top of the pass. Passing the final bend, they were disconcerted to find themselves the target of an Iranian anti-tank gun, and, turning quickly, they left the pass 'a good deal more briskly than we had entered it.'[95] Jack Masters was toiling up the hill with his convoy of Gurkhas when he was surprised to see a khaki saloon car, motoring quickly in his direction from the pass.

> The leading riflemen dropped and prepared to open fire. But the car was obviously unarmed and flying a red divisional flag from the radiator cap. It stopped beside us and General Slim got out. 'How the hell did he get past us?' I muttered. Willy* hurried forward. 'Morning, Willy,' the general said. 'There's nothing until you get round the fourth hairpin. They've got an anti-tank gun there.' There was a large hole through the back of the car body. Slim climbed back into his car, we saluted, and he drove on.[96]

* Lieutenant Colonel Willy Weallen, Commanding Officer of 2/4 PWO Gurkha Rifles.

Fortunately for the battalion, attacks by twelve Blenheims of 45 Squadron that afternoon, together with news of the advance of the southern column through Gilan, accompanied perhaps by the divisional commander's daring appearance at the head of his troops in an unarmed staff car, unsettled the defenders. During the following night the Iranians evacuated the position completely, leaving behind several empty anti-tank shell cases and piles of unexpended ammunition.

During 27 August the advance was held up at Zibiri, further along the route to Kermanshah, by well-sited Iranian positions. Just before attacks went in against these, however, at 9.15 a.m. on the morning of 28 August, Iranian officers carrying white flags advanced towards the British positions, seeking a truce. In the south-west Harvey's 8 Indian Division also began to move in the early hours of 28 August. Hurricanes of 261 Squadron and Blenheims of 84 Squadron had been softening up Ahwaz airfield and railway since 25 August. From before first light on 28 August a series of heavy bombing raids by Blenheims were made on troop concentrations around the town. The prospect of a long and bloody attack was lifted after only an hour of fighting, however, by the similar arrival of Iranian envoys at 10 a.m. with white flags. The Shah had ordered his troops to cease fire, and fighting ended shortly afterwards. The Indian Official Historian recorded the anti-climax that followed the formal agreement of an armistice, which robbed Harvey of what he rather disconsolately described as the 'full fruits of victory'.

> The Iranian troops returned to their barracks, the British hurried off for tea, while the Indians rushed into the cooling water of the Karun, not caring for the sharks who infested the river, and many suffered heavily. The inhabitants of the town showed a friendly attitude towards the British, and they appeared to have taken not the smallest interest in the affairs.[97]

This initiative came ahead of orders from the Shah in Tehran later that day to cease all resistance. On 27 August the Iranian Cabinet had resigned and on 28 August a new government was formed, led by Muhammed Ali Furuqi. It ordered the Iranian Armed Forces to cease resistance. The four-day war was over. The cost of the campaign for the Anglo-Indian force was twenty killed and fifty wounded.

Whilst these operations were underway, Soviet forces were entering the country from the north. One column moved towards Pahlevi and from there towards Kazvin, while another moved from Julfa towards Tabriz, and thence also to Kazvin via Mianeh. Little opposition was encountered, columns entering Kazvin on the fifth day of the operation. The British and Soviets met up at Sinna late on 29 August and to the south of Kazvin on the 31st.

The rapid success of these military operations, however, did not persuade the Shah to promise unequivocal compliance with Allied demands. He remained in denial about the severity of the situation his country faced. A further British note on 30 August now demanded the expulsion of all German citizens, less all those who had secured refuge in the German Legation. The Shah replied on 1 September, asking for clarity regarding the respective zones of occupation of the British and Soviets, and demanding reparations for the costs of the war to Iranian property. On 3 and 4 September Churchill urged both the Defence Council and the War Cabinet to take a strong line with Iran in terms of insisting upon taking over the road and rail routes through Iran to southern Russia, and maximizing the capacity of this strategic line of communication.[98] The Allies replied on 6 September, now demanding the expulsion of the German, Italian, Romanian and Hungarian Legations. The British were content to discuss reparations once these expulsions had been carried out, although the Soviets rejected them outright. The government persuaded the Shah to agree to these demands, although the Shah remained sullen and defiant, and throughout the various Axis legations showed by their inaction that they thought that the Allies would be unable to execute their demands on Tehran. They were wrong.

After accepting the Shah's plea for a cessation of hostilities, British and Soviet troops remained static for a week whilst waiting for Tehran to accede to all Allied demands. When it was apparent that these would not be forthcoming, on 15 September British and Soviet forces moved on the capital, precipitating the Shah's abdication. Because of this procrastination, the War Office ordered Wavell on 14 September to arrange a co-ordinated advance with the Soviets into Tehran. The advance into the suburbs was agreed for 3 p.m. on 17 September. On both the 15th and 16th the British placed heavy pressure on the Shah to abdicate. The BBC had broadcast from New Delhi and London suggesting to the Iranians that a change of national leadership was desirable. They reminded the Iranians of the autocratic nature of the Shah's 'Nazi-like' regime and blamed all the calamities of recent days firmly on his head. These results were successful. At 11 a.m. on 16 September the Shah abdicated and his 21-year-old son, Crown Prince Muhammed Riza, was proclaimed Shah in his place.

The invasion achieved its desired results, in dramatic fashion. The Iranian Armed Forces seemed in no way prepared to commit themselves to a decisive defence of their homeland. By 21 September the remaining Germans had largely been rounded up. The British had arrested some 400 suspects and the Russians 60, with the remainder allowed to evacuate to Germany via Turkey. However, the major German secret agents escaped capture, as did the Grand Mufti, who was reported to have sought sanctuary in the Japanese Legation as the first stage of his flight from the country.

Tehran was evacuated by both British and Russian troops on 18 October.

Great Britain's intervention was caused by Iran's unwillingness to understand the seriousness of the strategic pressures facing Great Britain in the summer of 1941. If Great Britain could not guarantee the security of its oil, and of its communications between the Middle and Near East through the Iranian and Arabian littorals, it would be forced to secure them for herself or lose out to Nazi Germany, which observed none of the niceties of international political discourse. Great Britain was at war for her life; though the invasion of Iran was of dubious legality, it was nonetheless of undeniable necessity. Iran's much-protected and valued neutrality became a stumbling block to its own security through the long, hot summer of 1941. If the Shah, who had approached London for a treaty in 1941, had been amenable in his response to British security concerns in June 1941, the country would never have been invaded at all. However, Iranian intransigence in June allowed the issue to escalate and result in a situation which left Great Britain with little choice but to pre-empt the certainty of German action. That lesson, at least, had been learned in Iraq. If Iran had reacted quickly and positively to the British perceptions of the threat facing its interests in Iran (the presence of so many Germany nationals in the country, a legitimate fear given German involvement in the recent Iraq affair), regardless of whether these Germans did in actuality present a threat, the issue would undoubtedly have gone away.

At no stage during the British and Soviet offensive was war declared on Iran: both British and Soviet ambassadors remained in Tehran throughout. Iranian sovereignty was impinged on only in terms of the invasion itself, and not in terms of her status as a sovereign state. A new Tripartite Agreement was not forced on the Iranian Government, but negotiated painfully slowly and agreed only in February 1942. This was not a self-serving invasion of national aggrandizement on the Nazi model, but one of survival, in which, as Churchill attested, inaction would have resulted in the perpetration of a greater evil. Wrote Churchill: 'Thus ended this brief and fruitful exercise of overwhelming force against a weak and ancient state. Britain and Russia were fighting for their lives. *Inter arma silent leges.**'[99] The small, weak state would have been swallowed by the larger, stronger predator if Great Britain had insisted on observing the letter of a legal principle. As Churchill acknowledged, this principle in reality only had veracity within an environment in which consenting states held to the general observance of international law. In a situation of international chaos, where the powerful sought to aggrandize themselves in spite of the law and at the expense of the weak, the principle had no force.

Despite this, it is clear that the invasion had indeed constituted a failure of diplomacy. Kennedy recalled that in London 'there was a general feeling that this short war had been unnecessary, and that our diplomatic action had been bungled.'[100] John Colville, Churchill's Private Secretary, agreed, observing in his diary that the invasion of Persia was 'an aggressive and not really warranted act, which is difficult to justify except on the, in this case dubious, principle of *Salus populi surprema lex.*†'[101] Despite these self-criticisms it is also clear that every opportunity had been provided to the Shah to address Great Britain's fears of German expansionism in the Middle East, but Iran had failed to act decisively to ally itself with good rather than with evil. The failure of diplomacy was profound, but only part of the blame can legitimately be placed at London's door, for in attempting to preserve

* 'In war there are no laws.'

† 'The safety of the people is the most important law.'

his country's independence the Shah involuntarily made his country more rather than less vulnerable. Defending his neutrality in isolation of any real appreciation that this created a dangerous security situation for Great Britain, and one in which the latter would be forced to defend its interests, was the direct cause of the invasion of Iran and thus of the Shah's own downfall. The Shah was clearly a nationalist of a high order, but not a geo-strategist. In attempting to defend his national prerogatives he fell foul of the swirling and competing interests of a Europe locked in flames, and suffered the very fate that he had tried to avoid.

Epilogue

So ended the four-day war for Iran. It was an unexpected culmination of four months of fighting across the Middle East, in Iraq, Syria and Iran, in which Great Britain had fought to enforce its strategic security prerogatives, even when these were opposed by the legal and moral sanctions of national sovereignty and neutrality, and constrained by an extreme poverty of resources. But in each case the justification for British action was clear: enemy intrigue at the heart of these states could quite easily, with the minimum of effort, have brought the Middle East into the German camp, with disastrous results for Great Britain, the integrity of her oil supplies and the viability of the line of communication to India. The absence in Berlin of any 'Oriental Plan' to rival that for *Barbarossa* should not lead to the conclusion that Germany would not have acted to exploit British weakness where it could. Indeed, the history of German foreign policy in the Middle East since the late 1930s, together with the vast sweep of the Nazi tide in 1940 and 1941, led policy makers in London to the only sensible conclusion at the time, namely that Hitler had designs on the Middle East and would drive on it when he was able. Dabbling in Iraq and Syria in April and May provided an undeniable surety of these intentions.

Somewhat unsatisfactorily in this context, Bullard concludes that 'No final answer can be given to the question whether the invasion of Persia was justified.'[1] This judgement is surely only true, however, in terms of the legality of the invasion. But in every other respect the war was necessary and justified. At a practical and pragmatic level, the invasion was crucial to eventual British victory in the Middle East. The campaign was designed to prevent the Germans exploiting Iran for their own nefarious ends, and in so doing to protect Great Britain's security interests, interests that had already been threatened by German action (real and perceived) in both Iraq and Syria. It is possible that without Nazi intrigue in the Middle East in late 1940 and early 1941, no British military action would have been necessary. However, it is also important to recognize that a beneficial consequence of this eradication of hostile influence was the opportunity provided for both Great Britain and the United States to create a supply route through Iran to the USSR. Churchill noted after the war that the invasion of that country 'enabled us to send to Russia, over a period of four and a half years, five million tons of supplies.'[2] For Churchill, this latter *consequence* of the war came in his own mind to be the dominant *justification* for action in the first place. He admitted that a hoped-for consequence of the campaign was 'more intimate and friendly relations with our new Ally'. With oil secure, the strategic dimension could now concentrate exclusively upon 'joining hands' with the Soviets, as he intimated in a note to General Ismay, for the COS Committee, on 27 August 1941: 'We do not simply want to squat on the oil fields, but to get through communication with Russia.'[3]

Iraq, Syria and Iran were equally crucial elements of the same strategic jigsaw in 1941, a puzzle that included a patchwork of states and interests from the Suez Canal to the defence of India. Syria provided a point of entry for Axis influence and intervention in both Iraq and Iran. Through the defeat of Iraq in May, the complete removal of Vichy and German influence from Syria in June and July and the eradication of the threat to Iranian oil in August, September and October, Britain was able to ensure that she could both stabilize her interests in a volatile region as well as fight on against Germany, independent of the goodwill of a United States still far from committed to the global struggle against fascism. The pieces of the jigsaw were, to mix metaphors, also tottering dominoes, one push of which would send them toppling into the Axis camp. If any of the countries in the region had fallen to Nazi control, the whole basis of British security in the area would have been threatened, perhaps even fatally, given Great Britain's profound military weaknesses in 1941.

Would Great Britain have been defeated had it lost control of the Middle East in 1941? The answer to this question depends entirely on what would have been the reaction to this defeat by the United States. Certainly, there were many in Great Britain who despaired of victory. The moral effect on the British public of yet another defeat at a time of otherwise almost overwhelming gloom should not be underestimated. If the British Army on the Nile had been lost, following hard after the devastation wrought at Dunkirk, what hope could have remained for those brave, elderly souls, armed with little more than pitchforks and shotguns, guarding Britain's shores? Many held no hope that the British would be able to overcome Rommel and save Egypt, as General Dill's comments to Kennedy indicated so desperately in late May. Indeed, over a year was to elapse before that first tentative victory outside a Libyan village at El Alamein. But the answer to the question about the reaction of the United States must remain conjecture. Certainly, there were strong voices in Washington urging the full-blooded involvement of the United States in what many recognized correctly as a global struggle against tyranny, but these voices were balanced equally by those urging the virtues of isolation.

The most that can be said, perhaps, is that if Great Britain had lost the Middle East in the summer of 1941 to Hitler, with its oil, and its ligatures of empire cut, the likelihood is that she would have been immeasurably weakened, to the extent that her continued survival would have been surprising, even with the focal point of German attentions now far to the east. The immediate and unequivocal declaration of war against Germany by the United States would have acted to save her, but the certainty of American commitment did not emerge until American soil had itself been violated, at Pearl Harbour in December 1941.

But this happily remains conjecture. What is certain is that three wars and three victories in five months had secured for Great Britain mastery of the Middle East during the hot and eventful summer of 1941. From April, when the advance units of Major General Fraser's *Force Sabine* nosed its way up the Shatt al-Arab waterway to dock at Basra, to 30 August when a ceasefire was agreed with Iran, Great Britain had, with pluck, imagination and bluff, seized the initiative that denied to Germany the fruits of its propaganda. By preventing Iraq – the first domino of three – from falling it had ensured, by aggressive pre-emptive action in both Syria and Iran, that these countries did not themselves fall to Nazi intrigue. The result of this boldness for London was incalculable. These actions closed the back door to the Suez Canal, destroyed decisively any hope of German military expansionism in Iraq, Syria and Iran, secured the critical sea and air communications to India, and allowed a vital conduit to open up from the Persian Gulf to the Caspian Sea, thus connecting a lifeline between the USA and the USSR that was to pump many millions of tons of supplies into Soviet veins in the three years that followed. And it also safeguarded Great Britain's precious supplies of non-American oil, without which the war would have undoubtedly been lost. As Wavell had seen so clearly in 1940, the war would be decided by access to oil. Britain's action in 1941 ensured, to paraphrase Hilaire Belloc's observation about the Maxim gun two generations earlier,* that she would eventually prosper against her foes, because 'We had the oil, and they had not.'[4]

* Belloc wrote of the Maxim gun, the first self-powered machine gun, 'Whatever happens, we have got / The Maxim gun, and they have not.'

APPENDIX

Comparison of Oil Production during the Second World War

Table showing annual oil production of combatants in million metric tons.[*]

Date	USA	USSR	UK	Total Allied[†]	Germany[‡]	Romania	Total Axis[§]
1940	–	–	11.9	13.0	8.0	5.0	10.1
1941	–	33.0	13.9	48.2	9.6	5.5	11.7
1942	183.9	22.0	11.2	218.4	11.2	5.7	14.8
1943	199.6	18.0	15.8	234.7	13.2	5.3	16.0
1944	222.5	18.2	21.4	263.4	9.5	3.5	11.1
1945	227.2	19.4	16.6	264.3	Negligible	Negligible	Negligible
Totals	833.2	110.6	90.8	1,043.0	56.8	25.0	67.0

[*] John Ellis, *The World War II Databook* (London: BCA, 1993), p. 275.

[†] Allied figures include those for Canada.

[‡] German figures include synthetic oil production.

[§] Axis figures include those for Italy, Hungary and Japan.

NOTES

Introduction

1. This was the substance of a discussion by the Supreme War Council on 28 March 1940. CAB 99/3. See also J.R.M. Butler, *Grand Strategy Volume II* (London: HMSO, 1957), p. 213.
2. John Connell, *Wavell: Scholar and Soldier* (London: Collins, 1964), p. 232.

Chapter 1 – Cairo

1. John Masters, *The Road Past Mandalay* (London: Michael Joseph, 1961), p. 25. Hopkins was President Roosevelt's deputy, architect of Lend–Lease and special envoy to Winston Churchill.
2. Ibid., pp. 27–8.
3. Ibid., p. 28.
4. Gilbert's account only transiently touches the facts. Martin Gilbert, *Second World War* (London: Weidenfeld & Nicholson, 1989), p. 168.
5. Freya Stark, *Dust in the Lion's Paw* (London: Century Publishing, 1961), p. 76.
6. Artemis Cooper, *Cairo in the War 1939–1945* (London: Hamish Hamilton, 1989), pp. 70–1.
7. The plans were *Operation Bilge* (destruction of the oil plant in Syria), *Operation Boatswain* (destruction of the oil terminal in the Lebanese port of Tripoli), *Operation Brass* (destruction of the oil plant at Kirkuk in Iraq), *Operation Bullion* (destruction of the modern oil plant at Haifa, built by British interests in 1939) and *Operation Clump* (destruction of the oil pipeline from Iraq, through Transjordan to Palestine). Martin Gilbert, *Finest Hour* (London: Heinemann, 1983), p. 889.

8. Stark, *Dust in the Lion's Paw*, op. cit., p. 81.

9. Ibid., p. 83.

10. Ibid., p. 77.

11. Haj Amin el-Huseini spent the remainder of the war as Hitler's guest in Germany, assisting where he could the killing of Jews, especially in Yugoslavia, and the recruiting of Muslim troops for the SS. He died in Egypt in 1974.

12. War Office, *PaiForce: The Official Story of the Persia Command 1941–1946* (London: HMSO, 1948), p. 1.

13. BL File L/WS/1/374.

14. This was certainly the view of John Glubb. See James Lunt, *Glubb Pasha: A Biography* (London: Harvill Press, 1984), pp. 100, 105–6.

15. John Connell, *Auchinleck, A Critical Biography* (London: Cassell, 1959), p. 191.

16. Connell describes Nuri es-Said as a 'statesman of calibre who . . . strove arduously, over some forty years, to contain the wild, extremist passions of his compatriots. When he was in power there was relative tranquillity, when he was out there was trouble.' Ibid., p. 191. The journalist Leonard Mosley, however, described him as a 'complaisant pro-British puppet'. Leonard Mosley, *Power Play* (London: Weidenfeld & Nicholson, 1973), p. 94. Nuri was murdered in a *coup d'état* in 1958. One of the new government's first actions following this *coup* was to invite the exiled Rashid Ali to return to Iraq.

17. Arthur Bryant, *The Turn of the Tide* (New York: Doubleday, 1957), p. 149.

18. Ibid., p. 150.

19. Geoffrey Warner, *Iraq and Syria* (London: Purnell, 1974), p. 37.

20. F.H. Hinsley, *British Intelligence in the Second World War*, Volume 1 (London: HMSO, 1979) p. 366.

21. Warner, op. cit., p. 96.

22. Ibid., p. 85.

23. Ibid., p. 94.

24. Ibid., p. 59.

25. WO/106 File 2620.

26. Major General John D. Frost, *A Drop Too Many* (Barnsley: Leo Cooper, 1994), p. 4.

27. The Iraq Levies comprised 17 seconded British Officers, 5 British Warrant Officers and Non Commissioned Officers (NCOs), 3 Medical Officers, 40 Assyrian Officers and 1,134 Levies.

28. A.C. Dudgeon, *Hidden Victory: The Battle of Habbaniya, May 1941* (Stroud: Tempus Publishing, 2000), p. 34. This is a revision of Dudgeon's *The War that Never Was* (Shrewsbury: Airlife Publishing, 1991).

29. Ibid., pp. 13–14.

30. When Frost departed Habbaniya in 1940 he was given an inscribed hunting horn as a farewell gift by the members of the Royal Exodus Hunt. It was with this horn that he rallied the men of his parachute battalion at Arnhem, the famous 'bridge too far', in September 1944. Frost, op. cit., p. 13.

31. Ibid., p. 10.

32. Ibid., p. 40.

Chapter 2 – New Delhi

1. Dharm Pal, *Official History of the Indian Armed Forces in the Second World War – Campaign in Western Asia* (Calcutta, 1957), p. 58.
2. Connell, *Auchinleck*, op. cit., p.193.
3. CA File 127. Auchinleck shortly changed the title of 'Army Head Quarters' (AHQ) to General Head Quarters (GHQ).
4. Connell, *Auchinleck*, op. cit., p.197.
5. Ibid., p. 187.
6. Ibid., pp. 188–9.
7. Ibid., p. 196.
8. Pal, op. cit., p. 51.
9. Compton Mackenzie, *Eastern Epic, Volume 1 September 1939–March 1943, Defence* (London: Chatto & Windus, 1951), p. 88.
10. Freya Stark, *East is West* (London: John Murray, 1945), p. 139. The American version, published simultaneously in New York by Alfred Knopf, is entitled *The Arab Island*.
11. Stark, *Dust in the Lion's Paw*, op. cit., p. 77.
12. Ibid., p. 78.
13. Freya Stark (in *East is West*) accuses Newton of incompetence and ignorance of the East. John Connell's verdict, however, is that Newton was merely 'weak and inexperienced . . .' John Connell, *Auchinleck*, op. cit., p. 191.
14. Lukasz Hirszowicz, *The Third Reich and the Arab East* (London: Routledge, Kegan & Paul, 1966), p. 141.
15. Mackenzie, op. cit., p. 90.
16. Connell, *Auchinleck*, op. cit., p. 199.
17. Butler, op.cit., p. 462.
18. Barrie Pitt, *The Crucible of War, Volume 1, Wavell's Command* (London: Jonathan Cape, 1980), p. 1.
19. Harold Raugh, *Wavell in the Middle East, 1939–1941: A Study in Generalship* (London: Brassey's, 1993), pp. 199, 215.
20. Ronald Lewin, *The Chief: Field Marshal Lord Wavell, Commander-in-Chief and Viceroy, 1939–1947* (London: Hutchinson, 1980), p. 134.
21. A.W. Tedder, *With Prejudice: The War Memoirs of Marshal of the Royal Air Force Lord Tedder GCB* (London: Cassell, 1966), p. 107. Tedder also commented unfavourably on the quality of the staff officers serving Wavell in GHQ Cairo.
22. Major General Sir F. De Guingand, *Operation Victory* (London: Hodder & Stoughton, 1947), p. 87.
23. The tragedy for Churchill was that, despite the advice of Dill and others, the man he chose to replace Wavell, Claude Auchinleck, displayed many of the same personal characteristics. A solid and thoughtful solider of considerable ability, Auchinleck did not have the charisma or imaginative ability of either Montgomery or Slim, Britain's two finest field commanders of the Second World War, and his time in command in Cairo was also to end in the 'Auk's' sacking in 1943.

24. This was the same problem that was to bedevil the British effort in Burma in the following year where it was the imagination of that unorthodox soldier, General 'Bill' Slim, that enabled the British, for the first time, to do in warfare what the Japanese had long practised.

25. Winston Churchill, *The Second World War: The Grand Alliance* (London: Cassell, 1950), p. 225

26. Dudgeon, op. cit., p. 28.

27. CA File 137.

28. Colonel Ouvry Roberts, his senior staff officer, described him as a 'charming man . . . with a distinguished career in the First World War.' OR, p. 226.

29. Connell, *Auchinleck*, op. cit., p. 201

30. Mackenzie, op. cit., p. 91.

31. Connell, *Wavell*, op. cit., p. 432.

32. Christopher Buckley, *Five Ventures* (London: HMSO, 1954), p. 8.

33. Stark, *Dust in the Lion's Paw*, op. cit., p. 75. She was not alone in this sentiment. See Edward Spears, *Fulfilment of a Mission: Syria and Lebanon 1941–1944* (London: Leo Cooper, 1977), p. 4.

34. Spears, op. cit., p. 5.

35. CA File 139.

36. Mosley, op. cit., p. 94.

37. Hinsley, op. cit., p. 411.

38. Connell, *Auchinleck*, op. cit., p. 207.

39. Gilbert, *Finest Hour*, op. cit., p. 1062.

40. N.L. Franks, *First in the Indian Skies* (31 Squadron Association, n.d.), pp. 71–5.

41. Buckley, op. cit., p. 9.

42. Stark, *Dust in the Lion's Paw*, op. cit., p. 81.

43. Gilbert, *Finest Hour*, op. cit., p. 1065.

44. Cable No. 62176 (MO5) Principal War Telegrams, Middle East 1940–43.

45. Connell, *Auchinleck*, op. cit., p. 207.

46. Churchill, *The Second World War: The Grand Alliance*, op. cit., p. 225.

47. Ibid., p. 226.

48. Warner, op. cit., p. 98.

49. Connell, *Auchinleck*, op. cit., p.209.

50. CA File 145.

51. Warner, op. cit., p. 99.

52. Hirszowicz, op. cit., p. 146.

53. OR, p. 236.

54. Connell, *Auchinleck*, op. cit., p. 210.

Chapter 3 – Habbaniya

1. Dudgeon, op. cit., p. 48.

2. T.E. Evans (ed.), *The Killearn Diaries, 1934–1946* (London: Sidgwick & Jackson, 1972), p. 167.

3. Ibid., p. 50.
4. Connell, *Auchinleck*, op. cit., p. 212.
5. Tedder, op. cit., p. 86.
6. Dudgeon, op. cit., p. 54.
7. Ibid., p. 55.
8. The British Official Historian mistakenly assumes that no warning was given. I.S.O. Playfair, *History of the Second World War. The Mediterranean and Middle East, Volume 2: The Germans Come to the Help of Their Ally, 1941*. London: HMSO, 1956, p. 183.
9. Dudgeon, op. cit., p. 57.
10. Translated from *Oriente Moderno*, pp. 552–3 and quoted by J.E. Katz at www.eretzyisroel.org.
11. Dudgeon, op. cit., p. 60.
12. Tedder, op. cit., p. 86.
13. Evans, op. cit., p. 167.
14. Stark, *Dust in the Lion's Paw*, op. cit., p. 91.
15. Quoted in Buckley, op. cit., p. 17.
16. Dudgeon, op. cit., p. 97.
17. Ibid.
18. He suffered concussion, a broken jaw, fractures of the sternum, ribs and left patella, severe bruising and the loss of two front teeth. Naida Davies (née Smart), *Unpublished Memoirs*, p. 170.
19. Dudgeon, op. cit., p. 87.
20. Tedder, op. cit., pp. 86–7.
21. Dudgeon, op. cit., p. 137.
22. OR, p. 232.
23. Hinsley, op. cit., p. 413.
24. John Glubb, *The Story of the Arab Legion* (London: Hodder & Stoughton, 1948), p. 312.
25. Dudgeon, op. cit., p. 99.
26. Gilbert, *Finest Hour*, op. cit., p. 1082
27. Dudgeon, op. cit., p. 104.
28. Stark, *Dust in the Lion's Paw*, op. cit, p. 96.
29. Ibid., p. 103.
30. CA File 156.
31. Ibid., p.160.
32. Connell, *Wavell*, op. cit., p. 435.
33. CA File 164.
34. Lewin, op. cit., p. 137.
35. Connell, *Wavell*, op. cit., p. 436.
36. Evans, op. cit., p. 169.
37. Ibid., p. 172–3.
38. Connell, *Wavell*, op. cit., p. 437.
39. Ibid., p. 438.
40. Ibid.

41. Churchill, *The Second World War: The Grand Alliance*, op. cit., pp. 228–9.
42. H.L. Ismay, *The Memoirs of Lord Ismay* (London: Heinemann, 1960), p. 207.
43. CA File 182.
44. Connell, *Wavell*, op. cit., p. 440.
45. Churchill, *The Second World War: The Grand Alliance*, op. cit., p. 230.
46. Ibid., pp. 230–1.
47. Ibid., p. 231.
48. CA File 129.
49. Ibid., p. 130.
50. Auchinleck's letter confirming Quinan and Slim's departure for Iraq on 4 May 1941 is in British Library L/WS/1/535.
51. CA File 199. Major General W.A.K. Fraser then became the British Military Attaché in Iran.
52. Masters, op. cit., pp. 44–5.
53. CA File 191.
54. Connell, *Auchinleck*, op. cit., p. 222.
55. Ibid., p. 223.
56. CA File 200.
57. Connell, *Wavell*, op. cit., p. 446.
58. Churchill, *The Second World War: The Grand Alliance*, op. cit., p. 231.
59. CA File 211.

Chapter 4 – Baghdad

1. Somerset de Chair, *The Golden Carpet* (London: Faber & Faber, 1944), p. 28.
2. The belief that the aircraft was Iraqi found its way into the Regimental History. See T.A. Martin, *Essex Regiment* (Brentwood: The Essex Regiment Association, 1951), p. 46.
3. De Chair, op. cit., p. 211.
4. Ibid., p. 21. For details of Enigma decrypts see Hinsley, op. cit., p. 413.
5. Field Marshal Lord Wilson of Libya, *Eight Years Overseas* (London: Hutchinson, 1948), p. 103.
6. Peter Bindloss, *Memories of World War Two* (Unpublished Memoir, 2001), p. 9.
7. R.J. Collins, *Lord Wavell: A Military Biography* (London: Hodder & Stoughton, 1948), p. 397.
8. Anthony Mockler, *Our Enemies the French* (London: Leo Cooper, 1976), p. 41.
9. Stark, *East is West*, op. cit., p. 118.
10. Ibid., p. 257.
11. De Chair, op. cit., pp. 32–3.
12. Collins, op. cit., p. 396.
13. Martin, op. cit., p. 46.
14. De Chair, op. cit., p. 211.
15. Sir Alec Kirkbride, *A Crackle of Thorns* (London: John Murray, 1956, p. 132) quoted in Lunt op. cit., p. 101.
16. De Chair, op. cit., pp. 16–17.

17. Ibid., pp. 36–7

18. Ibid., p. 37.

19. Ibid., p. 50.

20. Ibid., p. 15.

21. Warner, op. cit., p. 101.

22. See Niall Ferguson, *Empire: How Britain Made the Modern World* (London: Allen Lane, 2004), pp. 300–2.

23. Hinsley, op. cit., p. 413.

24. Spears, op. cit., p. 71.

25. Hirszowicz, op. cit., p. 161. A previous shipment of 100 tons of captured Dutch and French equipment was agreed on 24 April to be sent by five aircraft making ten trips each by air from Salonika to Syria at a future date. This consignment was prepared but never sent. It included fifteen thousand 6.6-millimetre Dutch rifles (with 5 million rounds), six hundred 6.5-millimetre Dutch Light Machine Guns (with 6 million rounds), two hundred 0.6-inch heavy machine guns (and 2 million rounds), together with fifty 81-millimetre French mortars (with 25,000 shells) and one hundred and ten 50-millimetre French mortars (with 75,000 shells). See Hirszowicz, op. cit., p. 147.

26. Stark, *Dust in the Lion's Paw*, op. cit., p. 100.

27. Dudgeon, op. cit., pp. 116–17.

28. De Chair, op. cit, p. 53. Roberts also comments critically on Clark and Kingstone, examples in his mind of an out-dated and cavalier amateurism in the Army. See OR, p. 242. Likewise, John Masters laughed at their expense. Prior to leaving England Major General Clark (according to Masters' probably apocryphal but amusing story) inspected one of his Yeomanry regiments. Asked whether everything was in order the colonel replied, 'Oh, I think so, George.' The general gently pressed for details – ammunition? Vehicles? Non-coms' training? Gas-masks? The colonel scratched his head and said, 'Dash it, I don't know about any of that, George . . . but we've got forty dozen of champagne, well crated, and the pack of foxhounds is in fine fettle.' Masters, *The Road Past Mandalay*, p. 39.

29. The command arrangements within Habbaniya after Smart's departure are not clear. This account is taken from OR, p. 231.

30. J.H. D'Albiac, *Report of Operations in Baghdad Area – 2 May to 31 May 1941.*

31. CA File 238.

32. Sir John Kennedy, *The Business of War* (London: Hutchinson, 1957), p. 136.

33. Somerset de Chair, however, regarded D'Albiac to be part of the new enlightened breed of RAF officer, describing him as 'the only Air Force Brass Hat in the Middle East at that time who believed that the role of the Air Force was to assist the Army. All the others were busy fighting their own Wars, and were surprised when the British armies, far below them on the ground, melted into retreat. D'Albiac proved for the first time that 100 per cent co-operation was possible.' This, however, was not borne out from his own observations of the Falluja battle. De Chair, op. cit., p. 54.

34. Mackenzie, op. cit., p. 103,

35. Stark, *Dust in the Lion's Paw*, op. cit., p. 106.
36. Ibid.
37. Buckley, op. cit., p. 27.
38. There are a variety of versions of this story. See Somerset de Chair, op. cit., p. 57; Dudgeon, op. cit., p. 126; Martin, op. cit., p. 50; and Wilson, op. cit., p. 107.
39. Martin, op. cit., pp. 50–1.
40. Wilson, op. cit., p. 108.
41. CA File 206.
42. Ibid., 230.
43. Ibid., 238. This was sent on 29 May 1941.
44. Raugh, op. cit., p. 215.
45. De Chair, op. cit., pp. 93–4.
46. John Glubb, *The Story of the Arab Legion* (London: Hodder & Stoughton, 1948), p. 243.
47. Stark, *East is West*, op. cit., p. 157.
48. PREM 3/309/5 Part 5 dated 28 May 1941.
49. Stark, *Dust in the Lion's Paw*, op. cit., p. 110.
50. Playfair, op. cit., p. 196.
51. De Chair, op. cit., pp. 71–2.
52. CA File 244.
53. Buckley, op. cit., p. 33.
54. Evans, op. cit., p. 178
55. Wilson, op. cit., p. 108.
56. Lunt, op. cit., p. 104.
57. Evans, op. cit., p. 181.
58. The Earl of Avon, *The Eden Memoirs: The Reckoning* (London: Cassell, 1965), p. 243.
59. PREM 3/309/5 Part 84 dated 5 June 1941.
60. PREM 3/309/5 Part 37 dated 31 May 1941.
61. TA Martin, op. cit., p. 59.
62. Stark, *East is West*, op. cit., p. 120.
63. Stark, *Dust in the Lion's Paw*, op. cit., p. 113.
64. The most certain figures are those provided by George Kirk, *The Middle East in the War* (Oxford: Oxford University Press, 1952), p. 75.
65. Slim, *Unofficial History* (London: Cassell, 1959), p. 152.
66. The Earl of Avon, op. cit., p. 244.
67. Tedder, op. cit., p. 83.
68. Playfair, op. cit., p. 197.
69. As told to Tony Dudgeon. See Dudgeon, op. cit., p. 139. Air Marshal A. W. Tedder formally replaced Longmore on 18 May 1941 although he had been in effective command since Longmore departed for London on 3 May.
70. Tedder, *With Prejudice*, p. 130.
71. Hirszowicz, op. cit., p. 144.
72. The full text of Directive No. 30 is at Appendix 2 to Playfair, op. cit., pp. 333–4.
73. Ismay, op. cit., pp. 207–8.

74. De Chair, op. cit., pp. 76–7. The Italian aircraft was shot down by a Gladiator of 94 Squadron, piloted by the squadron commander. See Dudgeon, op. cit., p. 132.
75. Playfair, op. cit., p. 197.
76. Hinsley, op. cit., pp. 413–14.
77. Winston Churchill, *The Second World War: The Grand Alliance* (London: Cassell, 1951), p. 237.

Chapter 5 – Beirut

1. Buckley, op. cit., p. 45.
2. Spears, op. cit., p. 31.
3. Gilbert, *Finest Hour*, op. cit., p. 1073
4. Churchill, *The Grand Alliance*, op. cit, p. 26.
5. CAB/95/1 1 July 1940.
6. CAB/95/1 8 July 1940.
7. Spears, op. cit., p. 33.
8. Ibid., p. 82.
9. Wilfred Thesiger, *The Life of My Choice* (London: Collins, 1987), pp. 359–60.
10. Quoted in A.B. Gaunson, *Anglo-French Clash in Lebanon and Syria, 1940–1945* (London: Macmillan 1987), p. 5.
11. Quoted in Mockler, op. cit., p. 234. See also Paul Webster, *Pétain's Crime* (London: Macmillan, 1990), pp. 1–34.
12. Ibid., pp. 17–18.
13. Spears, op. cit., p. 69.
14. Ibid., p. 26
15. Connell, *Wavell*, op. cit., p. 241.
16. J. Glubb, *The Story of the Arab Legion*, op. cit., p. 307.
17. Spears, op. cit., p. 14.
18. Ibid., p. 121. It should be noted, however, that de Gaulle had a very poor view of Spears as a chronicler. '*Les Mémoires du général Spears qui sont sujets à caution comme on l'a montré à maintes reprises.*' (*De Gaulle, mon pére*, Vol I, p. 141.)
19. Ibid., p. 97.
20. Quoted in ibid., p. 1.
21. J. Glubb, *The Story of the Arab Legion*, op. cit., p. 311.
22. In de Gaulle's Brazzaville speech of June 1944 he spoke of the need to provide reform and progress for France's colonies, allowing them to take their proper place in the French family of nations. This did not occur until de Gaulle's return to political power in 1958.
23. Gaunson does not believe that either man could have been unaware of this crucial distinction. I am not so sure.
24. Spears, op. cit., p. 105.
25. Gaunson, op. cit., pp. 24–5.
26. Spears, op. cit., p. 3.
27. PREM 3/309/5 Part 283 dated 29 June 1941.
28. De Gaulle, *War Memoirs Volume One: The Call to Arms 1940–1942* (London: Collins, 1955), p. 177.

29. Spears, op. cit., p. 35.
30. De Gaulle, op. cit., p. 179.
31. Spears, op. cit., p. 37.
32. Ibid., p. 32 and p. 64.
33. PREM 309/3 dated 27 April.
34. Quoted in Warner, op. cit., p. 125.
35. PREM 3/309/4 Part 25.
36. Wavell, *Despatch*, iv, para. 85.
37. PREM 3/309/4 Part 25 dated 4 May 1941.
38. PREM 3/309/4 Part 35 dated 6 May 1941.
39. Kirk, op. cit., p.93.
40. Spears, op. cit., p. 62.
41. Ibid., p. 64.
42. Ibid., p. 62 and 65.
43. Brian Roberts, *Randolph, A Study of Churchill's Son* (London: Hamish Hamilton, 1984), p. 209.
44. PREM 3 422/6.
45. PREM 3/309/4 Part 61 dated 9 May 1941.
46. Kennedy, op. cit., p. 116.
47. Ibid., p. 118.
48. PREM 3/309/4 Part 71 dated 10 May 1941.
49. Wavell, *Despatch*, op. cit., p. xx
50. Quoted in Warner, op. cit., p. 132.
51. Spears, op. cit., p. 84.
52. PREM 3/309/4 Part 83 dated 12 May 1941.
53. PREM 3/309/4 Part 84 dated 12 May 1941.
54. PREM 3/309/4 Part 103 dated 14 May 1941.
55. PREM 3/309/4 Part 95 and Part 97 dated 13 May 1941.
56. Quoted in Kirk, op. cit., p. 94.
57. PREM 3/309/4 Part 106 dated 15 May 1941.
58. PREM 3/309/4 Part 125 dated 17 May 1941.
59. Lewin, *The Chief*, op. cit., p. 140.
60. Tedder, op. cit., p. 93.
61. PREM 3/309/4 Part 139 dated 19 May 1941.
62. PREM 3/309/4 Part 136 dated 19 May 1941.
63. Tedder, op. cit., p. 93.
64. Quoted in Mockler, op. cit., pp. 62–3.
65. PREM 3/309/4 Part 141 dated 19 May 1941.
66. Tedder, op. cit., pp. 92–3, which is a fleshed out version of the original, in PREM 3/309/4 Part 140, dated 19 May 1941.
67. Tedder, op. cit., p. 93.
68. Ibid, p. 94.
69. Spears, op. cit., p. 84.
70. Eden, op. cit., pp. 246–7.
71. PREM 3/309/4 Part 142 dated 19 May 1941.

72. PREM 3/309/4 Part 151 dated 20 May 1941.
73. Quoted in Connell, *Wavell*, op. cit., p. 462. The original file appears to have been expunged from the record, or was never placed in the correspondence that now makes up the PREM files in the National Archives.
74. Kennedy, op. cit., p. 119.
75. Quoted in Connell, *Wavell*, op. cit., p. 462.
76. Evans, op. cit., p. 174.
77. Kennedy, op. cit., p. 124.
78. Quoted in Raugh, op. cit., p. 219.
79. PREM 3/309/4 Part 181 dated 21 May 1941.
80. Churchill, *The Grand Alliance*, op. cit., p. 291.
81. Spears, op. cit., p. 78.
82. Ibid., p. 86.
83. PREM 3/309/4 Parts 163 and 164 dated 21 May 1941 reinforced by information received on 22 May: Part 194 dated 23 May 1941.
84. Quoted in Mockler, op. cit., p. 32.
85. Kirk, op. cit., p. 95.
86. PREM 3/309/4 Part 182 dated 23 May 1941.

Chapter 6 – Damascus

1. PREM 3/309/5 Part 7 dated 28 May 1941.
2. PREM 3/309/5 Part 95 dated 6 June 1941.
3. PREM 3/309/5 Part 105 dated 7 June 1941.
4. Wilson, op. cit., p. 113.
5. PREM 3/309/4 Part 216 dated 25 May 1941.
6. PREM 3/309/5 Part 81 dated 5 June 1941.
7. Mockler, op. cit., p. 113.
8. Spears, op. cit., p. 100.
9. PREM 3/309/5 Part 67 dated 4 June 1941.
10. Buckley, op. cit., p. 54.
11. Kennedy, op. cit., p. 124.
12. Ibid, p. 126.
13. PREM 3/309/5 Part 81 dated 5 June 1941.
14. David Dilks (ed.), *The Diaries of Sir Alexander Cadogan, 1939–1945* (London: Cassell, 1971), p. 386.
15. Eden, op. cit., p. 249.
16. PREM 3/309/5 Part 61 dated 3 June 1941.
17. PREM 3/309/5 Part 67 dated 4 June 1941.
18. PREM 3/309/5 Part 23 dated 30 May 1941.
19. PREM 3/309/5 Part 94 dated 6 June 1941.
20. PREM 3/309/5 Part 120 dated 6 June 1941.
21. PREM 3/309/5 Part 150 dated 10 June 1941.
22. Spears, op. cit., p. 9.

23. Buckley, op. cit., p. 62.
24. De Guingand, op. cit., p. 87.
25. Gilbert, *Finest Hour*, op. cit., p. 1107.
26. Moshe Dayan, *Story of my Life* (London: Weidenfeld & Nicholson, 1976), pp. 43–51. The Official History records that this attack was made by '42 Australians', ignoring the role played by the Palestinian Jewish volunteers altogether.
27. Philip Guedalla, *Middle East 1940–1942: A Study in Air Power* (London: Hodder & Stoughton, 1944), p. 153.
28. Denis Richards, *Royal Air Force 1939–1945, Volume 1: The Fight at Odds* (London: HMSO, 1953), pp. 341–2.
29. Tedder, op. cit., p. 114.
30. Ibid., p. 124.
31. Spears, op. cit., p. 104.
32. Tedder, op. cit., p. 127.
33. Quoted in Mockler, op. cit., p. 171.
34. See ibid., pp. 106–9.
35. PREM 3/309/5 Part 146 dated 10 June 1941.
36. PREM 3/309/5 Part 162 dated 11 June 1941.
37. PREM 3/309/5 Part 176 dated 13 June 1941.
38. Quoted in Kirk, op. cit., p. 99.
39. Mockler, op. cit., p. 110.
40. Buckley, op. cit., p. 71.
41. Bernard Fergusson, *The Trumpet in the Hall* (London: Collins, 1970), p. 110.
42. Mockler, op. cit., p. 120.
43. PREM 3/309/5 Part 227 dated 17 June.
44. Quoted in Mockler, op. cit., p. 147.
45. Kirk, op. cit., p. 100.
46. Lieutenant Colonel Arthur Blackburn VC was in private life the Coroner for the City of Adelaide. He survived capture and imprisonment by the Japanese later in the war. Fergusson, op. cit., pp. 115–16.
47. Quoted in Buckley, op. cit., p. 102.

Chapter 7 – Deir-ez-Zor

1. Kennedy, op. cit, p. 133.
2. Glubb, *The Story of the Arab Legion*, op. cit., p. 309.
3. Spears, op. cit., p. 101.
4. Ibid., p. 89.
5. Glubb, *The Story of the Arab Legion,* op. cit., p. 312.
6. Ibid., p. 311.
7. Godfrey Lias, *Glubb's Legion* (London: Evans Brothers, 1956), p. 158.
8. Glubb, *The Story of the Arab Legion,* op. cit., pp. 317-18.
9. De Chair, op. cit., pp. 187-8.
10. Ibid., p. 198.
11. Glubb, *The Story of the Arab Legion,* op. cit., p. 322.

12. Lias, op. cit., p. 164.
13. Glubb, *The Story of the Arab Legion*, op. cit., p. 335.
14. Auchinleck's suggestion is PREM 3/309/5 Part 113 dated 7 June 1941; Dill's suggestion to Wavell is Part 141 dated 10 June 1941; Wavell's reply to Dill is Part 182 dated 14 June 1941.
15. Masters, op. cit., pp. 44–5.
16. Slim, op. cit., pp. 151–73.
17. OR, pp. 244–5.
18. Masters, op. cit., p. 48.
19. Ibid., pp. 47–8.
20. Ibid., p. 52.
21. Ibid., p. 50.
22. OR, p. 243.
23. Slim, op. cit., p. 173.
24. Spears, op. cit., p. 105.
25. Michael Dewar, himself an ex-Green Jacket, remarks surprisingly that 'Wilson demonstrated his not inconsiderable abilities as a negotiator and diplomat. De Gaulle was, even as this stage, notoriously difficult to deal with; Wilson seems to have handled him with consummate skill. Despite his direct manner and bluff exterior . . . [he was] a man who was capable of wise and balanced judgement and a degree of tact and sensitivity which was put to good use in negotiations with the Vichy French after their surrender in Syria and Lebanon and before their repatriation to France.' Michael Dewar, 'Wilson' in *Churchill's Generals* (London: Weidenfeld & Nicholson, 1991), p. 174.
26. Spears, op. cit., p. 126.
27. Gaunson, op. cit., p. 55.
28. De Gaulle, op. cit., pp. 177, 187, 188, 202, 210–12.
29. PREM 3/309/5 Part 175 dated 13 June 1941. These points were repeated in a personal message from de Gaulle to Churchill on the same day (Part 179).
30. Spears, op. cit., p. 117.
31. See Hinsley, Volume 1, op. cit., p. 424.
32. Quoted in Warner, op. cit., p. 160.
33. Eden, op. cit., p. 161.
34. Raugh, op. cit., p. 241.
35. Warner, op. cit., p. 162.
36. Thesiger, op. cit., p. 363.
37. PREM 3/309/4 Part 165 dated 21 May 1941.
38. Churchill, op. cit., p. 297.
39. Kennedy, op. cit., pp. 134–5. Both men were told on 21 June to change positions, Auchinleck to Cairo and Wavell to New Delhi.
40. Kennedy, op. cit., p. 122.
41. A. Danchev and D. Todman (eds.), *War Diaries 1939–1940: Field Marshal Lord Alanbrooke* (London: Weidenfeld & Nicholson, 2001), p. 165.
42. Ibid., p. 129.
43. Ibid., p. 137.
44. Spears, op. cit., p. 116. This point was made also by Wavell in a situation report sent to London on 11 June. See also Mockler, op. cit., p. 181.

45. Churchill, *The Grand Alliance*, op. cit., p. 296.
46. Hansard, 15 June 1941.
47. Pal, op. cit., p. 125.

Chapter 8 – Tehran

1. Kirk, op. cit., p. 131.
2. Kirk, op. cit., p. 130.
3. Pal, op. cit., p. 121.
4. Churchill, *The Grand Alliance*, op. cit., p. 423.
5. A fact noticed immediately by London. Chiefs of Staff Appreciation, 6 October 1939, CAB 66 (Volume 2) WP (1939) 73.
6. Iran, whose air force was built primarily of British aircraft, asked for the immediate shipment of sixty fighters and bombers. Chiefs of Staff Report, 23 February 1940, CAB 66, WP (1939) 73.
7. 'Review of Military Policy in the Middle East', December 1939, CAB 66 WP (1939) 148 and 'Military Policy in the Middle East' 13 January 1940, CAB 66 WP (1940) 18.
8. Chiefs of Staff Report, 23 February 1940, CAB 66, WP (1940) 66.
9. 'Military Implications of Hostilities with Russia in 1940', 8 March 1940, CAB 66, WP (1940) 91. See also Woodward, *British Foreign Policy*, Volume 1 (London: HMSO, 1970), pp. 71–6.
10. See ibid., pp. 109–12, and Hinsley, op. cit., pp. 198–9.
11. Stewart, op. cit., p. 22.
12. Woodward, op. cit., p. 473.
13. This story is very well told in Stewart, op. cit., pp. 28–31.
14. Connell, *Wavell*, op cit., p. 446.
15. Stewart, op. cit., p. 48.
16. Kennedy, op. cit., p. 157.
17. Prasad, op. cit., pp. 46–54.
18. Somerset de Chair, op. cit., pp. 53–4.
19. Eden, op. cit., p. 266.
20. Stewart, op. cit., p. 40.
21. Quoted in ibid., p. 43.
22. Bullard, op. cit., p. 226.
23. Pal, op. cit., p. 123.
24. PREM 3/309/5 Part 252 dated 21 June 1941.
25. Pal, op. cit., p. 124.
26. On 30 July 1941, a British intelligence summary dismissed fears of a *coup d'état* in Iran engineered by Nazi fifth-columnists. Hinsley, Volume 2, op. cit., p. 82.
27. Kennedy, op. cit., p. 154.
28. Churchill, *The Grand Alliance*, op. cit., pp. 331–2.
29. Stewart, op. cit., p. 55.
30. Pal, op. cit., p. 300.

31. Cooper, op. cit., p. 135.
32. Connell, *Wavell: Supreme Commander*, op. cit., pp. 23–4. [my italics]
33. Ibid., p. 26.
34. Ibid., p. 24.
35. FO/371/27230 File E3055.
36. Quoted in Pal, op. cit., pp. 301–2.
37. FO/371/27231 File E4141.
38. FO/371/27230 File E4065.
39. FO/371/27231 File E3995.
40. Pal, op. cit., p. 297.
41. FO/371/27231 File E4141.
42. Churchill, *The Grand Alliance*, op. cit., p. 424.
43. Ibid., pp. 424–5.
44. Ibid.
45. Sir Reader Bullard, *Britain and the Middle East* (London: Hutchinson, 1964), p. 133.
46. Kirk, op. cit., p. 133.
47. Stark, *Dust in the Lion's Paw*, op. cit., pp. 85, 87.
48. Hinsley, Volume 2, op. cit., p. 82.
49. FO/371/27231 File E4141
50. FO/371/27232 File E4478.
51. Kennedy, op. cit., p. 158.
52. Ibid., p. 159.
53. Eden, op. cit., p. 273.
54. Kennedy, op. cit., p. 159.
55. Quoted in Motter, op. cit., p. 21.
56. Ibid., p. 22.
57. Ibid., p. 15.
58. PaiForce, op. cit., pp. 66, 70.
59. Churchill, *The Grand Alliance*, op. cit., p. 477.
60. Churchill, *The Gathering Storm* (London: Cassell, 1949), p. 430.
61. FO/371/27201 File E4375.
62. FO/371/27201 File E4659.
63. Kennedy, op. cit., p. 157.
64. Eden briefed the Turkish ambassador in London on 19 August 1941. FO/371/27205 File E4830.
65. As Stewart affirms, the War Cabinet Minutes (CAB 66, Volume 18, WP [1941] 202) establish the date of this meeting as 11 August. Stewart op. cit., p. 76. HMS *Prince of Wales* was sunk, alongside HMS *Repulse*, at the end of 1941 by Japanese dive-bombers off the north-east coast of Malaya.
66. CAB 66, Volume 18, WP (1941), 202.
67. Pal, op. cit., p. 303. See also Hinsley, op. cit., Volume 2, p. 82.
68. Ibid.
69. Pal, op. cit., pp. 306–7
70. Quoted in ibid., p. 308.

71. NA/FO/371/27201 File E4860.
72. Quoted in Pal, op. cit., p. 310.
73. Churchill, *The Grand Alliance*, op. cit., p. 427.
74. Gilbert, *Finest Hour*, op. cit., p. 1171.
75. John Connell, *Wavell*, op. cit., p. 29
76. Pal, op. cit., p. 315.
77. Stewart, op. cit., p. 75.
78. See W. Langer and E. Gleason, *The Undeclared War, 1940–1941* (The Council on Foreign Relations. The World Crisis and American Foreign Policy series, second part, New York: Harper & Brothers, 1953), pp. 803–4. Hull's request to the British Ambassador, Lord Halifax, for further clarity of British intentions is in FO/371/27201 File E4717.
79. Stewart, op. cit., pp. 94–5.
80. FO/371/27208 File E4537.
81. Buckley, op. cit., p. 141.
82. Churchill, *The Grand Alliance*, op. cit., p. 428
83. Eden, op. cit., p. 273.
84. FO/371/27205 File E4812.
85. Kennedy, op. cit., p. 162.
86. Pal, op. cit., p. 313.
87. Kennedy, op. cit., p. 163.
88. Stewart suggests (op. cit., p. 98) that 120,000 Soviet troops were involved. This is surely an error. Motter (op cit., p. 10) cites the more reasonable figure of 40,000.
89. Kennedy, op. cit., p. 163.
90. Slim, op. cit., p. 182.
91. Ibid. 'Bundobust' is Hindustani for 'arrangements'.
92. Ibid., p. 181.
93. Ibid., p. 183.
94. OR, p. 251.
95. Slim, op. cit., p. 184.
96. Masters, op. cit., pp. 63–4.
97. Pal, op. cit., p. 330.
98. J.R.M. Butler, *Grand Strategy*, Vol III (London: 1964), p. 189.
99. Ibid
100. Kennedy, op. cit., p. 163.
101. John Colville, *The Fringes of Power* (London: Hodder & Stoughton, 1985), p. 430.

Epilogue

1. Bullard, op. cit., p. 227.
2. Churchill, *The Grand Alliance*, op. cit., p. 432.
3. Ibid., p. 428.
4. Hilaire Belloc, *The Modern Traveller* (London: Edward Arnold, 1898).

MAPS

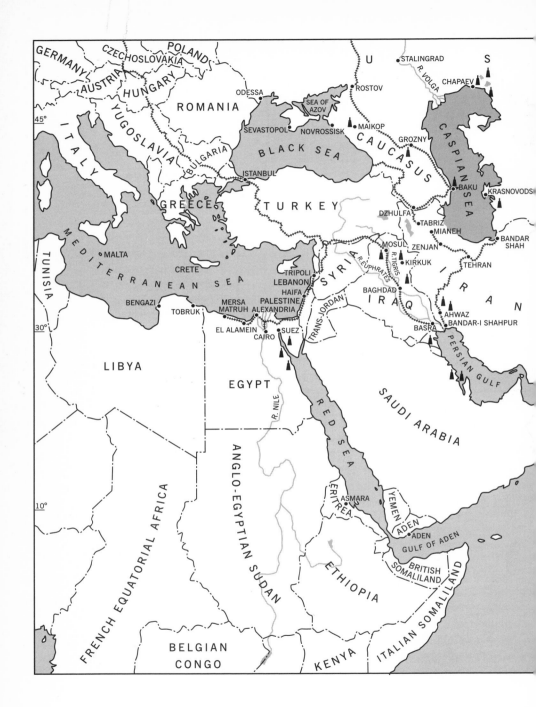

314

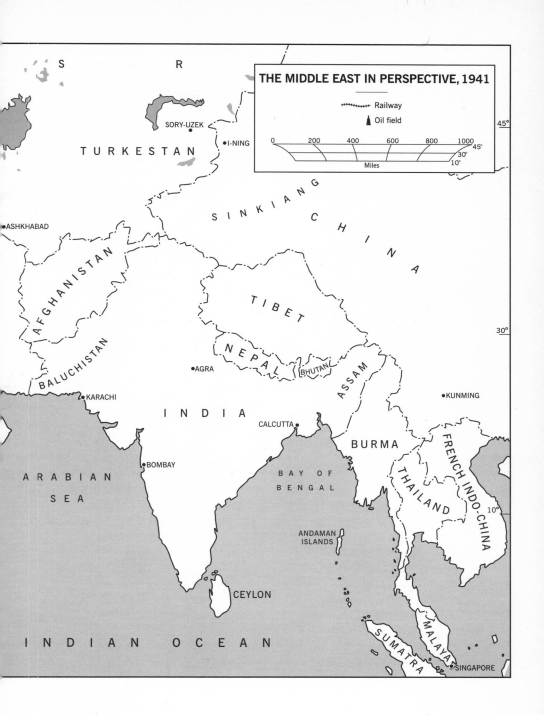

THE MIDDLE EAST IN PERSPECTIVE, 1941

Railway

Oil field

| 0 | 200 | 400 | 600 | 800 | 1000 |

Miles

S

R

TURKESTAN

SORY-UZEK

•I-NING

•ASHKHABAD

SINKIANG

CHINA

AFGHANISTAN

TIBET

BALUCHISTAN

NEPAL

BHUTAN

•AGRA

ASSAM

KARACHI

INDIA

CALCUTTA

•KUNMING

BURMA

•BOMBAY

A R A B I A N
SEA

BAY OF
BENGAL

THAILAND

FRENCH INDO-CHINA

ANDAMAN
ISLANDS

CEYLON

I N D I A N   O C E A N

SUMATRA

MALAYA

•SINGAPORE

45°

30°

10°

315

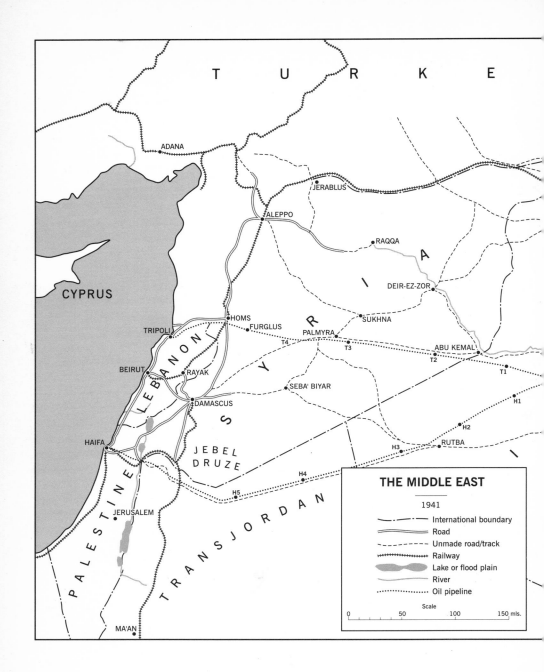

THE MIDDLE EAST

1941

— · — · — International boundary
═══════ Road
‑ ‑ ‑ ‑ ‑ Unmade road/track
+++++++ Railway
▬▬▬ Lake or flood plain
━━━━━ River
········· Oil pipeline

Scale
0   50   100   150 mls.

TURKEY

CYPRUS

ADANA

JERABLUS

ALEPPO

RAQQA

DEIR-EZ-ZOR

HOMS
FURGLUS
SUKHNA
TRIPOLI
PALMYRA
T4
T3
ABU KEMAL
T2
BEIRUT
RAYAK
T1
SEBA' BIYAR
H1
DAMASCUS
S Y R I A
H2
HAIFA
H3
RUTBA
JEBEL
DRUZE
H4
H5
JERUSALEM
PALESTINE
TRANSJORDAN
LEBANON

MA'AN

316

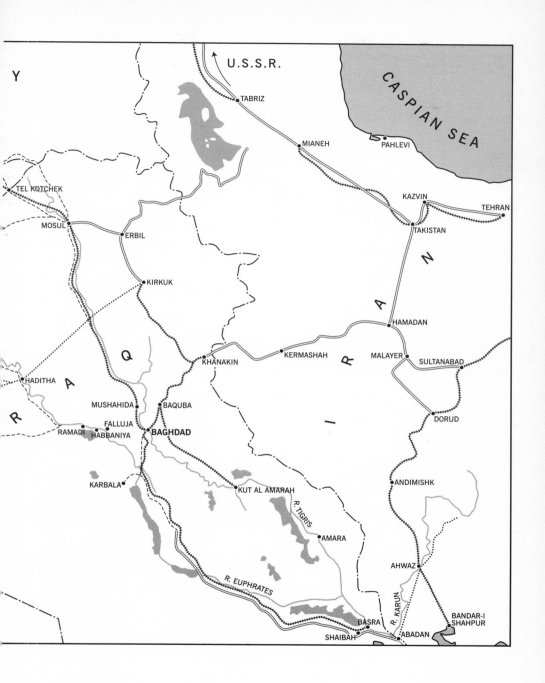

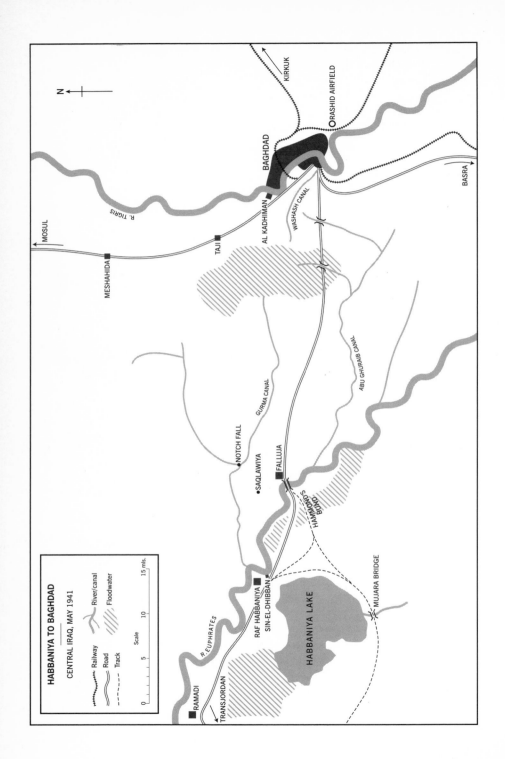

HABBANIYA TO BAGHDAD

CENTRAL IRAQ, MAY 1941

Railway
Road
Track
River/canal
Floodwater

Scale

0   5   10   15 mls.

N

BAGHDAD

RASHID AIRFIELD

KIRKUK

BASRA

MOSUL

R. TIGRIS

MESHAHIDA

TAJI

AL KADHIMAN

WASHASH CANAL

ABU GHURAIB CANAL

GURMA CANAL

NOTCH FALL

SAQLAWIYA

FALLUJA

HAMMOND'S BUND

MUJARA BRIDGE

HABBANIYA LAKE

RAF HABBANIYA

SIN-EL-DHIBBAN

R. EUPHRATES

TRANSJORDAN

RAMADI

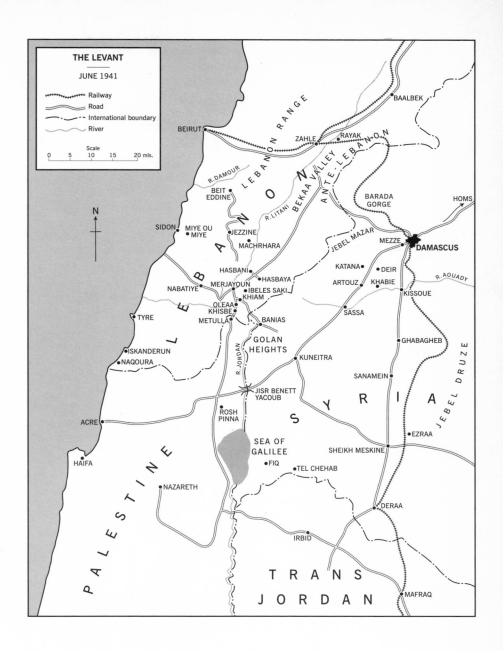

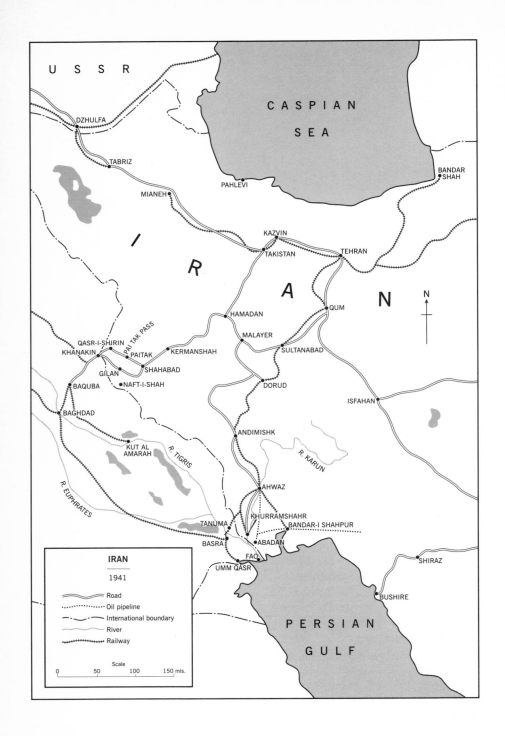

IRAN

1941

Road
Oil pipeline
International boundary
River
Railway

Scale
0   50   100   150 mls.

Select Bibliography

Manuscript Sources

AIR	Air Ministry papers, National Archives
BL	British Library (Asia, Pacific and Africa Collection)
CA	Claude Auchinleck papers, John Rylands Library
CAB	Cabinet papers, National Archives
FO	Foreign Office papers, National Archives
OR	Ouvry Roberts papers, Liddell Hart Military Archives
PREM	Prime Minister papers, National Archives
WO	War Office papers, National Archives

Prime Minister's Files

PREM 3   Operational Papers
            309/4- Principal Telegrams, Middle East, 30 April – 27 May 1941
            309/5- Principal Telegrams, Middle East, 27 May – 4 July 1941
            407A- Spears Mission, 1941–2
PREM 4   Confidential Papers
            32/5 Middle East, 1940–2
            32/6 Middle East Committee, 1940–1

Cabinet Papers

CAB 44   Mediterranean and Middle East: Iraq and Syria
CAB 65   War Cabinet Minutes, 1941–5
CAB 66   War Cabinet Memoranda, 1941–5
CAB 69   War Cabinet Defence Committee (Operations), 1941–5
CAB 95   Committees on the Middle East and Africa

War Office Files
WO106   DMO and Intelligence
                    2117, 2159, 2162, 2163 Middle East
WO169   War Diaries, Middle East Forces
WO201   Headquarters papers, Middle East Forces
FO371   Foreign Office files

British Library
L/WS   War Staff Series files, 1921–51

Despatches

Claude Auchinleck, *Operations in the Middle East, 5 July 1941 to 31 October 1941* (*London Gazette*, 1942).

John H. D'Albiac, *Report of Operations in Baghdad Area, 2 May to 31 May 1941* (*London Gazette*, 1948).

Arthur Longmore, *London Gazette Supplement. Air Operations in the Middle East, 1 January to 3 May 1941* (*London Gazette*, 1946).

H. Maitland Wilson, *London Gazette Supplement. Despatch on the Persia and Iraq Command* (*London Gazette*, 1946).

Archibald Wavell, *Despatch on Operations in Iraq, East Syria and Iran, 10 April 1941 to 12 January 1942* (*London Gazette*, 1946).

Archibald Wavell, *Despatch on Operations in the Middle East, 7 February 1941 to 15 July 1941* (*London Gazette*, 1946).

General

Christopher Buckley, *Five Ventures: Iraq–Syria–Persia–Madagascar–Dodecanese* (London: HMSO, 1954)

Sir Reader Bullard, *The Camels Must Go* (London: Faber & Faber, 1961)

J.R.M. Butler, *Grand Strategy, Volume II* (London: HMSO, 1957)

Winston Churchill, *The Second World War: Volume 3, The Grand Alliance* (London: Cassell, 1950)

R.J. Collins, *Lord Wavell: A Military Biography* (London: Hodder & Stoughton, 1948)

John Connell, *Auchinleck, A Critical Biography* (London: Cassell, 1959)

John Connell, *Wavell: Scholar and Soldier, To June 1941* (New York: Harcourt, 1964)

Colonel J.M. Cowper, *The King's Own: The Story of a Royal Regiment, vol 3: 1914–1950* (Aldershot: Gale & Polden, 1957)

Moshe Dayan, *Story of my Life* (London: Weidenfeld & Nicholson, 1976)

Somerset de Chair, *The Golden Carpet* (London: Faber & Faber, 1944)

General Charles de Gaulle, *War Memoirs, Volume One, The Call to Arms 1940–1942* (London: Collins, 1955)

Air Vice-Marshal Anthony Dudgeon, *Hidden Victory: The Battle of Habbaniya, May 1941* (Stroud: Tempus, 2000)

Major General Martin Farndale, *History of the Royal Regiment of Artillery, vol 5: Years of Defeat* (London: Brassey's, 1996)

Bernard Fergusson, *Trumpet in the Hall* (London: Collins, 1970)

A.B. Gaunson, *Anglo-French Clash in Lebanon and Syria, 1940–1945* (New York: Macmillan, 1987)

Martin Gilbert, *Finest Hour* (London: Heinemann, 1983)

John Glubb, *A Soldier with the Arabs* (London: Hodder & Stoughton, 1957)

John Glubb, *The Story of the Arab Legion* (London: Hodder & Stoughton, 1948)

F.H. Hinsley, *British Intelligence in the Second World War, Volume 1: Its Influence on Strategy and Operations* (London: HMSO, 1986)

Lukasz Hirszowicz, *The Third Reich and the Arab East* (London: Routledge & Kegan Paul, 1968)

Major General Hastings Ismay, *The Memoirs of Lord Ismay* (London: Heinemann, 1960)

John Keegan, *Churchill's Generals* (London: Weidenfeld & Nicholson, 1991)

Major General John Kennedy, *The Business of War* (London: Hutchinson, 1957)

François Kersaudy, *Churchill and de Gaulle* (London: Collins, 1981)

Majid Khadduri, *Independent Iraq: A Study in Iraqi Politics since 1932* (London: Oxford University Press, 1958)

Philip S. Khoury, *Syria and the French Mandate: The Politics of Arab Nationalism* (Princeton: Princeton University Press, 1989)

George Kirk, *The Middle East in the War* (Oxford: Oxford University Press, 1952)

Ronald Lewin, *The Chief: Field Marshal Lord Wavell, Commander-in-Chief and Viceroy, 1939–1947* (London: Hutchinson, 1980)

Godfrey Lias, *Glubb's Legion* (London: Evans Brothers Limited, 1956)

Gavin Long, *Greece, Crete and Syria* (Canberra: Australian War Memorial, 1953)

James Lunt, *Glubb Pasha: A Biography* (London: Harvill Press, 1984)

Compton Mackenzie, *Eastern Epic, Volume 1: Defence, September 1939–March 1943* (London: Chatto & Windus, 1951)

Norman MacMillan, *The Royal Air Force in the World War, Volume 3: 1940–1945* (London: George Harrap, 1950)

Colonel T.A. Martin, *Essex Regiment* (Brentwood: The Essex Regiment Association, 1951)

John Masters, *The Road Past Mandalay* (London: Michael Joseph, 1961)

Anthony Mockler, *Our Enemies the French* (London: Leo Cooper, 1976)

Leonard Mosley, *Power Play: Oil in the Middle East* (New York: Random House, 1973)

Vail Motter, *United States Army in World War II: Middle East Theater, Persian Corridor and Aid to Russia* (Washington DC: Government Printing Office, 1952)

Mohammed Reza Shah Pahlevi, *Mission for My Country* (London: Hutchinson, 1961)

Dharm Pal, *Official History of Indian Armed Forces in the Second World War. The Campaign in Western Asia* (Delhi: Combined Inter-Services Historical Section, 1957)

Major General I.S.O. Playfair, *History of the Second World War. The Mediterranean and Middle East, Volume 2: The Germans Come to the Help of Their Ally, 1941* (London: HMSO, 1956)

Harold Raugh, *Wavell in the Middle East, 1939–1941: A Study in Generalship* (London: Brassey's, 1993)

Denis Richards, *Royal Air Force 1939–1945, Volume 1: The Fight at Odds* (London: HMSO, 1953)

Aviel Roshwald, *Estranged Bedfellows: Britain and France in the Middle East* (Oxford: Oxford University Press, 1990)

S.W. Roskill, *History of the Second World War. War at Sea 1939–1945, Volume 1: The Defensive* (London: HMSO, 1954)

Joel Sayre, *Persian Gulf Command* (New York: Random House, 1945)

Gerhard Schreiber et al, *Germany and the Second World War, Volume 3: The Mediterranean, South-east Europe, and North Africa, 1939–1941* (Oxford: Clarendon Press, 1995)

Christopher Shores, *Dust Clouds in the Middle East* (London: Grub Street, 1996)

Sir Clarmont Skrine, *World War in Iran* (London: Constable, 1962)

William Slim, *Unofficial History* (London: Cassell, 1959)

Edward Spears, *Fulfilment of a Mission: The Spears Mission to Syria and Lebanon, 1941–1944* (London: Leo Cooper, 1977)

Freya Stark, *Dust in the Lion's Paw* (London: Century Publishing, 1961)

Freya Stark, *East is West* (London: John Murray, 1945)

Richard Stewart, *Sunrise at Abadan: The British and Soviet Invasion of Iran, 1941* (New York: Praeger, 1988)

A.W. Tedder, *With Prejudice: The War Memoirs of Marshal of the Royal Air Force Lord Tedder GCB* (London: Cassell, 1966)

Wilfred Thesiger, *The Life of My Choice* (London: Collins, 1987)

Martin Thomas, *The French Empire at War, 1940–1945* (Manchester: Manchester University Press, 1998)

Geoffrey Warner, *Politics and Strategy of the Second World War. Iraq and Syria, 1941* (London: Davis-Poynter, 1974)

War Office, *PaiForce: The Official Story of the Persian and Iraq Command* (London: HMSO, 1948)

Martin Wilmington, *Middle East Supply Center* (New York: New York State University Press, 1971)

Henry Wilson, *Eight Years Overseas, 1939–1947* (London: Hutchinson, 1950)

Sir Llewellyn Woodward, *British Foreign Policy in the Second World War* (2 volumes) (London: HMSO, 1970)

Humphrey Wyndham, *The Household Cavalry at War* (Aldershot: Gale & Polden, 1952)

Index